Wanted Women

CultureAmerica

Erika Doss
Philip J. Deloria
Series Editors

Karal Ann Marling
Editor Emerita

Wanted Women

An American Obsession in the
Reign of J. Edgar Hoover

Mary Elizabeth Strunk

 UNIVERSITY PRESS OF KANSAS

Assata Shakur, "Love," excerpted from *Assata: An Autobiography*, © 1987 by Zed Books Ltd. Used with permission of Lawrence Hill Books.

Published by the University Press of Kansas (Lawrence, Kansas 66045), which was organized by the Kansas Board of Regents and is operated and funded by Emporia State University, Fort Hays State University, Kansas State University, Pittsburg State University, the University of Kansas, and Wichita State University

Library of Congress Cataloging-in-Publication Data

Strunk, Mary Elizabeth.
    Wanted women : an American obsession in the reign of J. Edgar Hoover / Mary Elizabeth Strunk.
        p.   cm. — (CultureAmerica)
    Includes bibliographical references and index.
    ISBN 978-0-7006-1744-9 (cloth : alk. paper)
    1. Female offenders—United States—Biography. 2. Women outlaws—United States—Biography. 3. Crime—United States—History—20th century. 4. Hoover, J. Edgar (John Edgar), 1895–1972. 5. United States. Federal Bureau of Investigation—History—20th century. 6. Law enforcement—United States—History—20th century. 7. Sex role—United States—History—20th century. 8. United States—Social conditions—1918–1932. 9. United States—Social condition—1933–1945. 10. United States—Social conditions—1945– I. Title.
    HV6785.S77 2010
    364.1092'273—dc22   2010009290

British Library Cataloguing-in-Publication Data is available.

Printed in the United States of America

10 9 8 7 6 5 4 3 2 1

CONTENTS

Acknowledgments *vii*

Introduction: Ten Most Wanted *1*

1 The Girls behind the Man behind the Gun *16*

2 Mother Barker, Public Enemy No. 1 *53*

3 The Perfectly Ambiguous Bonnie Parker *85*

4 Radical Cheerleaders and a Frustrated PTA Type *108*

5 Panther, Prisoner, Poet, and Prize *139*

6 Glorious and Bitter Ends *171*

Epilogue *197*

Notes *207*

Bibliography *239*

Index *253*

Illustration sections follow pages 107 and 170

ACKNOWLEDGMENTS

Ma Barker and her sons were once forced to make a hasty retreat from their hideout on Minnesota's White Bear Lake. But on her way out of town, Ma took care to pay her ice bill. Like Ma, this project has accrued many debts, which I can only begin to repay by acknowledging the vital input and support of multiple people and institutions.

I began writing this book in the Twin Cities, where University of Minnesota Professors Sara Evans, Lary May, Elaine Tyler May, Riv-Ellen Prell, and David Noble all left their imprints upon it. Professor Rudy Vecoli offered important early guidance and put me in contact with his sister, Olga Gralton, who kindly shared her 1930s scrapbooks on the Lindbergh baby trial.

The University of Minnesota provided essential support in the form of grants and fellowships, including the Harold Leonard Memorial Fellowship and Study Grant for the study of film. An American Studies Travel Fund Award for archival research at the Academy of Motion Picture Arts and Sciences went much farther thanks to Elaine and Lary May, who generously arranged lodging at their relatives' home in California. I took sustenance (literal and otherwise) from the Mays' writing group and from a host of friends and colleagues, including Jacquetta Amdahl, Bill Anthes, Gary Aslakson, Josh Barkan, Matt Basso, Matt Becker, Jenn Blair, Karen Connelly-Lane, Benjy Flowers, Josie Fowler, Robert Frame, Steve Garabedian, Robin Hemenway, Brian Klopotek, Sharon Leon, Joyce Mariano, Dave Monteyne, Deirdre Murphy, Dave Noon, Susan Podelsky, Migdlena Tordova, Yuka Tsuchiya, Amy Tyson, and Melissa Williams. I feel a special gratitude for the fellowship of my smaller writing group chums Margot Canaday, Kimberly Heikkila, and Kate Kane.

While at Georgetown University, I received formative encouragement from Professors Dorothy Brown, Hubert Cloke, Emmett Curran, Bill McDonald, Elizabeth McKeown, and Patricia O'Connor, whose "Prison Literature" course was my first introduction to Assata Shakur. Professors Rupert Wilkinson and John Wilcox, from the University of Sussex, had an influential hand in this book's focus, as did two FBI agents who shared stories, lore, and a tour of the FBI headquarters in Philadelphia.

This work was buoyed by my colleagues from Hamline University, Syracuse University, and the Five Colleges Consortium, especially Heather Abel, Jenny Adams, Arlene Avakian, Steve Cohan, Elizabeth Cohen, Kris Deffenbacher, Veena Deo, Alexandrina Deschamps, Susan Edmunds, Ann Ferguson, Bob Gates, Mike Goode, David Hudson, Janice Irvine, Amy Lang, Karen Lederer, E. B. Lehman, Patricia Melzer, Lynn Morgan, Alice Moorhead, Mark Olson, Michael Reynolds, Jolynn Parker, Alan Silva, and Banu Subramaniam. Were it possible, I would have liked to reproduce in these pages a 2001 guest lecture/musical presentation by Mirjana (Minja) Lausevic and Tim Eriksen on the history of the outlaw ballad. Lucky were the students—and their speechless professor—who got to experience Tim and Minja's electrifying performance at Hamline University that day.

I owe a heartfelt debt to my students in Minneapolis, Syracuse, and Amherst. Their questions and interpretations enriched my own and gave meaning to the journey that was this project.

Jennifer King, head of Archives and Special Collections at Mount Holyoke College, offered this project both time and a dedicated workspace through Mount Holyoke's Scholar-in-Residence program. From 2005 to 2006, the Five College Women's Studies Research Center did the same. Finishing this book would have taken far longer without the professional and financial support of Five Colleges, Inc., particularly that extended by the Five Colleges' Cynthia Goheen and Marie Hess.

Parts of this work evolved from previously published articles. A section of Chapter 2 appeared in *Mob Culture: Hidden Histories of the American Gangster Film* (Rutgers University Press, 2005), and a version of Chapter 3 appeared as "Bonnie and Clyde's 'Other Side': The Good-Bad Outlaws of Larry Buchanan," *American Studies Journal*, no. 50 (Fall 2007).

One of the perks of writing a book such as this one was the opportunity to interact with the exceptional librarians and archivists who worked their magic on its behalf. I am indebted to Barbara Hall and Kristine Krueger of the Martha Herrick Memorial Library at the Academy of Motion Picture Arts and Sciences in Beverly Hills; Mark W. Falzini, archivist of New Jersey State Police Museum and Learning Center; and Mark Videbeck, a former graduate assistant to Marquette University's Professor Athan Theoharis, who graciously shared some of his FBI records on Ma Barker. For help with image procurement and general miracles, I must thank Charles Spetland and Jennifer Claybourgh-Torkelson of the University of Minnesota's

Special Collections; Ida Hay of the Five College Library Depository; and Amherst College librarians Michael Kasper and Susan E. Edwards. It was Susan who introduced me to Assata Shakur's friend, Rosemari Mealy, and arranged for an on-campus screening of Cuban director Gloria Rolando's *Eyes of the Rainbow* in a moment when the film was still banned in the United States.

This project found support and vital criticism from generous allies, including the independent researcher and SLA watchdog Greg Lang; the late Ron Clark, former editor of the *Pioneer Press;* and the Federal Bureau of Investigation's historian, John F. Fox. I drew inspiration—and a mighty useful set of resources—from Paul Maccabee, author of *John Dillinger Slept Here* and the donor of the Minnesota Historical Society's Paul Maccabee St. Paul Gangster History Research Collection.

I had the privilege of getting to know several creative people who responded graciously to inquiries about their work, including directors Fred Baker and Larry Buchanan, playwrights Dixie Lee Sedgwick and Brenda Kilianski, political cartoonist Steve Lindstrom, and author Stanley Hamilton. Thank you to Jimmy Bryan, the son of journalist John Bryan, for sharing his father's work and to Photofest President Howard Mandelbaum for making possible many of the film stills that appear in this book.

Joe Abbott, Sarah Doyle, Josna Rege, Ann Meeropol, Adam Sitze, and Amy Sitze all read parts of the book manuscript and made it much better than it would have been without their input. Bob and Chris Sitze patiently encouraged the long process of revisions with practical tips and thoughtfully assembled care packages. Dawn Wilson, a member of the "good SLA" (the Special Libraries Association), provided urgent last-minute research support and help locating images. Dawn also helped ready the book for production as a fact checker and indexer. For years, the clever Kevin Strunk sustained this project with his loyalty and know-how; he read and reread chapter drafts many more times than he would probably like to recall. Writing buddy and dear friend Danielle Bessett met me each summer morning at "our table" in Amherst College's Frost Library, lending momentum, good humor, and companionship to a sometimes lonely process.

From the start, I have been humbled and impressed by the team at the University Press of Kansas. It has been a pleasure to work with acquisitions editors Nancy Scott Jackson, Kalyani Fernando, and Ranjit Arab, editor in chief Mike Briggs, production editor Jennifer Dropkin, editorial assistant Hilary Lowe, copyeditor Monica Phillips, assistant director and marketing manager Susan Schott, and director Fred Woodward.

Like most books, this one grew up amid a web of other obligations and relationships. It owes a great deal to sympathetic neighbors like Jim Haefner and Jill Sherman, smart and wickedly funny friends like Quinn Hanzel and Laura Riddle, and exceptional babysitters like Michele Lauriat. It relied on the patience and moxie of my beloved Adam Sitze; the goodwill of our children, Daniel and Julia; and the support of our extended families.

Wanted Women is dedicated to my parents, Phil and Suzy Strunk, who gave us time, space, meals, childcare, and printer toner. They waited a long time for this book. Without their selfless encouragement, it would never have seen the light.

Wanted Women

Patty Hearst as "Tania." Courtesy of the National Archives.

Introduction

Ten Most Wanted

They were ten women one would expect to meet only in the pages of an eclectic novel:

- A teenaged heiress whose abduction made her a 1970s icon
- A former Black Panther who broke out of prison, fled the country, and published a best-selling memoir
- Five Berkeley women who gave up their middle-class lives (and husbands) and formed a paramilitary force to fight the "fascist insect" of the United States
- A "Machine Gun" missus whose flair for public relations earned both her and her mother two decades in the clink
- A sixty-year-old Missouri matriarch known for her devotion to religious hymns and her four jailbird sons
- A twenty-something waitress and divorcée cursed with dramatic ambitions and scant prospects for getting the hell out of Texas

They were celebrities. They were outlaws. They were thorns in the side of the Federal Bureau of Investigation (FBI). Taken together, their stories reveal what it takes—and just what it has meant—to be a high-profile female lawbreaker in the United States. Examining how these ten outlaws vied with law enforcement for the chance to control their stories at last explains our culture's complex fascination with the figure of the gunwoman —particularly the gunwoman who wields her weapon not in service to, but in defiance of, the law.

Apart from their sex, what unites Patricia Hearst, Assata Shakur, the five original women of the Berkeley-born Symbionese Liberation Army (SLA), Kathryn "Mrs. Machine Gun" Kelly, Ma Barker, and Bonnie Parker? All ten were improbable candidates for notoriety. In the parlance of modern law enforcement, each became a "person of interest" because of her willingness to toss aside a conventional and lawful life in pursuit of an existence she considered more worthwhile. All ten women became "wanted" criminals during, or just after, J. Edgar Hoover's forty-seven years as director of the FBI, and all would play a part in shaping his legacy and that of his Bureau. All ten saw themselves as struggling against an oppressive legal system and tried to persuade others of the same. Each woman renamed and reinvented herself; some did so multiple times. Each represented and misrepresented herself for the approval of an imagined audience, or "public," whom she regarded as potential victims of the state, just like herself. Deliberate distortion became the hallmark of all ten women's biographies, which intersect not only in FBI archives but also in the realm of entertainment and fantasy.

Both in the legal record and in the popular imagination, women's willingness to break the law has been read as biologically aberrant, sexually threatening, or politically charged. Depending on the criminal act, it may also be regarded as striking a blow for women's freedoms. The ten women of this book are "outlaws" because they became whatever various audiences have needed or wanted them to be. All have been the subject of films and seemingly endless media coverage. They have inspired stage plays, novels, reenactments, and fashion. Along the way, they became folk heroes and cautionary tales. More of an idea than a presence, they became the screens on which other women and men could project their anxieties and desires.

This book uses film and other popular culture–driven iconography to illuminate the collective cultural impact of its ten subjects in, and beyond, the two decades in which they became famous: the 1930s (Bonnie, Kathryn, and Ma) and the 1970s (the SLA women, "Patty" Hearst, and Assata). Sifting through the details of how, why, by whom, and *for* whom certain women outlaw pictures were made, or sometimes remade, demonstrates how mythologies attached to 1930s or 1970s outlaw subjects have echoed and reconstituted each other across time. It makes clear how headline-grabbing women lawbreakers in those two eras of economic and social crises became cultural flashpoints for their moments' uneasy reorganization of gender mores and federal law enforcement.

The 1930s and 1970s also bracket J. Edgar Hoover's long tenure as FBI director.[1] Some of the most enduring stories of these women—half of whom were killed at the hands of the law—are testaments to the success of the early FBI's publicity machine in establishing federal police power as a national asset. If the United States' "Gangster Age" of the early 1930s helped make the modern FBI, the FBI also deserves credit for having made legends of gangsters such as Al Capone and John Dillinger. All ten of the women featured in this book owe their reputations to Bureau interventions. Each woman's connection to the FBI began, at least in part, with her status as a public relations problem for law enforcement.

The abduction of the media heiress Patty Hearst from her Berkeley apartment in February 1974 posed an obvious set of challenges, especially after it was revealed that the FBI had failed to inform Patty that she was a potential SLA kidnapping target. The high-profile case became even more delicate for the FBI after Patty ostensibly joined her abductors. A few days after she declared herself a member of the SLA ("I have chosen to stay and fight"), Patty appeared to join them in an armed bank robbery. The bank's surveillance camera images, plus a widely circulated photograph of Patty transformed into the SLA's rifle-toting, beret-wearing "Tania," would become both a boon and a burden to the prosecution of her case. Patty's indelible outlaw image put ironic quotation marks around her plea of innocence. Yet Patty's emaciated body at the time of her trial hinted that the authorities had been confounded by a child-woman, albeit one who (it was speculated) had been intent on rebellion against her parents and bourgeois feminine conventions. Like the FBI's investigation of her kidnapping, Patty Hearst's abduction and trial reflected the tumultuous cultural politics of the middle 1970s, as well as a widespread disillusionment with state institutions. But Patty's complicated iconic cachet also had roots in an earlier era, in which three headline-grabbing women helped to shore up the boundaries of "respectable femininity" and to solidify the reputation of the FBI's G-men as the latter battled the gangster-outlaws of the 1930s.

An Echo of Guns and Cameras

The memory of the minor bandit Clyde Barrow would have dissolved quietly into history had he not died in the company of his girlfriend, Bonnie Parker. A few months before the 1934 ambush that took their lives, Bonnie, Clyde, and a third member of the Barrow Gang robbed a Texas

National Guard armory and photographed themselves with the stolen fire-power. In one photo, the diminutive, beret-wearing Bonnie props her foot on the bumper of a stolen Ford and draws to her jutting hip a revolver. A cigar hangs loosely from her mouth. That snapshot, and a few others like it, would be integral to the legend of Bonnie and Clyde. More memorable than any of the crimes the Barrow Gang committed, the cigar photo would be evoked and imitated countless times in film and fashion photography, both for its indefinable glamour and for its eloquent linkage of sex, violence, and the potential sexiness of violence. Four decades later, when the SLA released the propaganda photo of Patty Hearst with her gun and her beret, many in the public recalled Bonnie Parker.

The FBI had only an indirect hand in the case of Bonnie and Clyde, but the outlaws' deaths became, and remain, a prominent part of the modern FBI's nativity story and a turning point for the federal war on crime.[2] At the time that the Bureau began tracking the couple in December 1932, its federal agents were still forbidden to carry firearms. They could pursue Bonnie and Clyde only on charges that the pair had taken a stolen automobile across state lines. By the time the two most famous members of the Barrow Gang were brought down in a 1934 ambush made possible by an FBI tip-off, Congress had expanded the jurisdiction of federal agents to include the right to carry guns and make arrests. So the case of Bonnie and Clyde became another feather in the cap of the newly powerful G-man. The outlaws had gone to their deaths in a vehicle laden with stolen guns, which helped vindicate those who had wanted to arm the G-men. But, unlike the Texas posse that took some flack for it, federal agents never had to lift a gun against Bonnie, whose criminal transgressions did not necessarily warrant the death penalty and whom some remembered fondly for having stood by her man.

In 1933, the Bureau had apprehended another outlaw couple: Kathryn Kelly and her husband, George "Machine Gun" Kelly. The intimidating moniker belonged to George, but FBI director Hoover was more troubled by Kathryn, who allegedly seduced her dimwitted spouse into the gangster's life and a high-profile kidnapping scheme. Lest anyone feel pity for Kathryn, who was separated from her daughter and who would serve a long prison sentence alongside her mother for their role in "Machine Gun's" crimes, Hoover's 1930s-era speeches and writings repeatedly conjured Kathryn as an emasculating nag and George as a sorry specimen of compromised, criminal manhood. Hoover's account of George and Kathryn's unnatural partnership was designed both to shock and to deflate lingering affection for Bonnie Parker or any of the era's "gun molls." Over time, Bonnie's and Kathryn's stories have become jumbled together in popular culture, adding yet another layer of meanings to Bonnie's famous cigar photo.

In 1939, Hoover collaborated with Paramount Pictures on *Persons in Hiding*, a film based on George and Kathryn Kelly that is often misremembered as a film about Clyde and Bonnie. The movie's promotional campaign declared its female lead "The Girl behind the Man behind the Gun," a tagline that offers multiple interpretations. First, and most obviously, the film slogan neatly encapsulates Hoover's oft-enunciated belief that women could entice their male partners to break the law. Second, the slogan could be read as a sly expression of how the carefully leveraged scandal of female bandits and gun molls was helping to professionalize the once-struggling Bureau. The underworld "girl" made possible the success of *two* men behind guns—her man *and* the FBI's government agent, or G-man. Finally, the "Girl behind the Man" slogan reflected the multiple ways that the girl in its formula could be and was deployed in the 1930s and after.

Just as the prosecution in the trial of Patty Hearst had to downplay Patty's status as a kidnapping victim in order to produce a suitable villain, the official FBI script for the Kellys worked to extinguish the potential romantic appeal of outlaw-lovers. Identifying a woman as the "brains of an outfit" handily impugned both male and female gang members. Although the joke might today fall flat, as a gendered insult, it found traction for much of the twentieth century. It also tapped historic, racial anxieties when applied to the white SLA women (including Patty) alleged to be in thrall to a black male gang member, or to Assata Shakur, who in the 1970s was singled out as the "soul" of the Black Liberation Army and its "mother hen."

As a parent and a woman working among men, the former Black Panther Assata also drew unflattering comparisons to Arizona Donnie "Kate" Barker, the alleged 1930s gangland leader and mother to a set of male lawbreakers who played a seminal role in FBI history. The lingering notoriety of "Ma" Barker arose from a single, fatal encounter with federal agents in 1935. More infamous in death than in life, Ma would be touted by Hoover as "the most vicious, dangerous, and resourceful criminal brain" in the United States, as well as a symptom of the country's morally lax citizenry.[3] In 1936, the FBI began claiming her death as one of the proudest trophies of its success. However, the evolution of Ma's legend suggests that her reputation as a savage parent and as a ruthless, criminal mastermind was a Bureau invention—and one designed to conceal the G-men's accidental murder of a woman with no criminal record.

That is not to say that the FBI pursued Ma's family without cause or that Ma (or Bonnie or Kathryn or Patty or Assata) never stepped on the wrong side of the law. As with the other nine women in this book, details of Ma's life and motivations are difficult to ascertain. We may never know to what degree Kate Barker participated in or condoned her sons' crimes, which included two highly publicized adult kidnappings for ransom. Hoover dubbed her "Public Enemy No. 1." But a surviving member of the Barker gang later insisted that Ma had no knowledge of her children's exploits and that she was simply used by them as a cover. Ma herself remains a cipher, having left few records apart from pitiful letters written to prison wardens on behalf of her children.

Of the few photographs of Ma that exist, the most famous are of her sheet-draped corpse, posed as a grim trophy beside the dead body of her son. In the trophy photos, Ma's body appears short, plump, and—with her blunt, bobbed hairdo—sexually ambiguous. The ambiguity of her appearance, plus the ambiguity of her guilt, proved too delicious for fiction writers to resist. In subsequent popular culture representations, the reanimated Ma Barker has emerged as a cinematic cliché, a campy monster useful for revealing the social anxieties of the particular historical moment in which a film or television program about her was created. In one of the *Persons in Hiding* sequels, *Queen of the Mob* (1940), Paramount Pictures again teamed up with J. Edgar Hoover's Bureau to imagine a Ma Barker torn between a life of crime and the life of a doting grandmother. Significantly, Paramount's Ma *survives* the FBI shootout.

This is a book that is deadly curious about that survival, and the survival of stories about other women who seemed unlikely fodder for an outlaw legend. Under Hoover's direction, the Bureau worked with the popular press, and occasionally with Hollywood, to tell and retell the story of 1930s bandits brought down by the G-men. Amplifying a criminal's exploits could help keep public loyalty on the side of law enforcers, even as it made the law's ultimate victory all the more impressive. That, in itself, is interesting, but not as interesting as what happened to the fictional Mas, Bonnies, and Kathryns who slipped Hoover's grasp and who began mutating in response to the needs of new authors and new audiences. Following Hoover's *Queen*, Ma Barker's story was revived for at least three other Hollywood biopics and became the basis for dozens of other cinema "momsters," including

Ma Jarrett in *White Heat* (1958). Barker would never occupy the same cultural space as a Robin Hood, but her legend has yet tapped into the complex attraction of women outlaws stretching back to the American frontier's "lady wildcats."[4] That is one reason why members of the Marion County Sheriff's Department in Ocala, Florida, annually reenact Ma and Freddie's shootout by Lake Weir. "We're not commemorating Ma or Fred Barker," insists a representative from the Lake Weir Chamber of Commerce. "We're commemorating law enforcement."[5] That may be, but articles about the reenactment tend to focus on Ma and on the local woman chosen to play her. In one newspaper photo from 2000, a revived "Ma" inexpertly points her gun at the camera and grins.

Outside the Law, Inside the Lore

How can we explain the simultaneous horror, allure, and even comedy that are part of the cultural freight (and *fright*) attached to the image of the woman who commits, or threatens to commit, violence? One answer lies in knowing how to unpack that freight and how to make more intelligible that unwieldy category, "violent woman." Statistically, U.S. women commit fewer crimes than U.S. men, but novelty alone cannot explain why certain women lawbreakers linger in public memory while others fade into obscurity. It also cannot explain how any one, male or female, crosses over from an ordinary criminal to a folkloric outlaw in some corners of the public imagination, nor how the concept of "outlaw" is inevitably altered by placing the word "woman" before it. What makes a particular character mythogenic? Why do popular desires or stereotypes crystallize around her and not someone else?[6]

Two discoveries emerge right away. The first discovery is that these women's stories are attractive for the same reason that "true crime" remains an overwhelmingly popular, if frequently maligned, genre. Contested as they are, such stories call to the surface typically unacknowledged pockets of unease around class, race, sexuality, the family, and norms of femininity and masculinity. So, for example, as weird and wooly a tale as Ma Barker's can yet grip us because of the familiarity of its centerpiece: discomfort and confusion regarding the place of older, maternal bodies in our culture. Similarly, Patty Hearst and the other well-resourced white women of the SLA were alarming not only for their crimes but also for the implicit social privileges they rejected *and* for how successfully they could sometimes wield those privileges as a subterfuge for their illegal acts.

The second discovery is related to the first. The successful outlaw—or the outlaw whose reputation would seem disproportionate to her exploits—must attract the attentions of the law not merely because of her criminal acts but also for the cultural taboos she violates. The ultimate cultural significance of the woman outlaw depends on her ability to talk back to the law and to persuade others to talk back on her behalf. The ability to stir up talkback—to the law and to social norms—is what separates an outlaw from the run-of-the-mill gun moll, gangster, or self-styled revolutionary.

The term "outlaw" carries varied meanings, depending on the context. In its broadest interpretation, "outlaw" may refer to any individual or group that exists outside of prevailing norms, either by circumstance or by design. In this sense, outlawry would consist not of traditional criminal behavior (e.g., theft, murder), but of behaviors that have, by tacit consensus or legislation, been criminalized by a majority or ruling class. So there may be religious, political, ethnic, or ideological outlaws (among others) whose very existence helps shore up the borders of the mainstream, even as they begin to fracture mainstream assumptions.[7]

By definition, an outlaw evokes a divided response from the public, becoming both an object of loathing and an object of fantasy. In the Anglophone outlaw tradition that produced England's Robin Hood, Australia's Ned Kelly, and the United States' Jesse James, the outlaw is a folk hero who inhabits the murky zone between criminality and political protest.[8] Outlaws of this sort—or "social bandits," as the historian Eric Hobsbawm dubbed them—turn up frequently in folklore from cultures around the globe. In fact, they occur so frequently as to have become fairly predictable: a young man (the outlaw is typically young and male) and his community feel themselves mistreated by an oppressive power. Having no other recourse, the young man responds to that power with some combination of trickery and force. He briefly prevails, abetted by the loyalties of the social group that regards him (rightly or wrongly) as their representative. Then he dies, affording followers the opportunity to venerate his memory and granting detractors the moral satisfaction of his grisly end. This postmortem split is important. (It will be the hallmark of subsequent mass media reenactments, which, like many in their audience, will find it possible to embrace both positions.) Narrative dissonance makes possible the outlaw's immortality. From a remove of distance or of years, the outlaw will become at once greater and less than himself: a cauldron of percolating social tensions distilled into a single, charismatic biography.

The woman outlaw possesses her own version of this tradition, one that may follow the pattern above, but which is less able to imagine her as unencumbered by family ties, and which inevitably foregrounds her identity/ies as a woman. In focusing solely on women outlaws, this study would seem to remove sex as a variable for analysis, at least insofar as it excluded any male outlaws to whom the women might be compared. As it happens, the ten women scrutinized in this book can never be analyzed wholly apart from their male counterparts, since public interpretations of their actions so often hinged on the women's relationships with male partners or offspring. (And also with the almost exclusively male directors who re-created them in film.) In fiction, as in real life, the subjects of this book were all regarded as indices of a cultural unraveling that was the product of loosening social strictures on women. (For example, in the 1970s, prominent journalists and social scientists blamed the actions of the SLA and Patricia Hearst on the same culprit: "women's lib.")[9] Male gangsters and male countercultural radicals were frequently understood as products of their ethnicity or race, but for the most part the maleness of the outlaw remained so "natural" and obvious as to be nearly invisible. By contrast, with women outlaws—the need to add the "woman" qualifier marks them as an exception to the rule—their femaleness looms larger than any other trait. However motivated, women's social transgressions have consistently been interpreted first and foremost through the lens of their gender.

Because of this lens, tales of the woman outlaw are inevitably preoccupied with how and why she partook in acts of violence. The woman who uses a gun for anything other than self-defense or the protection of children is doubly deviant, for she threatens the comforting idea that women are intrinsically gentle, life-nurturing, and law-abiding. Unlike femininity and violence, masculinity and violence are not typically presumed in conflict. Violence, rage, and aggression are signifiers of masculinity, except when they are used as signifiers of a compromised or defective femininity. The woman outlaw therefore poses a dilemma to those who would theorize her. Do her aggressive acts show her to be mannish? Unsexed? Or are they just a product of biological proclivities that mark her as irrefutably female? The hunt begins for cracks in her commitment to the outlaw lifestyle. Had she no aspirations at all for a domestic or family life? Why and with whom did she travel? How well did she lie? Did she hate shooting a gun or did she love it? Any answer to those questions may serve as evidence of that which makes her quintessentially female, or volatile, or dangerous—or all three.

Here enters the importance of talking back. The woman outlaw who becomes a true outlaw, or social bandit, has tampered with a set of narrow gender expectations while also managing her story such that it reinforces them. Consider again Bonnie Parker's pose in her cigar photo, which reassures as it threatens. With the gun and the stogie, Bonnie might be claiming phallic power, but the rest of her stance telegraphs a conventionally feminine glamour and sexual availability. What's more, her slenderness and doll-sized proportions suggest a child-woman who is winking at her audience by playing at being a gangster or at being a man. Bonnie may not have been fully conscious of her photograph's dichotomous effects, but she did refer to a similar ambiguity—and to her own media savvy—in her one published poem, "The End of the Line," better known as "The Ballad of Bonnie and Clyde." Bonnie's ballad received widespread scrutiny for having established herself as Clyde Barrow's equal and for accurately predicting how she and Clyde would "go down together."

In outlawry, the most enduring cultural icons are those who, in life, were successfully self-promoting and who, in death, are sympathetically promoted by others. Bonnie's mother would eventually point to the gangster slang in her daughter's poems as representing "a strange and terrifying change in the mind of my child." After Bonnie and Clyde were killed, their family members immediately published their own recounting of the couple, one that emphasized Bonnie's early aversion to guns, her romantic devotion to Clyde, and her powerful yen for a child.[10] These were the engrossing character incongruities on which many a fictional adaptation would hang, most notably Arthur Penn's 1967 sleeper, *Bonnie and Clyde*.

Once Assata Shakur broke out of jail and became an international fugitive in 1979, both she and her loyal aunt, lawyer Evelyn Williams, published accounts of Assata as a precocious youngster who could "recognize a Van Gogh on sight" and who was interested, but not too interested, in boys.[11] The pressures on the African American Assata to perform the trappings of a respectable femininity were at once more and less intense than for her white counterparts. Assata's outlawry could more easily be configured as part of a general, capital-B black resistance rather than (exclusively) a by-product of her individual interests. But, depending on who was telling the tale, taking up the gun as a revolutionary outlaw might be an act of heroism, terrorism, cowardice, or hypocrisy. In her autobiography, Assata despaired at her grandmother's middle-class pretensions and favored armed revolution against the United States. Hoping to make her sympathetic to a mainstream audience, many of Assata's supporters (and certainly her legal team) were quicker to point out her striking good looks and her devotion as a mother.

A similar impulse would emerge with the SLA, the radical 1970s group remarkable for its copious writings and sometimes fatal obsession with political theater. Once the SLA's Angela Atwood (alias "Gelina"), Nancy Ling Perry ("Fahizah"), Patricia Soltysik ("Zoya"), and Camilla Hall ("Gabi") were confirmed dead alongside two male SLA members in a 1974 shootout with the FBI and Los Angeles police (Emily Harris/"Yolanda" was elsewhere at the time of the blaze), family and friends tried to soften the dead women's reputations as "domestic terrorists" by offering details from the women's promising, middle-class girlhoods. The subsequent outpouring of SLA-related journalism and fiction owes everything to those details, which stand in contrast both to the SLA members' FBI profiles and to the militant, "people name" personas they declared in their manifestos. Of course, most who take the SLA as a subject are most taken themselves by the SLA's story as scripted for—and later *by*—the enigmatic and temporary outlaw Patty/"Tania." Whether Patricia Hearst had willingly elected to join the SLA or was coerced remains a source both of ongoing debate and of her popular cachet.

The title of this book is "Wanted Women," a nod to the FBI's famous "Ten Most Wanted Fugitives" list. Like the "Public Enemy No. 1" designation that preceded it, the "Most Wanted" list had its genesis in the press. In 1949, a reporter for the International News Service asked the FBI for the names and descriptions of the "toughest guys" it would like to capture. The resulting story was so popular—and so effective in generating arrests—that Hoover made the list a standing FBI program. It became a formal expression of the Bureau's partnership with the media and with the general public, who grew accustomed to seeing FBI mug shots on display at the post office and later on television programs such as *America's Most Wanted*.

The wanted list built on the tradition of the wanted poster, hallmark of the early western outlaw and a tool used by the U.S. Department of Justice as early as 1919. The term "wanted" obviously refers to the law's desire to apprehend a criminal and bring her to justice. But for the purposes of this study and its ten women subjects, "wanted" also points to something more. Ten outlaws who were "wanted" by whom? And for what purpose? What can we learn from these women and their tracings on posters, in post offices, and on movie screens? How shall we interpret all that has been wanted for and wanted *from* the woman outlaw, such that those latent desires can lend fresh perspective on the historical organization of the law, on existing theories of gender and social deviance, and on the depiction of women's violence in entertainment?

All the women in this book are worth studying for the fictive elements that fed their preservation, as well as the cultural clues those fictive elements contain. With the possible exception of Ma Barker, each of the women spent enormous amounts of energy attempting to manipulate public opinion in her favor, or, at very least, to counter unflattering "official" portrayals circulated by the mainstream press and agencies of the state. So it should be clear that this is not a book that purports to locate the "real" Bonnie Parker, the "real" Ma Barker, the "real" Assata Shakur, or the "real" Patricia Hearst. It focuses instead on the fanciful and symbolic Bonnies, Mas, Assatas, and Pattys who have proliferated in popular culture from the first moment their names appeared in a headline and an FBI file. The outlaws' "real" stories are impossible to discern and even cease to matter because they were neither fueling nor indicative of corollary tensions and change around the moment of their reinvention.

That is why this book tracks the ten women whom private citizens— artists and activists, crime fiction buffs, and cinemaphiles—have wanted and needed them to be. Although this book is not a straightforward film history, movies are central to its arguments. Films about women outlaws serve as a reference point and a site for uncovering the political unconscious of law enforcement agencies, professional mythmakers, and various niche publics. Scrutinizing films and other ephemera helps to puzzle out the remarkable linkages among the ten women of this study, as well as their ongoing cultural utility. Obviously, the woman outlaw has been attractive to certain audiences—and frightening or confounding to others. Whatever her effect, the outlaw woman has proved *useful*—whether in terms of vindicating structures of authority, articulating a political challenge, or crafting a self-image. Outlaws of any sort have historically been most useful to those charged with preserving the favorable reputation and legitimacy of law enforcement. But outlaw women are also useful and inspiring to other real or potential women outlaws. Then there are the spaces in which the goals of law enforcement (to squelch the outlaw's appeal) and the goals of the outlaw (to be or to appear to be too noble to be "criminal") intersect with a broad array of popular entertainments. Certainly, outlaw women have been useful fodder for journalists, filmmakers, and other artists who find in the outlaw's story an expression of their own communities' fantasies and grievances.

How an outlaw's actions are remembered does not always depend on the original circumstances surrounding those actions. Just as an outlaw's tale may be recycled or adapted for some future purpose, so, too, may an outlaw's legacy carry forward elements of similar hero/antihero "types" who went before. J. Edgar Hoover certainly recognized this phenomenon and knew how to use it to the Bureau's advantage. The phenomenon also applied to the FBI's G-man hero (himself a derivative of the romanticized frontier lawman), whose cultural fortunes often correlated inversely with those of the public enemies he sought. Starting in the 1930s, Hoover and his public relations office propagated stories of noble, naive, and transgressive women to promote the FBI's mission and to help elevate the G-man into a new kind of national hero and masculine ideal. Piecing together iterative accounts of girls behind men behind guns shows how the FBI-originated woman outlaw who helped to launch Hoover's G-man in the 1930s had ironically helped to tarnish the Bureau by the 1970s.

Overview

The next two chapters draw out J. Edgar Hoover's lifelong preoccupation with women deviants, both in his articles and speeches and in the years that he dabbled in moviemaking. Chapter 1 describes how and why the legends of Bonnie Parker and Kathryn Kelly were stitched together to create the perfect female foil for the 1930s G-man. It also explains the phenomenon of the "good" badwoman by examining the split in the genealogy of cinematic female antiheroes who were based on real-life characters. The second chapter chronicles the invention of Ma Barker and the revealing films that Ma inspired in order to probe that most vexing ingredient of women's outlawry: her real or potential status as a mother.

The third chapter examines the symbolic political significance of the cinematic Bonnie Parker, especially in a moment of social upheaval and the FBI's precipitous decline in the late 1960s. Penn's 1967 film created a cultural sensation and still appears on critics' lists of the best and most influential films ever made. But, as Chapter 3 explains, there were other, allegedly *anti*–Bonnie and Clyde films that did just as much or more to seal the folk-heroic myth of the 1930s bandits, and that ensured the cultural phenomenon of "Bonnie Parker" would affect a later generation of women lawbreakers.

By the early 1970s, the FBI was scrambling to reinvent itself amid the aftershocks of Hoover's death and multiple federal scandals, including exposure of the FBI's abusive counterintelligence program (COINTELPRO). Once left-leaning college students and civil rights leaders became targets of the state, the FBI's G-man risked appearing equal parts bullying and irrelevant. Casting about for renewed moral authority while aggressively policing activist groups such as the Black Panthers, the FBI waged a public relations battle that bore the marks of the era's racial, sexual, and class tensions. Keenly attuned to the growing influence of the new mass media, the largely white and female SLA incorporated exactly those tensions into a recognizable outlaw formula when they kidnapped Patricia Hearst and made her their star. Chapters 4 and 5 focus on the self-conscious stylings of 1970s radicals whose deliberate biographical distortions and mythical iconographies echo those of the most enduring celebrity women bandits of the 1930s. The fourth chapter sorts though the films and memoirs that imaginatively reanimated five SLA women, four of whom perished in the fiery 1974 shootout and one of whom survived to help conceal Patty Hearst for another year. That the SLA were not the only ones preoccupied with the crafting of their public image shows how projection and sociopolitical "play" affect both the popular reception of the woman outlaw and the perceived legitimacy of the law.

Chapter 4 is framed by Patricia Hearst's almost four-decade journey from object of public sympathy to object of public resentment and back again. Chapter 5 examines the same set of decades in the life of the Black Panther-turned-exile Assata Shakur, whose experiences accentuate the different assumptions and assigned meanings that surround the woman outlaw of color. The precise origins of Assata's outlawry are difficult to pinpoint. Did her career as an outlaw begin with the six years in which she was multiply tried and eventually imprisoned for the fatal shooting of a state trooper during a traffic stop on the New Jersey turnpike? Or, as her autobiography suggests, did it begin earlier, with her civil rights–era childhood and burgeoning racial and political consciousness?

Assata escaped prison in 1979 and went underground. In response to the explosion of posters calling for the arrest of Joanne Chesimard (Assata's given name), citizens in New York, New Jersey, and other areas of the country plastered their windows with another message: "ASSATA IS WELCOME HERE." Five years later, Assata turned up in Cuba, where she was given political asylum and where she remains to this day. A 1998 NBC interview with Assata prompted the FBI to put her back on its "Most Wanted" fugitives list, until she was briefly displaced by the events of September 11, 2001.[12] A marker both of the FBI's shifting priorities and of the interplay of political symbolism, media, and law enforcement, Assata currently appears on the Bureau's "Featured Fugitives" list of domestic terrorists. (She also tops the list of New Jersey's "12 Most Wanted.")

Assata was still in her twenties when she became the "soul" of the Black Liberation Army (BLA). Now sixty-three, Assata is the same age as Ma

Barker when she became famous. November 2009 marked her thirtieth anniversary as one of the FBI's "most wanted." More than her surviving contemporaries who were once attached to the SLA, the former BLA member has been motivated to cultivate the potent political symbolism attached to her outlaw status, and to experience that status as reflective of historically racist structures of justice in the United States. Chapter 6 juxtaposes the twenty-first-century experiences of Assata Shakur and Patricia Hearst and the lingering controversies attached to their respective outlawries. This analysis opens with a snapshot of the public responses to Sara Jane Olson (formerly Kathy Soliah), the "second team" SLA-fugitive-turned-Minnesota-housewife whom the FBI captured in 1999 and sent to prison shortly after September 11, 2001. While Sara Jane Olson is not one of the "Ten Most Wanted" described in this book, one could easily make the case that she has aspired to be. Olson is useful for sorting out the ways that the accumulated lore of journalistic fiction, films, and federal law enforcement continues to shape the meanings imposed on these three very different women who will shortly reach the status of senior citizens. Their combined stories make clear what must happen to the outlaw who "breaks the rules" of a conventional outlawry by refusing to die.

In 2005, the FBI's award for information leading to Assata's arrest was raised to $1 million, a sum that her victims hope will bring an overdue reckoning and that her defenders decry as a blatant call to bounty hunters. The truth is that every person who encounters Assata and others like her will take away something that they want or need. Such has always been the public response to U.S. women outlaws and to the specter of women's violence more generally. The folklore and popular culture entertainments they inspire are very much like dreams, inviting us to sift through the symbolism and dross for those uncanny insights we could not find anywhere else.

1

The Girls behind the
Man behind the Gun

Whatever else they may be, violent women are marketable. Just ask Al
Bulling, owner of the Last Resort, a Daytona Beach bar once frequented by
Aileen Wuornos. Wuornos was arrested at Bulling's bar in 1991 and exe-
cuted by the state in 2002 for having murdered at least six men. Bulling sells
T-shirts declaring his joint the "world famous home of ice cold beer and
killer women." He also sells "Crazed Killer Hot Sauce" in bottles featuring
Wuornos's picture and a warning: "Not to be used by women with PMS."[1]

In 2003, Bulling and his bar appeared in *Monster*, a film about Wuornos's
murdering spree and her romance with the young woman who eventually
turned her in. Critics devoted less space to the film's serial killer story line
than to the dramatic physical transformation undertaken by actress Charlize Theron, who gained thirty pounds and wore a set of crooked yellow teeth in the leading role. Theron won broad praise for channeling
Wuornos's self-conscious bluster and deadening humanity. But her Oscar-
winning performance received the most attention for the attractive actress's
willingness to "play ugly."

Women's on-screen criminality had come in quite a different package
the year prior, in the movie musical *Chicago* (2002). A cynical send-up of
American fame and infamy, *Chicago* presents women's capacity for violence
both as a joke and a sexual asset. Like *Monster*, *Chicago* is based on a pair

of real-life women whose murder trials vaulted them to brief celebrity in the 1920s. But *Chicago*'s antihero protagonists are as beautiful as they are backstabbing and ambitious. Like *Monster*'s Wuornos, *Chicago*'s Velma and Roxie commit murder to get back at the men who hurt them. Also like Wuornos, they are desperate for love and hungry for the sorts of consumer goods that will validate them as worthy of others' envy and approval.

Genrewise, *Monster* and *Chicago* could not be farther apart. But together they suggest the range of predictable fetishes that emerge in recountings of women's violence. *Chicago*'s fetish is sex or, more precisely, the sexual appeal that is presented as both the cause and the *effect* of its principals' violence against men. Like all the other women killers in the film's prison sequence, Velma appears in strappy dominatrix costume, underscoring the seductiveness of hostility mixed with desire. Abetted by their show-women's instincts, Velma and Roxie exploit the titillating spectacle of aggression crossed with glamorous femininity. At film's end, the "scintillating sinners" dance onstage with a pair of glossy white tommy guns. When they point their guns into the crowd, the audience explodes with laughter and applause.

Monster takes a more sober tack. As its double-edged title suggests, the cinematic Aileen Wuornos is initially more of a Frankenstein's monster— brutalized, cast out, misunderstood—than a fiend. Like Velma and Roxie, she rewrites the traditional female victim role and becomes an aggressor. But her desires and appearance do not fit within sanctioned formulas of heteroromance and so cannot be repurposed as sexy entertainment. (Al Bulling's "Crazed Killer" advertising has a whiff of dangerous allure but is more nervous about the prospect of an inherently unstable female biology that might unleash a woman's anger.) The on-screen Wuornos is compelling, but not in a way that invites audience identification or fantasy. She is too needy to be slick and too brutal to be the avenging hero that she briefly fancies herself. That is one reason that the "restoration" of actress Charlize Theron to her successful movie-star self became so much a part of *Monster*'s story for the public. Theron's extradiagetic transformation from beast to beauty offered a sliver of redemption to the character Wuornos, whose opening line is an ironic confession: "I always wanted to be in the movies."

There are some who would argue that putting Aileen Wuornos in the movies is an affront to her victims and risks exalting her crimes. ("I have a problem taking these serial killers and making heroes out of them," Al Bulling told an interviewer in 2004.) *Chicago* chides its audience for making celebrities of killer women, but it does so with a winking plot that is clearly predicated on those same women's charismatic appeal. Both *Monster* and *Chicago* point to the fierce ambivalence that surrounds portrayals of women's violence, especially portrayals that are based on real-life people and events. This chapter explores the origins both of that ambivalence and of the entertainment formula that marks the boundaries of "appropriate" narratives of female deviance. *Chicago's* principals commit acts of violence according to this formula and then reassure an anxious public by performing a conventional femininity. That is why the audience guffaws when Velma and Roxie level their guns and why the duo ultimately escape punishment.

How does consensus arise around the notion of the "good" woman offender? What unwritten codes of conduct does she help reinforce, in tandem with her counterpart, the thoroughly "bad" woman offender? And, finally, what social forces must combine to create that rare woman lawbreaker who becomes something larger than herself—an outlaw symbol of the exhilaration and unease accompanying shifts in the cultural zeitgeist? The answers to these questions are complex, to be sure. But the most convincing explanation for the "good" or riveting badwoman hinges on a longstanding alliance between professional mythmakers and law enforcement. Of necessity, this chapter is selective in exploring that alliance, focusing exclusively on a tradition of women's outlawry in the United States and what happened to that tradition at the nexus of the Great Depression, New Deal reforms, and the expanding mission of J. Edgar Hoover's FBI. Women certainly were not the G-men's primary target in their 1930s war on crime. Yet a few women offenders became staples of the Bureau's narrative of itself, because they were useful tools for arousing public support of the movement to federalize crime control.

For an understanding of the "good badwoman" and her mutually constitutive relationship with Hoover's G-men, this chapter turns now to the tales of Bonnie Parker (of Bonnie and Clyde fame) and Kathryn "Mrs. Machine Gun" Kelly. Just as comparing the films *Chicago* and *Monster* reveals more than either of those two films could on their own, the stories of these two women bandits help illuminate how some women offenders are elevated to celebrity outlaw status while others are reviled as villains. The popular myths around Bonnie and Kathryn and the jumbling together of their two biographies are clues as to what 1930s audiences found most frightening and entertaining about each. Meanwhile, the Bureau's response to Bonnie, Kathryn, and other women like them reflected Hoover's conviction that U.S. citizens should have intimate knowledge of their "public enemies." In Hoover's view, staving off threats to domestic tranquility would require the scrutiny of individual citizens' personal conduct and reinforcement of the boundaries of "respectable" male and female behavior.

The Faithful Girlfriend: Bonnie Parker

Emma Parker fainted when the reporter called her Dallas home with the news. Her daughter, Bonnie, had been killed with her boyfriend by a sheriff's posse in Arcadia, Louisiana. Bonnie's older brother, Buster, later sought to comfort his mother, reminding her that rumors of Bonnie and Clyde's capture had circulated before but that the duo had never failed to escape. Other Barrow Gang members might be left behind in the lawmen's ambush, but the two most famous members of the gang, Clyde Barrow and Bonnie Parker, always got away.

On the morning of the phone call, however, the tables had turned. Bonnie and Clyde had been indirectly betrayed by one of the lesser Barrow Gang members, Henry Methvin. Henry's father, Ivan, had allegedly offered the sheriff information on Bonnie and Clyde's whereabouts in exchange for clemency for his fugitive son. At dawn on May 23, 1934, Ivan Methvin and an assortment of ex–Texas Rangers and Dallas deputies were lying in wait alongside the Louisiana back road that Bonnie and Clyde would travel on their way to rendezvous with the junior Methvin. Methvin's father's logging truck had been positioned to suggest that he was struggling with a flat tire; the posse was counting on Clyde to recognize the truck and stop to help.

All went almost exactly to plan. A stolen tan Ford V-8 came hurtling down the dirt road shortly after 9 A.M. As usual, Clyde was driving in his stocking feet. Bonnie was at his side with a Louisiana road map and a gun balanced on her knees. When the car slowed, the concealed posse opened fire, pouring round after round into the outlaws' sedan, which careened to an awkward halt and then rocked under the hail of bullets. Neither of the bandits managed to return fire. The windows shattered and the back of Clyde's head exploded. Shot multiple times in the hand, jaw, and forehead, Bonnie slumped forward, her face splattered with blood.[2]

Thus ended the inglorious criminal career of twenty-three-year old Bonnie Parker, a working-class Texas woman who had come of age in impoverished and crime-ridden West Dallas. At sixteen, Bonnie had abandoned the schoolwork at which she excelled to marry a man who soon deserted her and then went to jail for murder. Having lost her job as a waitress in the first year of the Depression, she was unemployed and dreaming of becoming an actress or a poet when she met Clyde Barrow in January 1930. Clyde, an escaped convict, was returned to prison shortly after this meeting but managed another breakout after coaxing Bonnie to smuggle him a gun. The romance that flared so rapidly stalled only two months after it began when Clyde was sent back to jail from 1930 to 1931, and then again when, during a failed car theft in early 1932, he left Bonnie behind to be captured and briefly imprisoned. Humiliated, Bonnie swore that she would never see Clyde again. But she also felt thwarted by the deepening Depression and the nearly three years in which she had struggled to secure steady work. By June 1932, Bonnie had rekindled her bond with Clyde and become an official traveling member of the Barrow Gang.

However much Bonnie Parker loved Clyde Barrow, her bleak prospects at age twenty-one probably spurred her willingness to join Clyde in a life outside the law. Given her well-documented love for drama and performance, she may have been desperate for the excitement and attention she had not found in Dallas. The stolen cars that Bonnie and Clyde left behind frequently contained newspapers folded to stories about themselves, indicating that they were following their own press. Clyde seems to have been motivated less by fame than by his determination to avenge the exceptionally harsh treatment that he and other prisoners had endured as inmates of the Texas prison system. But Bonnie reportedly spoke of "[her] public" and took pains to ensure that the people who read about her and Clyde in the papers knew that the fugitive couple were "just folks."

In death, Bonnie and Clyde would finally make national headlines. Before the fatal ambush, Bonnie was best known for the photo that she had not intended for the press, which showed Bonnie pretending to smoke a cigar. The image became one of the most publicized photographs of the twentieth century, and one that Bonnie unhappily obsessed over for the rest of her life. (When the Barrow Gang took as hostage a policeman whom they had wounded, Bonnie released the officer with an order: "That bit about me smoking cigars—it's bunk. Tell them I don't smoke cigars.")[3] An amateur poet, she wrestled with her self-image in two of her poems: "The Story of Suicide Sal," composed in a fury at Clyde during her short stint in prison, and the clear-eyed "End of the Line (Ballad of Bonnie and Clyde)," which predicted the couple's early death. The ballad also predicted that the families of Bonnie and Clyde would "bury them side-by-side," but that was not to be. Ignoring her daughter's wishes, Emma Parker refused to permit Bonnie's mangled remains to be interred beside her lover's. As Mrs. Parker reasoned, "Clyde had her for two years, and look what he did to her."[4]

Now, over seventy-five years after their deaths, we might more appropriately look at what Bonnie did to Clyde, and, in particular, how she ensured the outlaws' remarkable staying power as cultural icons. Grander underworld figures such as John Dillinger and Alvin Karpis scoffed at Clyde and Bonnie as "Goddamn Texas screwballs" and embarrassing "kids."[5] Compared to the scope, daring, and financial rewards of Dillinger's bank heists or Karpis's kidnapping ventures with the Barker brothers, the Barrow Gang's crimes—mostly filling station holdups and panicked shootouts with police officers—did seem amateurish and bloody. The Barrow Gang killed up to thirteen people, nine of whom were guards or police officers. Some of those deaths may have been avoidable but for Clyde and Bonnie's diminutive proportions. (He stood five feet six; Bonnie, only four feet eleven.) Puzzled by the growing number of slayings attributed to the pair, former gang member Ralph Fults relayed a message to Clyde to ask why so many people were dying. Clyde replied, "They think we're just school kids. They won't 'go up' for us. They don't think we're serious when we show them our guns. I guess because we're so small."[6]

Had Bonnie been a man, she and the rest of the Barrow Gang would likely have faded into obscurity with other Depression-era desperados who killed or stole for survival or amusement in the weakly policed mid- and southwestern United States. The novelty of Bonnie's tiny, feminine presence earmarked the Barrow Gang for celebrity—but why? Other rural gangs traveled with equally dedicated wives and girlfriends, and yet most of these women have been forgotten. Bonnie's cultural staying power began with the fact of her dramatic and, some argued, unjust killing at the hands of the law. That she went to her death in the exclusive company of Clyde made it possible to romanticize the couple as a combination of Robin Hood and Maid Marian (courageous champions of the poor) and Romeo and Juliet (doomed victims of fate and oppressive authority figures). Clyde was a killer, to be sure. But the record is murky on whether or not Bonnie ever had a direct hand in murdering anyone. By some accounts, Bonnie was the gang's fiercest aggressor and someone who either thrilled at the opportunity for bloodshed or was pathologically indifferent to it. She died with a rifle across her lap, but sources close to the outlaws insist that Bonnie left all the shooting to Clyde. According to former Barrow Gang member W. D. Jones, "She never fired a gun. But I'll say that she was a hell of a [gun] loader."[7] Contradictory accounts helped to fuel the Bonnie-and-Clyde legend. The *possibility* that Bonnie was more ruthless and violent than Clyde, crossed with the *possibility* that she was, instead, a devoted accomplice who left the killing to the men, became a key source of her—and Clyde's—ongoing cultural cachet.

Adding to that cachet was Fritz Lang's critically acclaimed *You Only Live Once*, released just three years after Bonnie and Clyde had died, and built around recognizable details from their lives. For his fatalist picture, Lang cast actor Henry Fonda—a beloved American icon even in 1937—as the "three-time loser" Eddie Taylor. Embittered by a sadistic U.S. prison system, Eddie at least has the love of a good woman, Jo (Sylvia Sidney), who happily becomes his wife. But the attractive newlyweds are forced to become fugitives after the ex-convict Eddie is shunned by "respectable" society and threatened with execution for a crime he did not commit. Once Jo's face begins appearing alongside Eddie's on wanted posters, more savvy lawbreakers blame their own crimes on the notorious couple. Although she is innocent, Jo repeatedly avows her willingness to die with Eddie, even going so far as to give over their newborn infant to her sister so she can remain with Eddie to the end. She breaks the law precisely once—to steal lifesaving bandages for her husband.

You Only Live Once echoed what Bonnie and Clyde's relatives had maintained about the outlaw lovers: that they were decent people, disinterested in luxury, and selfless in their devotion to each other. Eddie murders only when trapped and, above all, whenever the couple's quiet domestic life is threatened by an uncomprehending law. At film's end, an unseen gunman assassinates the lovers in a forest, just a few yards from the safety of the Canadian border. When Jo expires in Eddie's arms, she assures him that she has no regrets: "I'd do it again, darling." Eddie looks heavenward and hears the voice of the priest friend whom he accidentally shot in a panic. The priest's off-screen voice intones, "Open the gates!" suggesting that Eddie and Jo will be welcomed into paradise and granted, at last, the freedom denied to them on earth.

Film censors in Mexico objected to the dead priest's benediction, asking that it be struck from the film.[8] But even without the promise of a golden afterlife for its bandits, *You Only Live Once* did plenty to establish its protagonists' immortality. Attentive as he was to public attitudes toward crime, J. Edgar Hoover could not have been pleased, especially since Lang's film successfully skirted the Motion Picture Production Code's injunction that "the sympathy of the audience should never be thrown to the side of crime, wrongdoing, evil or sin." In the same month that Lang's film arrived in movie theatres, Hoover countered with the tale of another famous outlaw couple, a pair less likely to be resuscitated as sympathetic heroes.

The Domineering Wife: Kathryn Kelly

In 1933, a newly powerful Federal Bureau of Investigation wrapped up its first major case, which culminated in the trial of George and Kathryn Kelly. The couple was charged with the kidnapping and ransom of Charles Urschel, a wealthy Oklahoma oilman whom the Kellys and their confederates had held for ransom in Texas. Closing the net on the Kellys had not been easy, not even with the help of the savvy Urschel, who had managed to lead investigators back to his abductors' hideout. George, after all, was known throughout the country as "Machine Gun Kelly," the man who could write his name on a wall with machine gun bullets. In the wake of the Urschel kidnapping, he also became the Bureau's "Public Enemy No. 1." When authorities finally caught up with George in his native Memphis, he had been on the lam for almost two months, in which time he—or perhaps his wife?—had further terrorized the Urschels with letters that threatened to exterminate their entire family. The menacing letters may have been one reason that the FBI took liberties in their description of Kelly's arrest, claiming that agents had so panicked Kelly in a predawn raid that the gangster had coined for them a new nickname: "Don't shoot, G-men!" Kelly allegedly yelped. "Don't shoot!"[9]

Shaken from sleep by the raiding party, Kathryn Kelly feigned a bout of appendicitis. When that did not earn her escape, she tried instead to bribe one of the deputy sheriffs. The bribery attempt flopped in a room crowded with police officers and the press, so Kathryn reportedly switched tactics and began giving interviews. Weeping, she professed her innocence and said that George had promised to kill her if she did not partake in his crimes. Kathryn would later repeat this story on the stand, insisting that George had conceived of and planned the Urschel kidnapping on his own.

The trial judge was unconvinced. He broke courtroom protocol to warn jurors that Kathryn Kelly "was not wholly truthful" and, in fact, had contradicted earlier statements showing that she "knew about the kidnapping and knowingly participated." In the prosecuting attorney's final argument to the jury, he ridiculed Kathryn for pretending to be "a demure, loving, and fearful wife" in the face of evidence that she and her husband had used stolen cash to buy cars and expensive jewelry. Because Kathryn had purchased her husband's machine guns for him, the prosecutor derided her claims to innocence, pegging her as "the arch-conspirator."[10]

Kathryn Kelly was born Cleo Coleman Brooks in 1904 in the tiny town of Saltillo, Mississippi. Married at age fifteen, Cleo had a daughter with her first husband before moving back home to live with her mother. Before she met George Kelly, she had changed her name to "Kathryn" and had married twice more. Her third husband, the bootlegger Charlie Thorne, apparently took his own life, although his typewritten suicide note ("I can't live with her or without her") invited speculation that Kathryn had a hand in his demise.[11] She also may have helped plan a series of burglaries with a boyfriend in Fort Worth, Texas, but later argued that she knew nothing of her lover's criminal activities. The boyfriend vouchsafed for Kathryn's innocence and drew a five-year jail term. Kathryn was set free.[12]

Kathryn then married George Kelly, whom she had earlier remade as "Machine Gun" Kelly, a name she sensed would capture both headlines and the public imagination. George Kelly had once been George Kelly Barnes, the privileged son of a well-to-do insurance executive. After failed stints at college, marriage, and fatherhood, George drifted to Oklahoma, dropping his original surname along the way. Kathryn moved her new husband to her mother's ranch in Paradise, Texas, where she apparently helped transform the small-time bootlegger into a fearsome outlaw. According to lore, it was she who disciplined George to become a crack shot with a machine gun and she who slyly promoted Kelly by distributing his spent .45-caliber cartridges as souvenirs. As Machine Gun's reputation grew, so did his ability to recruit a more hardened element of the underworld to collaborate on bank heists. Soon the "notorious Machine Gun Kelly gang" had surfaced in local news reports. But the big bank jobs and national headlines remained out of reach, reserved as they were for more successful gangsters like Dillinger, Pretty Boy Floyd, and Baby Face Nelson. In search of better publicity and a bigger take, the Kellys began to dabble in kidnapping. Kathryn bought the signature guns with which George and some cronies snatched Charles Urschel from the middle of his bridge game in July 1933. Whatever else her role had been in the kidnapping, the machine-gun purchase—combined with the eloquence of the ransom notes—became the most damning evidence that Kathryn Kelly was the scheming pilot behind her husband and his gang.

Reflecting on the Urschel case five years later in his best-selling book, *Persons in Hiding*, Hoover wrote,

There was no doubt that the persons who had abducted [Urschel] were cold, cruel, accustomed to crime . . . Yet, when the ransom letters began to arrive, they carried an atmosphere of imagination and a casual use of hyphenated words entirely foreign to the average gangster . . . There was evidence of feminine thought and psychology. There was one conclusion: that the actual work had been done by a vicious gang, guided by some woman of superior intelligence.[13]

The formidable Machine Gun Kelly and the famous kidnapping for which he eventually received a life term are reduced to mere backstory in the case summaries published under Hoover's byline. For the rest of the decade, and for much of his long career, Hoover narrated the Urschel case with Kathryn Kelly as its primary antagonist. By Hoover's telling (or by that of the closely supervised ghostwriters who wrote in Hoover's name), George's wife seemed always to have a "longshoreman profanity" streaming from her "liquor-loosened lips," and it was she who became the true source of George's depravity. According to Hoover's team, it was Kathryn who could be counted on to "pac[e] and screa[m] hysterically until at last the man who was supposedly one of America's worse [*sic*] gangsters weakly assented to her demands." And whenever George lost his nerve, it was Kathryn who would call him a "cheap, sniveling blankety-blank-blank," but who would also promise him, "I'll take care of you, if you're so damned scared." Taking a cue from the FBI's official accounting of the Kelly case, many crime writers portrayed Machine Gun as a phony man-child, lost in the fantasy of the gangster movies whose style he copied. More than one publication described Kathryn as taking George to a movie house and plunking him in the back row, the better to placate her weak-willed husband and to get him out of the way while she rented a new hideout.[14]

While the typical gangster's woman, or "gun moll," was often derided as a materialistic airhead or romantically blinkered fool, Kathryn Kelly became famous as the alleged Svengali behind her puppet husband. Despite subsequent evidence that Kathryn may not, in fact, have written all the ransom letters for her husband or the eloquent threats to the Urschels that came later, her image as the "brains" of the Machine Gun Kelly gang stuck. Of course, Kathryn also had her weaknesses, claimed Hoover, among them a "maudlin streak which filtered through her cold-bloodedness."[15] Before she went to trial, Kathryn was known to dote on her fourteen-year-old daughter and to rank blood relations before spouses. Aware of her "almost weird clannishness for her own kin," the FBI at one point seized her mother and stepfather as bait. For her complicity in concealing Urschel at their ranch, Kathryn's mother, Ora Shannon, drew a life sentence, which indeed threw Kathryn into a panic. She may have cajoled George into composing the threats that bore his fingerprints. She fired off another set of letters condemning her husband and promising cooperation with the police if they would concede Machine Gun had coerced her parents' involvement. During her own trial, Kathryn even tried to cut a secret deal with the judge in which she would plead guilty in exchange for her mother's release. (The judge rebuffed the offer as inappropriate.)[16]

Hoover's *Persons in Hiding* borrowed liberally from E. E. Kirkpatrick's 1934 history of the Urschel kidnapping, which dubbed Kathryn a "consummate actress" for having postured as "the country girl who has fallen for the wiles of the city bred gangster." While conceding that Kathryn may once have been "a creature of the kindest impulses, lavish in her charities and tender in her sympathy for unfortunates," Kirkpatrick assured his readers that something monstrous lurked beneath her gentle facade. When a prosecuting attorney asked about her husband's guns, Kathryn's "falsely demure countenance changed to one of a cornered tigress." Under cross-examination, her eyes became "narrow slits of yellow venom. The sweet girlish smile had changed to a fiendish snarl. Her soft tones had changed to darts of forked lightning."[17]

Hoover and his ghostwriters also ran with the theme of a feminine predilection for deceit. According to *Persons in Hiding*, Kathryn had a red wig that was both a source and a symptom of her power. ("As soon as I get a red wig, I'll be alright," says Hoover's on-the-lam Kathryn.)[18] As Hoover later told the New York Round Table in apparent earnest, the female criminal "always has red hair . . . She either adopts a red wig or has her hair dyed red."[19] This hypothesis likely arose from centuries of lore around red hair as the mark of the libidinous, mischievous, or hot-tempered individual. It also reflected the FBI's prominent case files on Bonnie Parker, a natural strawberry blonde who sometimes tinted her hair a darker red, and on Kate "Ma" Barker, who did the same.

When the Kellys were cornered in Memphis, "the officers knew that of the two persons they sought, *the most dangerous by far was the woman.*"[20] For many years, true crime accounts of the Kelly tale seemed always to end on exactly the same joke as that repeated by Hoover: namely, that once revealed to the world as a henpecked, emasculated husband, Machine Gun Kelly became "Popgun Kelly."

The Home Front in the War on Crime

The scrutiny given to the Kellys' relationship and that of Bonnie and Clyde was symptomatic of a widespread unease around gender roles during the Great Depression. It also reflected the bandits' ongoing utility once they were dead or behind bars. Their criminal careers halted, Kathryn Kelly and Bonnie Parker became "wanted" as new formulas for outlaw fiction. At the same time, they helped solidify a new set of strategies for twentieth-century law enforcement, one that presumed that a woman could be just as corrupt as a man, and that sought to weaken the male lawbreaker by going after his female associates. Hoover's FBI would rely on the feminine-coded foibles of public enemies like Machine Gun Kelly to popularize and professionalize the 1930s G-men.

Of course, what became known as "Hoover's FBI" did not really exist before Hoover came to prominence during the Depression-era crime wave. A decade earlier, as head of the General Intelligence Division, Hoover had distinguished himself rather too zealously in the months leading up to the controversial Palmer Raids.[21] Following a rash of anarchist bombings in 1919, Hoover deployed every scrap of intelligence to round up radicals and immigrants suspected of endorsing violent political activity. Amid great public fanfare, he helped deport anarchist leaders such as Alexander Berkman and Emma Goldman to Russia. By 1921, Hoover had been named assistant director of the Bureau of Investigation. Just three years later, when financial improprieties rocked the Harding administration and sent political aftershocks through the Bureau, Director William Burns resigned in disgrace. So it was that the twenty-nine-year-old Hoover ascended to the post that he would hold for the rest of his life.[22]

Tasked with giving the scandal-ridden Bureau a thorough housecleaning, Director Hoover imposed stricter codes of dress and conduct on his agents. He purged the Bureau of nearly a hundred underperforming employees and political appointees, and he insisted that new hires undergo rigorous background checks and physical examinations. Hoover also required that agent recruits be between twenty-five and thirty-five years old, preferably with experience in accounting or the law. As a result, the new agents began to acquire a reputation much like Hoover's own—as highly competent bureaucrats. Their duties did not include enforcing Prohibition (there was a separate office for that), but the ban on alcohol had promoted a general atmosphere of lawlessness and a spike in gang activity that eventually extended the Bureau of Investigation's reach. In the meantime, Hoover quietly rebuilt his Bureau's image in a political climate that valued efficiency and limited government. In 1924, he created the Identification Division to consolidate the United States' two major collections of fingerprint files. Thereafter, "Ident" would serve as the nation's clearinghouse for prints collected by police agencies far and wide. Administering the prints lent the Bureau new authority, but without impinging on states' rights principles that regarded law enforcement as a local and state responsibility.

The stock market crash of 1929 and the economic ravages of the Great Depression scrambled the political landscape and set the stage for a much bigger role for the Bureau of Investigation. Once Franklin Delano Roosevelt had cinched the 1932 presidential election, his New Deal reforms ensured that the federal government would take on greater responsibility for the country's social welfare, especially in law enforcement. The 1932 Lindbergh baby kidnapping and the 1933 Kansas City Massacre, in which four lawmen and their prisoner were cut down by machine-gun fire outside a busy railway station, had ramped up pressure on Washington to do something about the violent crime that seemed to have intensified with the country's economic malaise.[23] The Roosevelt administration leveraged both the massacre and an outbreak of subsequent high-profile kidnappings to put dollars and political will behind a grassroots anticrime movement. As the gangster violence that had plagued the urban centers spread to the rural countryside, frightened citizens questioned the ability of local law officers to protect them.

In 1930, the Bureau of Investigation began disseminating its *Uniform Crime Reports*, an annual compilation of statistics that quantified crime rates and trends. These reports became an essential tool for local law enforcement agencies that wanted to hone their methods—and justify their budgets. In short order, the Bureau's own budget expanded rapidly, along with its jurisdiction. The newly enacted Lindbergh Law had made kidnapping a federal crime, which is why Hoover's agents could go after Machine Gun Kelly.[24] When gangsters like John Dillinger evaded capture by crossing over state lines, Congress passed a number of federal crime laws further enhancing Bureau powers. By 1934, Congress had decreed that the formerly unarmed agents could carry guns and make arrests. Suddenly, Hoover's "college boys" were the nation's top cops. The formerly unassuming Bureau of Investigation was renamed the Federal Bureau of Investigation (FBI), a title that suggested that it was the only federal agency of its kind.[25]

Between 1932 and 1939, the number of Bureau agents more than doubled, from 338 to 713. The same years saw an explosion of publicity for the FBI. Courting favorable press was nothing new in Washington, but in the push for New Deal legislation, federal agencies had dramatically stepped up their public relations efforts.[26] Declaring the notorious hoodlums of the early 1930s a threat to national security, President Roosevelt summoned both public outrage and "the strong arm of Government for their immediate suppression." Attorney General Homer Cummings, who had declared the nation's war on crime, sought to counteract gangsters' appeal by pitting them against a brand new idol: the FBI's G-man. Thus commenced an expensive and far-reaching campaign to sell the federal agent as an unimpeachable hero who "always got his man."[27]

As FBI director, Hoover soon found himself personally enshrined as a symbol of crime control. After offering a few weak objections, he was swiftly converted to the cause. Like Kathryn Kelly, Hoover well understood how the right public image could earn his organization greater respect, increased authority, and a steady stream of federal funds. Together with Cummings and publicists like Louis B. Nichols, Hoover forged a gallant archetype for his agents. The modern federal agent was a courageous crusader—clean-cut, dedicated, and morally upright. It was he (for the G-man was always a *he*) who had so frightened Machine Gun Kelly, at least in the story fed to the press.[28] And how better to draw media attention to the G-man's power than to assign the title of "Public Enemy No. 1" to a succession of high-profile criminals right before their capture or death? Hoover shrewdly designated John Dillinger as the number-one public enemy three months before agents ambushed him in front of Chicago's Biograph Theater.

Hoover grasped how the widespread fascination with the outlaw could be used in service of his own reputation and that of the law. When Chicago agent Melvin Purvis attracted accolades for his role in bringing down Dillinger in July 1934, Hoover responded by banishing Purvis and posing for the newspapers himself with Dillinger's hat, gun, and plaster death mask.[29] These remnants of the gangster's final moments, plus artifacts from other outlaws of the same era, soon became a part of the FBI headquarters tour in Washington, D.C. Visitors were invited to gawk at evidence of a vanquished criminal and then observe on-site agents peering into microscopes and poring over fingerprint indexes in the Bureau's cutting-edge "Crime Laboratory."

The juxtaposition of the gritty and impulsive outlaw with the scrupulous federal agent made for a compelling story. It was a story that Hoover and his Crime Records Division told over and over again. As one famous hoodlum after another fell or surrendered to the G-men's guns, the Bureau began feeding "authentic source material" to favored members of the press. Working with a stable of newspaper contacts and ghostwriters who sometimes affected a hard-boiled reporting style to mimic a gangster patois,

Hoover distributed colorful versions of the Bureau's best cases to newspapers, magazines, radio programs, and comic strips. Warring with crime had always made good entertainment, and the FBI scored a grand public relations coup with the release of the Oscar-nominated *'G' Men* in 1935. Brick Davis, James Cagney's streetwise special agent, sealed the FBI agent's status as a new American hero. Although Hoover had not originally endorsed the Warner Brothers project, *'G' Men* hit most of his talking points. It extolled the scientific detective work (ballistics tests, microscopic analysis, and fingerprint analysis) of which the Bureau was justly proud. The film even went so far as to rewrite the FBI's real-life embarrassments into triumphs.[30]

James Cagney's star turn as the G-man became an apt symbol for the pragmatic alignment of film industry formulas with the goals of the emergent FBI. The efforts of moralists and film censors aside, the gangster picture had become a popular movie house staple by the time of Prohibition's repeal in 1933. Gangster films had launched Cagney's career, and several of the very best featured Cagney as charismatic screen baddie—an urban, ethnic outsider determined to snare his piece of the increasingly elusive American dream. Repackaging the antihero-protagonist of Warner Brothers' *The Public Enemy* (1931) into a rugged federal agent lent some ironic spice to the straitlaced G-man. Cagney's straight-arrow agent had style, and it was built on his rogue's cachet.

Although the big-name bandits dubbed official "Enemies" of the middle 1930s indeed posed a threat to the public, certain subsets of that public had helped create them. Unlike the shadowy, urban, kin-based criminal syndicates that had preoccupied police and dominated movie screens in the late 1920s and early 1930s, lawbreakers like Dillinger and "Pretty Boy" Floyd had come of age in the rural Midwest and were of "pure American stock."[31] Widely feared for their violent acts, they also happened to be robbing banks at a moment when banks were unpopular.[32] The best-known bandits understood the importance of appearing the enemies of ruling-class interests and the allies of common folk who might be courted or bribed to conceal them. Generously reimbursing a rural family for meals and lodging and preventing the odd farm foreclosure was, for the new gangsters of the Midwest and Southwest, a worthy investment in preserving their liberty. Some of the "pure American" (white guy) public enemies invited comparisons to Robin Hood and to the not-so-distant hero-outlaws of the vanished American frontier. The more image-conscious bandits also evoked—and were influenced by—the era's most winsome movie stars. (For his habit of vaulting over bank counters, Dillinger was said to resemble the athletic actor Douglas Fairbanks.)[33]

This is not to say that every person hit hard by the Depression or in need of a little escapist fantasy felt sympathy for the homegrown gangsters whose misadventures the newspapers faithfully chronicled. But the *idea* of real people shucking the system, crisscrossing the country in their automobiles, and living by the gun could not help but send ripples through a national consciousness that had idealized the open country and a sometimes defiant self-reliance. To adapt Lizabeth Cohen's observation about Depression-era mass culture, each citizen's attitude toward 1930s lawbreakers therefore "depended on the social and economic contexts in which it developed and the manner in which it was experienced." If a celebrity outlaw came to prominence in the right way, then he—and, much more rarely, *she*—became the raw material that various subgroups could fashion to suit their own needs.[34]

Among those subgroups that used the outlaw for their own purposes was the FBI. Distressed at the lure of Depression-era bandits, and obligated to justify his own frequent retellings of their stories, Hoover reasoned "the best way to 'deflate' a criminal is to tell the whole truth about him."[35] Encouraging the press to follow his lead, Hoover vowed to "tell the truth about these rats." As he allegedly fumed to another member of the Department of Justice in 1934, "I'm going to tell the truth about their dirty, filthy, diseased women. I'm going to tell the truth about the miserable politicians who protect them and the slimy, silly, or sob-sister convict lovers who let them out on sentimental or illy-advised paroles."[36]

In 1936 Hoover collaborated with Universal Pictures on *You Can't Get Away with It*, a short documentary designed to showcase Bureau headquarters and the accomplishments of its highly disciplined—and highly anonymous—agents. (Hoover is the only FBI employee mentioned by name.) As the film's narrator explains, G-men were "soldiers in war while the world is at peace," and their dedication and know-how were the reason that the country had been released from the grip of gangland. The camera pans the FBI's carefully archived records, taking special note of the voluminous files devoted to women criminals—"400,000 of them—notorious female crooks and gangster females more deadly than the male."

In the years leading up to World War II, Hoover made women's potential criminality a focus of his lectures to women's groups, warning them how vital was their own moral example to their country's health. As he told the General Federation of Women's Clubs in Kansas City, Missouri, in 1938: "On two battle fronts we need the assistance of the women of the country: in the home and in civic life. The more important of these is in the home." As Hoover saw it, the country depended on homebound wives and mothers to apply their feminine influence to raise tomorrow's law-abiding citizens. As for women's role in the civic sphere, Hoover encouraged women to aspire to a "higher form of civic responsibility, so that the laws of our country may be efficiently enforced."[37] In other words, they should not insert a feminine sensibility where it did not belong—especially in efforts to reform the parole system, which Hoover regarded as having been weakened by naive, rich women too easily beguiled by the story of "a boy who never had a chance."[38] Public safety depended on these women (and the men who would be persuaded by them) to step aside in deference to more rational citizen leaders.

In the pages of the newly revamped *American Magazine*, Hoover lent his byline to a recurring feature that promised "never-before-told stories behind the most famous cases of our G-Men." Although it was billed as the "Secrets of the G-Men" and "the human stories behind the guns," the feature spent almost no time on the FBI's agents. Its didactic articles instead were built around criminal exploits and on choices made by ordinary people in modest circumstances. Citizens who partook in crimes, or who had tolerated or encouraged criminals, were shown lamenting their ruined reputations. The really wicked met with jail time or even a violent death—but not before Hoover had parsed the modern-day moral hazards that were the sources of their depravity.

The G-man series was a good fit in the 1930s for *American Magazine*, a men's magazine that had been converted to a "family magazine" shortly after the crash of 1929, when it gave up its Horatio Alger formula in favor of content that downplayed individual success and promoted the merits of a civic-minded self-discipline.[39] What *American Magazine* billed as true stories from the files of the FBI therefore became parables, especially for women. The "Secrets" series only rarely featured a woman criminal but frequently included warnings about the need to preserve women's virtue by saving them from their basest impulses, including a "misguided hero worship" of the moneyed male gangster. As Hoover theorized, women's increasing demands for fashions and new consumer goods could drive their men to thievery. Women's fondness for self-indulgent leisure pursuits and their susceptibility to excitement could make them careless parents who produced tomorrow's hoodlums.

In the narratives he cowrote with *American Magazine*'s Courtney Ryley Cooper, Hoover cautioned readers to check their individualistic desires, lest they follow the path of the gangland women who ended up ruined or dead. Occasionally, these warnings came in ironic contexts or from an unlikely source. For example, the November 1936 article "The Boy Who Wanted to Go Fishing" ostensibly profiled the notorious gangster Alvin Karpis but spent equal time on his romance with his girlfriend Dolores Delaney. Delaney had given birth to Karpis's son shortly after a police shootout in which Karpis left her behind with a bullet in her leg. For harboring one of the nation's top public enemies, she received a harsh sentence—immediate separation from her infant and five years in the steel cages of a prison for "female incorrigibles." *American Magazine* printed a letter that Karpis allegedly sent Delaney after her sentencing, one in which he reminded her, "All that glitters is not gold." Ignoring her avowals of continued affection, Karpis's letter urged Delaney to "stay the straight and narrow path" after her release and to "refrain from smoking cigars."[40] The deliberately unglamorous story line of Delaney's betrayal, imprisonment, and parentless offspring was meant to undercut the appeal of a gangland romance, especially for women. The cigar, of course, was made-up detail borrowed from the Bonnie Parker story. As Hoover and Cooper ventriloquized in the voice of Karpis, women were headed down the wrong path the moment they gave up honest living and subverted the natural family order.

Shake-Ups, Scapegoats, and Leading Ladies

Of course, much of what had been taken for granted as "natural" was passing away during the uncertain years of the Depression, when marriage rates had plummeted and fewer families were relying on a traditional, male breadwinner. By 1932, unemployment stood at a whopping 25 percent. Women workers lost their jobs at almost double the rate of men and tended to remain unemployed for longer. Married women who held jobs at the start of the decade were pressured to surrender them to male breadwinners.[41] The country's economic disaster revived a decades-old debate over women's physical and moral fitness for the nondomestic workforce. Never mind that the number of women working in industry or as "white-collar girls" had more than doubled since 1900, or that by the mid-1920s women had "invaded" nearly all occupations. Conservative detractors charged women who worked with threatening ideals of female purity and of the family as women's vocation. But voices from across the political spectrum were critical of female wage earners' "warfare on home life." As Laura Hapke has shown, Depression-era newspapers, mass-circulation magazines, and highbrow fiction found a common scapegoat in women who worked outside the home. Even protest authors like *The Grapes of Wrath*'s John Steinbeck "routinely extolled the home-front Ma Joad for knowing her place, shuddered at a companionate model of family earnings, scanted the single working mother, and looked askance at the self-supporting solo woman."[42]

With the political shake-ups at home and the rise of fascism abroad, categories of gender and class were overlapping in new ways. Many male, working-class novelists of the 1930s portrayed the working class as synonymous with virile, masculine ideals and disparaged the bourgeoisie as feminine and corrupt. This was consistent with recurrent anxieties over the defining characteristics of a "civilized" versus "rugged" American manhood in an increasingly urban society. It also ignored the experiences of labor-class women for whom domestic work in homes of their own had never been an option.[43] By the later 1930s the New Deal had created thousands of low-paying clerical positions for women workers in social services and education, sectors that had come to be regarded as "female work." An unprecedented number of women also began serving the New Deal government in high administrative positions. But such opportunities were not accessible to everyone and went mostly to well-educated and well-resourced white women.[44]

The controversies over women's roles inside and outside the home were therefore entangled in multiple systems of meaning, and these played out even in the world of crime. A working-class woman like Bonnie Parker needed her Clyde Barrow in order to take to the road and build a reputation as a bandit. So, too, did Kathryn Kelly need her Machine Gun as the male front to the couple's operations. Both women were sensitive to the social hierarchies of their day. Kathryn used fine clothing and cars to advertise her husband's success in a criminal network to which she had only indirect access. As a poor white woman from a disreputable part of Dallas, Bonnie was embarrassed to have once been jailed alongside a "crazy Negro woman." She always wore dresses, even when pants would have been far more practical, and she counted on the hostages whom she and Clyde "hosted" to attest to her feminine respectability.

Crime fiction reflected the social constraints that shaped the realities of working women's lives at the same time as they opened new spaces for social experimentation and fantasy. "Hard-boiled dames" proliferated in the pulp fiction magazines of the 1930s. Both the pulps and popular detective novels offered truly competent female characters on both sides of the law.

One pulp magazine editor explained the value of a female character who engaged in activities (such as gunplay) that were interesting to his mostly male readers: "When we first began to add females to the cast of characters, we found out, much to our surprise, that the circulation didn't diminish any. If anything, it went up higher."[45] As resolutely as Hoover and others might portray gang women as negative examples of womanhood, Depression-era women frustrated with their own lives could not have helped but notice that such women had ample money for clothes and amusement, apparent freedom from housekeeping or work responsibilities, and ostensible parity with the men in their lives. That such women had often replaced wayward husbands with new lovers of their own choosing not only evoked fantasies of uncommon sexual liberty, but also reverberated with women either dissatisfied with their mates or unhappy with the dearth of available marriage partners.

Historian Claire Bond Potter has written about the story of Marge Suskie, a nineteen-year-old housekeeper who became briefly famous in 1934 for writing a supportive letter to three of the Dillinger gang's gun molls. Suskie's correspondence illustrates how women criminals could be read as tantalizing, if romanticized, models of feminine empowerment.

> Good Girls: Don't talk. I hope John Dillinger never get[s] caught. Wish I could help him. If prayers help any he'll never be caught. P.S. I'll go the limit and then some. If you get this, please ans. and let me know. But perhaps you'd laugh and call me a damned fool. Maybe I am but I'd sure like to know you and help you just the same. this sure is a dead town.[46]

Suskie's letter sparked a minor investigation in which she confessed to the FBI that "she personally would like to have the experience of being a 'gunman's moll.'" She explained that she had gotten this idea from radio programs and movies, and that it was a common fantasy among the girls of Niagara Falls.[47] In exposing frustrations common to women of her generation, Suskie's letter revealed how a reproachful mainstream discourse around women gang members did not perfectly align with some citizens' private desires.

In a nonfiction book on Chicago's gangland, Walter Noble Burns anticipated the yearnings of Suskie and her contemporaries. His 1931 rumination on the charms of the gangster life analogized gang women to the "women of the old frontier" and "fair ladies in the days of chivalry" who thrilled at the bloody exploits of their rescuing knights. As Burns wrote:

If the lot of gangland women seems hard and woefully sad, they are far from viewing their situation in any such tragic light. Gangland has its fascinations. The women who breathe its tense atmosphere enjoy its thrill of danger and its raw drama and would not exchange it for the dull routine of more peaceful environments. . . . Gangland is romance, and the drab, stereotyped world beyond its dangerous borders is fit only for slaves of the typewriter, schoolteachers, or anemic feminine souls content to settle down with some white-collar clerk in dreary comfort and security. Gangland women are satisfied with gangland.[48]

Burns did not, of course, imagine his gang woman reaching the status of a Bonnie Parker or Kathryn Kelly. His emphasis was on the woman as passive romantic beneficiary of males' violent actions. However, in drawing the connection between gang women and the "women of the old frontier," Burns hinted that the gang woman was more authentically American than her law-abiding counterparts. Similarly, his denigration of "slaves of the typewriter, schoolteachers, and anemic feminine souls content to settle down with some white-collar clerk" rejected some previous feminine—and masculine—ideals of the period, recommending instead a model of womanhood based not on convention, but upon a philosophy of personal action and immediate gratification.

The link to the frontier and to a nineteenth-century tradition of all-American outlawry was significant for many an image-conscious public enemy. Male gangsters such as Alvin Karpis occasionally fancied themselves twentieth-century reincarnations of frontier legends like Frank and Jesse James; certain gangster films explicitly pondered that link.[49] Writing in 1943, Frederick Collins blasted Depression-era Hollywood for encouraging such associations: "Big-name gangsters—Robin Hoods they were called— became the heroes of the hour. Their names became household words . . . children were taken to the theater to see pictures of the pretty gangsters outwitting the snail-minded representatives of the law. This, then, was the situation which Edgar Hoover surveyed with anxious eyes and faced with fettered hands."

Collins lauded Hoover for having "taken the 'hood' out of Robin Hood and put it back into hoodlum."[50] In fact, Hoover had also endeavored to extend the category of hoodlum to the hoodlums' women, whom he regarded as the greater threat. He railed against the tendency of the courts to regard female accomplices as innocents, misled by their love for the wrong man. In 1938, some of the most popular of Hoover's *American Magazine* articles were reedited into a book, *Persons in Hiding*, which devoted multiple chapters to Hoover's message that a woman "has no more right to cheat the law than a man." In a characteristically acerbic argument for women's equality before the law, he took to task both female lawbreakers and the women and men who empathized with them: "The one quality which woman is supposed to possess is that of curiosity. Yet the gun moll seems always able to convince the world in general—especially those sentimental moo-cows of scant knowledge but loud voices who are forever interfering with businesslike law enforcement by their turn-the-other-cheek theories of crime eradication—that she was born entirely without the quality which made Eve eat the apple." "American chivalry is to blame for our gun moll," charged Hoover, and such sentimentality only encouraged "every cheap-minded little fool who thus is encouraged to believe that law and punishment were made only for men."[51]

Hoover and his agents despaired of the ability of women to rent hideouts, to provide their criminal partners with alibis, and to act as covers for a male gang that might normally have attracted suspicion. Of John Dillinger's girlfriend, Evelyn Frechette, Hoover fumed, "She's more dangerous to society than the desperado himself."[52] As he wrote in his *Persons in Hiding* chapter on Kathryn Kelly, "[Women of gangdom] are more than consorts. They are mainsprings. Gangs could not exist without them."[53] Hoover's regular collaborator, Cooper, echoed this opinion in one of his own books on gangland, in which he dismissed the "imaginative romanticists" who saw high purpose in the lives of the women he dubbed the "hussies in hiding": "I have found them to be nothing but a selfish, law-hating, piglike crew of filthy sluts, and the sooner they are so regarded by the general public, the sooner will the professional criminal lose one of his most valuable allies."[54] Together, the two men generated a relentless stream of publications that offered a collective portrait of the 1930s gang woman as a sexually voracious index of everything that could go wrong with the modern woman. As another author, Herbert Corey, concluded in a 1936 book for which Hoover wrote the foreword, "As a people we have not been paying attention to our business." Corey cataloged common theories as to why the public enemies flourished, among them the possibility that "the American wife is lopheaded and that Mother spends too much time playing bridge."[55]

But women with links to gangland ultimately were useful to the FBI. In a chapter titled "Dumb and Not Beautiful," Corey riffed on gang women's predictable feminine foibles—and particularly their attachments to their mothers—that the G-men had exploited to capture their gangster boyfriends and husbands. A gun moll could be the gangster's Achilles' heel in multiple ways. Made to feel jealous or faced with separation from kin or children, a gangster's girlfriend might be coaxed to testify against her man. The urban gangsters of the 1920s had been criticized for spending too freely on new consumer luxuries and thus becoming like women.[56] Such criticisms undercut the fantasy of the gangster as having preserved for himself a masculine power regarded by some as under assault. So, too, did negative attention paid to gangsters' girlfriends and wives. To deflate the image of "aggressive masculinity" attached to the rural, homegrown gangster of the 1930s, Hoover's team sometimes insinuated that the male gangsters' female companions were smarter, bossier, or more ruthless than they. Suggesting that certain women gang members were "mannish" as well as sexually diseased was a strategy designed to taunt the gangster and tamp down his appeal.[57] A woman like Kathryn Kelly, therefore, became the G-man's foil and his instrument. Her reputation for dominance helped assert the necessity of the G-man while also reinforcing the boundaries of "normal" men's and women's behavior.

Posited as representing a new paradigm of American masculinity, the G-man briefly enjoyed the same privileges as the gangster and the cowboy, other "men with guns" whom the cultural critic Robert Warshow identified as "the two most successful movie-made archetypes" of the U.S. male.[58] All three archetypes operated in womanless worlds, or rather in worlds made distinctive by the customary absence of "good" women. In fictional representations, the rare "bad" woman who operated in proximity to the gangster had the capacity to turn good, if only she were willing to be domesticated. (Joan Blondell's *Blondie Johnson* did just that in 1933, with the story of a hard-bitten female crime boss who is reformed after she falls in love with one of her targets.) By contrast, the woman who unrepentantly trespassed in the realm of "men with guns" endangered a coded-as-masculine space and identity that required women's absence and "otherness" to define itself.

Ironically, she who threatened to rob the gunman of his masculine authority could sometimes be the very source of his power. In 1937, just as *You Only Live Once* was arriving in theaters, *American Magazine* introduced "Crime's Leading Lady," Kathryn Kelly. By Hoover and Cooper's telling, Kathryn was a "talented girl who, if she hadn't been a gangster's gun moll, might have become a Hollywood star."[59] Posed with legs crossed and wearing a pair of sleek heels and a jaunty hat, Kathryn smiles pleasantly at the

American Magazine readers who would shortly learn how "one of the most attractive women ever to travel the crooked paths of the underworld" had used her appearance to manipulate George Kelly and create the "G-man." A more sober version of the same magazine feature reappeared one year later as a chapter in Hoover's *Persons in Hiding*. Retitled "The Woman behind the Crime," Hoover's second recounting of Kathryn's biography included many of the same details of the teenaged wife and mother from Oklahoma who had strategically married some of the richest men of her social stratum—Prohibition-era bootleggers. Like the magazine piece, Hoover's book deconstructed the female psyche that was not redeemed by love. Instead, he argued, Kathryn had used love as another of the feminine deceits that could draw and entrap a man to do a woman's bidding.

The Girl behind the Man behind the Gun

In 1939, in the pages of the *Motion Picture Herald*, Paramount Studios literally deconstructed a woman on Hoover's behalf. Six stark advertisements for the movie version of Hoover's *Persons in Hiding* introduced its female villain piece by piece. "THIS TENDER WHITE HAND . . ." blared the text above the image of a daintily manicured, disembodied hand, palm tilted upward in passive reception. Smaller lettering explained the hand's menace, for it had "held a man in its unyielding grasp and that man held the tommy gun that spread terror over the nation." To learn more about "the hand of America's queen of gangland," readers were urged to turn the page. Similar two-page ads instructed readers that a floating pair of "THESE LUSCIOUS LIPS" and "THESE BEAUTIFUL EYES" had managed to turn "a small-time crook into the nation's No. 1 killer!" The second page of each ad featured the face of the forty-four-year-old Hoover, originator of the *Persons in Hiding* screenplay, who promised to deliver "the *true* inside story of the girl behind the man behind the gun!"[60]

Lest readers miss the point, Dot Bronson (actress Patricia Morison) appeared fully assembled in a space below Hoover's face and next to the inscription, "She's beautiful . . . she's dangerous." Dot's supreme toughness derives from everything Hoover saw as treacherous about the gang woman. As an ambitious and sexually alluring "girl behind the man behind the gun," she gives her boyfriend both the motivation and the gumption to break the law. By extension, the *Persons in Hiding*'s audience could read male crooks as the puppets of a modern enemy: the assertive, hyperacquisitive woman whose class ambitions made her "ten times tougher than any man." As top G-man, Hoover was not just "any man," however, and so this new adversary's toughness could not outdo his. Clutching her tiny revolver, the promotional image of Dot appears to lean away from Hoover's looming gaze.

Persons in Hiding's advertising campaign promoted the newly legitimate FBI with a heavily gendered vision of the social ills the Bureau had disciplined itself to defeat. The campaign encapsulated the values and anxieties of an era, because Dot stood for any of the "girls" behind men behind guns who were key to the mid-1930s war on crime. Although its script was adapted from the Kathryn Kelly story in Hoover's book by the same name, the film *Persons in Hiding* is typically misremembered as a Bonnie and Clyde story.[61] But the discontented hairdresser Dot ("Molly" in the original script) prefers riches to the romance that allegedly motivated Bonnie Parker. Dot's desire for wealth is symbolized by her obsession with a certain expensive perfume, a brand dreamed up by Hoover himself, which he named "Tantalizing."[62] As her signature scent predicts, Dot is a tease who evokes desperate yearning and whose power relies on remaining just out of reach.

When a small-time crook, Freddy Martin, holds up Dot and her earnest, hardworking boyfriend, the boyfriend panics. Dot placidly taunts Freddy, egging him to violence. Frustrated, Freddy finally knocks the boyfriend unconscious and kidnaps the intractable Dot. But the kidnapping victim turns out to be a willing accomplice. She helps Freddy escape the police and then proposes that they join forces as a criminal team. Surveying her new partner, Dot muses that Freddy could be her thuggish Prince Charming: "I wonder if you are the man—the one I've been waiting for." She also warns him, "I think big. And that's the way I want to live. Big!" In the montage that follows, Dot forces Freddy to practice his marksmanship on a makeshift shooting range that she has set up with him. He shoots clumsily until she wearily kisses him and tells him she loves him; thereafter, his aim is perfect. Freddy's pathetic hunger for Dot's affection becomes the source of his weakness and malleability. Dot cultivates the latter as she schemes to transform him from a petty crook into an outlaw hero. Knowing that she cannot as easily become such a hero herself, she crafts for Freddy a dangerous new persona: "Gunner" Martin.

Dot and Gunner marry and embark on a profitable crime spree represented only by shots of an intense Dot behind the wheel of their getaway car. Flush with success, they drop in on Dot's elderly parents, the Bronsons, who are impressed with the rich appearance of their daughter and son-in-law until a radio broadcast reveals that their wealth is ill-gotten. After another crime spree, Dot and Freddy are briefly apprehended, but Dot orchestrates their escape by pretending to take a nap and then disarming a cop with a high heel pump. The escape makes headlines, possibly as a result of Dot's interventions. Her regular anonymous phone calls to the press publicize Gunner's exploits and inflate his gangster esteem.

Dot and Freddy's fortunes finally unravel when they branch out into kidnapping, inviting the attentions of an upstanding G-man, Pete Griswold, whose patient wife and modest household stand in stark contrast to the sordid world of the fugitives. Ignoring Freddy's advice that they should start saving so they can "go straight" and settle down like any other married couple, Dot squanders the kidnapping ransom on furs and other expensive items. While Freddie dreams of giving up crime in favor of a home and children, Dot repeatedly upends the trappings of domestic life. She delights in making Freddie do the cooking and cleaning, and, as running joke in the film, their flight from the law forces Griswold's cheerfully sacrificing junior partner to postpone his honeymoon, again and again.

Ultimately, Dot's telltale "tantalizing" scent leads to her capture and imprisonment when she cannot resist purchasing just one more bottle of her signature perfume before attempting to flee the country. Sporting a Bonnie Parker–style beret, she rails against the G-men who step in to arrest her and then offers them a souvenir cartridge shot by Gunner Martin. His carefully cultivated legend will stand as both Dot's proudest achievement and her personal disdain for "upright" people who settle for poverty and anonymity.

Like Hoover's published denunciations of women criminals, *Persons in Hiding* theorizes that the film's male crook would never have become so successful or so thoroughly deviant without Dot. Dot's most egregious crime is not her role in a kidnapping, but that of being a disruptive, rather than domesticating, influence, of having rejected motherhood, and of possessing an ambition and carnality that are beyond the control of her mate.[63] But the film's narrative suggests that even Dot's traditionally feminine attributes are a problem, and in some cases, provide the very conditions for Dot's downfall. For example, her feminine charms are excessive. Dot's physical allure allows her to manipulate the hapless men who would fall prey to her attentions, as demonstrated by the "snake charmer" music that sounds every time Dot applies her "Tantalizing" perfume. Her consumer desires also are excessive, in part because she does not want to work for what she covets but also because she has pegged a free-enterprise capitalist system as unjust. This is evident when Dot rejects her work-worn mother's admonitions to the straight life and insists that only the wealthy can afford moral principles. Finally, Dot's loyalty to her family is excessive. Her love for her mother ultimately makes her an unreliable partner in crime.

A Winning Strategy and a Losing Battle

The Motion Picture Herald raved about the "solid gold proposition" of cashing in on Hoover's name and endorsement. "If the people of the nation are agreed on any one thing it is that J. Edgar Hoover has done a good job as head of the Federal Bureau of Investigation and that the nation is better off for it." So began the *Motion Picture Herald*'s showmen's review of *Persons in Hiding* in January 1939, a month before the picture's official release. Then, in a twist that must have pained Hoover, the reviewer lauded the film as "impressively realistic . . . save for the key character, a singularly sinister young woman."[64] The reviewer's skepticism signaled what would be the FBI's losing effort to underscore the gang woman's menace while also making her wholly unsympathetic and unpalatable. That which the reviewer found unbelievable—the violence and avarice of *Persons in Hiding*'s female character—was precisely that which Hoover had wanted to convey to the public as true.

Over the next year, Paramount produced three more films adapted from the FBI cases in Hoover's *Persons in Hiding* book: *Undercover Doctor* (1939), *Parole Fixer* (1940), and *Queen of the Mob* (1940).[65] The last of these was adapted from Hoover's writings on Ma Barker. The Ma film and the Kathryn Kelly film fared better at the box office than *Parole Fixer* or *Undercover Doctor*, which were about peripheral male characters who had helped sustain the underworld but who were not a direct part of it.[66] None of the four films were "on message" in the way of the FBI's 1936 documentary, which had yoked the fascination with "real" gangster artifacts, such as a bullet-ridden Bonnie and Clyde car, in service of the FBI's might. Hoover's two films about thinly disguised gang women succeeded in leveraging the novelty and the spectacle of women's real or imagined violence. Ironically, that spectacle easily eclipsed the films' blandly righteous G-men. That is one reason why, as flashier gangster films crept back into fashion, theater owners of the later 1930s used Hoover's films as the first half of a gangster double feature; that is, as a B-movie offering that lectured on the importance of law and order, even though its message was often at odds with the A-production that followed.[67]

The ambiguous usage of the *Persons in Hiding* series portended its ambiguous effects. Posited as superlatively evil, and perhaps a bit mad, for having reached for male privileges of seduction and independence, Hoover's "girls behind men behind guns" reflected a cauldron of anxieties around forms of social organization that had been upended or called into doubt by the ongoing economic crisis. Along the way, the *Persons in Hiding* series peddled a heroic brand of American masculinity that was, like the FBI's G-man, supposed to be potent without being "vicious," and emotionally stable without being "cold."

In 1936, when nationwide arrests of women stood at 7.3 percent, Hoover fretted publicly that that statistic was a portent of even worse female behavior to come.[68] The *New York Times* ran this story, which occupied less than four square inches of text, all by itself in the upper-left corner of a full-page Macy's shoe sale advertisement. Hoover's exhortations to take seriously women's contributions to crime would never attract the same attention as the wicked women characters he helped launch for the screen. But he and his supporters would press doggedly on with the "girl behind the man" formula. Whether writing against gangsters, Nazi spies, communists, or Black Panthers, Hoover consistently sought to draw attention to these groups' women, how they might be useful to an investigation, and what their behaviors might reveal about the weaknesses of their male counterparts.[69]

Hoover's preoccupation with women criminals has occasionally been read as proof that he was the closeted gay man or vengeful pervert that some late-twentieth-century histories propose he may have been. His obsession with policing women's morals has been attributed to his status as a lifelong bachelor or the fact that he lived with his mother in his childhood home until he was forty-three. These tacitly homophobic theories for Hoover's professional misconduct are less convincing than the evidence that Hoover seems to have embraced a near-Victorian gender ideology, one that enshrined women as the moral center of domestic family life and that had very little tolerance for their potential failings. As he confessed in a 1939 interview: "I have always held girls and women on a pedestal. They are something men should look up to, to honor and worship. If men would remember this and keep them there, married life would be better. I have had that idea about women all my life." In that same interview, Hoover also spoke bitterly about his reaction to a woman who might disappoint him by failing to live up to his moral ideal.[70] A predilection to disappointment certainly may have helped Hoover's career in the long run. He was ready when Roosevelt's administration began encouraging the Bureau to monitor "subversive" activities as a part of the criminal activities that the administration had identified as a threat to internal security.[71] In the later years of Hoover's career, much of his power—and his ability to convince so many different presidents to retain him as FBI director—would rely on a lifetime of cataloging the private failings of public citizens as a source of real and potential political blackmail.

Hoover's keen interest in the women who consorted with male gangsters was ultimately as significant to the FBI's professionalization as the killing of John Dillinger in 1934 (a victory for the Bureau that had, after all, relied on the help of the informant "Woman in Red.") Stories of "gangster girl" transgressions not only added a dash of scandal and sex appeal to the prim morality plays turned out by Hoover and his team; they were also invaluable in the campaign to build up the G-men as symbols of moral inspiration and authority. But not all who had advocated for the campaign were happy with how Hoover had managed it. By 1938, even Homer Cummings was concerned that the Bureau was getting overexposed and asked Hoover to tone it down.[72]

In fact, the G-man, or something like him, had already proliferated in popular culture in copycat film shorts like the *Crime Does Not Pay* series (1935–1947) and in the *Gangbusters* radio serial that would later make the leap to television. These unauthorized representations of FBI culture were longer-lived than the ones with Hoover's imprimatur. In Bureau-sponsored films and writings, G-men were anonymous model citizens whose example and advice—particularly on parenting and teaching children respect for authority—were presented as holding out the possibility of eradicating crime altogether.[73] Theirs was a masculinity of tedious restraint and vigilance against the "contamination" of crime. Hoover was so fond of the contamination metaphor that he used it to open his *Persons in Hiding* book in an extended metaphor about the careful housewife who attends to the business of crime prevention in the same way that she attends to the dust in her rugs.[74] Hamstrung by their own dreary, worker-bee competence, the saintly agents in Hoover's stories ironically risked becoming confined in the same way as Hoover's ideal woman.

Meanwhile, Hoover's attempts to dampen the public's interest in gang women instead encouraged it and ironically helped to nourish a tradition of women's outlaw pictures in which the female lawbreaker could temporarily win some audiences' sympathies before meeting her inevitable punishment at film's end. Once the U.S. woman outlaw had become a recurring staple of the large screen, the individual women's stories that had mingled to create her no longer mattered. A product of the overlapping cultural space between the entertainment industry and law enforcement, Bonnie Parker (and other women outlaws who evoked her) would become but a cipher for a swirl of conflicted gender identities and individual frustrations. Unlike Kathryn Kelly, Bonnie had declared her identity through a romantic relationship that could be regarded as unending precisely because of its violent end. Never would she be packed off to one prison and Clyde to another. She offered a fantasy of self-reliance that was still wrapped up in her dependence on Clyde. So it was that Hoover's concern about the woman lawbreaker was justified, because, in relation to the G-man, women like Bonnie would get the last word. In the space of just a few decades, the outlaw women who had been so important to the FBI's professional ascendancy in the 1930s would also accelerate the Bureau's decline.

Two Fallen Women, One Rising Star

The crowds who came to gawk at Bonnie and Clyde's dead bodies on the day they were killed fell silent as the outlaws' remains were lifted from their car and hurried into the furniture store that served as a makeshift funeral parlor. One male observer uttered his disillusionment that Clyde was so small and slight, and a reporter hypothesized that everyone on the scene felt foolish and frustrated that such a little outlaw could have terrified the country for so long. Onlookers gasped as the coroner and his assistant removed Bonnie from the vehicle, making evident the extensive damage to the tiny woman's frame.[75] Here was tangible evidence of Attorney General Cummings's promise to "wipe out the public enemy" and restore the dignity of the law. Here, too, was stark proof that the woman outlaw should not expect gentler treatment on account of her sex. However, sentimentality for Bonnie and Clyde, the tragic love story, largely overshadowed any concern for "equal treatment before the law." So, too, did distaste for the all-male posse who hid in the bushes to execute a woman who may not have had a direct hand in any of the Barrow Gang murders. The ex–Texas Ranger Frank Hamer anticipated a potential backlash against his men when he told reporters, "I hate to bust a cap on a woman, especially when she was sitting down. However, if it hadn't been her, it would have been us."[76]

Another posse member recorded his astonishment at how many children—and how many more women than men—had crammed themselves into two different Dallas funeral parlors for a glimpse of the outlaws, who were memorialized separately. An estimated thirty thousand people streamed by Clyde's open casket; about forty thousand came to pay their respects, or simply stare, at Bonnie's remains.[77] The outlaws were curiosities, to be sure. The couple also had become "real" to many people who did not know them personally through the dissemination of stagey photographs and Bonnie's poetry. When Clyde was buried at sunset on a West Dallas hillside near his childhood home, souvenir hunters scrambled for the roses and peonies on his mounded grave as his wailing mother was led away.[78] Bonnie's private funeral across the city was more subdued. About 150 family and friends were on hand to hear the Reverend Andrews say that he loved Bonnie and that "though I never knew her . . . to help her now is a privilege." Bonnie's largest cemetery wreath was a gift of the Dallas newsboys, who had sold three times their normal volume of papers on the day that Bonnie and Clyde were killed.[79]

The *Dallas Journal* expressed contempt for its homegrown bandits with a political cartoon that advised its readers to forget about them: "The outlaw couple died like rats in a burning barn under the smothering fire of the sheriff's posse. The End."[80] A few weeks after the ambush, *Time* magazine ran an obituary on its National Affairs page. The notice appeared alongside the familiar image of "The late Bonnie Parker *Thornton*" posed with the cigar in her mouth. Clyde was nowhere pictured. Bonnie's photo caption, which underscored her status as a married adulterer, included this blunt appraisal from Bonnie's aunt: "She surely is in Hell."[81]

The barrage of negative publicity that Bonnie received during and just after her lifetime could not diminish her threefold advantage for making the leap from a small-time gangster's girlfriend to a potent outlaw legend in her own right. First, she possessed all the necessary autobiographical components of the social bandit, including her rural upbringing and an impoverished background symbolically overcome against great odds. Second, Bonnie achieved celebrity at the perfect historical moment, when certain Depression-weary citizens were still applauding bandits' anti-authoritarian daring. Third, Bonnie's story possessed the right mix of talkback and contradictions to make her a useful and strangely relatable outlaw. In death, the *concept* of Bonnie Parker became a therapeutic site for those who saw in her apparent transgressions a reflection of their own frustrations, fantasies, and ambivalences.

There would not have been any lingering fondness for the murderous Barrow Gang, of course, had Bonnie not done uncanny advance work to counteract their negative press. Mainstream publications self-consciously disparaged rural 1930s gangsters out of respect to their victims and the general public's genuine distress at their actions, and the Barrow Gang obviously was not immune to this ritual. But Bonnie Parker's famous "Ballad of Bonnie and Clyde" hinted that Clyde's experiences in prison were the original injustice that had driven him to desperation:

> I once knew Clyde
> When he was honest and upright and clean.
> But the laws fooled around,
> Kept taking him down
> And locking him up in a cell
> 'Til he said to me,
> "I'll never be free,
> So I'll meet a few of them in hell."[82]

In her "Ballad," Bonnie inaccurately portrays herself and Clyde as the sole members of the Barrow Gang and suggests they are heirs of the frontier outlaw Jesse James, who was widely remembered for fighting the law in the service of the weak members of society whom the law oppressed. Though misrepresented in the press as "cold-blooded killers," Bonnie assures her readers that she and Clyde "aren't so ruthless as that." In fact, she and Clyde are regular folks, hostile to stool pigeons, and weary at being chased by police:

> If they try to act like citizens
> And rent a nice flat
> About the third night they're invited to fight
> By a sub-gun's rat-tat-tat.

Bonnie seemed to understand how a good love story could make women's lawbreaking more palatable. She may have had a psychic dependency on the incorrigible Clyde, but, like her sympathizers, Bonnie suggested that this is healthy and, in fact, the proper source of a woman's identity. There is honor in her loyalty to her man. In just a few verses, her third-person poem makes it plain that she is no gold-digging gun moll and that she has no illusion about the future: "The law always wins." Bonnie throws her lot in with Clyde's and the two become tragic heroes, noble for their steadfast commitment to each other in the face of certain doom:

> The road was so dimly lighted;
> There were no highway signs to guide;
> But they made up their minds
> If all roads were blind,
> They wouldn't give up till they died.

Death is inevitable—"the wages of sin." Yet, as Bonnie asserts several times, death is not only chosen, it has been chosen by mutual agreement. The couple has chosen death over imprisonment and separation. They have chosen romantic love over the stifling, law-abiding existence that would have denied both. The self-sacrifice of this choice makes Bonnie powerful, and she who began as loyal helpmate becomes Clyde's equal at the end:

> Some day they'll go down together;
> They'll bury them side by side;
> To few it'll be grief—
> To the law a relief—
> But it's death for Bonnie and Clyde.

In placing her name ahead of Clyde's, Bonnie transposed the "Clyde-and-Bonnie" designation that most of her contemporaries habitually used to refer to the couple. The reversal obviously accommodated the rhyme. Consciously or unconsciously, it also reflected how essential was Bonnie to the Barrow Gang and its reputation. But Bonnie carefully keeps her ballad in a traditionally gendered universe where "it's fight man-to-man" and where "the women are kin and the men are men." Never does she suggest a leadership role for herself that is anything like that Kathryn Kelly supposedly occupied.

Bonnie's avowedly traditional relationship with Clyde stood in tension with her reputedly unconventional relationship with guns and cigars, two phallic symbols more "naturally" identified with men, especially in an era when respectable women smoked cigarettes, if they were caught smoking anything at all.[83] From the moment Bonnie's famous cigar photograph appeared in the press, reporters began discovering "a big black cigar butt" in every one of the Barrow Gang's alleged hideouts. Pro-Bonnie narratives took great pains to deny Bonnie's "cigar-smoking moll" image, echoing Bonnie's own protest that the cigar pose had been a joke. But the cigar detail was just too thrilling not to stick. One reporter claimed to have found a discarded cigar that bore the marks of "Bonnie's tiny toothprints."[84] The juxtaposition of "big black" cigar gripped between Bonnie's "tiny" teeth could be taken as either sexual innuendo or the suggestion that she was both female and male in her aggressions.

Contradictory interpretations of Bonnie's character underscore how her gender transgressions were perceived, recalled, and deployed by various of her "publics." The images of Bonnie posing with stolen firearms—in another widely distributed photo, she levels a rifle at Clyde's chest—suggested that she did more than partake in the *spoils* of violence; she also relished opportunities to engage in violence herself. In its account of the Arcadia ambush, the *Dallas Morning News* misidentified the rifle found across Bonnie's lap as a machine gun.[85] The Parker family objected, insisting that Bonnie had carried only a small pistol, which she had "cocked and ready to hand to Clyde at a moment's notice." (They also claimed that she had, at the moment she died, been absorbed in a magazine.)[86] Storytellers inclined to romanticize Bonnie describe her as having been flustered and afraid on the day she smuggled into Clyde's jail a gun that she had concealed between her breasts. In accounts less favorable to the outlaws, Bonnie coolly strode into the prison with the gun taped to her inner thigh.[87] The image of a gun smuggled between a woman's breasts clearly had much different connotations than did the gun as a surrogate penis between her legs.

In keeping with the Bureau's attention to personal respectability, the early files on the Barrow Gang included details of Bonnie's and Clyde's supposed sexual transgressions. Bureau documents alleged that Clyde was gay or bisexual and that Bonnie had insisted on bringing other males into the Barrow Gang to help cope with her "insatiable craving for sex."[88] (Like the cigar photo, this rumor was intended to be offputting and was another riveting detail for the pulps.) While federal and local law enforcement tried to degrade the public's opinion of Bonnie and Clyde, their families stubbornly sought to restore it. Clyde's mother created a small sensation when she tore down photographs of Clyde's and Bonnie's bodies from the Capitol Theater on Dallas's Elm Street. To counteract Bonnie's "official" reputation as promiscuous and manipulative, Bonnie's mother and Clyde's sister worked with a professional journalist to construct a highly sentimental portrait of the outlaw couple, one that includes this description of Bonnie shortly before she died: "There she sat, so lovely—only twenty three—with the May moonlight sifting through her yellow hair and making shadows on her cheeks—there she sat and talked to me of death as calmly as if she were discussing going to the grocery store. Bonnie looked up at me and smiled. It was a funny smile—as if she were a million years older than I was; as if she knew things I'd never learn if I lived for centuries."[89]

Like Bonnie's most famous poem, her family members' book leaves the impression that the two Barrow Gang's best-known members were physically attractive and basically decent young people driven into a life of crime by bad luck and an unshakable loyalty to each other. For their families, bad luck and loyalty seemed to go hand in hand. The couple's mothers each received thirty-day jail sentences for having harbored their fugitive children.

Bonnie's younger sister Billie drew a yearlong prison sentence for having cared for Bonnie after she was badly injured in a fiery car crash. In the wake of the ambush, Billie briefly became the closest substitute for her famous sister. Just two weeks after her sister's death, Billie told the *Daily Times Herald* that she was optimistically awaiting the "tenders of movie contracts in Hollywood" so she could set the record straight on Bonnie and Clyde.[90]

As Bonnie's own rendering of herself mingled with the rendering of many other storytellers, it was not long before Bonnie became "Bonnie," an imaginary goulash of several different women, including many a big-screen gangster's moll. One Bonnie was terrified of guns and left all the shooting to Clyde. Another Bonnie often influenced the gang's travel plans (they made surprisingly frequent visits to Bonnie's mother in Dallas) and felt free to defy Clyde's orders. For instance, one popular tale of the Barrow Gang's successful bank heist in Okabena, Minnesota, relates how numerous Okabena citizens turned out to block the robbers' escape. As one old man tried to ram their car with a railroad tie, Clyde allegedly gave Bonnie a pistol and an order: "Honey, shoot him before he wrecks us." But Bonnie ignored Clyde, forcing Clyde to veer the car sharply. She responded to his anger with a smile and said, "Why, honey, I wasn't going to kill that nice old man. He was white-headed."[91] This story may well have been fabrication, but it is still instructive. This is a version of Bonnie Parker upon whom escapist fantasies are easily projected. She is kindly, essentially antiviolence, pleasantly irrational, and blessed with the charming ability to avoid being killed herself. (Not coincidentally, this is the Bonnie Parker closest to the character immortalized in the famous 1967 film, *Bonnie and Clyde*.)

But for every story of Bonnie's mercy, there is another of her murderousness. In the Easter Sunday murder of two motorcycle police in Grapevine, Texas, Bonnie reportedly shot one of the fallen officers in the face at close range, relishing how his head "bounced just like a rubber ball!" The scene was witnessed by a farmer, who recorded Bonnie's alleged exclamation for posterity. One of the slain officers had been a rookie patrolman just a few days from his wedding, which meant Bonnie would have been guilty of destroying another couple's dreams. The farmer's testimony was later discredited, and a Barrow Gang member confessed his own guilt in the killing, but the image of Bonnie Parker coldly executing a policeman added one more contradictory episode to the outlaw's legend.[92]

Despite, or more likely *because* of, Bonnie's and her family's attempts to control her public image, the exact tenor and extent of her gang activity are difficult to ascertain. So much of what we know about her has evolved almost entirely from the few, sometimes conflicting personal accounts of witnesses or her former criminal consorts, the questionable research efforts of zealous crime reporters, and various newspaper and fictional representations that prioritized dramatic effect over historical record.

Therein lies the secret of Bonnie's persistence as a cultural icon. Unlike Kathryn Kelly, about whom there was never circulated a story of mercy, only stories of betrayal and violence (Hoover's articles described Kathryn as having urged her husband to kill their kidnapping victim after collecting his ransom), Bonnie Parker had plenty of supporters to "talk back" on her behalf. Because she never went to trial, she never had to forfeit the outlaw's most important asset: public aid and sympathy. Whatever her capacity in the Barrow Gang, there is no doubt that Bonnie helped to terrorize law-abiding citizens in the Southwest. But Bonnie's apparent devotion to her family and to Clyde made it possible for certain of her contemporaries to imagine a well-intentioned Bonnie who was appealingly modern and supportive of her man.[93]

Thus, working-class women like Marge Suskie, who felt little or no connection to any articulated feminism, might regard Bonnie as representing appealing freedoms not typically afforded to someone of her sex or modest social station. Bonnie did not need to have any political agenda to become a potent cultural symbol for many rural, working-class, Depression-era women (and men) who felt that they and others like them had been wronged by law enforcement. In this way, Bonnie was not only a social bandit but also an example of what historian Jacqueline Dowd Hall called the "venerable tradition of 'disorderly women,' women who in times of political upheaval embody tensions that are half-conscious or only dimly understood."[94]

It helped, of course, that Bonnie was dead. She and Clyde had not been gone a year before their family members had declared them "legends up and down the land." As the family would boast, "Pretty Boy Floyd was crowded into oblivion. Machine Gun Kelly was an also-ran."[95] Writing forty-five years after the ambush of Bonnie and Clyde, one member of the posse that killed Bonnie and Clyde recorded his irritation at the 1930s-era habit of comparing them to George and Kathryn Kelly. As Ted Hinton reasoned, the Kellys had "surrendered without a struggle—the way John Dillinger had surrendered so many times. In this, they were pikers, compared to Bonnie and Clyde." Hinton ended his memoir by complimenting the couple in whose presence even much more successful gangsters were "pikers": "They stuck together and they loved each other. That just about tells it."[96]

There was no one left to compliment or "tell it" for Kathryn Kelly, who did not have the ironic good fortune of "going down together" with her mate. Kathryn instead drew a life sentence just like Machine Gun, who told newspapers he was glad to be rid of his wife. Kathryn's newspaper columnist mother, Ora Shannon, would have had a platform from which to launch a different image of Kathryn for the public, but that was not to be. Both Kathryn and Ora were sent to jail in 1933; Kathryn's fourteen-year-old daughter went to live with distant relatives. Unlike Bonnie, whose romance with Clyde drew comparisons to Romeo and Juliet and who was reincarnated sympathetically in Hollywood, Kathryn was tapped only to play the nagging female villain and a fleeting role in a 1935 newsreel documentary. In the latter, she appeared as herself, sitting unhappily at a prison sewing machine. Identified only as "the first woman to be sentenced to life imprisonment under the new Federal Kidnapping Law," Kathryn declined to address the camera. While another prisoner spoke up to express her regrets, Kathryn stayed silent.

Over twenty years later, Kathryn hired an attorney to reopen her case. When he demonstrated that the handwriting testimony used to convict Kathryn was false, both she and her mother were acquitted. Kathryn told reporters that she might go on the "truth-telling" lecture tour around the country, but the conditions of her release required that she keep a low profile instead. She was offered a job as a hospital bookkeeper, provided she never spoke about her past or her case.[97] She died in 1985 and was buried in Oklahoma, along with whatever truths she had wanted to tell.

2

Mother Barker,
Public Enemy No. 1

On April 3, 1936, Bruno Richard Hauptmann was executed for the kidnapping-murder of Charles and Anne Morrow Lindbergh's two-year-old baby boy. Yet Hauptmann, who had been denounced in court as "Public Enemy Number One *of the World*," was not commanding the attention of law enforcement the world over. In that same month, J. Edgar Hoover disclosed the identity of the "*Real* Public Enemy No. 1." The readers of *American Magazine* were the first citizens privy to the story, which previously had been "locked in the archives of the Federal Bureau of Investigation." According to Hoover, America's worst villain was not Hauptmann, or Al Capone, or the still-at-large Alvin "Creepy" Karpis. Instead, Hoover's article declared, "the most vicious, dangerous, and resourceful criminal brain this country [had] produced in many years" was none other than "Mother Barker."[1]

What made the timing of Hoover's pronouncement most peculiar was that by April 1936, "Mother Barker" had been dead for over a year. On January 16, 1935, Kate "Ma" Barker (as she was better known) and her youngest son, Fred, had been shot and killed in a gun battle with FBI agents at Lake Weir, Florida. Fred Barker's criminal activities were well documented. But, whether it had intended to kill her or not, the FBI would have more difficulty accounting for the death of Fred's diminutive, sixty-three-year-old mother, who had never in her life been fingerprinted, arrested, or officially charged with any crime. Eyewitness reports of the shootout varied wildly, reflecting the tumult of the encounter. Depending on who told the story, Ma Barker was too obstinate, too ignorant, or maybe too frightened to obey the lawmen's orders that she and Fred emerge from their cottage hideout. The only certainty is that Ma died out of sight, thus concealing both her reaction to the standoff and the true manner of her death. (The FBI was reluctant to claim credit for the bullet that allegedly pierced Ma's heart, attributing it instead to a self-inflicted gunshot wound or a mercy killing at the hands of her son.)

With the appearance of Hoover's *American Magazine* article fifteen months later, Ma Barker was reborn. The sparse outlines of her meagerly documented life were altered and amplified to cast Ma as a criminal queen bee whom the FBI was *forced* to destroy. Hoover's article denouncing Ma and justifying her demise ultimately launched her as a potent icon: that of an outrageous, unnatural mother whom the magazine proposed as "a lesson to every foolish woman who overindulges her children."[2] To this day, Ma's name remains a part of the vernacular, an idiom most often used to denigrate an older woman as coarse, violent, or domineering.

As a woman, a mother, and, by 1930s standards, an elderly person, Ma's apparent violation of cultural stereotypes endowed her with greater celebrity than would have been accorded her had she been a male outlaw or, say, a father traveling with his infamous "Barker Boys." Like Bonnie Parker and Kathryn Kelly, Ma would become a symbol of Depression-era anxieties around shifting gender roles, especially as they were manifest within the family. In Hoover's writings and elsewhere, she became a dramatic parable on the need for women to focus on the domestic and childrearing priorities that Hoover repeatedly invoked as an antidote for crime. Painting Ma as the iron-fisted leader of the Barker-Karpis Gang also demeaned its male membership and diminished their exploits. By virtue of their mother's overbearing reputation, the Barker "boys" were virtually absolved of the very real crimes they committed. But Hoover's "*Real* Public Enemy No. 1" profile was meant as a special humiliation to Alvin Karpis, the final holdout of the 1930s public enemies who was fast becoming Hoover's personal nemesis. For the rest of his life, Karpis would gripe about the "legend of Ma Barker," which he swore "only grew up in the years after her death and only then in order to justify the manner in which she met her death at the hands of the FBI."[3]

It is easy to see how discrepancies could form around the biography of a woman who left few, or deliberately falsified, records; who kept no diary; and whose only known jottings are letters written to prisons and lawyers on behalf of her oft-incarcerated sons. The embellishments and incongruencies in Ma Barker's life story have been essential to her status as a malleable legend, one predicated on the mix of sentimentalism and unease that accompany the figure of "mother." In the pages of the *American Magazine*, Hoover and his collaborator, Courtney Ryley Cooper, strategically launched the "official" Ma, who would become the foundation for Ma Barker, the recurring screen icon. For the next few decades, Ma's FBI-embellished story would serve exactly the purposes for which it was originally intended: to justify state authority and to recommend that women—and especially mothers—be excluded as direct enforcers of that authority.

Origins of the Enemy

The FBI's formal record calls Ma by the name she used after marriage, Katherine "Kate" Barker. Born in 1872 to a poor family near Springfield, Missouri, she began life as Arizona Donnie Clark, and it is the child, "Arrie," who is the prelude to the monster in Hoover's "*Real* Public Enemy." Hoover's article described Ma's childhood as "that of the ordinary Missouri farm—church, Sunday school, picnics, hayrides, candy pulls, and the little red schoolhouse." Whether this detail sprang from real research or a nostalgic view of rural life in the late 1800s, it brilliantly evoked the scandal of a "normal" community that had nurtured and concealed a lurking evil. "Crime travels into strange places for its recruits." The young Ma adored hymns and Bible study.[4] Her parents were Scotch-Irish, although her FBI file and most subsequent biographies noted that she also had "some Indian blood in her veins."[5] Of the "dark, mysterious brilliance" in Ma's eyes, Hoover and Cooper mused, "Perhaps it spelled fierceness, for Kate Barker was a fierce woman, in her crime and in her affections."[6]

At twenty, Ma married George Barker. Within a few years, the couple had four sons: Herman, Lloyd, Fred, and Arthur, whom everyone called "Doc." Though all four Barker children ran seriously afoul of the law, only Fred and Doc were active in what later became the Barker-Karpis Gang. Herman killed a Kansas policeman in 1927 and may have committed suicide immediately afterward. Although Herman's death was attributed to a self-inflicted gunshot wound, Ma insisted that this was a cover-up and that the police had executed her eldest son.[7] Lloyd Barker was incarcerated for

most of his adult life. From 1922 to 1947, he was locked up in Leavenworth prison for a post office robbery. In 1949, he was killed in a domestic
dispute.[8]

Hoover and Cooper described Ma's family as "a spawn of hell." In a set
of internal Bureau edits, one of Hoover's agents requested that Hoover
change that phrase to "a spawn of *criminals.*" Hoover disregarded the plea,
and the editors of *American Magazine* apparently decided to ignore it as
well. As a storytelling detail, the image of four Barker boy hellions worked
beautifully with Ma's reputed willingness to harangue the authorities on
her sons' behalf, even when they had broken the law.[9] Hoover and Cooper
trumpeted Ma's advocacy on behalf of other delinquent boys besides her
own sons as evidence of why she could later have become a shrewd crime
consultant sought out by "criminals from a dozen penitentiaries."[10]

The *American Magazine* article depicted Ma as the physical embodiment
of growing avarice. To "Mother Barker, slowly growing fat and dumpy. . . .
George Barker's remonstrances [that she stop serving as a crime consultant]
counted for nothing." According to her FBI file, Ma grew tired of her husband because their meager existence had made her obsessed with wealth:
"She began to long for luxuries that George could not provide." Later in
Hoover and Cooper's article, Ma grows rich off her criminal instincts and
raises tens of thousands of dollars by running a regular hideout for escaped
cons and wanted robbers: "To feel money stream through her fingers, to
know it could buy whatever she desired, to order extravagantly—all these
were great solaces to Ma Barker. She demanded increasingly heavy fees for
the hiding of a convict or for her counsel in a major job of lawbreaking."
The "*Real* Public Enemy" insinuated that, for the purposes of manipulating
sympathetic judges and parole board officers, Ma may have fraudulently
posed as a destitute single parent who needed her sons released so they
could support her.[11]

Hoover speculated that the four Barker children might have become law-
abiding if only the Barker patriarch had been able to exert his rightful place
as head of the household. His *American Magazine* article foregrounded the
sorrow of the displaced father. When neighbors complained about his sons'
petty crimes during their youths, George Barker would allegedly say, "You
have to talk to Mother. She handles the boys . . . She would never let me do
with that what I wanted to." In "The *Real* Public Enemy," George "talked
wistfully of the days when he had tried his own methods of reform" with
his wayward sons, trying to interest them in "clean pursuits, the fun of
tramping across the country in search of rabbits, of hunting for squirrel."

But Ma had her own way with the children, and so, "unable to reconcile his sense of right and the life of his family, [George] gave up his family and went away. Ma grew fatter, shrewder, and prospered."[12] Hoover and Cooper characterized George Barker as a figure of great pity, brokenhearted and reluctant to speak of "the boys" except as children. Again and again, the father's influence is tied to the wholesomeness of nature and masculine sport: "[George] tries to remember only those days when, gun in hand, he led the youngsters over rolling meadow or through leafy woods . . . 'They were good boys then.'"[13]

Abridged versions of the *American Magazine* biography appeared instantly in the *Nashville Banner,* the *Hartford Courant,* the *Tulsa Daily World,* the *Milwaukee Journal,* and the *Kansas City Star,* where Cooper originally worked as a crime reporter before he joined the *American Magazine* staff. (Some of the contemporary newspaper articles mention a recent visit from Cooper, whose "lecture tour" on celebrity criminals fueled curiosity about Ma.)[14] The unabashed poaching by these newspapers and the geographically disparate urban audiences they reached demonstrate the successful and speedy proliferation of the FBI propaganda machine. The FBI's archive on Ma Barker includes photocopied collections of the 1936 newspaper clippings on Ma, indicating that the Bureau closely monitored its influence on public opinion. In the case of the "*Real* Public Enemy" feature, its influence was easy to trace. References to Ma's charmingly "ordinary Missouri farm" and "lusty" hymn singing were reprinted verbatim again and again, not only in contemporary newspaper accounts, but also in crime biographies written decades later. Reporters relished the image of Ma dragging her sons to church each week and her alleged ranting against the hazards of liquor and girlfriends. Thereafter, Ma's religiosity and potentially perverse love for her male offspring became a staple of her biographies.

By Hoover's telling, Herman Barker's death and the simultaneous imprisonment of Ma's three surviving sons changed Ma Barker "from an animal mother of the she-wolf type to a veritable beast of prey."[15] Whether or not this harsh characterization was warranted, Ma did abruptly make several drastic changes in her life in the years that she was separated from her children. At age fifty-five, Ma left George Barker and moved across town. There, wrote Hoover and Cooper, she allegedly raised tens of thousands of dollars by running a regular hideout for escaped cons and other wanted persons. The exact details of how she supported herself may have been exaggerated, but Ma did continue to press for her sons' release by hounding the parole boards, wardens, and governors. Her efforts finally paid off in

March 1931, when Freddie was released from Lansing Prison, and in September 1932, when Doc was paroled from McAlester. Fred returned home with his former prison cellmate, Alvin Karpis, who had also been set free.

By all accounts, Ma took an instant liking to Karpis, and her acceptance of "Old Creepy," as Karpis was dubbed for his sinister smile, fueled speculation about what Ma and Karpis might have meant to each other. Hoover and Cooper claimed she had taken Karpis into her "queer, fierce range of affections," which phrase suggested a range of interpretations.[16] As Richard Hirsch wrote in a 1940 *True Detective* piece on Karpis, "Ma was proud of her adopted son. He could not have been more vicious if he had her own corrupt blood flowing through his veins."[17] Subsequent crime journalists painted Karpis as Ma's star pupil in crime; others posited him as her chief rival for control within the gang.

In his 1971 memoir, Karpis was adamant that he and Ma shared a simple friendship based on his willingness to finance Ma's trips to the movies and other small amusements such as bingo. Karpis claimed that when he met Ma, she had been subsisting in a run-down shack. Soon after, she went to live with Karpis and Fred Barker and began accompanying them on road trips. As Karpis wrote, "Whether she was aware of it or not, Ma made a nearly foolproof cover for Freddy and me and Doc. When we traveled together, we moved as a mother and three sons. What could look more innocent? We usually told our landlords and apartment house superintendents that we were salesmen, taking care of our widowed mother . . . [T]he cops were always thrown off by our family appearance."[18]

Karpis characterized Ma as "an old-fashioned homebody from the Ozarks" who spent her free time doing jigsaw puzzles and listening to the radio. He insisted that Ma "knew we were criminals and that we'd spent time in prison. But she was never informed of the specifics."[19] When Karpis and Fred Barker were sought for the murder of a Missouri sheriff, they fled to the protection of St. Paul, whose crooked police force was hospitable to fugitives. Ma followed them to Minnesota and, according to official FBI accounts, began dying her graying hair dark red. (Or, if St. Paul residents' recollections are given priority, she dyed it blond.) By February 1932, Ma, Fred, Karpis, and Ma's boyfriend, Arthur "Old Man" Dunlop, had set up housekeeping in St. Paul and began calling themselves the "Andersons."

Camouflage and Talkback

Crime historian Jay Nash saw Ma's childhood as having shaped her destiny, since she had grown up in the same heartland that nurtured Jesse and Frank James. Jesse James was killed when Ma was ten, but, according to Nash, "she never forgot the handsome bandit. She had seen him ride through nearby Carthage once with the Younger brothers at his side."[20] Whether or not the story is true, it points to the connections a person of Ma's generation might easily have drawn between the rural midwestern gangsters of the 1930s and the outlaw bandits of her childhood. Perhaps Ma was as oblivious as Karpis claimed and unwilling to "concern herself with the younger generation's problems."[21] Perhaps she regarded her sons and Karpis as modern-day outlaws taking from an unfair system. Could she have fancied herself as an outlaw, too? What would it have meant for her to use an alias and to alter her appearance? Her Minnesota neighbors recalled her as kind. She gave out candy and nickels to the children who helped walk her dog. Each time the Barker-Karpis Gang was discovered and forced hastily to relocate, they took care to settle accounts with the paperboy, the iceman, and the garbage carrier on their way out of town. Ma also made good on a promise to deliver another family's twenty-five-cent ice payment. This gang had stolen tens of thousands of dollars from banks around the Midwest. They kidnapped two prominent Minnesota business-men—bloodying one of them just blocks from his young daughter's school. Yet the story of how they risked capture to pay off tiny debts lingered for decades, evidence of their supposed allegiance to the "little guy."[22]

By Hoover's account, Ma had lived a double life in St. Paul. As was her habit, he said, she established contact with some of the city's most dan-gerous underworld denizens. But she also made connections in St. Paul's wealthier neighborhoods, where she and her family knew the police would not be looking for them. "Ma Barker was an actress. She appeared to most people to be a demure, friendly, smiling person. Throughout her life, she frequently took advantage of reputable people whom she met, in obtaining letters of reference. She used such references in renting hideaways among respectable people in many different cities and states . . . Thus, the old woman, with an air of age and respectability, led the way [for the rest of the gang]."[23]

When Ma, Fred, and Karpis left St. Paul for Kansas City, they rented an apartment in an exclusive residential area, the better to avoid the atten-tions of the police. In St. Paul, their cover was blown when their landlady's son saw pictures of Karpis and Fred in a detective magazine. Then Ma's boyfriend, Arthur Dunlop, was found shot to death on the shore of a Min-nesota lake. "Not far away," claimed Hoover and Cooper, "was a woman's bloodstained glove."[24]

The "*Real* Public Enemy" article also alleged that it was Ma's idea that the gang should abandon bank robberies and take up kidnapping. Karpis denied Ma's involvement in the gang's successful kidnapping of the wealthy St. Paul brewer William Hamm in 1933, or its kidnapping of a prominent Minneapolis banker, Edward Bremer, a year later. (Indeed, Twin Cities researcher Paul Maccabee places Ma in Chicago at the time of the Bremer snatch.)[25] FBI agents on the Bremer case traced Doc Barker's fingerprint from a fuel can, and the culprits were identified. By the spring of 1934, pictures of Doc, Fred, Alvin Karpis, and other gang members were again prominently displayed in such magazines as *True Detective*, as well as upon thousands of FBI wanted posters.

Seeking a fresh start through plastic surgery and fingertip alterations, Fred and Karpis unwisely trusted themselves to the underworld doctor Joseph P. Moran, who literally mutilated them. They emerged from the botched operation in serious pain and with no appreciable difference in their identifying features. Assisted by Karpis's girlfriend Dolores Delaney, Ma Barker nursed the wounded pair back to health and, several months later, Moran turned up dead. Fred and Doc Barker were named as the killers, although never formally charged. Fiction writers later capitalized on the story of criminals scarred by the bungled surgery, a "just deserts" narrative that was all the more salacious for the scandal of the corrupt physician. Moran's murder also added another delicious storytelling detail to Ma's legend. In some fictional accounts of the gang's activities, Ma brutally slays Moran and anyone else who dares harm her children.

Ma's real-life attachment to her offspring was amply documented in the letters she wrote for years on their behalf. Her correspondence with the family's attorney, and her self-presentation within it, suggest that she and her husband were indeed feeling vulnerable in 1927–1928, when all three of her surviving sons were incarcerated. Her reference to financial hardships was corroborated by Karpis's description of Ma's evident poverty at the time he first met her. Leaving aside Karpis's repeated assertions of Ma's "naiveté," it's also possible that Ma knew what was expected of her when negotiating with the parole system:

Dear Mr. McGhee:

This is Mrs. Barker riting. I am going to tell you some more of my troubles, Mr. McGhee. I heard today they have been punishing Dock something affel. I heard they did have him chained up and the rats had nawed on him and there was some boy got out down there and he went up and told the govner and he went down there. I just wondered if you would rite down there to that party you no and find out if it is true or not.

My sister heard this from a boy that knows Dock. It seems like they could be something done. I haven't any money to do anything with. Mr. Barker is having the rumitism affel bad I heard today. It seems like I sure do have my share of trouble Mr. McGhee. Do you think there is any chance to get Freddie out? It does seem like they has got to be something done as Mr. Barker hant able to work and I have worked myself nearly to death this summer to try to make ends meet. We do kneed Freddie home so bad to help us. We are right up against the real thing in a finiancle way. Mr Barker said you did take care of Bert's [Herman's] grave. I sure do thank you for it Mr. McGhee. How is Mrs. McGhee and the boys. Tell them hello for me. Let me hear from you soon.

As ever, Mrs. G. E. Barker[26]

Cooper reproduced this letter as part of his research for "The *Real* Public Enemy," but noted that he "[saw] no use for it." It conveyed too mundane and pathetic a portrait of Ma to include in the *American Magazine* article, except as another index of her twisted maternal instincts. The hand-wring-ing, near-illiterate Ma Barker also contradicted the article's claim that the Barker-Karpis Gang had relied on Ma's cunning to pull off their bank jobs. As Hoover and Cooper theorized, Ma not only exploited her "nice little old woman" appearance to case each bank, she also had plotted the gang's escape after the commission of their crimes. "Ma's 'getaway charts' were amazing in their minute attention to detail. . . . 'Ma' would have one of the 'boys' drive her over the route selected for the escape. With one eye on the speedometer, she would mark down in code every turn and twist of the road, every obstruction, every dangerous curve. . . . She made her road tests in wet weather and in dry, to be ready for any emergency at the time of the actual flight."[27]

If meticulous scientific research and planning were the hallmarks of the midcentury G-man, *American Magazine*'s Ma Barker became a worthy adversary. To maintain her disguise as a helpless little old lady, Ma was, Hoover and Cooper wryly noted, "still at it, writing doleful 'mother' letters to prison authorities . . . only a short time before she, herself, was killed, a bullet-heated machine gun in her aged hands."[28]

The Battle for Mother Barker

It was no accident that Hoover approved *American Magazine* as the forum for his bulletin on Ma Barker. By the late 1930s, *American's* primary competitors were *Redbook* and *Cosmopolitan*. The recently revamped "family magazine" was tilting more heavily toward a female readership and promised its audience "a complete mystery novel" in every other issue. As avid consumers of mystery fiction, *American Magazine* readers were the logical targets for series of true crime reports—touted as the "Secrets of the G-men"—that censured women's deviance and extolled the achievements of the FBI.

When the *"Real* Public Enemy" article hit newsstands in April 1936, the FBI was still riding the crest of public approval from its string of successes in the war on crime. The drive to sell a heroic image of the G-men had gained momentum in 1934 with the Bureau of Investigation's expanding powers and its massively publicized successes in bringing down a long list of public enemies, from Bonnie and Clyde to John Dillinger. These victories explain why, taken out of context, the *American Magazine's* artist's depiction of an FBI agent might have been mistaken for a gangster. As Hoover's Bureau regulations required, the crouching G-man accompanying the "Public Enemy" article is clean-shaven and wears a suit. But, in the illustration he also clenches a machine gun in his hands and a drooping cigarette in his menacing, downturned lips. Topping off the picture is a broad-brimmed hat, tilted rakishly in the style of the villains James Cagney was famous for portraying on screen.

The G-man's gun is trained on a photograph of the real Ma Barker, which appears on the opposite page. The plump contours of her person are evident in her drop-waist sailor dress and her head is half hidden by a cloche hat. Ma stands in a field of waist-high wildflowers that cannot entirely conceal what she grips loosely in her right hand: a walking cane. Given the FBI's solid public standing in 1936, it is possible that Ma's benign appearance may not have mattered. Still, one wonders whether the danger Hoover attributed to the cane-toting Ma was met by some readers with laughter or skepticism.

Illustrations aside, any careful reader might notice inconsistencies in the *"Real* Public Enemy" narrative. The article implied that Hoover had stared into Ma's eyes, which had, in the language of the article, "always fascinated me." As the voice of Hoover mused, Ma's eyes "were queerly direct, penetrating, hot with some strangely smoldering flame, yet withal as hypnotically cold as the muzzle of a gun. The same dark, mysterious brilliance was in the eyes of each of her four sons."[29] The phrasing was Cooper's, and Cooper's research relied heavily on an interview with Ma's estranged husband, George Barker. But correspondence with Hoover and other Bureau members indicates that Cooper did not conduct this interview himself and in fact had never met any of the Barkers. That did not stop Cooper from including in the article a few first-person flourishes to suggest to readers that J. Edgar Hoover had personally spoken with George Barker and also spent time in the company of Ma and her children, even though she never had direct contact with anyone in law enforcement until the shootout in which she was killed.[30]

In fairness, some of the embellishments to the Ma Barker legend appear not to have been the work of Cooper or Hoover and were instead the invention of the magazine editors. For example, the article repeatedly asserts Ma's talents as a social chameleon: "Ma Barker was an actress . . . She could weep with the ease of a movie star and much more convincingly."[31] No such observation appeared in the original article draft. The magazine editors may have wanted to reassure readers that the lack of evidence connecting Ma to any of her sons' robberies or kidnappings was, in fact, evidence of her supreme duplicity.

When author Herbert Corey wrote about Ma Barker in *Farewell, Mr. Gangster!* (1936), his Hoover-endorsed paean to the FBI, even he could not quite accept the idea of Ma as an underworld mastermind. But he did record her as a tasteless "harridan" and dictatorial parent.

In her latter days, Ma Barker was described as a red-eyed, wattle-necked harridan, fond of hanging cheap beads and ten-cent-store gimcrackery on her bulging person. She was as vicious as a Gila monster and yet she was able to successfully pose as a nice old woman when in the presence of strangers. She was no she-genius in crime, but she was a stern mother. She made her boys behave. They might rob and murder, but they could never bring their loose women into her house. She kept them from getting too drunk. She made them check in at nine o'clock most nights, and above all she taught them not to talk.[32]

If Karpis is believed, Ma was but a decoy for the gang and had no interest in the activities of her male traveling companions. By Hoover's published accounts, Ma was their ringleader and a criminal genius. But these opposing characterizations did align on one subject: Ma's antagonism toward her sons' girlfriends. Whether or not Hoover exaggerated in his assertion that Ma Barker "shuddered in jealous trepidation when a new gun moll threatened to steal the love of one of her boys," this was the one and only point on which Hoover and Karpis agreed.[33] As both Karpis and Herbert Corey allowed, Ma's determination that her sons keep free of romantic entanglements may have been spurred less by maternal jealousy than by her concern that their girlfriends would turn them in to the law. In the years after her death, Ma's supposed prohibition on booze and dames would be used alternatively to ridicule her or to praise her as more sensible than the rest of the Barker-Karpis Gang. Either approach worked to amplify the *American Magazine*'s Ma, who had "ranged through the Midwest like a tempestuous, whim-struck queen, storming at the slightest disobedience to her rulings."[34]

The more excessive renderings of Ma's story had the greatest staying power. Many of the potentially fabricated details from "The *Real* Public Enemy" became the centerpiece of Hoover's best-selling 1938 book, *Persons in Hiding*, and so she entered the historical record as another power-hungry and entitled woman who provided the "roots of crime."[35] It was more interesting to imagine Ma as an updated Lady Macbeth than as the diminutive woman Karpis recalled as a "slightly nutty old queen" who needed an air cushion to see over the dashboard of a car.

After the murder of the quack doctor Joseph Moran, the Barker-Karpis Gang scattered about the country. On January 8, 1935, federal police located Doc Barker in Chicago and captured him without a fight.[36] Through a marked map discovered in Doc's apartment, the FBI tracked Ma and Freddie's retreat to a resort in Oklawaha, Florida. At dawn on January 16, a team of federal agents surrounded the house that Ma and Freddie had rented by Oklawaha's Lake Weir. Herbert Corey's *Farewell, Mr. Gangster!* describes a decorous confrontation in which a G-man very politely rapped on the cottage door and advised the Barkers to come out peaceably.

> "Go to hell," said Ma Barker. A machine gun was propped against the inside casing of the door. Ma Barker slammed the door shut with her one hand and picked up the gun with the other. She was firing before the agent could get off the porch . . . Fred Barker went into action from the second floor.[37]

Most accounts at least agree that Ma Barker did the talking on the morning of the standoff. So it happens in Hoover and Cooper's *American Magazine* feature, in which a special agent bravely reveals himself to Ma and Freddie so they have fair warning that they are surrounded.

"Fred!" he shouted. "Ma Barker! We are officers of the United States Department of Justice!"

There was no answer. The special agent went on: "We want you to come out one at a time. You will not be injured."

There was still no answer. Again the special agent called, "Unless you come out, we'll have to use tear gas to force you out!"

Silence. Then the special agents began to call from every side, reiterating the fact that the place was surrounded. At last Ma Barker answered; the tone was firm, cold: "All right; go ahead."

In a move that ratchets up the suspense of the early morning encounter, the agents on the scene misinterpret Ma's response as an admission of defeat.

The officers believed she was telling Fred to surrender. Still in the open, not thirty yards from the house, the special agent in charge again shouted, "All right; you won't be hurt. Come out one at a time. You first, Fred."

The answer was a burst of machine-gun fire from Ma Barker, at an upstairs window. Then a rifle was fired by Fred from downstairs. The agent in charge was surrounded by whipping dust, raised by the bullets of the machine gun. But he reached cover, miraculously escaping at least thirty-five shots aimed at him by the woman.

Ma Barker may have been the brains of the outfit, but apparently she was a lousy shot. Hoover and Cooper's description of the standoff emphasizes Ma's outrageousness and the FBI's clever professionalism.

Then the battle truly began, lull and burst, flaring flame followed by silence. But there was no surrender in the heart of Ma Barker or that of her dominated son. . . . At last, the special agents figured out the distances from the windows, and approximate places at which mother and son concealed themselves. They began to shoot through the walls of the house at these points.[38]

Six hours later, the cottage was reduced to a sieve. The Barkers had stopped firing. So had the FBI agents, who had run out of ammunition. Meanwhile, a number of local residents had gathered to watch the shoot-out. A few of the more eager spectators found themselves pressed up against trees in the midst of the battlefield, terrified of catching a stray bullet.[39]

Stories diverge as to what happened next. In the official FBI account, agents "kick down the door" and find Ma beside a machine gun with its "barrel still smoking."[40] E. J. Connelley, an FBI agent on the scene, told newspaper reporters that once the shooting from within the house had subsided, the agents had dispatched an elderly black handyman, Willie Woodbury, to enter the house and confirm that its occupants were dead.[41] The FBI's Melvin Purvis, who was also on the scene, tried to put a positive spin on "the darky" Woodbury's involvement. As Purvis explained, once the return gunfire had halted,

> there was no way for the special agents to know whether the people in the house were dead or whether they were waiting and preparing to kill any agents who attempted to rush the house. The darky, named Willie, volunteered to go into the house if the agents would call out to him in a loud and abusive voice, as if they were forcing him to go in. He was a pretty smart darky.[42]

The FBI's gunfight with the Barkers "held the headlines in American newspapers for a long time," wrote Purvis.[43] In *Persons in Hiding*, Hoover sought to correct the impression given by "lurid writers" that Ma had been the "pathetically defiant leader of a small group of courageous men." Hoover disapprovingly recalled how souvenir hunters ripped apart the Barkers' rental house at Oklawaha. "Finally the owner charged admission, and the curious paid, as though this were a circus instead of a tragedy of misused lives."[44]

Ma and Fred Barker were both found dead in an upstairs bedroom. Fred was holding a submachine gun and had been hit eleven times. A .300 gas-operated rifle with forty of its ninety-four rounds gone lay next to Ma. (Herbert Corey imagined how it might have happened that, "with one final filial gesture, Fred Barker had given his old mother the gun which carried . . . one hundred rounds . . . and kept the 50-shot machine gun for himself.")[45] Ma's body had taken three bullets, including one directly through the heart. The Bureau recorded her death as having occurred at the hands of sharpshooting agents who needed to defend themselves. Several accounts highlight the fact that Ma's handbag contained $10,200 in large denominations.[46]

J. Edgar Hoover assured the press that now that "the backbone" of the Barker-Karpis Gang had been eliminated, the other gang members would soon be "knocked off." Lest some readers regard the killing of a sixty-three-year old woman with her son as cruel, Hoover also reminded journalists that "Ma told her boys never to be taken alive."[47] It took George Barker eight months to raise the funds he needed to ship back to Oklahoma the bodies of his former wife and son. In that time, hundred of locals and tourists streamed through the Florida mortuary for a glimpse of the Barkers, whose bodies were kept oiled for preservation and display.[48] Ma and all her sons were interred in an open field in Welch, Oklahoma, not far from where George Barker ran a filling station.

Ma's grave marker is modest—just a tiny metal sign holder with a typewritten notice. The inscription references the long time her body was on display and also prioritizes the role most central to her legend:

"MOTHER"
KATE BARKER
DIE [sic]: Jan. 16- 1935
Buried October- 1935
The Darkest Night, Shall end
In bright Day

Raising the Dead

Eleven months after Ma died, movie audiences were riveted by another machine-gun mama, an invention of Twentieth Century Pictures. In *Show Them No Mercy* (1935), a plucky couple and their baby girl are taken hostage by an unsympathetic gang of thugs. One of their abductors goes so far as to shoot the little family's dog as it tries to run for help. At film's end, G-men finally move in to save the day. But it falls to the young mother (Rochelle Hudson) to slaughter the most sadistic gang member (Cesar Romero). When he threatens to kill her husband, she grabs a machine gun and rakes the villain with bullets. He drops to his knees, blood oozing from a line of gaping holes across his torso. *Show Them No Mercy* reflected the Depression era's deepening anticrime mood and distaste for kidnappings like those associated with gangsters Alvin Karpis and the Barker brothers. Applauding the machine-gun scene in *Show Them No Mercy* as a call to arms for America's wives and mothers, film censors lifted their strict ban on visible wounds to allow the gory climax. Here, after all, was a mother hero who would never take up a gun, save to defend the safety and stability of her family.

A few months later, in the same month that *American Magazine* subscribers were reading about a maternal antihero who was "The *Real* Public Enemy," a U.S. Senate committee publicly lambasted Hoover for never having been directly involved in any of the arrests for which his Bureau was taking so much credit. Hoover therefore put the word out to his agents that he would personally snap the handcuffs on Alvin Karpis whenever he was found. His opportunity came swiftly. On May 1, 1936, agents located Karpis in New Orleans, and Hoover flew down to oversee the capture of the nation's final, big-name public enemy. In the official FBI account, Hoover leaned into Karpis's car and collared him before he could reach for a rifle. Karpis maintained that Director Hoover had hung back until a team of agents immobilized Karpis, and only then stepped forward to declare the arrest. Either way, Karpis's capture was a public relations victory for Hoover, although he had to satisfy himself with seeing Karpis bound at the wrists with an agent's necktie. No one had remembered to bring a pair of handcuffs for the arrest.

Karpis spent most of the next thirty years imprisoned at Alcatraz. Shortly after his release from prison in 1969, he published a memoir full of fury at the "old practice of the FBI to dress up the truth with lies that make them look more clever and powerful than they really are . . . the story of Hoover the Hero was false." Karpis devoted a chapter of his book to his own account of Ma Barker, but admitted that the FBI's version of Ma was too firmly "entrenched in North America[n] . . . books, kids' comics, detective fiction and movies" for him to alter Ma's legend. In 1968, the *New York News* crime reporter Henry Lee had dubbed Ma Barker one of the "Ten Most Wanted Criminals of the Past 50 Years," because this "fanatically possessive and loving mother" had relentlessly defended her children in the face of accusations she knew to be true. Lee based his account on "long and detailed discussions with leading crime enforcement officials throughout the United States." Of course, by 1968, few, if any, of those officials would have had direct exposure to the Barker case. Most could only have known it from the institutional lore first invented by Hoover and Cooper in the pages of *American Magazine*.[49]

The suggestion in "The *Real* Public Enemy" that Ma had been an actress proved prophetic, for she was destined for a starring role in Hoover's *Persons in Hiding* film series. Like the Kathryn Kelly–inspired *Persons in Hiding* film from 1939 that bore the series' name, *Queen of the Mob* (1940) was a morality tale drawn from highly recognizable elements of Ma Barker's life. Press packets for *Queen* followed the same formula as the first *Persons in Hiding* movie, but this time promised a "Reign of Terror! Ruled by a Queen of Crime Ten Times Tougher than the Toughest Man!" Hoover's face again appeared on film posters, a little larger now that his *Persons in Hiding* series had become established. The film's official promotional materials situated Ma and gang within a larger tradition of Anglo-Celtic outlaw-heroes, including Robin Hood. Having thus established Ma's outlaw pedigree, the film's press sheets sternly noted that most of history's notorious bandits were "sordid, vicious egotists, basking for a time in the limelight of publicity." This ambiguous promotional strategy made sense in the wake of the huge critical and financial success of Warner Brothers' *The Adventures of Robin Hood* (1938).

Correspondence between FBI headquarters in D.C. and the writers at Paramount indicates that the FBI director kept close tabs on the adaptation of his book into screenplays. These letters reiterate again and again that Hoover would withdraw his support—and use of his image—unless he personally approved the final script. After the Motion Picture Production Code Administration dispatched an early version of the *Queen of the Mob* script to the Department of Justice, an assistant to the district attorney wrote Production Code Administration Chief Joseph Breen a frank letter in which he condemned the script for "exploiting the accomplishments of a Ma Barker type of lawbreaker and for no good purpose." The assistant earnestly warned Breen, "No one seriously engaged in law enforcement would approve the picture." Four days and a spate of testy memos later, word arrived from D.C. that "Mr. Mulcahy was wrong in his comments since J. Edgar Hoover, who *is* seriously engaged in law enforcement, has read and approved the script." This correspondence further noted that the district attorney's assistant had been "eliminated from the Department of Justice a few days ago."[50]

Hoover did not always get his way, however, especially with the Ma Barker script. For instance, the censors would not accept Hoover's title, *The Woman from Hell*, and so Paramount released the film as *Queen of the Mob* in 1940. *Queen's* "Ma Webster" (as she was renamed for the film) is far tamer a character than the Ma Barker whom Hoover and Cooper described in *American Magazine*. The adapted screenplay by William R. Lipman and Horace McCoy reimagined Ma's eldest son as having been lost not to a suicide but to the "straight" world. Redeemed by the love of his upstanding wife, Ethel, Ma's son Bert has built an honest life and become a lawyer. To Ma, this defection rankles, as does her displacement in Bert's affections by another woman.

Ma Webster (Blanche Yurka) plans her crooked sons' crimes and frequently identifies herself as the leader of her sons and their gangland associates. ("So long as we're workin' together, I'll do the thinking. . . .

Somebody's got to have a brain around here.") But she is distracted by her need to arrange clandestine visits with Bert's baby son, her only grandchild. In the final sequence, she readies her home for a children's Christmas party and persuades her son Eddie to dress up as Santa Claus. "Tell [the kids] to be honest," she coaches him. "Tell 'em not to do anything they would be ashamed of. Lay it on thick!" Eddie never gets a chance to dispense ironic advice, because G-men surround the house before the party starts.

In the original Hoover-approved script, *Queen of the Mob* ended with Ma bidding the federal agents a bitterly defiant "Merry Christmas, G-men," as she lies dying beneath her Christmas tree. But this ending so appalled test audiences that it had to be reshot. In the final cut, Ma does not die in an FBI shootout. Instead, she surrenders and concedes, "All right, Mr. G-man. You win," before bidding a sorrowful farewell to Eddie, who, still dressed as Santa, lies dead beneath the Christmas tree.[51] The G-men who lead Ma from the house take chivalrous care first to put away their guns. While critics who reviewed *Queen of the Mob* made clear that audiences had not forgotten the real Ma Barker and her violent death in the Florida standoff, the revised ending still represented another success for the FBI. Audiences got the film's message that Ma had been as corrupt as the G-men were righteous. Not public outrage at the FBI's actions but a squeamish aversion toward seeing grandmothers get shot seems to have dictated the new ending—one that made the federal agents greater heroes than before.

Apart from its tidied-up finale and more temperate villain, *Queen of the Mob* was largely faithful to Hoover and Cooper's *American Magazine* account, especially as it enacted certain traits that would forever be associated with the "real" Ma Barker. These traits articulated the contradictions of the older female aggressor, who is simultaneously an object of comedy, derision, and danger. In *Queen*, Ma distrusts all other women, especially younger female rivals. She forbids her sons to associate with women and tears Bert's wife out of a family photograph. Ma also craves expensive consumer goods, but does so, the film intimates, because she is keen to the prejudices of a legal system that make the world of high society one of the safest places for a criminal to hide. (As Ma reasons in the film, "The last place the G-men'll look for us is in the social register.") A wily manipulator, she uses her appearance of vulnerability and innocence to rent hideouts and case banks. Ma therefore employs what is coded in her body by way of her sex, age, and whiteness to garner power in precisely those arenas where older women are presumed to have none. She "fronts" for her sons and they, in turn, front for her as the male bodies she needs to gain access to "the things we want, not just the things we need." In this way, she precisely echoes Hoover's argument that women not be underestimated in their capacity both as criminals and as criminal-enablers.

In keeping with Hoover's published denunciations of gangland women, *Queen* condemns underworld women for more than breaking the law. Ma feels entitled to the material comforts she spent most of her life without and possesses an ambition—and skill for moneymaking—far beyond those of the men around her. Paradoxically, traditionally feminine attributes and practices function as the very condition for Ma's capture. Like Dot in *Persons in Hiding*, Ma's criminal ambitions are undone by her family attachments, in this case, an overwhelming devotion to her grandson. *Queen of the Mob*'s revised ending suggests that separation from the child, and not death, was for Ma the ultimate punishment. Cultural norms double as a strategy for the enforcement of the law.

By the time the *Persons in Hiding* series went into production in 1939, Germany had invaded Poland and U.S. involvement in World War II seemed imminent. Suddenly, the gang-busting G-men found it necessary to morph into the spy-busting G-men. *Queen of the Mob* had done a reasonable box office, but, by the time agents led her gently off-screen in 1940, Ma Barker, the gangster nemesis, was becoming something of an outdated symbol. It would only be a few years, however, before Ma took on a new relevance in the realm of popular culture. Hoover's *"Real* Public Enemy" would prove an apt icon for wartime and postwar cultures preoccupied with rigid gender roles enacted in relation to child rearing, the nuclear family, and domestic space.

Generation of Vipers

In 1942, Farrar and Rinehart published *Generation of Vipers*, Philip Wylie's splenetic treatise on the "cancer of the soul" that was ruining the United States. Wylie unleashed his fury on just about every American subgroup—businessmen, academics, the military, and more. But he reserved a special venom for "Mom" and the "momism" that was Wylie's word for the unhealthy reverence accorded to her. As Wylie wrote,

> Let us look at mom. She is a middle-aged puffin with an eye like a hawk that has just seen a rabbit twitch far below. She is about twenty-five pounds overweight, with no sprint, but sharp heels and a hard backhand which she does not regard as a foul but a womanly defense. In a thousand of her there is not sex appeal enough to budge a hermit

ten paces off a rock ledge. She none the less spends several hundred dollars a year on permanents and transformations, pomades, cleansers, rouges, lipsticks, and the like—and fools nobody except herself. If a man kisses her with any earnestness, it is time for mom to feel for her pocketbook, and this occasionally does happen.[52]

Wylie lamented such women's longevity, yearning for a time when "mom folded up and died of hard work somewhere in the middle of her life." He also credited thirty-five years of national decline to the fact of women having gotten the vote in 1920.

Mom's first gracious presence at the ballot-box was roughly concomitant with the start toward a new all-time low in political scurviness, hoodlumism, gangsterism, labor strife, monopolistic thuggery, moral degeneration, civic corruption, smuggling, bribery, theft, murder, homosexuality, drunkenness, financial depression, chaos and war.[53]

By 1954, *Generation of Vipers* was in its twentieth printing, having sold more than 180,000 copies and having stirred up a furious debate. "Mom" was a sacred American institution but also a figure of profound ambivalence in a moment when women were living longer and further encroaching on formerly male professions, especially during World War II. Compared to a previous generation, middle-class mothers and grandmothers may also have seemed the clearest beneficiaries of an expanding consumer culture. In Alfred Hitchcock's thriller, *Shadow of a Doubt* (1943), the "Merry Widow" serial killer gets his comeuppance, but not before he explains why his murders of rich women are justified.

The cities are full of women. Middle-aged widows; husbands, dead. Husbands who've spent their lives making fortunes, working and working. And then they die and leave their money to their wives, their silly wives. And what do the wives do, these useless women? You see them in the hotels, the best hotels, every day by the thousands, drinking the money, eating the money, losing the money at bridge, playing all day and all night, smelling of money, proud of their jewelry but of nothing else. Horrible, faded, fat, greedy women . . . Are they human or are they fat, wheezing animals, hmm? And what happens to animals when they get too fat and too old?[54]

In his revised introduction for *Vipers*, Philip Wylie redefined "momism" as the dangerous product of a wartime tendency for "mother-worship."

Women thereafter came to dominate and infantilize their offspring, rendering their male children particularly vulnerable to what Wylie characterized as a self-serving "gynecocracy."[55] This theory was the engine behind the Oscar-nominated *White Heat* (1949), about the mama-obsessed gangster Cody Jarrett (James Cagney, returning to the genre he helped create). The sociopathic Cody suffers from debilitating Oedipal headaches, product of a mother who is at once corrupt and overindulgent. Blinded by pain, he runs for "Ma Jarrett," who takes grown-up Cody in her lap and soothes him like a baby. As one of *White Heat*'s screenwriters would later recall, "we synthesized Ma Barker down to having one son instead of four and we put the evil of all four into one man."[56] When, at the film's climax, Cody stands astride a flaming oil tank and screams, "Made it, Ma! Top of the world!" he is addressing the Ma Barker–inspired character who was his strength and his torment.[57]

Fears of the "gynecocracy" and the potentially destructive power of mothers over their husbands and sons injected fresh relevance into Hoover's "Mother Barker." In a special 1955 edition celebrating the achievements of the FBI, *Look* magazine reenacted Hoover and Cooper's 1936 *American Magazine* article on Ma Barker. The *Look* feature presented "The *Real* Public Enemy" article as real news, intimating that photos of the actors portraying Ma and her sons were candids of the actual Barker family. A few years later, Hoover collaborated on another fictionalized FBI retrospective, *The FBI Story* (1958). The film starred the venerable actor Jimmy Stewart as Chip Hardesty, an agent who must balance his responsibilities as a family man with his responsibilities to the Bureau. Critics scratched their heads at how much time the film spent on the family dramas versus the G-men action. In fact, *The FBI Story* might have been subtitled "The Girl behind the Man behind the Gun," since its narrative thread centers on Chip's long-suffering wife, Lucy (Vera Miles), and her constant sacrifices in support of her husband's career. When Lucy finally attempts to separate from Chip, she finds that she is helpless without him and resigns herself to a life married to the FBI as well as to one of its agents. The intelligent but gentle Lucy is the anti-Ma, the anti–Bonnie Parker, and the anti–Kathryn Kelly. Devoted to her country, her children, and to making a home for Chip, she is the ideal woman Hoover described in his 1938 book, *Persons in Hiding*. Meanwhile, the contrast between Chip's benevolent, paternal G-men and destructive, out-of-control Ma Barker is bluntly enacted in a montage representing the gangster era. Armed, angry, and dark-complexioned, Ma appears in the upstairs window of a cottage surrounded by cool-headed agents. Stewart's voice-over sarcastically refers to Ma as a "sweet country gal" as he carefully aims his rifle and executes her. The antithesis of saintly, blonde Lucy, Ma dies an awkward death at the hands of one of the United States' most beloved movie stars, further solidifying Hoover's "official" myth of Ma Barker as an underappreciated peril.

Three more feature-length films about Ma Baker emerged at roughly the rate of one a decade from 1950 to 1970: *Guns Don't Argue, Ma Barker's Killer Brood,* and *Bloody Mama.* Each film stretched her character to more violent proportions, and each reached new generations that could only know "Ma Barker" and the early FBI through their on-screen portrayals. Ironically, the man who once rejected J. Edgar Hoover as lacking an understanding of show business happened to consider Hoover's "Mother Barker" rather well suited for it.[58] Radio personality and producer Phillips H. Lord wrote the script for Ma Barker's next on-screen incarnation, *Guns Don't Argue.* First broadcast piecemeal on television in 1955, the story was reissued by Visual Drama Inc. as a feature-length film in 1957, by which time rural gangland stories were nostalgia pieces representative of a simpler time. But the Ma Barker story line perfectly reflected contemporary fears around a surge of juvenile delinquency and the overbearing mothers and ineffectual fathers who might be behind it. *Guns Don't Argue* also enacted Wylie's "momist" vision of a deviant woman with the power to produce deviant men—either by dominating them or by giving birth to them.

Unlike *Queen of the Mob,* which avoided direct mention of the real-life characters on whom it was based, *Guns Don't Argue* purported to be a documentary about Ma Barker and other prominent underworld figures of the 1930s. (This absurd claim to authenticity is unintentionally opened to question by the film's tagline: ". . . and dead men tell no tales.") The story opens with an FBI agent's voice-over dedication "to the men who overcame a period of gangster violence unmatched in criminal history." While the camera pans a quaint 1950s-style neighborhood, an off-screen voice intones how in 1934 "your town, my town, *any* town in the USA" was in peril as criminals freely roamed the countryside. The film culminates with a fictional heist involving a who's-who list of 1930s baddies: John Dillinger, Homer Van Meter, Baby Face Nelson, and the Barker-Karpis Gang. This final heist is contrived and directed by a Ma Barker closely matched to the Ma whom Hoover described in *American Magazine.* Actress Jean Harvey plays Ma as the violent puppeteer behind her "spawn of hell."

Ma and two of her grown sons first appear assembled around the kitchen table. Son Doc Barker lifts a machine gun from the table and brandishes it admiringly before his brother, Fred. "What a saxophone!" he whistles. The camera pulls right to reveal Ma, who jerks the gun from Doc's hands: "Make way for a music lover!" Physically, the 1957 "Ma" who snatches the symbolic phallus from her sons presents a stark contrast to the small and frail Blanche Yurka who played Ma in 1940. *Guns'* Jean Harvey is a massive, wide-shouldered, broad-hipped woman who appears even larger with the help of black, thick-soled orthopedic shoes. Her costume is consistent throughout the film; she wears plain housedresses and aprons, with her hair pulled severely off her face into a gray-white bun. After seizing the gun, Ma appears in close-up against a vacant backdrop. She shoots wildly and scowls into the camera as the voice of the FBI agent-narrator intones: "Crime breeds crime. And one gang of outlaws was linked to another. In the Middle West there was a church-going woman with four sons. To make certain her fierce pride in them would be justified, she taught them all she knew." Emphasized here are Ma's religious background and convictions and the contaminated nature of what Ma had passed on to her progeny, by way of knowledge or genetics.

"As a planner and caser of jobs, Ma Barker had no equal," says the narrator. Several scenes depict Ma as a criminal genius for whom all other outlaws aspired to work. In one especially improbable moment, Dillinger and Baby Face Nelson watch intently as Ma gives them orders on how to rob a bank she has cased. She demonstrates the particulars of the plan with a three-dimensional map, complete with toy cars. The success of the bank job depends upon Alvin Karpis successfully delivering a baby carriage filled with guns. The carriage, apt trademark for a matriarchal gang, could be read as symbolizing the concealed menace of maternal caretaking and influence. It may also have been a deliberate nose thumbing at Karpis, who, as the only one of the film's real-life gangsters still alive and still imprisoned, had vowed to kill and discredit Hoover.[59]

Fred, Doc, and Lloyd Barker come across as puerile and weak-willed. Ma must coerce them, with shouting and blows, to enact the schemes she designs. When Ma declares that their next job will be a kidnapping, the "boys"—in spite of their advanced ages the "Barker boys" never became men—worry about committing a federal crime and the possibility of being pursued by "those G-men who can carry guns!" Ma scoffs at their fear: "The FBI . . . college boys! Get one of 'em in front of a machine gun, his hide's no tougher than the local laws." In this and later Ma Barker films, the agents whom Ma disdains stand for the paternal authority she has usurped. Ma's power lies in the sentimentality evoked by her older mother status, against which the G-men heroes must remain constantly on guard. The film concludes with an exchange between the narrator and another FBI agent, who confesses he is apprehensive about capturing Ma. The second agent sadly strokes his hat, noting: "'Ma,' that's what I call my mother." "Yeah, well, don't get sentimental about this one—it could kill ya," retorts the agent-narrator.

In fact, the men in Ma's life prefer death to the possibility of tangling with her. Eldest son Herman kills himself to avoid arrest because his mother taught him that the "worst sin in the world is to get caught." Ma's real-life boyfriend becomes, in the film, her perpetually drunk second husband, Arthur, who consents to his own murder to escape her unpleasantness. Only gang member Alvin Karpis displays any hint of rebellion. At one point, Ma smashes Karpis's bottle of beer against a wall with the stern order, "In my outfit, no liquor and no dames!" Karpis starts from his chair, fists clenched, but the conventions of sex will not permit him to strike the elderly woman who is also his boss. Teeth gritted in frustration, he resumes his seat. But the "conventions of sex" have actually been muddied and *that*, the film intimates, is Ma's primary crime. When Ma declares her outfit free of alcohol and "dames," she may be renouncing (for reasons of religion and self-discipline) two things her male compatriots are supposed to enjoy. But the no-dames rule also marks Ma out as not fully female and thus as a gender-confounding member of what Wylie dubbed momism's "thundering third sex."[60]

As really did happen, Ma and Fred are ultimately cornered in their Florida cottage hideout. But *Guns Don't Argue* presents one significant inaccuracy: two agents stage the ambush alone. Sensing the lawmen's presence, Ma orders her son to start shooting, but Fred protests, saying he would rather surrender and live. Ma becomes enraged: "You gutless little punk! Start shootin' or I'll slaughter you!" Even after Fred is hit by a bullet, she admonishes him to get back on his feet and keep firing. Only when Fred dies does Ma temporarily give up the fight, dabbing her eyes with her apron. Solemn music sounds as the narrator's voice chronicles the change: "Ma Barker, for a moment, softened. She became like a normal mother. Tenderness—a real sorrow—showed through the callus of viciousness."

Lest viewers feel any pity for Ma, her mourning lasts no more than a few seconds. In a flash, she is back on her feet, shooting determinedly from the cottage's front window. The audience watches her from a vantage point within the house, as though they, too, were members of her gang. With the FBI men off-screen and silent, Ma has the last word in the fight: "Those dirty butchers! Butchers! Dirty butchers!" She keeps shooting even when, presumably hit many times, she begins sinking slowly to her knees. A small painting of an American Indian on the rear wall—a reference to the belief that Ma possessed a "touch of Indian blood"—becomes the camera's final focus as Ma slips out of view.

Mother to Monster

Only three years elapsed between the theatrical release of *Guns Don't Argue* and its near-remake, *Ma Barker's Killer Brood* (tagline: "No. 1 Female Gangster of All Time!"). The two films shared the same director and co-producer but left the script to F. Paul Hall, a little-known writer a *Los Angeles Times* review chastised for not having done more with "all the history" behind the nonfiction Ma Barker.[61] In fact, Hall drew his material from what were supposed to be the best "historical sources" available to him— the *American Magazine* article and the Ma Barker stories from Hoover's book, *Persons in Hiding.* Hall's script therefore imagines what the Barker boys might have been like when they were truly little boys, as well as speculating about the dynamic between Ma and the boys' father. Actress Lurene Tuttle's Ma Barker, though more emotive and physically vulnerable than Jean Harvey's creation, exhibits all the same traits of momism as her predecessor; she is domineering, selfish, and materially acquisitive. But *Killer Brood*'s Ma plays to other of Philip Wylie's famous complaints about moms, ratcheting up the character's parasitism, hypocrisy, and wiles. Tuttle's Ma also owes some of her dominance to the cloaks of religious piety and hysterical tears, which she slips on and off with slithering ease.

As *Guns Don't Argue* implied with its pseudo-documentary format, *Killer Brood*'s producers boldly declare that their story is true: "This story is true, documented from police records, newspaper files, and eyewitness reports. It is the sadistic career of Katherine Clark Barker, master of crime who taught her sons that the only crime was to 'get caught.' So cunning was this evil genius that in almost two decades of robbery, kidnapping, and murder, she herself was never once arrested. Ma Barker, mother to the underworld and Public Enemy."

The *Los Angeles Times* entertainment reporter could not resist a joke about how thoroughly "Mother Barker . . . the FBI's all-time pin-up girl," would appall child-rearing expert Dr. Benjamin Spock. "To think she isn't a fiction. Ugh!"[62] The *Los Angeles Mirror-News* echoed this sense of revulsion: "Miss Tuttle [as Ma] presents a strong case against maternity."[63] By 1960, the Ma Barker tale's authenticity was accepted without question. The "evil genius" had also become the stuff of parody and camp (Ma as unappealing "pin-up girl" or as superlative parenting "Don't"). But Ma Barker still represented ongoing anxieties surrounding female sexuality and motherhood as dangerously destabilizing when not contained by a system of masculine preeminence and reproduction in service to the state. Any "case against maternity" was a case not only against the vision of a criminally violent Ma Barker, but against any mother who, like Ma, challenged a cold war–era domestic ideology that relied on economically and politically subordinate women to serve as guardians of public morality.[64]

Killer Brood opens with the Barker family assembled in a church pew, the perfect family. Her smiling husband on one side and three neatly dressed little sons on the other, Ma casually confiscates a slingshot from her youngest, with a knowing "boys-will-be-boys" glance. Both parents watch with pride as the eldest Barker child, Herman, plays the violin before the congregation. But when the Barkers return to their shabby home, all personalities except Mr. Barker's are instantly transformed. The boys throw off their church clothes with bitter complaints. Ma begins screaming at Herman for shaming the family at the service. Violins, she says, are only for the sissies she despises. When an ineffectual Mr. Barker attempts to stand up for his son, Ma grows angrier, grabs Herman's instrument, and breaks it over her knee. She orders her husband, who encouraged Herman's musical training, to take a look at their other, more productive sons. The three younger boys triumphantly step forward with the fistfuls of money their mother directed them to steal from the church's collection plate.

The audience is meant to sympathize with Herman, the only "good" son and, not coincidentally, the only one influenced by his father. When Herman is caught engaging in a petty theft that his mother ordered him to commit, Ma sobs and smothers him with kisses while in the presence of the sheriff. She also proudly asserts her son's regular church attendance. As soon as Ma gets Herman back to the house, however, she drops the loving mother act and strikes the boy fiercely. "Don't . . . get . . . caught!" There is a blow accompanying each word. The audience sees a downward, close-up shot of Herman's face from Ma's viewpoint; the little boy looks terrified and then resigned. As emblem of the Oedipal mother who prompts her son's self-destruction, Ma will continue to test and mercilessly taunt her oldest son until he is driven to suicide.

When Mr. Barker suggests that he will begin whipping his sons for their misdeeds and reluctantly unfastens his belt, Ma swings at him with a flyswatter—a clear reference to his diminished status in the household.

Having established her dominance over her husband, Ma voices her dissat-isfaction for all forms of ineffectual paternal influence—both in the nuclear family and in the church. When a fearful Mr. Barker warns Ma that God will strike her down for corrupting their sons, Ma mocks her husband's faith and argues that their children's delinquency owes to their father's fail-ure as a male provider. Citing her own humiliating childhood poverty as justification for her boys' crimes, Ma ridicules her husband's reliance on Bible scriptures as a signature of the assenting poor: "Too much Bible and too little beef. Too many psalms and too little sowbelly. We don't need your chicken feed and we don't need *you*. So why don't you beat it?" The guilt-ridden Barker patriarch agrees to move out and will not consent to Herman's frantic pleas that he go along. Much later in the film, the Barkers are reunited at Herman's funeral. Mr. Barker tentatively approaches Ma, saying, "Katie, this didn't have to happen." She wails in response: "I know. If only you'd been a better father!" Mr. Barker's face contorts and he slips out of the frame for the final time.

Ma arranges for another funeral in dispatching her second husband, Ar-thur, whose lush ways have blown the gang's cover. She does not have her sons kill him, as happened in *Guns Don't Argue*, but instead forces Arthur to play Russian roulette. Laughs Ma, "I'm just about to divorce you—the quick way!" Her sons are delighted: "Ma, you are the slickest!" Ma's slick-ness in this film again extends to her role as the master planner and caser of bank robberies. But, in a departure from any written record, *Killer Brood* imagines Ma as also participating in her sons' various holdups and kid-nappings. Ma's presence adds an extra note of sadism to the Barker-Karpis Gang's crimes, as in the moment when an enraged Ma crushes a guard be-tween her automobile and his armored truck and then twice runs over him to ensure that he is dead.

In one final horrific crime, Ma kills the doctor who botched Alvin Kar-pis's and Fred's plastic surgery. Her method of death is as cruel as possible. The doctor is trussed with ropes in the backseat of an automobile, doused with gasoline, and set aflame. Delirious with fear, the doctor pleads with his anonymous killer, represented only by a pair of male hands. When the doctor begins to burn, he reveals the name of she who ordered the killing: "It was Ma Barker," he squeals. "Ma Barker!" The flaming car hurtles off a cliff. The producers also utilized this scene under the movie's opening credits, but edited differently so as to imply that the off-screen assassin is, in fact, Ma.

The final Florida cottage scene in *Ma Barker's Killer Brood* resembles that in *Guns Don't Argue* but has far more dialogue and an extra scene in which the hubris of a pair of local police officers ("I'm gonna get the Barkers!") leads to their swift extermination. Ma also attempts to snare two FBI agents by making it appear that Fred is holding her hostage. The agents are skeptical, however, especially when Ma, as purported victim, whips out a rifle from beneath her apron. A shootout ensues, and Fred repeatedly tries to surrender. Ma's reaction, by this time, is predictable: "You gutless punk, you're as yellow as your old man! Stop shakin' and start shootin.' Start shootin' or I'll drill ya myself. I'd rather see one of my sons dead than a coward!"

When Fred dies, Ma has no moment of tender sorrow as she did in *Guns Don't Argue*. She weeps over his bloodstained form, but her reaction is still one of rage at the barriers of class and at the lawmen she regards as having unjustly murdered her offspring. She rips madly through the cottage's screen door, blindly firing her weapon and screeching: "They was always against us. Don't you see we had to fight? I'll kill you, ya butchers!"

Symbolically, at least, the discarded Barker father reclaims his authority and has the last word. At film's end, Ma's narrative voice-overs are replaced by those of a stern-voiced male reciting scripture in the style of Mr. Barker. "For a good tree bringeth not forth corrupt fruit. Neither does the corrupt tree bringeth forth good fruit." Referring to the Barkers and other underworld characters, the voice concludes: "None left his mark. Each left his stain." But, as with all other Ma Barker movies, Ma leaves no literal stain at all. Unlike Fred, Ma never bleeds, perhaps because that image might lend truth to her characterization of the G-men as "butchers." Filled with bullets, Ma merely sinks to her knees and then flops dramatically into a swamp. The FBI agents stand with expressions of distaste over the dead body:

> *First agent*: "If you didn't know the old witch, you'd think she was somebody's sweet old grandmother."
> *Second agent*: "Yeah—like the wolf in Red Riding Hood!"

Ma's memory might have ended there but for the success of another outlaw picture. In 1968, a studio famous for churning out youth-oriented horror flicks, American International Pictures, commissioned a Ma Barker script that might cash in on the success of Arthur Penn's 1967 *Bonnie and Clyde*. Postponed in the wake of the Robert Kennedy assassination, the studio's Ma movie was finally produced under the direction of Roger Corman in August 1969, just as the Manson family murders hit the headlines. Suddenly, *Bloody Mama*'s tagline, "The family that slays together stays together," seemed less a parody of the real slogan about family prayer and more a tasteless exploitation of current events.

American International Pictures had long specialized in monster and exploitation pictures, and *Bloody Mama* delivers both. Shelly Winters's Ma Barker, who speaks approvingly of lynching and sports an oversized cross around her neck, is a caricature of southern Ozark prejudice and warped religiosity. The 1970 release features the usual host of Ma Barker traits, but magnified to the level of outrageous perversion. For example, Ma's love for her unsavory sons goes beyond possessiveness. The Barker sons are presented as infantilized and sexually confused by the hyperbolized Oedipal love behind Ma's habit of alternately bathing or bedding them. In an early scene establishing Ma's contradictory relationship with her offspring, she chastises the boys for cursing, lies to protect them from rape charges, and then chastises them again—for raping a woman below their social class. She does all this while washing the "boys" (all grown men) in a wooden tub.

Ma's strange devotion to her children is explained by the near-silent opening sequence, in which teenaged Kate Barker is accosted in a forest by her father and two brothers. After the implied incestuous rape, a tearful Kate fumes: "Gonna have me some boys and it wasn't any one of 'em who wouldn't kill for me and didn't kill for me or me for them. That's what you call family. Mama's boys!" With this line, the film draws on a classic Freudian interpretation of a victimized and frustrated woman as having given birth to sons to make up for her own "lack." However, Ma Barker ends up more often killing for her sons than they for her. And she takes particular satisfaction in torturing other women. For instance, to effect her sons' escape from a bank holdup, Ma forces four "fat ladies" of her own age to cling to the outside of the speeding getaway car. Citing the need to get rid of dead weight, Ma then pushes the largest and most frightened of the old women off into the road, where she is subsequently struck by a police car.

When perpetually high Barker son Lloyd (Robert De Niro) reveals the gang's identity to a young female vacationer, Ma insists that this security risk be eliminated and drowns her in a bathtub. The murder is eerily shot from an impossible viewpoint beneath the tub; the camera looks up at the panicked young woman's face, held underwater by Ma, whose own face is bathed in unnatural light. Ma's sons are also visible, standing around the tub in passive attendance of what their mother seems to be experiencing as a moment of religious rapture. Unlike previous versions of Ma, who consciously used piety as a disguise, *Bloody Mama*'s Ma is a true believer and master of twisting biblical teachings to her own ends. Whereas other cinematic Ma Barkers had moments of misgivings about their criminal activities, Shelley Winters's Ma never falters in her conviction of her own righteousness and state of persecution.

The Barker son's prostitute companion, Mona, confronts Ma after the drowning, backing down only when Ma threatens to drown her also. "There's nothin' you won't do, is there, Ma?" says Mona. Ma responds philosophically: "It's supposed to be a free country, Mona. But unless you're rich, it ain't free and you know that. So I aim to be freer than the rest of the people." To cheer her family after the killing, Ma plays the piano, singing the pro-peace anthem "I Didn't Raise My Boy to Be a Soldier," and insisting that the others join in.

Condemned as a "vile exercise" and "Mommie and Clyde," *Bloody Mama* yet earned the praise of a few critics who lauded it as "more honest than *Bonnie and Clyde*" for refusing to mythologize its subjects.[65] One such defender, writing in 1980, quoted Hoover's *American Magazine* article as proof that *Bloody Mama* got it right.[66] But *Bloody Mama* dramatically departs from the Hoover-endorsed Ma, in that the G-man had become irrelevant, a stale symbol of antiyouth authority on par with Ma's out-of-touch parent. In previous films, the Barker Gang relied on its innocuous image as a multi-generational family. *Bloody Mama* subverts this logic, implying that, to the contrary, the family is an insidious social structure. Although the Barker sons do exhibit an intense loyalty to their mother, they also chafe under her control, and this tension seems manifest in the sons' various foibles: alcoholism in Arthur ("Doc"), drug addiction for Lloyd, and psychopathic urges in Herman. Pegged as the homosexual lover of his former cellmate, Kevin Dirkman (Bruce Dern, playing a character clearly meant to be Alvin Karpis), Fred is furious when his mother insists on sampling Kevin's affections. Unable to decide if it will embrace or condemn the younger characters' countercultural impulses, the film ultimately does both, urging audiences to despise Ma's children for their excesses, but to despise even more Ma the "square."

Unlike previous Ma Barker films, in which the G-men step in as paternal disciplinarians who set things to rights, *Bloody Mama*'s FBI is a nondescript, almost incidental force in the film, appearing only minutes before its conclusion. By the time agents move against the Barkers, the family has already started to disintegrate from within, thanks to the interventions of another surrogate father figure, the millionaire and Barker kidnapping victim, Samuel Pendleberry. Pendleberry disturbs the sons with blue eyes that resemble their real father's; he also indirectly chides Herman for being cowed by his mother/boss: "It's a hell of a thing to be without power, sonny boy." Herman is less infuriated than he is deeply moved by this observation and by Pendleberry's promise that, "if I were your father, I'd take each one of you over my knee and give you the whaling of your lives."

After collecting Pendleberry's ransom, Ma spitefully insists that they kill him anyway because he rebuffed her amorous advances and rebuked her for swearing. Ma's reign as gang leader officially ends when the boys take Pendleberry into the woods and fire off their guns but set the prisoner free. Herman then officially wrests control of the gang by knocking Ma to the ground when she tries to give him an order. "You're an old lady, Mama. You just can't go beatin' up on grown men like they was little babies. It just ain't ladylike." Sprawled in an unflattering pose on the floor, Ma reacts with a bewildered senility that will remain with her until the movie's end: "Herman? That's not you, Herman?" Herman takes his girlfriend's hand and leads her from the room, reasserting a "natural" order of male-led, heterosexual relations.[67]

In a surreal re-creation of the final Florida shootout with the FBI, Ma is trapped in the cottage with all her surviving sons and Kevin, the Karpis figure. Kevin remains but tries to bargain with the G-men. "I'm not a Barker!" he screams. "You bet your sweet ass you ain't," Ma says coldly and guns him down. One by one, the remaining Barker brothers fall, until only Herman and Ma are left. In a twisted and delayed version of Herman Barker's real-life suicide, Herman very deliberately kills himself in front of his mother. A crowd of picnicking families gather outside the besieged cottage and clap as Ma breaks a second-story window, props her submachine gun on a needle-pointed Bible verse pillow, and begins firing with a vengeance upon the agents. The film freezes at the moment she is shot; Ma is never shown dying and, despite the title, never bleeds. *Bloody Mama* ends with a shot of a three-cent postage stamp depicting *Whistler's Mother*. The stamp logo bears sardonic witness to the film's message: "In Memory of the Mothers of America."

In the first twenty-five years after her death, the cinematic Ma Barker went from corrupt grandmother, to unnatural amazon, to wily, class-conscious coquette. In these earliest films, Ma never stood as protagonist, but neither was she a clear-cut villain. She was, instead, a screen upon whom the deepest anxieties of a particular age could be projected. Ma therefore stood for mothers deemed responsible for their complicity in an increasingly consumer-oriented world, for their encouragement of the "male weakness" accompanying shifts in sexual roles, and for raising children not to embrace—or to embrace too fervently—a capitalist, democratic system.

Regardless of the time or style in which Ma was imagined, almost all films about the Barkers underscored the necessity of a heroic FBI. Each dramatization may have offered, for its audience's pleasure, the spectacle of the Barkers' grotesque behavior. But each also rearticulated the need for a state power that could defuse threats to a father-centered, heteronormative family unit by destroying inherently violent aberrations in that unit. In this way, the Ma Barker films perfectly mirrored a half century of Bureau philosophy under the direction of J. Edgar Hoover. That formula broke down by 1970, however, by which time both Ma Barker and Hoover's G-men were repositioned in popular culture as menacing, out-of-touch zealots.

3

The Perfectly Ambiguous
Bonnie Parker

Alvin Karpis died in 1979 of an overdose of sleeping pills. He who had vied with J. Edgar Hoover for the right to tell Ma Barker's story managed to outlive his nemesis by seven years. During Karpis's twenty-five years as a prisoner at Alcatraz, he became a rare surviving icon of the United States' gangster age. By chance, he also gave guitar lessons to fellow inmate Charles Manson, who became a criminal icon in his own right.[1] Karpis was paroled in 1969, one year after American International Pictures (AIP) hurriedly shot *Bloody Mama* in response to Warner Brothers' breakout hit *Bonnie and Clyde*. By the time *Bloody Mama* finally reached theaters in 1970, some Americans regarded it as they had the Berkeley-born Manson Family: as a chilling indictment of the late 1960s counterculture.

In fact, *Bonnie and Clyde* and *Bloody Mama* reflected different sides of a widening political chasm in the United States. The first film is often remembered as a forerunner of the countercultural explosions of 1968–1970 and an outlet for impatient and disillusioned youths in an increasingly violence-soaked culture. The second film mocked the hypocrisies of the country's elders while presenting the boomer generation as infantilized, drug addled, sexually deviant, and morally dissolute. Ma's victims—and at times Ma herself—stood for a backlash against the counterculture, embodied in those Richard Nixon dubbed the "forgotten Americans" in his second campaign for president.

Like their resurrected principals, neither *Bonnie and Clyde* nor *Bloody Mama* had much love for institutionalized authority, which was ironic since neither of the two films would have existed without the FBI's war on crime. J. Edgar Hoover's aggressive public relations blitz on behalf of the Bureau had done more than invent the G-man. It also had ensured a steady parade of public enemies—Bonnie and Ma among them—who had helped sell the concept of police power as a social asset. This chapter uses the recurrence of the cinematic "Bonnie Parker" (or, rather, the mishmash of 1930s-era women and anxieties that created "Bonnie") to demonstrate how she affected the self-consciously *political* women outlaws of the early 1970s. It tracks Bonnie's pop-culture refracted influence on a new generation of radical feminist lawbreakers by examining the FBI's flagging status in the latter decades of the twentieth century; the adaptability and durability of the Bonnie and Clyde formula amid stark shifts in the mass entertainment industry; and a 1968 B-movie knockoff that provides fresh insights into Arthur Penn's much-revered, much-dissected *Bonnie and Clyde*. Together, these analyses begin to explain why the poster girls of the FBI's Depression-era professionalization efforts found their echo in the very different women the Bureau was pursuing forty years later. The chapter also underscores the reliance of the outlaw phenomenon on the mutability of its characters and on the talkback that may begin as the stuff of fantasy yet has real and consequential effects.

Culture Wars and the Domesticated G-Man

When Nixon took office in 1968, Hoover was seventy-three years old. He had been at the FBI's helm for forty-four years and had served eight different presidents. His leadership had shaped the twentieth-century Bureau. It also had helped define the United States by giving form to its enemies and then using those enemies to enforce the boundaries of good citizenship. In the decades that Alvin Karpis was behind bars, Hoover's Bureau had traded gangsters for other threats like fascism and communism—two "evangelistic doctrines" that prompted the FBI to conduct surveillance on American citizens. By the time Karpis left prison in 1969, the infiltration programs begun as a method for rooting out communism's "fellow travelers" had expanded to contain other members of the country's political left, notably civil rights activists, Black Power groups, and antiwar demonstrators.[2]

During the Depression and afterward, Hoover had convinced a large constituency to regard the Bureau and its agents as exemplars of morality and efficiency. The FBI's most faithful supporters were the children of the 1930s, many of whom were, as adults, still receptive to Hoover's "great sell." As the journalist Robert Sherrill explained it, the "Junior G-men" grew up to fight in World War II, whereupon the Bureau supplied a regular stream of magazine articles and movies to convince them that "J. Edgar Hoover and his clean-cut men were wise to every move the saboteur rats were trying to make." Then came the 1950s, when "some of us let down our guard; we were tired of the international tension . . . we were willing to tolerate the dangerous radicals in our midst, excusing their perfidious ideologies in the name of freedom of speech. Not J. Edgar Hoover. Not the FBI. They knew it was no time to relax. They knew that was what the international conspirators wanted us to do. Through the untiring vigilance of Hoover and his men, Americans made it safely into the 1960s."[3] Addressing the 1970s youths who marveled at their parents' regard for Hoover "as the same wonderful man who protected us from gangsters and un-American gremlins," Sherrill reminded them that three decades of the Bureau's "Perfect Image" was "well-nigh impossible to erase from the mind."[4]

The FBI had assiduously cultivated that image during the cold war, collaborating with Hollywood on the family-centered plot of *The FBI Story* (1959) and on such semi-documentary/thrillers as *The House on 92nd Street* (1945), *Walk a Crooked Mile* (1948), and *I Was a Communist for the FBI* (1951). Even more than the *Persons in Hiding* films, these were FBI productions, because everything—from the script to the style of acting—had to be approved by FBI agents assigned to each film. In 1954, Hoover successfully advocated for a federal law prohibiting the use of the FBI's name, or any of its files, without the express authorization of its director. Those protected files and cases ultimately became the basis of ABC's successful television series *The F.B.I.* (1965–1974), starring Efrem Zimbalist Jr. as a mild-mannered senior agent whose office was supposedly right next door to Director Hoover's.[5]

Zimbalist's Inspector Erskine reflected what Richard Gid Powers has described as Hoover's "domesticated agent" of the 1950s and 1960s. As suited a mainstream audience then more attuned to private than public interests, the G-men of *The F.B.I.* were stalwart advocates of family life and the status quo. In keeping with Hoover's intensifying campaign to promote moral reform as the best defense against crime and communism, scripts for *The F.B.I.* were almost completely free of violence and devoid of sexual innuendo.[6] This gentle approach won a loyal following for the program, which became a valuable recruiting tool for the Bureau.[7] But the popularity of *The F.B.I.* during its nine-year run could not completely obscure the rumblings of the imminent cultural divide.

However much more "domesticated" the G-man of popular culture might appear, not much in Hoover's formula had really changed from the early 1930s. The difference was that Hoover had achieved eminence and experience enough to exert tighter control over representations of the Bureau. His ideal agents were actually the same civic-minded do-gooders in the 1960s as they had been in the 1930s, although, in keeping with a family-minded entertainment industry at midcentury, they were more likely to have wives and children in tow. A perfect G-man like Inspector Erskine and *The FBI Story*'s Chip Hardesty reassured many in the public of their safety. Yet, without an irrefutable villain to serve as the G-man's opponent, he could become too blandly certain to function for long as entertainment. Like the morally perfected women of Hoover's books and articles, the saintly men of the fictional FBI had no margin for error. Any stain on the G-man would be his undoing. So it was that the real FBI ultimately found itself trapped by the success of its own image making, especially as certain of its self-promoting tales from the gangster era began to be used against it. Against a backdrop of Vietnam, ongoing civil rights struggles, and the incipient women's rights movement, stories about the public enemies of old began to move in new directions, particularly after some of the G-men's less savory tactics became known. Characters like Bonnie and Clyde were going through changes, both as symbols of a burgeoning youth culture and as intimations of the coming assault on the markers of "respectable" manhood and womanhood. For three decades, the story of the short-lived Texas duo had been recycled and reimagined in film, with each new iteration adjusting the female character to suit audiences' needs for an escapist fantasy and/or a cautionary tale. Each retelling persisted in punishing its outlaws, but not before it gave them a chance for the talkback that helped erode the authority of Hoover's FBI and that lent the Bonnie and Clyde genre its commercial appeal.

Outlaw Love and the Making of Bonnie and Clyde

Bonnie Parker and Clyde Barrow made their film debut on the morning that they died, on a stretch of highway near Gibsland, Louisiana. Just minutes after Frank Hamer and his posse shot the couple and their vehicle to pieces, posse member Ted Hinton shot the couple and their car *in pieces* with his 16-millimeter movie camera.[8] In nearby Arcadia, where the couple was autopsied, a local photographer shot Bonnie and Clyde again, taking flash pictures of their bloody, disfigured bodies and then selling the prints for five dollars to individuals and fifty dollars to members of the press.[9] Some of those on the scene began ripping away buttons and bits of cloth from the dead couple's clothing and used pocketknives to saw off pieces of Bonnie's blood-soaked hair. A few of the boldest souvenir seekers tried to amputate fingers and ears from her body and Clyde's.[10]

The meaning of those gruesome artifacts—and, by extension, of Bonnie and Clyde—depended on who regarded them and in what circumstances. Attentive as the couple had been to self-image, it would now fall to others to determine which of their photo-images would prevail: that of Bonnie and Clyde, daring, romantic outlaws, or that of Bonnie and Clyde, despised and mutilated bandits.

The bandit couple was cinematically "reincarnated" just three years later in Fritz Lang's tragic *You Only Live Once* (1937), the first feature-length film inspired by their story. Less sympathetic reenactments followed, including the FBI-sponsored *Persons in Hiding* (1939). Writing in 1980, film critic Carlos Clarens described the film, which was really a Kathryn Kelly–Bonnie Parker mash-up, as a "foreseeable Hoover[-driven] debunking" of Bonnie and Clyde's "disproportionate build-up in the Hearst papers." He theorized that *Persons in Hiding* offered a window onto "the way that America thought about Bonnie and Clyde in the thirties—as picturesque but unglamorous second-raters." Still, Clarens conceded, the little B-picture "could not quite suppress the romantic aspect of an outlaw couple meeting by the roadside or hiding out in shabby rented rooms."[11]

What explains the pull of the Bonnie and Clyde picture, or of any of the subsequent films identified, or *mis*identified, as such for the sake of their hetero-criminal romance? Movies about such "picturesque . . . second-raters" tend to evoke conflicted responses, just like Clarens's. That is because the ostensibly simple story line could be used to speculate on universal questions about love and loyalty, power dynamics in men's and women's relationships, and whether women might be morally superior to men, or vice versa. As Clarens alludes, audiences could also take vicarious pleasure in the doomed couple's "us-against-them" adventure. Inevitably, filmmakers and their audiences projected different meanings onto the transgressions of the woman lawbreaker according to the political context in which a film was made and shown.

In whatever genre or era it appeared, the spectacle of a Bonnie and

Clyde story typically hinged on the tragedy and contradictions of the Bonnie character's "unfeminine" attractions to guns, money, and ready sex. In 1949, the King Brothers released the noirish *Gun Crazy* (1949), about a menacingly unstable beauty who shares with her mate a deadly lust for firearms. Its "Annie Laurie Starr" is equal parts Belle Starr, Kathryn Kelly, and Bonnie Parker, a mythical amalgam that makes her a foe to the domestic life that *Gun Crazy* acknowledges as both an ideal and a trap. Almost a decade later, *The Bonnie Parker Story* (1958) wrung part of its pulpy plot from the sentimental memoir written by Bonnie and Clyde's families after the couple's death. Convinced that Clyde Barrow (or "Guy Darrow," as the screenwriters cheekily renamed him) was a loser, the film mourns Bonnie Parker as a sassy, fallen heroine whose bombshell sexuality has thwarted her desires for a respectable life.

Once the revised Production Code of 1956 had lifted the ban on films about the lives of real-life criminals, moviemakers began finding ready plotlines in the 1930s public enemies, who suddenly seemed quaint compared to the specter of Nazis, communists, and spies. Of course, Depression-era baddies could also resonate with midcentury fears. *The Bonnie Parker Story* played as half of a teen-oriented double feature with Roger Corman's *Machine Gun Kelly*. Both movies portrayed their big-name gangsters as 1950s-era juvenile delinquents, a comparison J. Edgar Hoover himself had drawn. (Interestingly, the real-life Kathryn Kelly was acquitted and released from prison the same year that *Machine Gun Kelly* was released. Corman's film worked around that problem by giving Machine Gun a domineering girlfriend, "Flo Becker," the daughter of gang matriarch "Ma Becker.") When Hoover sniped at "opportunistic elements" in the film industry for corrupting young audiences in their "pursuit of profits above all else," Samuel Arkoff retorted that Hoover was out of touch, since the Motion Picture Association of America Code still guaranteed that gangster characters were never presented as heroes.[12] (Not that the target audience for Arkoff's American International Pictures had ever required traditional heroes. Commercially, AIP's *The Bonnie Parker Story* fared well in 1958 and was bringing in even better receipts a decade later, after the release of Penn's *Bonnie and Clyde*.)[13]

From the start of the 1950s, movie audiences were skewing younger than ever before. A Bonnie-and-Clyde romance therefore became a natural for the new realities of the film industry. Certainly, it worked well in the cheap and rapidly produced B-films, which became ubiquitous after the major Hollywood studios lost their near-exclusive movie distribution rights and movie house attendance dropped precipitously with the rise of television culture. By the middle 1950s, a significant segment of the struggling film business was catering to the United States' 4,000 new outdoor movie theaters, which served a mostly teenaged, car-infatuated audience less interested in the show than in the social scene made possible by the drive-in theater.[14] The staples of such venues were the exploitation pictures, a genre defined by *Variety* in 1956 as "low-budget films based on controversial and timely subjects that made newspaper headlines." As Thomas Doherty has shown, commercial filmmakers attracted their new, younger audience by doing things that TV still could not do, dramatizing subjects that were "outlandish, mildly controversial, and a little licentious."[15]

Variety further identified the new style of filmmaking as holding the greatest appeal to "uncontrolled" juveniles, which must have fueled the chicken-or-egg debate over whether popular entertainments influenced or merely reflected youth violence and criminal activity. In 1958, just before the release of *Machine Gun Kelly* or *The Bonnie Parker Story*, nineteen-year-old Charlie Starkweather and his fourteen-year-old girlfriend, Caril Fugate, killed eleven people in Nebraska and Wyoming. The young couple's mutually destructive romantic relationship and aspirations to celebrity (Charlie fancied himself another James Dean) became the focus of media reports. So, too, did the couple's brutality, since their victims included Caril's parents and her two-year-old sister. After they were captured alive, Charlie and Caril's alliance disintegrated, with each trying to pin blame on the other. Caril went to prison; Charlie was executed by the state of Nebraska. Like the crimes of George and Kathryn Kelly, the Starkweather-Fugate killing spree later inspired multiple films misremembered as Bonnie-and-Clyde pictures.

Starkweather and Fugate enhanced the potential appeal of Bonnie and Clyde, who could, through the haze of years, appear kinder and gentler by comparison. The Barrow Gang's murders may have been just as senseless, but never had they turned against family or children or each other. The 1930s bandits' own deaths also made possible a film like *The Bonnie Parker Story*, which could revel in the bad behavior of its title character and then appease the censors by killing her off by film's end. In *Gun Crazy*, the Bonnie character actually dies at the hands of her Clyde, who recognizes that her killer instinct has driven her mad. In *The Bonnie Parker Story*, she expires in a police ambush, whispering the name of the respectable man who might have been her redemption.

Paradoxically, it was the fact of the original Bonnie and Clyde's violent deaths that made it possible to remember them as so vital. However people might have clucked at the circa 1933 photograph of a pistol-packing, cigar-smoking Bonnie, that indelible image became all the more potent after she died, when it was released into the "afterlife of the imagination."[16] It helped to seal Bonnie Parker's place in film history and as part of a new image-driven prescription for women's outlawry. Like the male outlaw, the woman outlaw in the model of Bonnie Parker had to appear to offer more style than threat. Yet, compared to her male counterpart, she was at once more and less open to interpretation. Deciphering the cinematic Bonnie in a moment of social upheaval—and deploying her as a political symbol to justify the authority of law enforcement—would become the centerpiece of a pitched battle over Bonnie and Clyde's legacy in the late 1960s.

Bonnie and Clyde's *Other Side*

Arthur Penn's *Bonnie and Clyde* (1967) deserves the most credit for having launched its eponymous bandits as tragic, countercultural heroes. Its stars, Faye Dunaway and Warren Beatty, personified the couple as glamorous and charismatic. Indeed, Dunaway's and Beatty's young faces became synonymous with the title characters and, arguably, remain the prevailing images associated with the historical Bonnie and Clyde. Never mind that Penn's film famously concludes with a graphic, slow-motion reenactment of the couple's death in a barrage of gunfire. Contemporary audiences left theaters in a solemn hush, but their silence was born of horror rather than of a sense of justice done.[17] That is because the preceding 110 minutes of screen time privilege Bonnie and Clyde's vantage point, encouraging empathy for the pair's frustration and their self-importance. Yes, the 1967 Bonnie and Clyde commit reckless acts of violence, but they *look so good* doing it. Against the film's stagy Depression-era backdrop, the couple becomes the embodiment of youth, romance, and yearning. By contrast, their victims barely register, save as faded cardboard cutouts lacking names or narrative. The camera affirms Bonnie and Clyde as the only living things on an otherwise inert and colorless landscape.

Given the importance of photography to Bonnie and Clyde's celebrity, it is fitting that Penn's movie begins with a reference to a camera. The film's opening credits are interspersed with sepia-toned still photographs from the 1930s. Over the slow rise of a scratchy phonograph recording, the photos "click" as they appear against a black background, suggesting a historical slide show. Photo images of actors Beatty and Dunaway, identified as Clyde Barrow and Bonnie Parker, are included with the authentic period photographs, lending verisimilitude to the story and characterizations that will follow. Of course, screenwriters Robert Benton and David Newman took generous liberties with the biographies of their subjects, downplaying certain details (the nine law enforcers slaughtered by the Barrow Gang; Bonnie's marriage to another man) that would have detracted from their tale of Bonnie and Clyde as doomed lovers, destroyed at the hands of a resentful Establishment generation.[18]

Initial critical disgust for *Bonnie and Clyde* rapidly gave way to critical acclaim, and no less a mainstream outlet than *Time* magazine embraced the film as herald of the anti-authoritarian "New Cinema."[19] Audiences from the 1960s onward would read the film as commenting on everything from civil rights to the war in Vietnam. Arthur Penn suggested that *Bonnie and Clyde* was a social justice picture, with special appeal to oppressed groups who, like the Depression-era bandits, had nothing left to lose.[20] But the film did not need a clear politics to revive Bonnie and Clyde as folk heroes, or to spark an international appetite for 1930s-style fedoras and double-breasted suits. The sudden ubiquity of young people in Bonnie berets and other gangster-inspired fashions represented another set of artifacts snatched from the bodies of dead outlaws, albeit on a new, mass-culture scale. Thanks to Penn's film, Bonnie and Clyde had become symbols for a youth culture—and brewing counterculture—suspicious of those in power. Screenwriters Benton and Newman denied that politics had motivated the script, but observed that their film had captured the modern zeitgeist: "If Bonnie and Clyde were here today, they would be hip. Their values have become assimilated in much of our culture—not robbing banks and killing people, of course, but their style, their sexuality, their bravado, their delicacy, their cultivated arrogance, their narcissistic insecurity, their curious ambition have relevance to the way we live now."[21]

If *Bonnie and Clyde* succeeded because of its relevance in 1967, it also drew the ire of those who were old enough to have known the real-life Bonnie and Clyde or who had known Bonnie and Clyde's victims. To revel in the outlaws' style without acknowledgment of their crimes seemed to many a worrisome index of the culture's growing immorality. Among those most unhappy with Penn's film was the family of the late Frank Hamer, whom the film employed as its title characters' homely, villainous foil.

Enter Larry Buchanan, the maverick director of low- and no-budget B-movies who grew up in Dallas, just like Bonnie and Clyde. A self-described "guerrilla filmmaker" who often did contract work for the self-consciously outrageous AIP, Buchanan had been planning a remake of *The Bonnie*

Parker Story when Arthur Penn hired him to scout Texas locations for *Bonnie and Clyde*.[22] Buchanan did so and supplied Penn with extras from his stock acting company.[23] He also smelled opportunity and quickly converted his Bonnie Parker project into *The Other Side of Bonnie and Clyde* (1968), a "personal, out-of-pocket send-up of Arthur Penn's classic."[24] Buchanan's sixty-minute documentary examines the runaway success of *Bonnie and Clyde* as a social problem, incorporating stories and photographs of the real-life Bonnie and Clyde as a corrective to Penn's film. *The Other Side* also won the cooperation of the estate of Frank Hamer, whose biographer, widow, and son were eager to counteract the portrayal of Hamer as an opportunistic bounty hunter.

Like Penn's *Bonnie and Clyde*, Buchanan's *The Other Side of Bonnie and Clyde* also opens with a simulated slide show, albeit one that takes the tone of a police briefing. Mug shots from the wanted poster of the real-life Clyde Barrow, young and jug-eared, are "projected," slide-show style, with a loud click onto the screen. In voice-over, the avuncular folksinger and native Texan Burl Ives intones: "Wanted for murder in three states. Clyde 'Champion' Barrow. Age 25. 5 feet, 7 inches. 130 pounds. Hair: dark brown and wavy. Eyes: hazel. Light complexion."

The next image is a close-up of the real Bonnie Parker. The "slides" click twice more to reveal the fuller photograph, in which Bonnie playfully points a rifle at Clyde. Again, the voice-over: "Bonnie Parker, companion of Clyde Barrow. 4 feet, 10 inches. 85 pounds light. Hair: dyed red. This pair is dangerous and their car is known to be an arsenal on wheels. She reads romance and movie magazines and writes poetry. He fancies himself a musician, plays the saxophone."

Larry Buchanan loved the detail of Clyde's saxophone, an incongruous item that turned up in the "arsenal on wheels" that became Bonnie and Clyde's death car.[25] A former actor and contract player for Twentieth Century Fox, Buchanan gravitated to all such quirks and clues of character, especially those that improved the theatricality of his subjects.[26] The youngest son of a widowed Texas constable, the charismatic Buchanan had once considered the ministry before he discovered the movies. The strict Baptist orphanage in which he grew up made use of his showman's instincts and put him to work as their traveling ambassador, touring rural churches to rile up the faithful and drum up donations. Buchanan's script for *The Other Side* reflects Buchanan at his entrepreneurial best, shrewdly framing his film in opposition to Penn's *Bonnie and Clyde* and using that film's own rhetoric against itself.

The mug shots that open Buchanan's *The Other Side* shortly give way to a color image of a bank foreclosure sign: "Property of Midlothian Citizens Bank. Trespassers Will Be Prosecuted." Penn's *Bonnie and Clyde* featured an identical sign, and in that film it was both an impetus and symbol of Bonnie and Clyde's empathy for the dispossessed. Upon meeting a homeless farmer and his family who have lost their farm to the Midlothian Bank, Beatty's Clyde shoots the bank's sign and declares his new profession: "We rob banks." *The Other Side* relies on audiences' memory of this scene. Following a tight shot of bullets splintering the Midlothian sign, the film cuts to a 1930s Ford V-8 speeding down a rural highway. The sleek, golden hair of the vehicle's female occupant suggests that this is the car of Bonnie and Clyde (or at least of actors Dunaway and Beatty), and it is they who abruptly halt the car to shoot at a "Chism for Sheriff" sign on a telephone pole. Narrator Ives sighs: "When viewers in Tokyo, New York City, and London applaud and cheer at the death of law enforcement officers on the screen, is it just more fuel for the violence that grips our cities?" The film then flashes a preview of a sequence that will appear again later in *The Other Side*. Bonnie raises her rifle through the car window and shoots an unarmed police officer in the face. The officer slaps his hands to his injury, then slumps and falls in agonizing slow motion, bleeding from the eyes.

Ives conjures the "cult" of *Bonnie and Clyde* and its "instant and spontaneous global influence on young people" over a montage of 1960s models in gangster- and gun moll–inspired fashions. (One male model wields a machine-gun prop.) Next appears the elderly, bespectacled Mrs. Frank Hamer, widow of the Texas Ranger. She reads aloud a letter from a twelve-year-old girl who laments her peers' response to the 1930s outlaws: "My friends think the [Ranger] Captain was so cold to kill Bonnie and Clyde because they were so much in love," says the girl. "I tell you, if Captain Hamer were alive I would congratulate him on his actions, and since he is not, I must congratulate his wife instead."

Juxtaposing the frankly earnest (letter-reading widow) with the frankly evil (officer-slaying Bonnie), *The Other Side* plunges ahead with two predictable aims: to deglamorize the bandit lovers and to recuperate the figure of the law. Buchanan's *Other Side* editorializes with reversals—reversals recognizable to anyone familiar with *Bonnie and Clyde*. The Midlothian Bank sign appears just before Bonnie and Clyde shoot a symbolic lawman (the sheriff poster) and then slay a real one. As in the original film, the bandits' Ford bounces across the countryside to jaunty musical accompaniment. But it also seems forever to be driving past a graveyard.

Having schooled himself as a director through careful study of others' movies, Buchanan insisted that Arthur Penn had lifted his Barker brothers' reunion scene, shot for shot, from AIP's *Bonnie Parker Story*. As he wrote, "The fisticuff exchange is, *cut to cut*, an identical sequence! The similarity is remarkable." (Warren Beatty confirmed the theft.)[27] It is no accident that Buchanan filmed parts of *The Other Side* by turning Penn's sequences inside out, foregrounding the vantage point of the law or of Bonnie and Clyde's victims. For instance, *The Other Side* includes a reenactment of the 1933 standoff between the Barrow Gang and authorities in Platte City, Missouri. In Penn's film, the shootout scene privileged the experience of the gang, trapped and frightened in their motel. There is no such opportunity to identify with the nondescript officers who have them surrounded. By contrast, in *The Other Side*, Bonnie and Clyde are the ciphers, represented primarily by the gun barrels that smash the motel windows and poke, anonymously, through Venetian blinds. The camera creeps along the ground with a lawman as he tentatively approaches the building where the shooters have concealed themselves. The audience therefore feels the lawman's tension and vulnerability as he scrambles to avoid the outlaws' bullets.

In another sequence, Clyde harangues an elderly gas station owner in the middle of the night. The camera avoids Clyde's face, representing him only by a pair of legs as he steps out of his automobile, and by a pair of fists as he pounds the old man's door. A moment later, the gas station owner's frail wife steps out into the moonlight, more curious than concerned. The camera zooms in on the woman's lined face, as she placidly brushes her long, silver hair. "Give us some gas!" Clyde commands the station owner, off-camera. "And your money!" says the faceless "female with Clyde." (*The Other Side* hints that Clyde may have cheated on Bonnie.) The unnamed female, who appears only as a torso and skirt in the passenger seat, levels a gun at the station owner, and his surprise and fright register in tight close-up. She shoots, and as he pitches forward, the camera cuts to the anguished face of the silver-haired wife, who gasps and faints in horror. The outlaws' car roars off, and, as never happens in *Bonnie and Clyde*, the audience is left behind with the bloody aftermath of a violent encounter.

Buchanan also reversed and reframed *Bonnie and Clyde*'s storytelling by foregrounding the faces and recollections of people who had encountered the real-life Bonnie and Clyde. So it is that *The Other Side*'s audience meets Sophia (Stone) Cook, one of two people impulsively kidnapped by the Barrow Gang in April 1933 for having witnessed a car theft. According to lore, Bonnie chatted eagerly with the captives and was amused to learn that one of them, H. D. Darby, was a mortician. "You probably recognize us from seeing our pictures everywhere," Bonnie reportedly said. A frightened Darby and Cook were eventually released after hours of driving along country back roads at speeds exceeding ninety miles per hour. Once the captives disembarked, Bonnie may also have grandly tossed from the car window a five-dollar bill to help the pair make their way back home.[28]

The 1967 *Bonnie and Clyde* screenplay tweaked this anecdote to underscore the Barrow Gang's geniality and loneliness. So desperate are they for company, they treat their captives like party guests and soon have them laughing and at ease. Bonnie approvingly declares them in allegiance with the gang because they, too, are "just folks." She reminds them, "It's not like you was the laws or something." The disclosure of the mortician's profession is used to tragicomic effect when a shaken and superstitious Bonnie abruptly orders him from the car. The scene telegraphs her character as sympathetic—and keenly aware of the early death her love affair with Clyde has made inevitable.

The Villain Makes the Hero

Because Bonnie Parker died young, she remains frozen in time, forever twenty-three. Had she survived, she would have been in her late fifties in 1968. In *The Other Side*, Bonnie's onetime captive and contemporary, Sophia Cook, is middle-aged and matronly, a reminder of the "typical West Dallas" woman Bonnie might have become.[29] Buchanan uses Cook as a voice of reproach and replays several of her comments over footage of Bonnie and Clyde's death car. ("They wanted something for nothing and they knew that the officers stood for what was right.") Cook's recollection of the kidnapping recalls Penn's fragile and romanticized Bonnie and rewrites her as hard and unsentimental. According to Cook, when Mr. Darby revealed his profession, "Bonnie laughingly said, 'We know one of these days that we'll get it, but we'll have one last request and we'll request that you get to embalm our body.' She said, 'now won't you get a big kick out of that?' and she gave a '*ha ha ha*.'"

If Cook seems pleased to testify in Buchanan's movie, it may be because the 1967 *Bonnie and Clyde* had portrayed her character as such a silly thing.[30] *The Other Side* positions Cook as a sober moral authority, the home demonstration agent who taught Depression-era families about canning and self-sufficiency. Sewing as she talks to the camera, Cook muses, "To them [Bonnie and Clyde] a life didn't mean anything. They would just as soon kill as to talk to you. Honor comes first. If you are hungry, most people will help you as they did here. I was working for the public here and there were many people that were helped [and] they didn't rob banks and they didn't kill and do things of that kind."

While Cook worries for "the young people" who might take the wrong message from Penn's movie, she also exhibits some ambivalence toward the outlaws who made her briefly famous. Proudly relating how she and Mr. Darby were asked to identify Bonnie and Clyde's bodies in Louisiana, she says, "I don't know that Mr. Darby really helped with the embalming but *he was there*. He had his finger in the pie enough to know that he was there anyway." Leaving aside the distasteful image of an undertaker's "finger in the pie" of an autopsy, Cook's comment suggests that she regarded the figurative honoring of Bonnie's embalming request as having contributed to the outlaws' punishment. But Cook's emphasis also asserts that having had a connection to Bonnie and Clyde was itself an honor.

Larry Buchanan would not have disputed the special status of such a connection. Indeed, the success of his film depended on deflected glory—from Arthur Penn, from Bonnie and Clyde, and also from the legendary Texas Rangers. *The Other Side* parrots *Bonnie and Clyde*'s rollicking soundtrack. But the outlaws' jaunty theme is undercut by the "noble frontier hero" harmonica music accompanying the film's homage to Frank Hamer, the longtime Texas Ranger who patrolled the U.S.-Mexican border during the time of the Mexican Wars through World War I and Prohibition. *The Other Side* draws heavily from the 1968 biography *I'm Frank Hamer*, so named because of Hamer's ability to calm a volatile situation just by announcing his presence. As narrator Ives sums up, "If all the criminals in Texas in 1934 were asked to name the man they would most dread to have on their tail, they would all have named Captain Frank Hamer. There was not an outlaw of the period that did not fear and respect him."

In 1934, J. Edgar Hoover had pronounced Hamer "one of the greatest law officers in American history," a testimonial Hamer's biographer could still cite without much irony in 1968. *The Other Side* also boasts that Hamer was "known to have participated in 100 individual gunfights and to have killed 53 men defending himself in the line of duty. [He was] wounded 17 times and left for dead on four occasions." Hamer was, in short, "the best, most fearless, and most efficient peace officer Texas ever had."

Brawny, autonomous, and taciturn, Hamer might have gone down in history as a classic western lawman-hero had he not orchestrated the ambush of Bonnie and Clyde. The fact that Hamer had tracked the outlaws for 102 days, or that he had done so at the behest of the Texas governor who begged him out of retirement, meant little once Bonnie and Clyde were brought down not in Texas, but in Louisiana. Reviled by some as an opportunistic bounty hunter, Hamer's reputation took an even worse turn a decade after his death. In 1967, the actor Denver Pyle played Frank Hamer as an ugly and humorless snake of a man, with stained teeth and traditional villain's mustache. Pyle's Hamer spends the film in a state of simmering hatred for Bonnie and Clyde, especially after they take him prisoner, photograph him in their mocking embrace, and distribute the photo to the press. Although many movie viewers assumed otherwise, no such humiliating encounter ever happened between the real-life Hamer and the Barrow Gang. But the screenwriters' invention did reflect the very real public relations battle between 1930s bandits and law enforcement. It is Dunaway's Bonnie who dissuades the gang from killing Hamer, urging them instead to "take his picture!" She alone intuits what the gang's apparent mercy will recoup in talkback by humiliating Hamer in the press. Later, Pyle's reptilian Hamer schemes to recuperate his image by killing Bonnie and Clyde and then having himself photographed with the trophy of their dead bodies. He scowls and pledges to "have my picture taken with them once more."

Hamer makes good on his promise, but *Bonnie and Clyde* denies him his moment of triumph. The film ends in a moment of silent shock, just seconds after the outlaws' death. The camera peers through the automobile's shattered rear window and over Bonnie's bloodstained white dress. The final shot, before the screen goes black, is of Hamer in his bad guy's black shirt. Gun in hand, he stands before his posse, grimly surveying the carnage they have wrought. *Bonnie and Clyde* abounds with adult heavies. Frank Hamer is what Nixon and Hoover soon became—the quintessential enemies of a youthful counterculture. Like the sixtyish character Malcolm Moss, who clobbers his son, C.W., for getting a tattoo and then berates him for failing to achieve the same notoriety as Bonnie and Clyde, Hamer stands for the corrupt and out-of-touch father figure who makes the Barrow Gang look like innocents by comparison. In the 1967 film, young characters who play by the older generation's rules are dupes. Hamer uses the lure of propriety to con the blinded "preacher's daughter," Blanche Barrow, into giving up information. Hamer and Moss conspire to slaughter Bonnie and Clyde by setting a trap that exploits their kindness. The lovers go to their deaths completely unarmed, with no chance of firing a return shot.

By contrast, the living principals of Buchanan's *The Other Side*— Sophia Cook; Mrs. Frank Hamer; Frank Hamer Jr.; and John Jenkins, coauthor of the Hamer biography—lament the late sixties' prevailing distrust for authority. Jenkins sees a parallel between circa 1968 suspicions and a Depression-era disenchantment with law enforcers: "In our time, they call them the fuzz. In those days, they called them the laws." It is Jenkins who most strenuously asserts Frank Hamer as honorable hero by reminding viewers that 80 percent of Bonnie and Clyde's victims were law officers: "It wasn't disrespect for the law; it was an absolute psychotic hatred for the law that these two people had."

Jenkins's statement is bracketed by two reenactments, one of an Oklahoma shooting from April 1934 and one of the Easter Sunday murders of the two police officers at Grapevine. Although Bonnie was never conclusively attached to the latter crime, *The Other Side* dramatizes the eyewitness account that was later recanted.[31] Bonnie (represented only by a pair of women's shoes and the hem of her long dress) shoots one officer in the face and then leaves the car to shoot a second, fallen officer point-blank in the head. Her gloating, off-screen voice repeats the infamous line about making the officer's head bounce like a rubber ball.

In the next reenactment, a middle-aged constable and his deputy approach Bonnie and Clyde's automobile, which is stuck in the mud in the middle of a graveyard. "You folks seem to be needing some help," says the constable. The camera zooms in on Bonnie's angry face. Although her lips do not move, the audience hears her shout, "We don't need any help from the law!" "Go!" yells Clyde. He ducks, and up comes Bonnie's shotgun. She shoots and kills the deputy. Clyde fires a pistol at the constable, who writhes on the ground, clutching his bloodied shoulder. The camera's shot/countershot shows him making direct eye contact with Bonnie, whose gun is still raised.[32] On these events, the film's voice-over gives Hamer the final word: "She was, begging your pardon, a bit of a female dog." The sequence then cuts to the famous image of the cigar-smoking Bonnie Parker.

Where Penn's *Bonnie and Clyde* garnered sympathy for the bandits by privileging their motives and family ties, *The Other Side* moves to obscure those elements, foregrounding instead the most revolting versions of their crimes. All positive traits are ascribed exclusively to Hamer, whose family and admirers structure the film's narrative. Director Buchanan also found in his interview subjects—and in photos of the outlaws—insinuations about Bonnie and Clyde that were calculated to repel 1960s audiences. For instance, an image of Clyde Barrow holding hands with another member of the Barrow Gang, Raymond Hamilton, becomes proof both of Clyde's bisexuality and of Bonnie's promiscuity. (As Ives archly explains: "Hamilton was one of a succession of men who would, for a time, be a friend to *both* Bonnie and Clyde.")

The Tender Killers

The real Bonnie Parker was badly disfigured in a fire that resulted from Clyde having fallen asleep at the wheel of their automobile. She walked with a pronounced limp ever after and frequently had to be carried by Clyde. This was not a tale that made it into the script of *Bonnie and Clyde*, but *The Other Side* makes much of it. *The Other Side* also mentions the possibility of Bonnie's alcoholism (she "turned to whiskey for the strength to go on"), Clyde's infidelity, and, most damning of all, the couple's vanity and bad taste. A photo of Clyde hoisting Bonnie on his shoulder gives way to a fanciful re-creation of Bonnie's world. A woman's disembodied hands brush enamel on her toenails, then twist the knob on an old radio. Screen magazines with the faces of 1930s starlets litter the floor. Ives signals his disapproval by continuing wearily: "She read magazines of romantic confessions, painted her toenails pink, and upset color conscious people by trying to match her dyed-red hair with red hats, dresses, and shoes. It was said she had a loud mouth."

In *Bonnie and Clyde*, Clyde marvels at the publication of Bonnie's poem "The Ballad of Bonnie and Clyde." "You made me somebody they're gonna remember," he crows. The scriptwriters got that right. Without Bonnie, Clyde and the rest of the Barrow Gang would likely have faded into obscurity with other Depression-era desperados who stole for survival or amusement in the weakly policed mid- and southwestern United States. The novelty of Bonnie's diminutive, feminine presence earmarked the Barrow Gang for celebrity and was crucial to the fascination surrounding her and Clyde's dramatic end.

Both *Bonnie and Clyde* and *The Other Side of Bonnie and Clyde* fetishize Bonnie, her death, and her relationship to violence. Previous cinematic representations of the Bonnie and Clyde story had the Bonnie character expiring bloodlessly, even if she were shown to die in a hail of bullets. In the 1967 film, however, not only does Bonnie bleed, the whole gory process of flailing limbs and contorted expressions is presented in slow motion. Arthur Penn claimed that he directed actress Faye Dunaway's dying movements to resemble orgasm.[33] For *The Other Side*, the death car is the film's literal climax, to which the film's entire narrative builds. Images of the outlaws' ravaged bodies, slumped in the automobile and laid out on improvised coroner's slabs, serve as ghoulish morality tales. But Buchanan cannot resist sneaking in some titillation in the form of the exposed bosom of Bonnie's corpse.

By 1968, the forty-four-year-old Buchanan had cowritten, produced, and directed eighteen of his own films, including *The Naked Witch* (1957), *Naughty Dallas (A.K.A. A Stripper Is Born)* (1958), and *Mars Needs Women* (1966). His 1996 autobiography, *It Came from Hunger! Tales of a Cinema Schlockmeister,* lovingly describes the various screen actresses with whom he fell in "movie-love." It also relates an apparently formative incident in which the young Buchanan happened upon a couple making love in a Baptist church's baptismal font. ("With a whoosh of delight, a pretty girl in a clinging wet dress shot up out of the real water.")[34] For much of his career, Buchanan was drawn to stories with three ingredients: sex, piety, and an unconventional female lead. His attraction to Bonnie Parker makes sense in the context of a filmography that included cinematic ruminations on Marilyn Monroe (twice), Janis Joplin, and Mary Magdalene.

The Other Side's ersatz documentary established Frank Hamer as its protagonist. Yet the film was not marketed as a film about the Texas Ranger. Penn's *Bonnie and Clyde* had this tagline: "They are young, they are in love, they kill people." Ads for *The Other Side* also focused on the outlaws, promising, "Their thing revealed like it happened! Love! Perversion! Blood and Death!" Bonnie's tousled head occupies the bottom half of *The Other Side*'s poster. She reclines, one hand draped over her slack mouth. The image is deliberately ambiguous; Bonnie may just have been killed, or she may be about to lick her trigger finger in a moment of eroticism. Buchanan knew well that a soft-porn-style poster would sell movie tickets, even if it did not match the content of the film it advertised. There is no sex in *The Other Side*. There is, however, a charged hatred between Bonnie and the lawmen she, and she alone, is shown to massacre. Part fetish, part storytelling foil, a murderous Bonnie accentuates the heroism of Hamer, the only lawman shown to survive his encounter with her.

The 1967 film took precisely the opposite tack with its Bonnie character. It imagines her as conventionally feminine, which is to say that violence is not supposed to come naturally to her. Glamorous and sentimental, her primary flaw is her devotion to Clyde. Whenever she holds a weapon, the gesture smacks of playacting or sexual provocation. *Bonnie and Clyde* permits Bonnie to own a tiny gun (Clyde gets her one to "fit [her] hand, see?"), but she mainly uses it as a prop in the bank holdups. The killing of lawmen is left to Clyde or, more frequently, to Clyde's brother, Buck. By contrast, and by design, *The Other Side*'s Bonnie shows no compunction about wielding a rifle and, as a matter of fact, wields it more lethally than Clyde. The 1968 Bonnie is more caricature than character, but even that cannot drain her of the rebel gunwoman's magnetism. As Larry Buchanan hypothesized years later in his DVD commentary, "She led him [Clyde] down the path, and he went, joyfully."[35]

Ambiguity and Reversals

In its final reel, the 1967 *Bonnie and Clyde* symbolically condemns the law as having destroyed something lovely and beautiful. Penn literally aligns his audience with the dead outlaws at the end of his film. That his Bonnie and Clyde died unarmed and trying to help a friend obscures the memory of the people they murdered—victims who, according to Benton and Newman's script, they killed out of desperation rather than malice.

In *The Other Side*, the law owns the story of Bonnie and Clyde. "There are many conflicting versions of the last hours of Clyde Barrow and Bonnie Parker," concedes narrator Ives, before reading aloud an account from Hamer's biography, one that accentuates Hamer's own fortitude and fairness. Having resolved to "take Barrow and the woman alive if we could," Hamer recalls himself as having stepped out from a hiding spot in the bushes to demand that they surrender. He carefully insists that the deadly shootout was inevitable: "Instead of obeying the order as I had hoped and prayed, they grabbed for their weapons and all hope for a capture alive perished."

In Buchanan's reenactment, Bonnie's head snaps to the direction of the camera. She swiftly raises her rifle, and the camera zeros in on her face and the gun barrel. The barrel points squarely at the audience, who are, for a moment, symbolically threatened along with the concealed posse. Then the film cuts to the discharge of Hamer's gun, which points away from the audience, and which appears to save viewers from Bonnie's bullet. After several seconds of gunfire from the rest of the posse, there is silence. The camera tilts up and arcs to the left, to pan a row of pine trees against the sky. When the shot swoops down again to the road, it is taken from the 16-millimeter footage recorded on the day of the ambush. Grainy and green, the wreck of the real Bonnie and Clyde's automobile appears. The camera zooms in on the bodies, still in the car's front seat, but mangled beyond recognition. Posse members mill about the automobile and remove its contents—including fifteen different firearms—which are inventoried on-screen.

Hamer was "applauded by the press, and honored on the floor of

Congress," although *The Other Side* acknowledges that he also received some harassing letters in the wake of the ambush. Ives reads aloud a portion of one such letter from Clyde Barrow's father, who wrote to demand that his son's guns be returned to the Barrow family. The Texas state legislature denied the request and awarded the guns to Hamer. (In *The Other Side*, Hamer's son proudly exhibits the guns, one of which, he claims, bears a smear of Bonnie Parker's own blood.) The documentary ends with a shot of Hamer's formal oil portrait, a few defensive statements on behalf of the Texas Rangers, and a final reminder of *The Other Side*'s purported aim: "If the film you have just seen has given you a new awareness and appreciation of law enforcement, then Frank Hamer would have been pleased that you saw it."

Today, over forty years after the release of Arthur Penn's *Bonnie and Clyde* and its "schlockmeister" critique, one film routinely makes reviewers' Top 100 Films lists. The other has languished in obscurity. Until recently, one of the only ways to see *The Other Side of Bonnie and Clyde* was to travel to Washington, D.C., to request the faded print archived by the Library of Congress. That all changed once Mel Gibson announced his intention to film *The Passion of Christ* (2004). Sensing another business opportunity in the wake of Gibson's film and the widespread popularity of Dan Brown's 2003 book, *The Da Vinci Code*, Larry Buchanan left retirement to tackle his "magnum opus," *The Copper Scroll of Mary Magdalene*.[36] It was his last film before he died in 2004. While promoting his film about the biblical bad-woman, Buchanan was happy to talk about *The Other Side*, Bonnie Parker, and the 1930s outlaws he had once worried would take the life of his constable father.[37] Although *The Other Side* had sought to dim the outlaws' legend, Buchanan's memories of shooting the film "on the exact spot they died" took him back to the youth he spent in a Texas orphanage. "After lights out on a summer's evening, we would look toward Highway 80, a mile away, and watch the speeders and imagine Clyde at the wheel and Bonnie at his side. It was very romantic. Please remember this was a time of hunger and 'them against us.' These were our heroes. We were rooting for them!"[38]

In the final year of Buchanan's life, Something Weird Video (SWV) released a DVD of *The Trial of Lee Harvey Oswald*, Buchanan's oft-copied "what if?" documentary from 1964. The company included Buchanan's *The Other Side of Bonnie and Clyde* as the disc's second feature. Suddenly, Bonnie-and-Clyde aficionados could screen as bright and clear a version of *The Other Side* as had once been shown in drive-in movie theaters all over the Southwest and New York state. Buchanan approved: "Through the years, none of my pictures . . . has generated as much response as [my film about] 'Bonnie.'"[39]

In 1996, Buchanan described *The Other Side* as a "send-up" of Penn's movie, which suggests that he regarded his documentary as more coy than cutting toward the film it burlesqued. While *The Other Side* remains but a footnote to Arthur Penn's far more successful film, Buchanan was, on some level, much more aware than Penn of the instability of outlaw storytelling. He also may better have understood the manipulability of an image. *The Other Side* was, after all, responding to *Bonnie and Clyde* as a manipulation. In its desire to capitalize on the success of that film and to recuperate the law, *The Other Side* reached for the "truth" about Bonnie and Clyde. Yet, once the duo had been released to the "afterlife of the imagination," their story was refracted through whatever lens matched the needs of a contemporary audience. To paraphrase the *Time* magazine reviewer who was among the first to defend Penn's movie, Buchanan's hunt for the "real" Bonnie and Clyde was a crowd-pleasing exercise, but also an irrelevant one.[40] There was no clear "Other Side" to the 1967 *Bonnie and Clyde*, not least because the meaning of that film, like the meaning of Bonnie Parker, was anything but static.

Penn's film is still gorgeous—each frame a canvas, striking in its composition and thick with period details. Faye Dunaway's obviously fake eyelashes may scream 1960s, and at times the blood looks embarrassingly fake, but *Bonnie and Clyde* remains a work of art. Contrary to many viewers' recollections, the film does not really champion its outlaws, who are beautiful but dimwitted and too often shown in moments of depression and doubt. By contrast, *The Other Side* attentively searches out the details of period photographs that did not become iconic, and inadvertently uncovers moments of apparent normality and tenderness: Bonnie and Clyde on a picnic blanket, Bonnie and Clyde lounging in intimate embrace.

Both *Bonnie and Clyde* and *The Other Side of Bonnie and Clyde* have their scolds. *The Other Side* has Burl Ives, although his disapproving narrative is undone by many of the photographs, which do too much to humanize the outlaws. These many years later, Ives is also undercut by Buchanan's circa-2003 DVD commentary. "The yeast of a thing is poverty," Buchanan observes, hinting that Bonnie's and Clyde's actions were not entirely without just cause. He also professes admiration for Clyde's musicianship and Bonnie's beauty. *Bonnie and Clyde*'s Cassandra is Bonnie's mother, Mrs. Parker, who points out the obvious to her daughter and her lover:

"You try to live three miles from me and you won't live long, honey. You best keep running, Clyde Barrow. And you know it!" The actress Mabel Cavitt delivers the line with a hopelessness that is chilling. Nothing in *The Other Side* is so unambiguous or so bleak. Hindsight makes visible a startling truth: The 1968 film that set out to deflate the Bonnie and Clyde myth is ultimately less critical of the real-life outlaws than the film that supposedly romanticized them.

New Heroes, New Enemies

Screenwriters Newman and Benton saw the real-life characters that inspired their *Bonnie and Clyde* as deeply contemporary. Their movie projected an "American sensibility." "Today, in a time when everybody likes to talk about being 'aware,' we have inherited a legacy from [the] underworld," the screenwriters reasoned. "What we now call 'the underground,' what the hip people do and are and feel, stems in great part from 'the underworld.'"[41]

Many years later, the *Economist* echoed Newman and Benton's assessment. Describing Bonnie Parker's cigar image as a "proto-modeling photograph," the magazine singled it out as one of the original "gangster chic" photographs of the 1930s that have exerted a strong influence on fashion and entertainment photography ever since: "Many of the fashionable snarls, grimaces, and growls that appear in today's music and film magazine could have been lifted from one or other of the FBI 'Wanted' posters that have been tacked up in the post offices around America in the past 50 years."[42]

By the 1970s, a new generation of women lawbreakers were making headlines, among them the kidnapped heiress Patricia Hearst, the Weather Underground's Bernadine Dohrn, and Charlie Manson's creepy acolytes, the "Manson Girls." In 1974, *U.S. News & World Report* ran photographs of all these women, plus Bonnie Parker and her cigar, next to an article that fretted over the fact of "Women Catching Up with Men in One More Field: Crime." But for Arthur Penn's movie and the cultural fallout reflected in Larry Buchanan's *The Other Side*, the image of Bonnie in her outdated garb might have seemed incongruous in an article that worried about the dangerous effects of "women's lib" on late-twentieth-century American women. The photo caption informed readers that Bonnie Parker was one of the "forerunners of today's women outlaws."[43]

As women lawbreakers appeared on the rise, the reputation of the G-man was sinking. The FBI had always had its critics, even major ones, but none of these had generated any long-term outrage on the part of the greater public.[44] However, in the wake of Hoover's 1972 death, Watergate, and a Senate investigation into the Bureau's illegal surveillance techniques, the time was ripe for a backlash against the FBI and its carefully cultivated image. The success of Hoover's self-promoting enemy formula had enabled a politicized law enforcement agenda. Indeed, one could argue that crime itself had been gradually redefined to include the personal habits of high-placed public figures and anyone suspected of being a "subversive." By dint of Hoover's leadership, crime prevention included the habitual monitoring of individual citizens' behavior in the name of domestic security. His domesticated G-man would therefore become a punching bag during the countercultural split—a split deepened by revelations of the G-men's improprieties. As the Bureau struggled to reinvent itself in the turbulent Watergate years, Hoover's enemy "formula" was again taken up—and taken down—by a violent youth counterculture trying to be outlaws of a different sort.

Bonnie Parker's infamous cigar photo. © Bettman/Corbis.

Sylvia Sidney and Henry Fonda play outlaw lovers on the lam in *You Only Live Once* (1937). Courtesy of the Academy of Motion Picture Arts and Sciences.

THE CHIEF OF THE
G-MEN PRESENTS

CRIME'S leading

A talented girl who, if she hadn't

been a gangster's gun moll, might

have become a Hollywood star

PETTY holdup men and big-shot gangsters are of the same insignificant breed. Both are weaklings and cowards. They differ principally in build-up—in the way they are staged and advertised in the underworld and in the country at large. You can turn a skulking sneak thief into a national terror if you give him the right kind of producer and press agent.

Not so very long ago the name of George (Machine Gun) Kelly brought a shiver of fear into the homes of wealthy families in every city of the land. This trade-mark of crime—Machine Gun Kelly—was a symbol of kidnapping, of brutal power, ruthlessness, and cunning. But when we stripped off his make-up we found behind it a craven, blundering blowhard, who better deserved the vaudeville name of "Pop Gun" Kelly than the dramatic and formidable title that he bore. But he didn't invent it. It was the creation of his manager, press agent, and leading lady—Kathryn Kelly, his wife—one of the most attractive women ever to travel the crooked paths of the underworld—and one of the most vicious.

When Kathryn Kelly met George Kelly in Oklahoma City not many years ago, he was a weak, loud-mouthed, over-dressed bootlegger, whom the aristocrats of crime held in contempt as "small fry." An actress by instinct, with a remarkable gift for showmanship, she sized him up—a thickset, powerful man with sleek hair and a weak, round face. He would do, she thought. He could be staged as a super-villain—the part she had longed to play. And, as the star criminal of America, he would bring her wealth.

Persistently she built him up. She embarked upon a popularity campaign in gangdom, where she was indisputably the best-looking and best-dressed gun moll of the lot. She rode in a sixteen-cylinder car, her silver fox furs floating from her shoulders. Apparently, whispered the underworld, Kelly must be a big shot—must be making good. She bought him a machine gun and kept score for him in practice until he was able to strip a fence-top of a row of walnuts. Upon at least one occasion, she collected the bullets and passed them out among her criminal friends like cigars, remarking, "Here's a little souvenir for you—a bullet from George's machine gun—Machine Gun Kelly, you know."

HIS fame increased. Here was a man for a gangster to know, to work with. Under Kathryn's management he found himself a master of crime, directing gang activities, bank robberies, and kidnappings! And at last his name was emblazoned across the land as the star of one of the most daring but most stupid spectacles in the theater of crime—the kidnapping of Charles F. Urschel, Oklahoma oil millionaire, who was seized at his home and held for $200,000 ransom. But the real brains of the crime was Kathryn Kelly, leading lady, producer, and press agent for her henpecked husband.

If you had met Kathryn Kelly casually you might have thought her a very nice person. She appeared to possess such ready sympathies, especially for children. Her own daughter by a previous marriage appeared to be the most important thing in her life. Then, there was her aging mother, whom she apparently adored. But perhaps it was pretense. She was always acting.

She played the piano with moderate ability. She used English that was far better than the average. She was attractive to look upon, of good carriage and pleasing manner. She usually dressed with excellent taste, especially when driving. She was the best example I ever have encountered of the fact that present-day crime often wears the habiliments of honesty.

The crimes of Kathryn were the culmination of a lifetime and were the expression, partly, of thwarted ability. Born in 1904 in Saltillo, Miss., Kathryn was the only child of a somewhat strange union: a father of good family and a mother who, while intelligent and talented, nevertheless had criminal relatives. The mother once worked in a bank, was an expert typist, and earned odd money at times by writing articles for farm magazines. But she lived to run afoul of the law.

A dark-eyed, dark-haired child, Kathryn was spoiled and "made over." She

Lady

BY J·EDGAR HOOVER
with
COURTNEY RYLEY COOPER

WIDE WORLD PHOTO

Kathryn Kelly

had been christened Cleo, but, actress that she was, she changed her name. Her parents let her have her way. Alert and wildly imaginative, she made her way swiftly through eight grades of school; then, at fifteen, went away to Oklahoma and was married. When a baby daughter was born to her, she suddenly returned to her mother in Saltillo and sued for divorce, which was granted.

When her mother moved to Coleman, Texas, a town and district largely populated by her own relatives, Kathryn went along. She was seventeen now, slim, well-formed, chic, and almost beautiful. And she was clothes-crazy. Residents also said she was man-crazy. Soon she began making extended trips to the nearest metropolis, Forth Worth, while the baby was left at home with Kathryn's mother. This, however, was not a case of imposition upon a dear old innocent woman. The mother had developed shortcomings of her own. She had opened a small hotel which soon be-

gan to gain an unsavory reputation. When home, Kathryn acted as the establishment's bootlegger.

INNOCENT and demure in appearance, with a fondness for playing the part of an ingénue, Kathryn made friends with law-abiding people and eventually found employment in Fort Worth. But she had bad friends, too. One of these was a woman accused of shoplifting, of consorting with criminals, of assault, and even of burglary. They became in-

separable. Finally Kathryn dropped all pretense of work. Police said she lived by the same methods as her companion. But Kathryn outwardly remained the sweet young girl from the country who liked to talk with glowing pride about the future of her little daughter.

"I want my little girl to grow up to be the finest woman that ever God gave breath to," she told a sympathetic policeman one night in Fort Worth. It was during an interrogation regarding why she had (Continued on page 74)

Kathryn Kelly as "Crime's Leading Lady" in the February 1937 *American Magazine*. Courtesy of the Five College Library Depository.

Multipage ad for *Persons in Hiding* in the 1939 *Motion Picture Herald*. Courtesy of the University of Minnesota.

...She's beautiful
...She's dangerous

...blasting her way from the amazing, true pages of J. Edgar Hoover's "PERSONS IN HIDING" ...the most sensational crime drama ever to explode on the screen!

J. EDGAR HOOVER
Director of Federal Bureau of Investigation

"Unquestionably top-of-the-bill quality from every angle. The real, authenticated article. All other previous excursions into this field have been ordinary 'cops-and-robbers' stuff."
—*Hollywood Reporter*

Adapted from **J. EDGAR HOOVER'S**
"PERSONS IN HIDING"

LYNNE OVERMAN · PATRICIA MORISON · J. CARROL NAISH · JUDITH BARRETT
A Paramount Picture · Directed by LOUIS KING · Screen Play by William R. Lipman and Horace McCoy

The real

"Ma" Barker

AS director of the so-called G-Men —we much prefer to be called Men of the F. B. I.—a part of my task is the attempt to learn what lies behind criminality. All too often, the ardent "good citizen" of today may be the menace of tomorrow. It was so with the most dangerous lawbreaker in my experience.

And, strange as it may seem to some people, that person was not John Dillinger, Baby Face Nelson, nor any of the rest of our so-called No. 1 public enemies, but a woman. The most vicious, dangerous, and resourceful criminal brain this country has produced for many years belonged to a person called "Mother Barker" by scores of satellites.

In her sixty or so years this woman reared a spawn of hell. Of her four sons, one was a mail robber, another a holdup man, and the remaining pair were highwaymen, kidnappers, wanton murderers. To a great extent their criminal careers were directly traceable to their mother; to her they looked for guidance, for daring resourcefulness. They obeyed her implicitly. So, too, did the other members of the Barker-Karpis gang of hoodlums, highwaymen, kidnappers, and murderers which she headed.

With the calm of a person ordering a meal Mother Barker brought about bank robberies, holdups, or kidnappings and commanded the slaying of persons, some of whom only a short time before had enjoyed what they thought was her friendship. Yet she liked to hum hymns, and at one time in her life, at least, she was deeply religious and a regular church attendant.

Crime travels into strange places for its recruits. For Mother Barker it reached into a farmhouse in a pocket of the Ozark Mountains some eighteen miles from Springfield, Mo., where a

*BEGINNING—Never-before-told stories be-
hind the most famous cases of our G-Men*

Public Enemy No. 1

By J. Edgar Hoover

WITH COURTNEY
RYLEY COOPER

This article, the first of a series by the head of America's Scotland Yard, offers the most vivid picture from behind the guns of crime I've ever encountered. It's sordid. It deals with sinister human beings. It is motherhood at its worst. But it portrays graphically some of the contributing causes of crime. And it has a lesson for every foolish woman who overindulges her children. It's a story that until now has been locked in the archives of the Federal Bureau of Investigation. But—don't read it if you're easily shocked.—*The Editor*

dark-haired girl of less than usual stature reached the age of marriage some time in the middle '90s. She was the daughter of parents predominantly Scotch-Irish. Friends knew her as "Arrie" Clark; she had been christened Arizona, for what reason is undetermined.

The life of her childhood had been that of an ordinary Missouri farm—church, Sunday school, picnics, hayrides, candy pulls, and the little red schoolhouse. Somewhere she had gained the nickname of Kate, again for no ostensible reason. Her family was circumspect and remained so.

A young farm laborer named George Barker came along when Arizona Clark was barely out of her teens. They were married at Aurora, Mo., where Kate

Barker was known as a good wife, devoted to the Presbyterian church, a fair housekeeper, and averse to back-fence gossip. There her sons arrived, Herman, Lloyd, Arthur, and the favorite, whom she called Freddie. Herman and Lloyd grew to school age in Aurora; the others were still babies when the family moved to Webb City, where the father worked at various jobs in the lead and zinc mines. Kate Barker, always somewhat secretive, had few close friends.

She went to church and to Sunday school, dragging her brood with her, to sing the hymns with the same lustiness as the rest of the

*George Barker
"forgotten father"*

congregation. With her, of course, went George, her husband, a mild, inoffensive, quiet man who seemed somewhat bewildered by his dominating wife. This was especially true when he attempted to assume the guidance of his growing boys. There was a feline intensity about Kate's determination that no one but herself should be their mentor; and in her eyes they could do no wrong.

The eyes of Arizona Clark Barker, by the way, always fascinated me. They were queerly direct, penetrating, hot with some strangely smoldering flame, yet withal as hypnotically cold as the (Continued on page 118)

The first article in Hoover's "Secrets of the G-men" series in the April 1936 *American Magazine*. Courtesy of the Five College Library Depository.

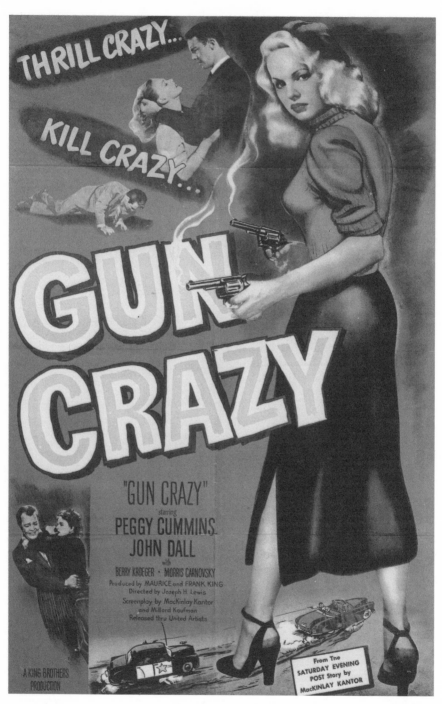

Poster for *Gun Crazy* (1949). Courtesy of the Academy of Motion Picture Arts and Sciences.

Poster for *The Bonnie Parker Story* (1958). Courtesy of Photofest.

The original Bonnie and Clyde are often "just folks" in Larry Buchanan's *The Other Side of Bonnie and Clyde*. Courtesy of the Academy of Motion Picture Arts and Sciences.

Promotional material for Arthur Penn's *Bonnie and Clyde* (1967). Courtesy of the Academy of Motion Picture Arts and Sciences.

Faye Dunaway as Bonnie Parker. Courtesy of the Academy of Motion Picture Arts and Sciences.

Promotional still for *Queen of the Mob* (1940). Courtesy of the Academy of Motion Picture Arts and Sciences.

Advertisement for *Bloody Mama* (1970). Clip art from American Independent Pictures.

4

Radical Cheerleaders and a Frustrated PTA Type

If she had come of age in a different era, Bonnie Parker might have dreamed of a career in television. As it happened, the most famous actress ever to incarnate Bonnie Parker on-screen later morphed into television producer Diana Christensen, the captivating antagonist of Sidney Lumet's *Network* (1976). As Christensen, Faye Dunaway brokers a ratings-boosting deal with the Ecumenical Liberation Army (ELA), whose most dedicated member is a kidnapped heiress with more than a passing resemblance to Patty Hearst.[1] Christensen coaxes the ELA and an Angela Davis figure to star in a new series built around the ELA's own obsessive footage of themselves robbing banks and committing other "authentic acts of political terrorism." Subsequently heralded as having forecast the coming of reality TV, *Network's* satirical plot mocked the real-life SLA for courting celebrity over revolution. It also skewered the television industry for cheerfully profiting from such groups' empty but telegenic violence.

Network was released the same year Hearst went to trial for crimes committed after her abduction by the SLA and her apparent conversion to their cause. The United States was celebrating its bicentennial, but the mood in the country was grim. Many who had watched the bizarre details of the Hearst case unfold on television were skeptical of claims that Hearst might have been brainwashed by her captors. Indeed, *Network* imagined its pretty heiress as having naturally become the most fanatical member of her group, drawing on a widely held perception that countercultural children of elites were always more desperate to prove their radical-populist credentials. Ironically, *Network* skewered television audiences as the real victims of a collective brainwashing. When the veteran TV news anchor Howard Beale (Peter Finch) directs his viewers to run to their windows and join him in a chorus of "I'm mad as hell and I'm not going to take it anymore!," the spontaneous uprising is a jolting but ultimately ineffectual piece of political theater. By film's end, the shallow political terrorists are in bed with the immoral gods of new media. Together, they hustle their prize—the radicalized former good girl—before the cameras in an effort to draw the kind of ratings that will undo the grip of the Establishment. Audiences may denounce the spectacle as empty exploitation, but they also find that they cannot look away.

The story of the SLA, which had neither the membership nor the duration of radical groups like the Panthers or the Weather Underground, would not seem to warrant all the attention it has received. But for the symbolic seizure of the granddaughter of media magnate William Randolph Hearst, the SLA would likely have receded into Bay Area history. As many others have pointed out, the senior Hearst's style of "yellow journalism" indirectly made it possible for the SLA to win the publicity it craved. The SLA was also a product of a paranoid subculture fueled by its founders' experiences in Vietnam and the far left's deepening distrust for law enforcement, particularly the disgraced FBI. As the G-man's reputation continued to tank, the mostly white, mostly female SLA attempted its own "great sell," self-consciously casting themselves—and Patty Hearst—as noble outlaws who fought not against the oppression of their people but against the *privileges* of their skin and social class.

Artists, journalists, and scholars have long been fascinated with the undeniable drama of the nineteen-year-old Patty Hearst's apparent metamorphosis from "beautiful heiress" to "Tania," gun-toting bank robber and revolutionary. But her eighteen-month stint with the SLA may actually be less remarkable than her forty-year journey from victim to villain and back to victim again. Adding a specific and fresh angle on a well-trod history, this chapter considers how Patty's outlawry was constructed and then made useful by two different groups—the FBI and the five women of the SLA—both of whom were in a moment of crisis and reinvention. The story of the kidnapping victim, her SLA captors, and the struggling 1970s FBI is shot through with all the social and economic tensions of its era. It is also a story replete with the kind of self-conscious image-making that was both a product of, and a boon to, an emergent television news industry. This chapter sifts through the coincidences and converging social forces that made the SLA's attempt at a *politicized* women's outlawry—particularly Patty's—so important. It also explains why the chameleon-like, post-SLA Patricia Hearst ultimately succeeded as an outlaw, despite having violated the normally hard-and-fast rule that the outlaw must die.

The Rise of the Symbionese Liberation Army

The SLA is frequently misidentified as a sixties group by those who would remember radical political activism as belonging exclusively to that decade. In fact, the SLA could not have existed before the early 1970s, fueled as it was by the convictions of its members that too little had yet been done to change a United States that they saw as employing imperialist tactics abroad and encouraging a racist class war at home. The few who were admitted to the SLA's secretive, Maoist, military group had all rejected nonviolent resistance in favor of "necessary violence" because—in the words of one SLA document—"All the reforms of the '60s had failed, or been taken back, or were inadequate to start with."[2]

By the end of the 1960s, a substantial number of young Americans were feeling cut off from what they regarded as the conventional aspirations of their parents, which they criticized as materialistic or meaningless. For those who had supported the civil rights and antiwar movements, 1968—the "year of rage"—was also a year of profound disillusionment. Tensions spiked with the assassinations of Martin Luther King Jr. and Robert Kennedy, the deepening war in Vietnam, and yet another summer of widespread urban violence—culminating with the mayhem between protestors and police at the Democratic National Convention in Chicago. Meanwhile, the student protests at Columbia University had presaged a wave of campus struggles between college students and administrations across the country. In September, FBI Director J. Edgar Hoover described the Black Panthers as "the greatest threat to the internal security of the country," and he continued to supervise the Bureau's covert counterintelligence program (COINTELPRO) against it and other "dissident" groups.[3] In November, Republican Richard Nixon won the presidency by a narrow margin, carrying with him the hopes of many conservative and working-class Americans who were uneasy with the rising counterculture.[4]

In the fall of 1969, a small faction of Weathermen took over the Students for a Democratic Society (SDS) from within, on a platform that the

SDS had not been doing enough to end the war or to support groups like the Black Panthers in the fight against white privilege. Bernadine Dohrn, a twenty-seven-year-old lawyer and the Weathermen's most prominent leader, alarmed the Establishment with her declaration that U.S. high school students were on the verge of revolt and could, at any moment, abandon their schools and families to join a youthful revolution against the U.S. government. One call to arms was the October "Days of Rage," designed to "bring the war home" through acts of vandalism in affluent sections of Chicago. Two months later, when FBI agents and local police killed the charismatic Panther Fred Hampton in his Chicago home, Dohrn publicly mused that the Manson family's slaughter of innocent people in the Hollywood hills should be an inspiration to her fellow "honkies," who were frightened by the call to violent struggle against the wealthy and the powerful.[5] Shortly thereafter, she and other key members of the Weathermen went into hiding and became the Weather Underground.

In early 1970, Hoover issued an FBI report that singled out "extremist, all-Negro, hate-type organizations" and communist-sympathizing student radicals as two of the most serious challenges to social stability.[6] In the pages of *PTA Magazine*, he warned parents that SDS agitators were trying to gain access to their children's schools to woo young ones with anti-authoritarian Marxist rhetoric.[7] For the countercultural New Left, as for a generation of leftists before them, Hoover's cautions were a joke, further evidence that the FBI would use any means necessary to stamp out nonconformist behavior. Plenty of Americans still admired the heroic, pop-culture G-man, but the Bureau had lately come under fire for having done too much to fuel anticommunist hysteria and not nearly enough to enforce the legally ensured protections due to civil rights protestors. As Richard Gid Powers has pointed out, the FBI was the counterculture's most obvious symbol of the authoritarian state, and becoming an official FBI enemy only strengthened the resolve of those who suspected the Bureau of perpetuating economic and racial injustice.[8]

On April 30, 1970, Nixon went on television to announce the invasion of neutral Cambodia. The news was met with a surge of antiwar protests, which resulted in the killing of four white students by National Guardsmen at Ohio's Kent State. Ten days later, two black students were killed in a similar protest at Jackson State in Mississippi. Those who had been predicting a holocaust of student and black dissenters had their proof. In September, Brandeis University students Kathy Power and Susan Saxe were part of a team from the "National Student Strike Force" that set fire to the National

Guard Armory in Newburyport, Massachusetts, and made off with a truck and ammunition. To protest the Vietnam War and finance weapons for the Black Panthers, they robbed a bank with the help of three ex-convicts, all of whom had been enrolled in a special Brandeis program to help prisoners get a college education. On the day of the bank heist, the former convicts were captured, but not before one of them killed patrolman Walter Schroeder, a father of nine children. Power and Saxe joined the thousands of other radicals who were going underground, using dead infants' birth certificates to create aliases and new identities.

By October 1971, eight of the fourteen people on the FBI's "Most Wanted" list were either New Left or revolutionary types, including Power, Saxe, and the photogenic Bernadine Dorhn, whom Hoover had declared "the most dangerous woman in America." With this shift in the FBI's priorities came a reduction of their power. In 1971, Attorney General John Mitchell abruptly took over Hoover's longtime responsibility of reporting the nation's crime statistics. For the first time in four decades, Hoover no longer had complete control over the crime figures, and the story he had told about a decrease of crime under the new Republican administration proved untrue. (Before 1971, Hoover had also characterized predominantly black D.C. as a criminal hotspot. Once the crime stats were in Mitchell's hands, the city suddenly became "normally criminal," much like the rest of the country's urban areas.)[9] Hoover died in 1972, still embroiled in a battle with the underground radicals who saw themselves as warrior-outlaws, exacting retribution for the government's sins. An accidental explosion that killed several of their members in 1970 convinced the Weather Underground to bomb "symbols or institutions of American injustice" rather than human targets. They later argued that their nonlethal bombings had yet managed to deflate the government's "aura of invincibility, to show that the FBI didn't always 'get its man.'"[10]

By the summer of 1973, the Watergate scandal was breaking around Richard Nixon. The country was learning about COINTELPRO and the extralegal behaviors of the FBI and other surveillance organizations.[11] The war dragged on, although most U.S. troops had pulled out of Vietnam. Many of the civil rights, student, women's, and antiwar movements had splintered, partly due to the FBI's success in infiltrating the leftist organizations it regarded as a threat.[12] But the FBI would soon concede failure in its hunt for the Weather Underground. An internal FBI memo lamented the fact that potential informants were impervious to the lure of reward money.

COINTELPRO abuses would make it impossible to pursue Weather Underground members on federal conspiracy and riot charges, and so those charges were dismissed.

Meanwhile, the SLA had officially become known to the FBI in the late summer of 1973, when the former released its "Declaration of Revolutionary War" against the United States.[13] The Symbionese Liberation Army took the first part of its name from the word "symbiosis," or the cooperative living together of two dissimilar organisms.[14] It declared itself a "United Front and Federation of members from the Asian, Black, Brown, Indian, White, Woman, Gray, and Gay Liberation Movements," together mounting an assault on what they rejected as a genocidal capitalist system.[15] The SLA's symbol was a seven-headed cobra, the part-serpent, part-human *naga* of Hindu and Buddhist mythology.[16] (An FBI agent noted in his report that a similar design appeared on the cover of Jimi Hendrix's 1967 record album, *Axis: Bold as Love*.)[17]

Reconstructing the SLA's politics was not difficult. Indeed, as one journalist put it, "They wrote down *everything*. . . . [They] were terrorists with the habits of graduate students."[18] The SLA would write and broadcast literally hundreds of detailed pages on their objections to what they saw as an exploitative, unresponsive government that refused to end an immoral war. They expounded on racism, sex and sexism, the energy crisis, the need to protect the environment, and what they argued were the parallels between the U.S. education system and its system of prisons. They critiqued the FBI, the police, private property, the faltering 1970s economy, and even what they regarded as the coming evil of computers. There seemed to be no issue on which the SLA would not comment and which they could not somehow judge within their much-recorded Symbionese ideology. Mixed in with their loftier goals for equality and an anticonsumerist revolution were other radical tenets that became the SLA's hallmarks, including a vitriolic hatred of the "pig-fascist" police and a romantic commitment to "the People." The SLA regularly paid homage to the latter in their signature line, "Death to the Fascist Insect That Preys on the Life of the People."

Like *Network*'s solipsistic ELA, the SLA were more concerned than the Panthers or Weathermen in trying to manipulate contemporary media in their favor. While they would later accuse the "pig press" of spreading lies, the SLA's influence depended almost entirely on the newspaper and television coverage that had helped to make them a household name. In the wake of Patty Hearst's 1974 kidnapping, the SLA won their demand that the press publish in full their lengthy communiqués and that they broadcast multiple audio recordings in which SLA members expounded on the aims and philosophy of their "army."

In early 1974, that army consisted of one black escaped convict, thirty-one-year-old Donald DeFreeze ("Cinque"), and his six twenty-something disciples, all of them college-educated and all of them white. Two other white members of the group—Joe Remiro and Russ Little—had gone to jail for the fatal shooting of Marcus Foster, the black superintendent of the Oakland Public Schools. The Foster murder was a senseless act in which neither man had been directly involved, and it earned the SLA the enmity of many left-leaning groups in the Bay Area.[19] Remiro (known within the army as "Bo") and Little ("Osceola") frequently drop out of Patty Hearst's abduction story, even though the SLA had taken Hearst as a "prisoner of war" in hopes of securing Bo and Osceola's release.

On February 4, Patricia Campbell Hearst was getting ready for bed in the Berkeley, California, apartment she shared with her fiancé, Steven Weed. When Weed opened the door to a woman begging to use the telephone to report a car accident, two men burst into the apartment, savagely beat Weed, and dragged Patty into the night. Stuffing her into the trunk of their waiting car, they drove her to a suburban San Francisco hideout. Once there, Patty was kept for six weeks in a tiny closet, blindfolded and bound, while the group bombarded her senses with music and read to her from various revolutionary tracts. The SLA informed Patty that she was their prisoner of war, taken in retaliation for crimes committed by her parents and other ruling-class elites. Over the next few weeks, they released audiotapes in which Patty repeated these charges and assured her parents that she was being treated fairly, in keeping with the rules of the Geneva Convention. California prison officials swiftly denied the SLA's demand for a prisoner exchange but did grant the incarcerated Bo and Osceola rather exceptional privileges, including that of being allowed to send out messages for radio and newspaper distribution. "Patty," they wrote, "we feel that we have already done the most concrete thing we can do to assist in your safe release, by exposing the true intentions of the FBI [to kill rather than save you]."[20]

The SLA also ordered the Hearst family to donate $70 worth of groceries to every poor person in California—a "good faith gesture" that, if fully implemented, would have cost up to $400 million. Patty's father, Randolph, the chairman of the Hearst media empire, declared that sum beyond his capacities and offered instead to give away $2 million worth of free food, with another $4 million to follow his daughter's safe release. As part of the hastily organized "People in Need" (PIN) program, volunteers helped distribute boxes of foodstuffs stamped with the SLA's seven-headed snake logo. This Robin Hood–style coup stymied many high-profile activists who had roundly condemned the SLA for "hamper[ing] the course of the revolution by bringing government repression and harassment to leftist groups."[21] In a joint statement, the six left-wing organizations designated by the SLA to run the food giveaway agreed to cooperate but insisted, "We do not condone terrorist activity."[22]

The first PIN giveaway led to violence, as recipients fought and clawed each other at one of the distribution centers. Like the drama of Patty's parents speaking to the reporters encamped on the lawn of their Hillsboro mansion, the spectacle of the food riots made all the television news channels. Displeased by the unfavorable media coverage and by the Hearst family's failure to meet their original demands, the SLA released another tape in which Patty complained that the giveaway program had been too stingy and that the quality of the meats had not matched those regularly enjoyed by the Hearst family. In the SLA's next communication, on April 3, Patty declared her intention to "stay and fight" with her kidnappers, accusing her parents of having deliberately wasted time, "time which the FBI was using in their attempts to assassinate me." Accompanying the announcement of her recruitment was the now-famous photograph of the beret-wearing Patty posed with a heavy-duty firearm in front of the SLA's seven-headed cobra.[23]

Twelve days later, security cameras photographed an armed Patty Hearst in the center of San Francisco's Hibernia Bank. Only now she was "Tania," SLA soldier, working with Cinque and three other SLA women to net almost $11,000 in stolen cash. Earlier assertions that Hearst had been acting and speaking under duress now became more difficult to defend, particularly after U.S. Attorney General William Saxbe made public his opinion that Hearst had become a "common criminal." The FBI's official wanted poster for the Hibernia robbery listed Patty as only a "material witness" to the crime. But this did not prevent many in the public from reevaluating Patty as an ungrateful child, a political and sexual adventuress who may even have arranged her own kidnapping.

Among some audiences, however, the bank robbery and the Tania coup had helped the SLA shake off some of the taint of the Foster murder. Retimah X, a young black woman who had helped hide the SLA, explained that she did so because "All these white people came from good homes. They didn't have to become revolutionaries, but they chose it themselves."[24] Some journalists confessed they had begun to recognize themselves in the SLA women and in Patty Hearst in particular. *Newsweek* columnist Shana Alexander called Patty "the country's first big-time all American girl," and one who acted out middle-aged Americans' "most secret fantasies."[25] The *New York Times'* Sara Davidson concurred in her reflection on Berkeley's mellowing counterculture. As she wrote: "They [the SLA] offered [Patty] a heroic name, a rebirth . . . the affair seemed to set off in me and everyone I encountered powerful fantasies and fears. It was a screen which reflected our private plots."[26] Reproductions of gun-toting Patty Hearst's SLA portrait began appearing around Berkeley, printed with the slogan "We Love You, Tania."

"The SLA Is Women"

In the weeks leading up to the Hibernia bank heist, FBI agents on the Hearst kidnapping, or HEARNAP case, had been struggling to learn more about the rest of the SLA members and their motivations. Antipathy toward law enforcement was commonplace in the Bay Area, particularly among those scattered revolutionary cells that had decided to abandon peaceful protest within the system in favor of all-out confrontation. Ironically, the success—or perceived success—of the FBI in infiltrating and covertly derailing left-wing groups had only served to make some of those groups more violent and secretive.

There was some evidence to suggest that the SLA was a reconstituted version of Venceremos ("We Shall Win"), another radical Berkeley group, which had taken its name from Che Guevara's battle cry. Anxious about the possibility of informants, Venceremos members had to prove their commitment to armed uprising through petty burglaries and bombings—initiations designed to weed out both the weak-willed and anyone who might be working for the feds. Before the dissolution of Venceremos in 1973, the group had publicized a five-plank program that called for community control of police (i.e., a disarmed police force and armed citizenry), the formation of a People's Liberation Army, and the right of racial and ethnic minorities to set up their own nations if they wished. The SLA communiqués echoed these goals, along with Venceremos's strong support of women's rights, twenty-four-hour child-care centers, free abortion and birth control, total job equality between the sexes, and total sexual freedom.[27]

In their copious writings, the SLA was less clear on their vision for the future than on what they wanted to destroy. Most clear was their opposition to everything "bourgeois." Private property, family ties, marriage, and monogamy were deemed oppressive and antirevolutionary. The SLA scorned the Panthers, who had run as Democrats in the 1973 Oakland elections, as traitors belonging to the "pseudo-left."[28] Their critiques of the Panthers, Weather Underground, and similar radical groups reflected the SLA's habit of taking inspiration from other organizations' causes and then crafting themselves in opposition to what they saw as those organizations' faltering commitment to the People. A combination of idealism and ego seems to have convinced the SLA that they could discipline themselves to be the most sincere brand of outlaws and that they, at last, would perfect revolutionary leadership.

Taking a cue from Donald DeFreeze's "Cinque," each of the SLA members cast off their "slave names" upon joining the army. Their new "People names" signified their solidarity with an American minority underclass whom they planned to politicize through the violence that "phony revolutionaries" like the Weather Underground had been too cautious to attempt. Bill and Emily Harris, a married couple who had both taught high school in Indiana before migrating to Berkeley in the early seventies, became "Teko" and "Yolanda." Like Bo, Teko had served in Vietnam and had been radicalized by the experience. He and Yolanda coaxed to Berkeley another Indiana University couple and were eventually recruited by the wife, Angela Atwood ("Gelina"), to the SLA. Nancy Ling Perry ("Fahizah") was a former chemistry major who had contemplated a career in medicine and who had once campaigned for the right-of-Nixon presidential candidate Barry Goldwater, but her personal goals and politics were turned inside out by the time she kicked a drug habit and took a job working at a Berkeley fruit stand. Willie Wolfe was a doctor's son from Pennsylvania who put off his anthropology degree to work for racial equality; he became the SLA's "Cujo." Patricia Soltysik ("Zoya") also disrupted her language studies at Berkeley to work for various radical political movements, including labor organizing and women's rights. She brought to the SLA her onetime girlfriend Camilla Hall, a poet and artist who became "Gabi."

That was the complete roll call for the original army: three men and six women, counting Patty Hearst. The thinness of their ranks startled Patty, since the SLA audiotapes frequently boasted about the might of its medical and combat units. Kate Coleman, a former member of the self-consciously zany, media-oriented Yippies, saw the SLA's tiny membership as a sign of the nervous times. "[The SLA] knew they weren't infiltrated because they didn't have a broad-based organization. But that was also their downfall.

Because if they survived, how could they grow? They could only build up myth."[29] Attuned as they were to their own publicity, SLA members seem to have regarded the building of their own myth as the SLA's most important asset.

It mattered that the SLA had so many women members, not only to how law enforcement responded to their crimes but also to perceptions of their "recruitment" of Patty Hearst. Writing in 1974, Sara Davidson insisted that Patty's apparent transformation was less bizarre than it was familiar, because conservative, privileged women frequently reinvented themselves upon moving to a countercultural hotspot like Berkeley. In the farewell tape to her family, Patty had dumped fiancé Steven Weed, saying, "I've changed, grown. I've become conscious and can never go back to the life we led." As Davidson observed, "In how many homes across the country recently has a woman delivered that message?"[30] Two years later, in the pages of *Newsweek*, a psychiatrist attributed the strange attraction of the doomed SLA members to their implicit role as America's wayward offspring. They "struck a note that everyone responds to," and, in the case of Patty, "the note was the strain between parents and children—and the political overtone that those relationships took on in the sixties."[31]

The April bank robbery had been sensational not only for the sight of SLA soldier Tania, but also for the image of three other women bank robbers on the scene with Tania and Cinque. Patty had by then been thoroughly dissected in the press as the Hearsts' slightly rebellious, decidedly apolitical middle child, an art history major who had been poised to marry her former high school math teacher against the wishes of her family. Now attention swiveled to Emily Harris (Yolanda), Angela Atwood (Gelina), Nancy Ling Perry (Fahizah), Patricia Soltysik (Zoya), and Camilla Hall (Gabi), with an emphasis on the latter three, who had been caught on the bank's security tape.

When the FBI and the press sought out the SLA women's families in California, Minnesota, Illinois, and New Jersey, the interviews revealed a group of well-educated women with a radical-activist bent. All had opposed the Vietnam War, joined in street demonstrations, food communes, and other features of Berkeley's antiestablishment life. All but one of them had been cheerleaders, prompting FBI profilers to surmise that, as "joiners" and "boosters," they were natural recruits to the self-assertive SLA. (Patty Hearst had also been a cheerleader.) Lacey Fosburgh, who covered the SLA-Hearst kidnapping case for the *New York Times*, marveled at how the SLA women had "ceased to be routine products of their middle class backgrounds."[32]

Hoping to learn what had compelled each of the SLA women to reject the privileges of her upbringing, FBI agents carefully took inventory of the women's personal and political activities. In keeping with the Bureau's habit of surveilling groups linked to 1970s feminist activism, it recorded with interest the SLA women's involvement in "women's lib groups that show masturbation movies," their estrangement from "Goldwater Republican parents," and their romantic relationships with other women or with nonwhite husbands and lovers. FBI informants described the SLA women as "lesbians with possible suicidal tendencies," but singled out Angela Atwood as "a frustrated PTA type."[33] Over the months of intelligence gathering, agents at first resisted, and then puzzled over, the notion that the five women would accept a black man and ex-convict as their leader. FBI profilers initially deduced that "Jalena" (their spelling of "Gelina") was a black woman who was married to Cinque and "the brains, the thinker, the planner" of the group. They also wondered if Nancy Ling Perry (Fahizah) might be the real leader of the SLA because she had been married for seven years to a black man and because she had handled all the early communications.

The FBI's criminal experts further speculated that all of the women had undergone "psychosexual crises" in the summer of 1973 that had prompted their vulnerability to "self-destructive revolutionary impulses." As evidence, profilers noted that the two women in a lesbian relationship had twice broken up that year. Three of the five women had recently ended their marriages. One had opened her marriage to include sex with "the beautiful black man who . . . conveyed . . . the torture of being black in this country and being poor."[34] Sex and the crossing of racial boundaries and assumed class and gender norms were central to most of the FBI psychiatrists' theories on the motivations of the group. So, too, were comparisons to Charles Manson, who allegedly held his female followers in a sexual trance. In a leap that infuriated the SLA women, the SLA was sometimes imagined as an interracial Manson family, with Cinque as their charismatic leader. In the 1979 book *Anyone's Daughter*, Shana Alexander theorized that Cinque had given the guilt-wracked women of privilege "a black totem pole to dance around." Thanks to Cinque's influence, "the middle class white girls had become 'bad,' so bad that two of them were able to walk up to Marcus Foster and shoot him in the back at close range."[35]

In her own evaluation of the SLA, Sara Davidson read the tape of the Hibernia bank robbery as having refuted the image of the SLA women as sexual slaves. After all, four women had marched ahead of Cinque into the bank while two white men waited in the getaway car. Also, the SLA women identified themselves as combat soldiers with military-style rankings, just like the men. The group's self-consciously evenhanded treatment of its male and female members struck some as definitive evidence that Cinque was not in charge, but just a front for the group's female masterminds.[36]

TV reporter Marilyn Baker had been one of the first to cast doubts on Cinque's role as leader of the SLA. Baker, whom the FBI publicly acknowledged as having underground contacts superior to their own, had combed an abandoned SLA safe house and told investigators what she thought they were up against.

> My sources all said the same thing. "The SLA is women!" and "Check heavy lesbian contacts!" . . . We couldn't say how we knew. But it was there [in the safe house], in their own handwriting, in the purloined papers. The only major editorial correction that appeared in them, again and again, was the reversal of the order of man and woman and men and women every time they were typed. Also, when they had written of the Ages of Man, Man became people. The woman always came before the man in Symbionese rhetoric. No man would have made these editorial changes, and few women would have either, even the most radical women's libbers. We were beginning to see the human forms behind the seven-headed snake.[37]

Baker regarded Cinque's feminism-infused speeches as conclusive evidence that he was under the women's thumb. As she mockingly wrote, "I remembered the taped voice, the affected lilt, the attempt by a ninth-grade drop-out to sound intellectual—Cinque's voice declaring the equality of women, the importance of women, the dignity of women."[38] Having discovered the SLA's stash of face-darkening makeup, Baker also reported that the mostly white SLA might be trying to pin their crimes on black citizens.[39]

Like the Harrises (Teko and Yolanda), Angela Atwood (Gelina) had aspired to a life in the theater. It was she who helped dress and disguise her comrades with eyeglasses and wigs and theater-grade blackface makeup to conceal white skin. This was not, as initially speculated, to put the blame for their actions on people of color, but rather an expression of both self-loathing and a fervent reverence for blacks as the more authentic revolutionaries. It also was an effective way to stay ahead of the law. Steven Weed told police that he had been beaten by two black men, but the beating had actually come courtesy of Cinque and Teko, with the latter wearing blackface. For many of their critics, the white SLA members' desire for communion with a black underclass and their emulation of black patterns of speech inevitably recalled Norman Mailer's 1957 essay, "The White Negro," which riffed on the tendency of marginalized cultures to become models for those alienated from the culture at large. As Mailer reasoned, two black eighteen-year-olds who had murdered the white owner of a candy store were "daring the unknown" by entering into a new relationship with police while also protesting the injustice of private property. So it was the white SLA members who used Cinque as a remonstrance against their own bourgeois privilege, as well as a license to commit acts of violence that would be politically meaningful rather than merely brutal.

While the SLA fetishized race, it struggled to downplay gender and sex difference. The SLA women attempted to craft for themselves outlaw personas divorced from bourgeois conventions of gender, which meant that they would live as equals with the male members of their team and take as many physical risks as the men, especially in situations of "combat." (The assassination of Marcus Foster was originally planned as an all-female hit, but backup gunman Cinque had to begin the action after Zoya and Fahizah froze on their triggers.)[40] Sexual exclusivity was forbidden, as was declining requests for sex from male members of the group.[41] The SLA women's preoccupation with gender and gender equality was manifest in the way that they coached Patty to respond to the press conferences held by her father and mother. It affected the way they wrote or cowrote her taped statements to her parents and the press, and the way they initially concocted (and costumed) her outlaw persona. Tania therefore became a fascinating index of the group's fantasies, since she was not only a product of the SLA's failure to force a prisoner swap, but also an opportunity to custom-design a woman outlaw to suit their revolutionary feminist ideals.

Historian William Graebner has written that among the things the SLA held out to Patty were "a variety of new, intense forms of identity, a righteous political and social agenda; membership in a small group; a shared feminism, expertise in firearms; a harder, better conditioned body; the mysteries of the underground; a deviant sexuality; a dramatically heightened level of celebrity; [and] the risks and titillations of life as a criminal."[42] Graebner's reference to a "deviant sexuality" seems a little tin-eared given Patty's status as a rape victim—albeit one who was given over to her rapists by women convinced they were freeing her from sexual oppression. But certainly Patty's "deviance" in having chosen—or in giving the *appearance* of having chosen—sexual relationships with Cinque and perhaps all the other members of the SLA became a prominent part of the outlaw tale that the SLA helped craft for her. Patty's/Tania's rejection of a genteel life, her facility with guns, and her apparent sexual liberties were intended to demonstrate how readily an individual could transform herself into someone new by adopting "a radically different gender script."[43] If managed in a disciplined enough fashion, the SLA women reasoned, such a transformation would help erode the social strictures attached to biological sex difference.

Yet the women of the SLA were never considered outside their sex, particularly as law enforcement worried over an apparent spike in female lawbreakers. In 1968, Ruth Eisemann-Schier had become the first woman on the FBI's "Most Wanted" list for her part in a ransom kidnapping. Five months later, a second woman made the list. By 1973, the list included three women, all of them student radicals. Between 1968 and 1973, arrests of women for "serious" crimes (everything from car thefts to murder) had risen 52 percent, while the same category for men had risen by only 8 percent. While some experts suggested that the increase in arrests reflected a growing willingness on the part of male police to arrest and convict women, many suspected that other factors of contemporary life were inciting women to the sorts of violent crimes that had once been the near-exclusive province of men. In the fall of 1974, *U.S. News & World Report* set out to discover why "violent crime committed by women is marching upward more than at any time since headlines of the 1930s dwelt on the exploits of such gun-wielders as 'Ma' Barker and Bonnie Parker."[44]

The allusion to two Depression-era personalities hinted that an increase in women's lawbreaking might have roots in the sorts of economic and social upheavals that had been under way when Bonnie and Ma first came to prominence. In 1974, as in 1934, birthrates had plummeted and women were remaining single longer than in previous decades. Women from both eras were incentivized into the workforce by the need to support themselves and their families in periods of economic downturn, when many marriages were breaking down. In the 1970s, as in the 1930s, "natural" roles for men and women were thought by many to be slipping away as women entered the workforce in greater numbers and again "invaded" formerly male occupations. Female workers met with pushback from ambivalent supervisors and colleagues, and another round of hand-wringing articles on what the uptick in women's employment might be doing to children and to American masculinity.

During the 1970s, the percentage of working women rose from 43.4 percent to an unprecedented 51.2 percent. For the first time in U.S. history, more women were inside the paid workforce rather than outside of it. But that slow revolution carried with it endless struggles for the rights of women to earn the same pay as their male counterparts, to ascend to managerial positions, and even to get a line of credit without a male cosigner. These and other issues fueled the liberal (and legislation-focused) branch of the women's movement that had been dominated by white, middle-class women from the early 1960s onward.[45] Liberal feminism's achievements—and its blindnesses—had also fueled activists' determination to expand the women's movement to work for a broader cross section of women (minority women, poor women, nonheterosexual women) and to push for even more drastic social reforms. In the words of a popular 1970s slogan, sisterhood was powerful. One Chicago attorney told *U.S. News & World Report* that it was obvious that feminist activism had emboldened women to lawbreaking. "This is the first decade in which large numbers of women have had their consciousness raised enough so that they feel capable of carrying out a crime," he said. In the same article, sociologist Georgette Sandler concurred that women's criminal activity might be an expression of widespread disillusionment at their rising but still frustrated expectations in the working world.[46]

On the SLA tapes, Patty insisted that she had not been drugged, brainwashed, or otherwise confused into becoming an SLA soldier. Nor, it seemed, had any of the other women who had joined the army of their own volition. Were the SLA women in thrall of a male compatriot (as Kathy Power was said to have been) or were one or more of them the manipulative queen bee within a terror cell (as Bernadine Dohrn was supposed to be)? In her 1975 book, *Sisters in Crime*, Freda Adler used the example of the SLA to argue that women's criminality was in fact rising in tandem with women's liberation and claimed that the "bizarre, tumultuous, and seemingly short-lived era of the SLA may have marked a major turning point for American women." In Adler's perspective, the formation of the SLA coincided with the peak of the women's movement, when the fervor of women's political desires provoked an explosion of violence among some high-achieving "All-American Girls." *Sisters in Crime* was one of the first criminological texts to discard the long-held theory that a woman's criminality stemmed from all that was supposed to be wrong with her biology. But antifeminists seized the book's claim of a supposed cause-and-effect relationship between women's rights and women's lawbreaking to suggest that relegating women to domestic duties was not merely a social convention—it was a matter of public safety.

Many who have tried to make sense of the Patty Hearst kidnapping have noted that it occurred just weeks after the release of a highly popular horror movie about the demonic possession of a young girl. In *The Exorcist*, a devil animates and speaks through the girl's body, until her frightened mother enlists the help of two priests to cast it out and reclaim her daughter's soul. Patty's first year with the SLA also coincided with the publication of Stephen King's breakout novel, *Carrie*, about a teenager who unleashes terrifying secret powers on the peers who were cruel to her. The themes of a "good girl" who suddenly snaps, or whose body is overtaken by a hostile power, reflected 1970s anxieties around changing gender roles. They also happened to reflect the two primary theories on what might have happened to Patty Hearst. Either Patty had been dragged off by a scary, countercultural fringe group and then "possessed" by them and made to do and say as they dictated,[47] or, as Patty maintained in her later SLA recordings, that same fringe group had disabused her of her white, bourgeois illusions, which set free her retributive inner revolutionary. Had the SLA comprised only men or men and women from less privileged backgrounds, the latter scenario might not have seemed as plausible. As it was, the tantalizing mystery of whether Patty was a victim or a convert always came down to the fact and influence of the other former "good girls" in the group.

From the outset, the SLA women's attempts to downplay gender and to assert their and Patty's equality as soldier-outlaws were roundly rejected by the press and by law enforcement. The SLA's crowing assertions of its own triumphs proved less gripping than tidbits about the SLA women's failings and the evident contradictions between who they really were and who they professed to be. Newspaper features written in the wake of the Hibernia bank robbery inevitably mentioned Camilla Hall's poetry and avowed pacifism, Patricia Soltysik's pre-SLA decision to change her name to "Mizmoon," and Nancy Ling Perry's brief career as a topless dancer. These were precisely the sorts of intriguing character incongruencies on which all future literary and cinematic accounts of the SLA would hang. Meanwhile, the FBI had also put out word that Perry (Fahizah) had a phobia of excess body hair and that Hall (Gabi) suffered from a hereditary kidney ailment that had killed all her siblings.[48] Such details might be relevant to the FBI's investigation. They also worked to reinforce the message that the SLA women were all damaged or slightly crazy.

Happy Hunting, Charles

The SLA was not the only group struggling to defend itself in the court of public opinion. The FBI's HEARNAP case files reflect the disillusionment of a public grown wary of Bureau authority and skeptical of agents' competence and intents. By the early 1970s, the FBI was hamstrung by its own image, one that had become particularly confining in the final years of J. Edgar Hoover's forty-eight-year tenure as director. Illegal programs such as COINTELPRO had grown out of Hoover's desire to maintain the Bureau's creaky image as the country's moral flagship—albeit one increasingly identified with smearing or intimidating citizens who might protest the war or organize for civil rights. As several FBI historians have noted, the public largely ignored allegations or evidence of FBI abuse before Hoover's death. After his death, the pendulum swung in the other direction and many Americans became quite receptive to the suggestion of scandals connected to the Bureau.[49] Eighty-four percent of those surveyed gave the FBI a "highly favorable" rating in a Gallup poll conducted in 1966. But public confidence in the Bureau dropped precipitously in the next decade, with approval ratings tumbling from 71 percent in 1970, to 52 percent in 1973, and to a dismal 37 percent in both 1975 and 1979.[50]

By the time Hearst was snatched from her Berkeley apartment in 1974, Hoover was two years gone. However, because the radical, racially integrated, heavily female SLA so aptly embodied the "subversive activities" that Hoover had built his Bureau against, his influence remained. The FBI's battle with Patty Hearst's abductors and eventually with Patty herself was largely symptomatic of the Bureau's internal conflicts between the loyalists who sought to preserve Hoover's legacy and the reformists working to temper or dismantle it.[51]

Under Acting Director L. Patrick Gray in 1972, agents had at last been permitted to wear colored (nonwhite) shirts and to have coffee and snacks in the office. Gray relaxed the standards for the Bureau's transfer policy, weight requirement, and daily reports. In the months immediately following Hoover's death, the FBI even began employing women as temporary agents. (Women and minority agents were not recruited to permanent appointments until 1978.) But Gray had not been in office a year before he was forced to resign for having destroyed documents in the course of the FBI's investigation of the Watergate scandal. As a result, morale in the Bureau had hit a new low by the time San Francisco's Special Agent Charles Bates was tapped to lead the SLA kidnapping case. It did not help, of course, that the Bureau seemed always to be a step behind the SLA and that Patty's taped messages grew increasingly belligerent toward the FBI. When the SLA fled to Los Angeles, they left behind a cyanide-spiked bathtub stew of documents, disguises, urine, and other slop. Just above the mess, they scrawled a mock greeting to Bates: "Happy Hunting, Charles."

Agents found few willing sources on the Berkeley scene, where they met with suspicion or open hostility. Ironically, the HEARNAP investigation was further impeded by the FBI's attempts to show a new and open face to the leery public. The SLA had come into being just as the Bureau was overcompensating for Hoover's relentless focus on the Communist Party by putting the word out that its agents were "only interested in individuals; we don't go after groups." Criticized for being too accommodating of the SLA's demands, Bates and his agency were charged by state officials with hampering worldwide efforts to combat political terrorism.[52] Bates's field office had also infuriated the Hearst family with its admission that it had failed to inform them that Patty's name had appeared on a list of potential SLA kidnapping targets that police had recovered a month before the abduction.

The widespread perception of the 1970s G-men as duplicitous, corrupt, and disorganized proved useful to the SLA on multiple levels. It fed their fantasies about becoming martyrs in a fight against a police state. It also became a central tenet in the SLA's reeducation of Patty Hearst. Cinque repeatedly warned Patty that the FBI would not regard her with any sympathy and would more likely assassinate her than rescue her. As Patricia Hearst later wrote in her memoir:

> I knew nothing about [the FBI], except for fictional accounts on television. . . . They [the SLA] told me story after story of the FBI storming radical hideouts, shooting through doors, killing everyone inside, asking no questions. The FBI could kill with impunity. They had a license to kill. And they would shoot and kill in order to wipe out radical movements in the country. But, said Cin, the SLA would not be ambushed and slaughtered like the others. The SLA would be ready to do battle with the pigs. Then I would surely die in the crossfire.[53]

In the course of their investigation, the FBI checked 50,000 tips and spot-checked or interviewed 30,000 people in the Bay Area. Some 8,500 agents, or 75 percent of the agency's field force, had at one time or another been committed to the search for Patty Hearst.[54] Paradoxically, law enforcement *prolonged* the lifespan of the SLA organization when it finally caught up with the group on May 17, 1974. On that date, the SLA's core membership perished in a deadly fire initiated by a gun battle with FBI agents and the Los Angeles police. The fierce shootout and resulting conflagration were perfectly timed for live, full-color coverage on the evening news, thanks to a brand-new generation of portable TV cameras. One of the correspondents shouted to evening viewers, "You are witnessing the biggest gunfight in the history of the West!"

From his jail cell, Joe Remiro (Bo) listened to the television coverage of the two-hour-long battle and compared it to what he had seen as an enlisted soldier in Southeast Asia. John Bryan, a former *San Francisco Chronicle* reporter, recalled his colleagues as having the same reaction: "Dozens of Namvet newscasters watched a small army of Namvet-trained cops use typical anti-VC fire-fight tactics against a holed-up band of guerrilla fighters in an epochal two-hour battle and immolation. 'It's just like Vietnam,' they said almost in chorus. 'The war has come home.'"[55] The *Chronicle's* Tim Findley later marveled that the normally savvy SLA had, for once, failed to capitalize on a media opportunity. "The SLA could have given themselves up and made a speech right there," said Findley. "They had the whole world watching them."[56]

Patty Hearst's parents were among those in the broadcast's audience, and, like most viewers, were watchful for evidence that their daughter might be trapped in the flames. Because the SLA refused to surrender, no one on the scene appeared to have any idea whether Patty might be one of the white women reportedly still firing their weapons from beneath the floorboards of the burning house. It was another twenty-four hours before the coroner's report could positively identify the two male and four female bodies pulled from the rubble after the blaze. Most were grossly disfigured by the gas masks that had fused to their faces and by the bandolier shells that had exploded in the massive heat.

Through it all, Patty—who the previous day had sprayed the front of a sporting goods store with submachine-gun fire—was hiding out in a hotel room near Disneyland with Bill and Emily Harris. She later described her terror as she witnessed six of her former SLA comrades go to their deaths in the devouring flames. All that the SLA had told her about the FBI's wrath appeared to be coming true. Weeks earlier, Cinque had rebuked those who doubted the SLA and had eerily predicted how "even in death [the SLA] will win, for the very ashes of this fascist nation will mark our very graves."

In fact, the Los Angeles fire evoked more sympathy for the SLA at Berkeley than had ever been shown to them before. True, police had repeatedly urged the SLA to give themselves up, and the SLA had responded by firing almost four thousand rounds into a residential neighborhood. But the image of the doomed SLA soldiers resisting surrender and grimly fighting to the end made villains of the police, who had greatly outnumbered the SLA and who were accused by some of using excess force. The FBI was also criticized anew for having consented to the shootout and for permitting the SLA-occupied house to burn to the ground. In June, friends of Angela Atwood organized a memorial service in honor of her and her fallen SLA comrades. From a nearby building, FBI agents filmed memorial participants as they conferred on the dead the blessings of the righteous outlaw. The event eventually produced the second-team SLA, which helped conceal Patty and the Harrises for another sixteen months. The three remnants of the original SLA released a final tape, in which Patty/Tania declared, "I died in that fire." Her outlaw mystique now stronger than ever for having pulled the television-assisted trick of a death without dying, Patty eulogized each of her former SLA comrades.

> Gelina was beautiful. Fire and joy. She exploded with the desire to kill the pigs . . .
>
> Gabi crouched low with her ass to the ground. She practiced until her shotgun was an extension of her right and left arms, an impulse, a tool of survival . . . Zoya wanted to give meaning to her name and on her birthday she did. Zoya, female guerrilla, perfect love and perfect hate reflected in stone-cold eyes . . . Fahizah was a beautiful sister who didn't talk much but who was the teacher of many by her righteous example. She, more than any other, had come to understand and conquer the putrid disease of bourgeois mentality . . .
>
> Cinque loved the people with tenderness and respect. They listened to him when he talked because they knew that his love reflected the truth and the future.

In a move that came back to haunt her, Patty also claimed to have discovered true love with Cujo, "the gentlest, most beautiful man I've ever known." Their relationship was based on their "commitment to the struggle and our love for the people," she said. "I was ripped off by the pigs when they murdered Cujo, ripped off in the same way that thousands of sisters and brothers in this fascist country have been ripped off of people they love. We mourn together and the sound of gunfire becomes sweeter."[57]

The Trial of Patty Hearst

In its rumination on the surprising success of *Bonnie and Clyde*, *Time* magazine proposed that the first generation to have grown up with television were experiencing the world differently than their parents and grandparents.[58] "Television's abrupt leap from news about Viet Nam to *Gomer Pyle* to toothpaste ads expands people's vision," observed a former television director quoted in the article.[59] *Time* hypothesized that younger citizens had grown comfortable with the "sudden shifts of reality" that were becoming a staple of the new media age. The SLA had certainly grown up with television, and they compulsively tracked their own celebrity on the radio and television that they kept on all day. Patty later recalled how excitedly they flipped the dials to catch every possible mention of their exploits.[60] The *San Francisco Chronicle*'s Jerry Belcher and Don West credited the SLA with having "provided the nation's newscasters with a magic formula: the beautiful, pampered princess stolen away by evil forces. And the media pulled out all stops in reporting on her plight."[61]

But the princess-in-peril story was too simple a narrative for whatever had happened to—or perhaps been chosen by?—Patty Hearst between the night of her kidnapping in February 1974 and the day the FBI finally burst into her San Francisco apartment in September 1975. She had deployed a weapon to free Bill and Emily Harris when the former was hassled for shoplifting. She had crisscrossed the country with minimal supervision and had spent a long season with the Harrises in a remote Pennsylvania farmhouse, where, by her own account, she spent her days walking and jogging alone. As prosecutors in Patty's trial later emphasized, Patty had never once attempted to get word to her parents, or to anyone in the outside world, despite having become remarkably adroit with firearms (as a result of the SLA's training) and having been left in situations where it should have been easy for her to escape. In their chronicle of the SLA, Les Payne and Tim Findley deduced that the kidnapped Patty had found herself "caught up in the guns and planning, the love, the sex . . . Patty the soft, pale heiress would become Tania, the tough gun moll."[62]

Patty's turn as an outlaw depended on the "sudden shifts of reality" that made her a sort of Rorschach test for the press, the FBI, and her various publics. Although she had repeatedly been a mouthpiece for the SLA's politics, and although her "Tania" had been modeled on a Latin American revolutionary, most audiences brushed aside the long-winded SLA rhetoric to interpret Patty either as a modern-day "gun moll" or as the tragic heroine of a soap opera plot. Janey Jiminez, who guarded Patty Hearst during her trial, recalled having built up a mental image of Patty as "a hard-swearing, gum-chewing lady bandit out of *Bonnie and Clyde*." Instead, her prisoner had turned out to be "about as threatening as a baby rabbit." The emaciated child-woman Patty "could never be drawn into a bank hold-up simply because she was turned on by the 'romance' of the idea," Jiminez insisted. "That's too loony—Okay for *Bonnie and Clyde* or an episode in 'Kojak,' but not for Patty Hearst."[63]

But Patty had consented—or perhaps been coerced?—to collude with the second-team SLA in their haphazard efforts to revive the first team's revolution in 1975. With Patty driving the getaway cars, the new, all-white SLA at first tried quietly robbing banks without announcing who they were. But their hit on the Crocker National Bank turned tragic when the SLA's Emily Harris accidentally shot Myrna Opsahl, a forty-two-year-old mother of four who had been in the bank to deposit her church's collection monies. Opsahl was raced to a nearby hospital and expired in the operating room, where her husband happened to be the surgeon on duty. Because the second-team SLA had not identified themselves, it was years before the murder caught up with them. They switched tactics and began plotting to blow up police cruisers with homemade pipe bombs.

The FBI stormed Patty's apartment on the same day that they had pounced on Bill and Emily Harris while the couple was out on their daily jog. Most of the rest of the second-team SLA had managed to skip town, but the arrests were still a victory for Special Agent Bates. As Patty later wrote in her memoir: "The FBI, after having been the laughingstock of the radical left, and much of the press and public, had won out in the end." At the moment of the raid, Patty first wet her pants out of fright and then tried to emulate recent press pictures of the captured fugitive Susan Saxe. As agents pulled up alongside the San Francisco Federal Building, Patty smiled broadly at the horde of reporters and photographers who had gathered outside. From the backseat of the agents' vehicle, she raised a clenched fist in salute. Writing in 1982, Patty explained her actions as a result of her SLA conditioning. "This is how I'm supposed to act now, I thought. Those pictures would show me being taken off to a fascist concentration camp, like a true revolutionary. I had a role to play and I knew my part well."[64] She continued to play that role as she was processed at FBI headquarters by the federal clerk. Asked to state her profession, Patty laughingly responded: "Urban guerilla." Like her subversive power salute, this flippant answer immediately was reported in newspapers and on television news programs around the country.

Patty's September 19 arrest made headlines in what was to be a busy month for gun-wielding women radicals. Twenty-six-year-old Lynette "Squeaky" Fromme had been arrested on September 5 for the attempted assassination of President Gerald Ford. Fromme had been another middle-class white girl from Santa Monica, California, before taking up with Charles Manson in 1967. On September 22, forty-five-year-old Sara Jane Moore, a much-married aspiring revolutionary and occasional FBI informant, made her own failed attempt on President Ford's life. Neither Fromme nor Moore ever ascended to the same prominence as Patty Hearst, but their stories helped amplify the suggestion that she was another deranged female opportunist, equal parts scary and pathetic. Shortly after her show of defiance at the Federal Building, Patty pled "not guilty" to charges of armed robbery and of having used a firearm to commit a felony at the Hibernia Bank. Her lawyers convinced her to sign a statement that said, in essence, that her many weeks in a closet had left her insane.

A week after Patty's arrest, the FBI released a partial transcript of her conversation with a childhood friend, Trish Tobin, who had come to visit Patty in prison. During the conversation, Patty had cursed freely and told Tobin, "My politics are real different from way back when." She said she hoped she might be released on bail, so she could issue a personal statement from a "revolutionary feminist perspective." The "Tobin transcript" proved damaging to Patty's trial and to her reputation. By the spring of 1976, a Mervin Field poll showed that 68 percent of Californians wanted her to do prison time if found guilty. Two-thirds believed she had joined the SLA of her own volition and had not been forced to make any of the audiotapes. Almost half thought it likely that she had colluded with the SLA to plan her own abduction.

Jiminez argued that Patty confounded most Americans, who would have preferred her to behave like a victim, or at least as a compelling heroine for her own story. Stony-faced in her daily jaunts to and from the courthouse, Patty did not match any of the prevailing options for women in the spotlight and so became an object of resentment for all sides. As Jiminez wrote,

> She wasn't a cheery working girl like Doris Day or Mary Tyler Moore; not a bereaved widow (Jackie Kennedy Onassis) or a loyally suffering wife (Pat Nixon); nor was she a sunny hoyden with a heart of gold (Shirley MacLaine). The leftists denounced her as a traitorous publicity hound; the squares said she should be disowned by her parents. She

even inherited some of the anger left over from the pardoning of Richard Nixon.[65]

Had Patty publicly expressed her gratitude to the FBI or some remorse for her actions, she may have fared better in her trial. Although she had been reluctant to go on the stand, her attorney, F. Lee Bailey, insisted that she testify anyway. On his advice, she took the Fifth Amendment forty-two times to avoid answering questions about her activities with the SLA. State Attorney James Browning made good on his promise to decimate her defense. He reminded the jury that Patty had not exploited opportunities to escape or to contact family members. He showed them enlarged stills from the Hibernia bank security camera, which supposedly showed Patty cursing at bank customers. He punched holes in the brainwashing theory by drawing attention to the five other white, upper-middle-class young women who had joined the SLA of their own free will. Why then could Patty Hearst not have done the same?

Finally, Browning called into doubt Patty's claims to having been sexually assaulted, by repeating what she had said on tape about her love for Cujo/Willie Wolfe. In a rare show of emotion on the stand, Patty spat that she "couldn't stand" Cujo and had only read those words at the insistence of the Harrises. Yet, on the day of her FBI capture, Patty still had in her possession a carved monkey necklace that Cujo had given her. Cujo himself had worn a similar amulet, which had been recovered from beneath his dead body in Los Angeles. "She couldn't stand him," Browning noted sarcastically in his closing argument. "And yet there is that little stone [monkey] face that can't say anything; I submit to you that it can tell us a lot."

The trial of Patty Hearst began on February 4, 1976—precisely two years to the day of her SLA abduction. In those twenty-four months, she had been featured on five *Newsweek* covers. In March 1976, she appeared on her sixth and seventh. The last of these showed a close-up of Hearst's face with "GUILTY" stamped across her forehead in bold letters. One female juror later told the press that Browning's monkey necklace argument had been essential to their verdict. "That was what changed my mind," said the juror. "I really saw how much she was lying. It just had to be lying, through and through."

In the years after her trial, Patty attempted the type of image rehabilitation that she had left to her legal team in the months after her arrest. First in magazine interviews and later in *Every Secret Thing*, Patty retold the story of her captivity, emphasizing how fearful she had been of both the SLA and the FBI. She characterized herself as having been exploited by both organizations, as in this recounting of the notorious "Tania" photo shoot: "The [SLA] girls brought out what seemed like combat fatigues and Fahizah put her beret on my head, cocked to one side, and they handed me a sawed-off M-1 carbine to hold as I posed. Then Cin got the idea of tying a rifle scope to the carbine to make it look more awesome and to confuse the authorities." According to Patty, she had been present only in body for her SLA "coming out" party. The SLA posed and prepped her like a mannequin, but she was still the same Patty inside:

> Zoya aimed a Polaroid camera at me, as Teko tried to push me into the proper belligerent pose. "Look really mean," someone told me.
> "Bend your legs more."
> "Smile a little, not too much."
> "Get into a shooting stance . . . make like you're goin' to shoot someone . . . crouch . . ."
> I did not like it one bit, being used like that.[66]

Patty also accused the FBI of conspiring to frame her, figuratively and literally, by cropping the edges of the bank security camera images. The stills shown in court had omitted evidence that the other SLA members' guns had been pointed directly at her throughout the robbery.[67]

In her memoir, Patty never fully consents to the idea that she might have been brainwashed or have suffered from Stockholm syndrome, in which a kidnapping victim develops warm feelings for her captors. Instead, she describes herself as having learned to agree with the SLA and acquiesce to all their demands as a strategy for self-defense. When Gelina arranges for Cujo and later Cinque to have sex with Patty in her closet while the other SLA members sit and listen nearby, Patty is humiliated but reminds herself, "You're still alive." Convinced that she has been abandoned by her parents and the FBI, she adopts a tactic of mental discipline fed by resignation. She will neither feel nor think, but only do what she is told: "There was no point objecting anymore, not even in my thoughts. I would have to do anything they wanted in order to survive."[68]

By the time the SLA entrusted her with guns and ammunition, Patty claims she had suppressed her true feelings for too long to have any grip on reality. Left all alone in the SLA van, she botches a perfect chance for escape. As Bill and Emily Harris squabble with a store security guard who has already snapped a handcuff on Bill, Patty reflexively fires her weapon over their heads "like Pavlov's salivating dog," responding to a much-rehearsed cue. Narrating the experience from the future, Patty cannot resist granting herself a flicker of clarity before she reverts to her role as a robot for the SLA:

> All during the training I had never quite believed that it was for real. I had thought it was all a game of some sort, a make-believe designed by these people whom I had to humor in order to win their approval and stay alive . . . That flash of insight into what I had done and the significance of it was at the time but a brief glimpse of reality, like a sudden streak of sunlight through a hole in dark, rolling cumulus clouds, there one instant and gone the next.[69]

The Ambiguous Outlaw

In 1979, President Jimmy Carter conditionally commuted Hearst's seven-year prison sentence on the grounds that she likely would not have broken the law were it not for her degrading experience at the hands of the FBI. The kidnapping, trial, and twenty-two months in prison had eaten up five years of her life. She married her bodyguard and moved with him to Connecticut, where they live quietly to this day.

In a 1974 interview, the Hearst family cook told *Ladies Home Journal* that it would have been best had Patty died in the Los Angeles "holocaust." Doing so, the cook explained, would have transformed Patty into a "modern Joan of Arc . . . cleansing herself of the sin of having disgraced her parents."[70] Fred Soltysik, older brother to the SLA's Patricia Soltysik (Zoya), wished instead for Patty's safe return, dubbing her "the SLA's own Persephone." Patty had been taken in winter but would be released (the elder Soltysik had hoped) by spring.[71] Of course, carrying the Persephone metaphor to its logical conclusion implied that Patty, having had a taste of hell's pomegranate seeds, would never be fully free of that underworld and would in fact be obliged to keep returning to it.

So, too, in a fashion, would the FBI. A few weeks after the commutation, ABC rushed to broadcast its television movie *The Ordeal of Patty Hearst*. A retelling of Patty's kidnapping, the drama unfolds mainly from the perspective of the soon-to-retire Agent Charles Bates (Dennis Weaver). A widower with a teenaged daughter of his own, Bates is a dedicated, no-nonsense G-man hero in the old mold. Much of the dialogue is set up to demonstrate the passing of a taciturn, paternal style of leadership that is nowhere in evidence in the young males of the 1970s. Bates is an honorable, hardworking foil to the dissolute and rapacious SLA men. Patty's father, Randolph, dresses down her whiny boyfriend, Steven Weed, for "go[ing] to pieces every time somebody puts a camera on you." Meanwhile, the menacing SLA women provide a shadowy enemy to all mankind, swapping lesbian love poems and promising Patty that Bates and his agents were planning to "splatter you around the room."

As Patty, actress Lisa Eilbacher does not have much to do besides act petrified. She says little but cringes and weeps each of the multiple times that she is shown on the verge of another sexual assault. Back at FBI head-quarters, Bates exhorts the cynical younger agents to remember that they are in a "race for this girl's life." He maintains that Patty is still innocent until proven guilty, even after the local police have turned against her. (The police review the Hibernia bank tape and declare Patty a turncoat because "I'll tell you what, Captain—she's not crying.")

As the case stretches on, Bates faces the threat of mandatory retire-ment and the opprobrium of being the agent who "can't even catch Patty Hearst." In a candid exchange with his daughter, he complains that the FBI has become a laughingstock, and she gently informs him that the FBI may need to adapt with the times:

Bates: In the old days, people used to believe in the FBI. They used to call us. They used to help us. This younger generation, they seem to think *we're* the criminals. How are we supposed to find the SLA if young people won't talk to us? . . .

Becky: Dad, the kids at school have a saying. "Different strokes for different folks." See, kids nowadays need to do their own thing. Maybe things aren't right the way they are.

Bates: You're agreeing with the SLA, are you?

Becky: No. All I'm saying is that things change.

After months of humiliation and a scuffle with the jaded, new Bureau leadership in D.C., Bates finally gets his moment of glory. To the pace of a quickening soundtrack, he and his agents doggedly piece together the slim-mest of clues to apprehend Patty and the Harrises. Bates arranges for Patty to be brought to him, expecting that she will express thanks. He greets her heartily ("I'm Charlie Bates, Miss Hearst. I rather imagine that you're glad that this is all over!"), but she is silent and expressionless, her eyes a creepy blank. Bates's smile fades as it dawns on him that the FBI has failed Patty Hearst. The final credits note that the real Bates retired shortly after the close of the HEARNAP case and that he had written letters in support of the suspension of Patty's prison sentence.

Patricia Hearst's 1982 memoir, *Every Secret Thing*, took its title from a verse in Ecclesiastes: "For God shall bring every work into judgment, with every secret thing, whether it be good, or whether it be evil."[72] In 1988, the book was reissued as *Patty Hearst: Her Own Story*, just in time for the release of the movie it had inspired. Paul Schrader's *Patty Hearst* is entirely sympathetic to its subject, who is both hostage and plaything for a band of violent paranoiacs. From the moment she is taken, thrashing and screaming, from her Berkeley apartment, Patty (Natasha Richardson) is certain that her death is imminent. When the SLA toss her in a car trunk, she thinks she is being buried alive. For the rest of the film, Patty's mental images will continue to intrude meaningfully on the action, as in the moments when she envisions the FBI breaking into the SLA safe house with rifles drawn. When Cinque offers her the choice either to join the SLA or to return home, Patty's mind flashes repeatedly to the image of her dead body being flung into an earthen grave. We also see the neck of a wine bottle that Cinque taps on Patty's thigh, an unmistakable symbol of the sexual brutality that will be her punishment for a wrong answer. As in the memoir, Patty embraces a practical form of "live burial," smothering her impulses to be anything but a puppet for the SLA.

In Schrader's film, the SLA are precisely the deluded, broken people that *Every Secret Thing* made them out to be. The one exception is sunny Angela Atwood (Dana Delany), but even she is a victim of her devotion to the egomaniacal Cinque (Ving Rhames). As happened in *The Ordeal of Patty Hearst*, Fahizah (Olivia Barash) rants about her hatred for her furniture-salesman father and her relief at having escaped her putrid, bourgeois upbringing. Cujo (Pete Kowanko) is a fat-faced man-child who talks incessantly of killing pigs and of dying for the revolution. He is smitten with Patty, who shudders at his wish that they might go down in history together as lover-revolutionaries. Throughout the film, Patty is tormented by the Harrises, especially Emily (Frances Fisher), who cackles at Patty's observation that the public seems to hate her. "Yes, but they *love* to hate you," Emily retorts.

Emily's "Yolanda" is at once the best and the worst SLA sister. She is the most vocal about women's equality, and her villainy sometimes turns on this commitment. At one point, Patty inadvertently embarrasses Emily when she catches her singing sweetly and kneading bread in the safe house kitchen. Furious at her humiliating lapse into domesticity, Emily snaps that *she* will lead the next SLA action, whereupon the film cuts to Emily gunning down a female bank customer. Myrna Opsahl is not named, but viewers familiar with the case could deduce for themselves that Emily's crackpot feminism had led her to extract vengeance on a "traditional" mother and homemaker. (In *The Ordeal of Patty Hearst*, the murdered bank customer is a visibly pregnant woman, a likely allusion to reports that another of the SLA women had kicked a pregnant teller in the abdomen, causing her to abort.)

Following Patty's arrest, several lawyers sit around a table discussing her fate. Dismissing the possibility of a plea bargain on the grounds that "the public wouldn't stand for it," they argue over whether Patty is a symptom or a scapegoat of an era. Patty's attorney, F. Lee Bailey, has a pointed exchange with Prosecutor Browning:

Bailey: How are you going to get a fair jury? In the sixties, every parent sent their nice normal kid off to college and bingo! It was like the kid got kidnapped by the counterculture. Turned into a commie and said "screw you" to society and his parents. Lived in a commune and had free sex with negroes and homosexuals.

Browning: So?

Bailey: So, they think Patty did the same thing.

Browning: Didn't she?

Once she is in custody, Patty's troubles have only just begun. She writhes and cries during an examination by an unsympathetic OB-GYN and sighs at the prurient male psychiatrist who repeatedly asks if she witnessed any "lesbian activity." One of the psychiatrists, a specialist in lie detection, tells Patty he is convinced she is telling the truth precisely because she has not tried to make her story more favorable for herself. "A very strong man under similar conditions would have just curled up and died," he tells her. "Is that supposed to make me feel better?" Patty sardonically replies.

Patty Hearst made its debut at the Cannes Film Festival. It was not a box office sensation, but it did gross well over a million dollars during its international run in the fall of 1988. In his *New York Times* review, film critic Vincent Canby warned American audiences that Schrader's film "doesn't make for the kind of neat movie in which one immediately knows how one is supposed to respond. . . . Instead, the movie makes scary demands on the audience."[73] The same could be said of the entire saga of Patty Hearst.

In fact, Schrader's film departs significantly from Hearst's memoir in its conclusion, which imagines an uncharacteristically forceful Patty having a frank talk with her father in a prison waiting room. She tells him of her plans to lobby for a presidential pardon and says that the real reason that she is in prison is for the crime of having survived her captivity. That was her one mistake, she says, because it had been "emotionally messy" for the general public. "People fantasized me for so long they thought they knew me. When I finally surfaced—a real person, a real story—I was inconvenient. But I'm here, and I'll let them know it, too. I made it worse, hiding from the press. I let people keep their fantasies." Schrader insisted that Patty had to deliver a defiant speech at the film's end because "people can't watch a movie about a character who does nothing."[74] Ironically, the real Patricia Hearst insisted that her survival had everything to do with "nothing." Doing nothing (to offend her captors). *Being* nothing (except what others wanted her to be). Surviving her captivity indeed had been a problem for Patty, who technically violated the rule that "the outlaw must die." In repudiating "Tania" as the expression of a desire not her own, Patty retreated into a characteristic blankness or ambiguity that would, at times, cause injury to her reputation. But remaining an enigma has more often been an asset to Patricia Hearst, even as it bewilders the filmmakers and federal law enforcers who have tried to make meaning from her case.

While helping to promote *Patty Hearst*, Patricia Hearst (she insisted on shedding the "Patty" as soon as she left prison) praised the film but admitted she found Schrader's tacked-on resolution "dishonest." Unlike her on-screen double, Hearst has never vowed "to let people see the real me, to demystify myself." Her post-SLA strategy for survival—the one that has served her well—is better reflected in *Patty Hearst*'s final line: "Pardon my French, Dad, but fuck 'em. Fuck 'em all."

5

Panther, Prisoner, Poet, and Prize

As Joanne "Joey" Byron, she was a precocious, teenaged runaway, navigating New York City and her burgeoning social consciousness as a child of the civil rights era. As Joanne Chesimard, she worked for the Black Panther Party until she became fed up with the Party's internecine disputes. In 1971, she went underground, abetted by a host of aliases and the suspicion that the "whole Black community [was] on the FBI's Most Wanted list."[1] As Joanne Deborah Chesimard, alias Assata Shakur, she has remained one of the FBI's most wanted for over three decades.

Today, Assata Shakur is a fugitive, the subject of two hagiographic "documentaries," and (to some) an outlaw-hero whose significance is continually evolving in relation to local and world politics. But in 1971, many residents of New York would have known Assata/Chesimard as an alleged bank robber for the BLA, or Black Liberation Army. By 1973, the former deputy commissioner of the NYPD, Robert Daley, had dubbed Assata the "soul of the gang" and the BLA's "mother hen, who kept them moving, kept them shooting."[2]

Assata would maintain that her high profile in this period had everything to do with her gender. As she observed in a 1973 radio broadcast, "I am a Black revolutionary woman, and because of this I have been charged with and accused of every alleged crime in which a woman was believed to have participated. The alleged crimes in which only men were supposedly involved, I have been accused of planning."[3] Assata's story inevitably fore-grounds the different assumptions and assigned meanings that surround the outlaw of color.[4] It also reiterates the difficulty of the outlaw who "breaks the rules" of a conventional outlawry by growing old.

Technically, Assata first chose the path of the outlaw while in her early twenties, as a result of her Panther activities in Harlem. But this was a still largely anonymous and local brand of outlawry, and one then predicated (at least by her own account) more on rhetoric and populist programs than on flouting the law. Her outlawry deepened when she joined forces with the BLA, a black nationalist-Marxist organization that declared its intent to take up arms for the liberation and self-determination of black people in the United States. Because of its explicit embrace of violent and ille-gal means of protest, the membership and organization of the BLA were shrouded in secrecy. Like the SLA it helped inspire, the BLA's clandestine activities were also a reaction to the extreme paranoia bred by the FBI's COINTELPRO program and the Bureau's successful infiltration of the Black Panthers and other New Left groups.

Assata was undoubtedly surveilled by COINTELPRO in her years as a Panther. After becoming an associate of the BLA, she became a focus of the Bureau's NEWKILL and CHESROB investigations into the murder of several New York City police officers. Meanwhile, surveillance photos from an apparent BLA holdup of a Queens borough bank were enlarged into wanted posters, and these were hung in subways across the city. "Joanne Chesimard" was the only woman on the posters and the only suspect iden-tified by name.[5] Although a jury later ruled that she was not the woman in the photo, Assata's reputation as the leader of New York's BLA grew.

After Assata's capture in May 1973, the *New York Daily News* summed up the twenty-five-year-old's career this way: "In a 15-month period, Chesi-mard's criminal reputation exceeded such female felons as Bonnie Parker and Ma Barker. She became the most wanted woman in New York City history."[6] To compare Assata with two white, Depression-era outlaws who had lived and died in the middle- and southwestern plains may initially seem odd. But the analogy was apt. Just a few years prior, both Bonnie and Ma had been reanimated via the latest cinematic interpretations of their legends. Like Assata, they were—or were made out to be—women who not only had consorted with outlaw men but were those men's equals or betters in using violence to get what they wanted. Like Assata, Bonnie and Ma loathed the police and the privileged classes, or at least became synonymous with that loathing. Thus, like Assata, they became figures of political fantasy and social unease—upending gender and class hierarchies, and, especially after their deaths, becoming sites of the possible, the pleasurable, and the taboo. Taken together, the myths that accumulated around Bonnie and Ma represented the spectrum of potential for an outlaw like Assata: she might be read either as the sexually appealing icon of a righteous counterculture or as an irrational, cop-killing monster.

In the course of her lifetime, Assata Shakur/Joanne Chesimard has occupied both of those fantasies and dozens of others in between. By the 1970s, the FBI was collaborating with local police on the Joint Terrorist Task Force (JTTF), which, among other efforts, was invested in enhancing Assata's negative image through campaigns such as the subway wanted posters.[7] Like Bonnie and Ma, she owed her reputation as an antihero to Bureau interventions designed to tamp down her appeal. (Along with the Weathermen's Bernadine Dohrn, she was one of the last women ever sought by J. Edgar Hoover before his death in the spring of 1972.) Also like Bonnie and Ma, Assata was highly self-conscious and attentive to her public audience, whom she addressed through the savvy distribution of her speeches, biographical details, and poetry.

Of course, Assata Shakur is also quite *unlike* Bonnie Parker and Ma Barker, neither of whom ever wished for the dismantling or reform of the capitalist system that drove them to criminal acts. Like the women of the SLA, Assata was more explicitly political, and so her story was far less adaptable to mainstream commercial entertainments. As a black woman whose outlawry arose from a desire for racial and economic justice and the violent redress of oppressive government actions, her reputation more closely parallels those of such "outlaws" as Harriet Tubman and Angela Davis, symbols of how women marked as racial minorities have historically been both more impacted by the U.S. criminal justice system and more outside of its protections.[8] Far more than for any of the white women outlaws in this book, Assata's outlawry is complicated by the intersection of her gender and her race. These were the lenses through which all of Assata's actions have been interpreted, even—and most self-consciously—by herself.

Telling the Story of Assata

Most accounts of Assata's life, including her own autobiography, begin with her capture by the New Jersey State Police, when she and two compatriots were stopped by police just after midnight on May 2, 1973.[9] The details of this encounter are still in bitter dispute. What is clear is that the traffic stop turned into a shootout, by the end of which one New Jersey state trooper and one of the car's occupants, another former Black Panther, had both been shot dead. Assata was shot twice, with one of the bullets shattering her clavicle and another dropping into her chest cavity and lodging near her heart. In the next six years, years in which Patty Hearst was famously kidnapped and then found guilty for her involvement in SLA activities, Assata spent most of her time in prison, awaiting multiple trials for her alleged role in two New York City bank robberies and a kidnapping.[10] She was brought up on eight different sets of criminal charges, only four of which went to trial. But it was during one such trial that a judge banished Assata and her male codefendant from his courtroom for their deliberately disruptive behavior. Held together in isolation, they conceived a daughter, whom Assata delivered while in prison. Pregnancy-related health concerns, plus the scandal of the prisoner having become an expectant mother, forced the postponement of Assata's trial in connection with the New Jersey trooper's death. She would not be tried for events connected to the 1973 traffic stop until 1977, when she was convicted as an accomplice in both deaths. For her role as accomplice, she received New Jersey's mandatory life sentence, plus twenty-six to thirty-three years in prison.[11] Yet, to this day, the official records of the U.S. Congress, the FBI, and the state of New Jersey all insist that Assata was *directly* responsible for the trooper's death. Her allies, of course, vehemently deny that Assata was in any way responsible for the murder, citing expert testimony that claimed she had not fired a gun that evening, as well as physical evidence that she had been shot with her arms raised in surrender.

In November 1979, a small band of supporters successfully conspired to help Assata escape prison in full daylight and slip "underground." On the first anniversary of her escape, Assata released a taped message "From Somewhere in the World," in which she decried acts of white supremacist violence that had occurred in the twelve months since her prison break. Posters defiantly professing that "ASSATA IS WELCOME HERE" turned up in sympathetic New York City neighborhoods. For the next five years, Assata remained in hiding until she was granted political asylum in Cuba.

It was in these elements of theater and daring (the prison break, the disembodied communiqué, the prolonged evasion of the FBI and police), and *not* as a direct result of the 1972 Turnpike shootout, that Assata's outlawry ascended to the level of myth. One day after her prison break, she made the FBI's "Most Wanted" list. With the publication of her self-titled 1987 autobiography—a lyrical rumination on her experiences in prison and on the racism that affected her childhood and choices—Assata achieved one of the most effective examples of outlaw talkback to state and federal law enforcement. Living at such a short remove from the United States, but protected as a political refugee by Fidel Castro, Shakur was ideally positioned, geographically and otherwise, to become a larger-than-life political symbol and fantasy.

Any study of Assata Shakur/Joanne Chesimard requires an understanding of her years on trial and in prison, as well as the heightened racial tensions and mounting paranoia toward (and *within*) law enforcement institutions of the 1970s. To comprehend Assata as a female outlaw who became iconic when she made the FBI's "Most Wanted" list also requires an understanding of the mythologies that have surrounded her in the decades hence. As is typical for a celebrity outlaw—and for the woman outlaw, in particular—Assata's fame hinges on the perpetual convolution of her story, which is to say, the inability of anyone to produce a definitive account of the events that led to the two Turnpike deaths and her arrest. Had there been more or better witnesses to determine who shot whom that night, the story would have ended there, a tragic footnote to the era's tensions. Instead, in the ensuing decades, an intricate set of circumstances has only grown more complex. One thing is certain: Assata/Joanne became a symbol of injustice. But whether she represents the injustice of a racist police brutality or the injustice of an unrepentant, escaped convict remains a source of protracted controversy.

The 1968 trial of Black Panther Party founder Huey Newton for the killing of a white police officer invigorated the original Black Panther movement, even as it intensified the FBI's resolve to destroy the Panthers. In similar fashion, Assata/Joanne became a uniquely polarizing outlaw—and one who has subsequently been used both by the radical left *and* by state and federal police. Like Newton and even Patty Hearst before her, the real-life Assata risks falling short of the imaginative projections of both her admirers and detractors. The reason for this is simple: Assata is still alive. The ways she narrates her life and its meaning have inevitably evolved in the years since May 1973, when she was just twenty-five.

The Outlaw Invents Herself

Assata's self-narration has also evolved since the 1987 release of *Assata: An Autobiography*, an accessible and dramatic text that has been a popular bestseller for the Independent Publishers Group for over two decades. (The Independent Publishers Group still sells 8,000 to 9,000 copies of *Assata* each year.)[12] Lawrence Hill's decision to publish the book met with howls of protest from the New Jersey State Police, as did the book's fairly positive critical reception. Authorities' concern over the book was justified. Not only did the autobiography represent an official thumb-of-the-nose at the state by the former prisoner, it also guaranteed that many of those too young to remember the Black Liberation Army would get to know Assata as "Assata" rather than Joanne. The book's title reflects a deliberate split from Assata's "slave name" and former self. It erases the woman who became infamous in New York and New Jersey while also elevating Assata to the ranks of those who are so prominent as to go by a single name.

Assata's recounting of her life swings back and forth between the miserable conditions of prison and her precocious childhood. The racism she encountered at her grandparents' home in South Carolina and as an adolescent in New York City makes the trajectory of her life from middle-class black child to member of the BLA seem almost inevitable. As a political biography, *Assata* becomes an opportunity for its author to reinvent herself and to offer up her personal life as the basis for transformative political action.[13]

The coming-of-age Assata is supremely confident, if also prone to moments of self-criticism that are meant to be instructive to her readers. She has star quality, twinkling with an energy and audacity that alternately charm and infuriate those around her.[14] The young woman who emerges in Assata's autobiography is much like the fonder portraits of the girl Bonnie Parker: she is the precocious child of permanently hard times. She is theatrical, sensitive, and bright. She also dabbles in poetry. Most of Assata's chapters conclude with her own blank-verse poems, which express her personal and political convictions about a particular event. Assata's grown-up politics (or middle 1980s politics) are everywhere in evidence throughout the narrative. Her refusal to capitalize the first letter of proper names (e.g., u.s., new jersey, leavenworth) and her deliberate substitution of the Germanic "k" for the letter "c" in her references to "kourt" and "amerika" are meant to subvert the authority of those institutions she wants to reveal as racist and oppressive. Meanwhile, her book's consistent lowercased rendering of the first-person pronoun, "i," is a marker of humility, a political gesture to signal an understanding that she does not regard herself as more important than anyone else.[15]

Although Assata strongly identified with the aims of the Black Panther Party (BPP), she was reluctant to become an official Party member.[16] In her book, she ascribes to herself a moment of courage in explaining this reluctance to the Oakland Panthers, whom she visited in the summer of 1970. ("It was hard for me to say it because i felt so much love and respect for the sisters and brothers seated there, but i knew i'd hate myself if i didn't say what was on my mind."[17]) The anecdote becomes a tribute both to her own candor and to the rationality of the Panthers, who listened to Assata's criticism of the New York BPP's "arrogant, fuck-you style" and pledged immediate reforms.

Assata opens the chapter on her California summer with two seemingly unrelated recollections. The first describes her fury at the assassination of Martin Luther King ("I'm tired of bulletins. I want bullets.").[18] The second distills into one paragraph her short-lived marriage to her fellow City College of New York student-activist, Louis Chesimard. King's murder and Assata's divorce pushed her toward Berkeley, "where everything was happening," and where she would make a study of radical politics and urban guerrilla warfare. In the weeks that she lived in the Bay Area, Jonathan Jackson, the seventeen-year-old brother of the incarcerated Panther author George Jackson, stormed a Marin County courthouse with an automatic weapon and took five hostages in an attempt to free his brother.[19] By Assata's account, it was Jonathan's earnest, but suicidal, mission that ultimately galvanized her to become a Panther. His funeral becomes for her a moment of epiphany: "What kind of rage, what kind of oppression, and what kind of country shaped that young man? I felt guilt for being alive and well. Where was my gun? And where was my courage?"[20]

In the wake of the Marin courthouse incident, Angela Davis was charged with murder because some of the guns used by the younger Jackson and his accomplices were registered to her. Expressing her admiration for (the ultimately acquitted) Davis, on whom Assata had been keeping "clippings,"[21] Assata writes,

> We were very glad they hadn't caught [Davis]. I hoped they never would. The air was charged, everything was happening so fast, and I wasn't blind anymore. I was seeing things straight, seeing them more clearly than ever before . . . Of all the things i had wanted to be when i was a little girl, a revolutionary certainly wasn't one of them. And now it was the only thing that i wanted to do.[22]

She describes traveling home with a single, burning goal, "to struggle on a full-time basis."

Back in New York City, Assata officially joined the BPP, to which she was immediately valuable for her office skills and her connection to a college campus. Elated by her work for the Free Breakfast Program and the Afrocentric Saturday Liberation School, she was less pleased with her duties as a defense committee fund-raiser at the white support groups.[23] As she recalls her participation in these events:

> I was the perfect angry Panther. I hated standing around while all these white people asked me to explain myself, my existence. I became a master of the one-line answer.
>
> "What made you become a Panther?"
>
> "Oppression."
>
> "What do you think about Huey Newton?"
>
> "He's a right-on Black revolutionary leader."
>
> "What do you think white people should be doing?"
>
> "Organizing other white people in their communities, supporting Black and Third World liberation struggles, and helping to free the Panther 21."
>
> Once a guy asked if I was really going to off the pigs.
>
> "Not tonight."[24]

Assata's regular appearances at such fund-raising events may have had long-reaching effects. In addition to making her the female face of the BPP for certain well-heeled left-wing supporters, her "angry Panther" routine surely helped heighten her profile among the law enforcement agencies that were tracking the Panthers' every move.

Her public statements to the contrary, by 1971 Assata was increasingly disenchanted by the awkward leadership of Huey Newton. When Newton resumed leadership of the BPP after two years in prison, he found it much different than the Party he had inspired. According to a former BPP associate, by the time Newton was released on bail in 1970, the Panthers were "no longer just a few wild guys with guns who were willing to go the limit." In Huey's absence, the BPP "had grown into a large organization that served free breakfasts for children, ran health clinics, set up schools, and distributed free chickens to celebrate Newton's birthdays."[25] The New York City Panthers had also spent two years fighting for the release of twenty-one members who had been arrested in the spring of 1969 and charged with a conspiracy to blow up the New York Botanical Garden, among other targets. Although the Panther 21 were heroes to many in the Party, Newton ultimately expelled them from the BPP after they released a letter from prison that was critical of his leadership.[26] As more and more of her friends were expelled from the Panthers and deemed "enemies of the people"—and as the surveillance on her apartment became an open secret—Assata finally decided to leave the Party, convinced that she would herself soon be expelled.[27] In her book, she mourns the loss of the BPP's former pageantry.

> This [1971] Party was a lot different from the Black Panther Party i had fallen in love with. Gone were the black berets and leather jackets . . . Gone were the Panther marches, the Panther songs. . . . Everything felt different. The easy, friendly openness had been replaced by fear and paranoia. The beautiful revolutionary creativity i had loved so much was gone. And replaced by dogmatic stagnation.[28]

What could only be understood with the benefit of hindsight—and of the circa 1975 findings of the Church Committee Investigations—is how intermeshed the faltering of the BPP was with the activities of the FBI. As Assata points out, BPP membership had grown quickly and chaotically.[29] But there is little question that the original Black Panther Party, as it was developing in Newton's absence, would have lasted longer and evolved differently had the FBI not intervened to the extent that they did. Starting in the 1950s, the FBI had expanded the counterintelligence program it used to harass communists to include a massive offensive against civil rights leaders such as Martin Luther King Jr.[30] By 1968, J. Edgar Hoover had declared the BPP "the greatest threat to the internal security of the country" and called for its "neutralization," which became a code word for Panther frame-ups, imprisonments, assassinations, and public vilifications.[31] Thereafter, the FBI intensified its counterinsurgency program against the BPP, colluding with local police to encourage rancor and disorder within the Party ranks. In his study of police repression, Frank Donner reported that, by the end of 1969, an "estimated 30 Panthers were facing capital punishment, 40 faced life in prison, 55 faced terms up to thirty years, and another 155 were in jail or being sought." In 1969 alone, police conducted over thirteen raids on BPP offices, including the predawn attacks that produced the Panther 21 and that killed the Panthers' charismatic Fred Hampton in Chicago.[32]

The Hampton murder relied on the assistance of an FBI informer who had infiltrated the Panthers and posed for months as Hampton's bodyguard. Assata relates her own encounter with another undercover operative, Cotton, an intimate of the BPP leadership who slowed construction on a new Panther headquarters and sneakily sowed mistrust between Assata and her associates.[33] A January 21, 1971, FBI memo from headquarters reminded agents that "the present chaotic situation within the BPP must be exploited," and exhorted them to "further aggravate the dissension within BPP leadership."[34]

This moment represented a point of no return for Assata. In her book, she expresses no regrets at having gone further into radicalism by joining the BLA. Warned not to go home by a friend who reports that her apartment is "crawling with pigs," Assata imagines the terrors that might befall her at the hands of the police.

> What would they do to me if i went home? I hadn't done anything.
> I thought about the Panther 21. They hadn't done anything either.
> Anyway, they [the police] can do anything they want . . . Maybe they
> would charge me with harboring a fugitive or with conspiracy to harbor
> a fugitive . . . maybe they would try to interrogate me, beat and torture
> me until i signed some phony confession or something. I decided one
> thing right then and there. I definitely wasn't going home.[35]

She had no thought of reasoning with the police because she had no evidence that the police could be reasonable. All of her Panther contacts were then in the grips of the same rampant paranoia bred by the FBI's counterintelligence efforts in cooperation with local police departments. The Harlem Panther leadership had gone so far as to fortify their BPP office as a military stronghold, a move that foreshadowed the actions of the SLA in Watts, and which Assata regarded as ridiculous. "One of the Party's major weaknesses," she writes, was "its failure to differentiate between aboveground political struggle and underground, clandestine military struggle."[36]

The BLA offered vigilante justice for internal enemies of black communities. For example, the BLA's "Deal with the Dealer" program called for roughing up, kidnapping, or even killing anyone who tried to sell drugs in New York's black neighborhoods. However, among most U.S. whites and nonradical people of color, the BLA would become better known for its campaign of retributive violence against urban police. Between 1971 and 1973, nearly 1,000 black people—including two children and a teenager—were killed by U.S. police. BLA members responded with a "defensive/offensive" campaign meant to defend blacks against their own police. In the two years after the dissolution of the BPP, the U.S. government credited the BLA with the deaths of twenty police officers.[37]

In her autobiography, Assata lambastes the media for exacerbating racial tensions between black communities and their police. She decries the legacy of slavery and black oppression that makes it possible for gun ownership to transform any dark-skinned person into an instant thug. "Nobody gets upset about white people having guns, but let a black person have a gun and something criminal is going on."[38] She urges blacks to arm themselves, saying that to be without a firearm in the United States would be "suicidal."[39] Presumably, Assata followed her own advice and armed herself as a member of the BLA, but, in the noble outlaw tradition, Assata carefully narrates herself as having been forced by the state to take up the gun. Her book offers only the barest outline of her early activities underground, hinting that she began working in some capacity for the "railroad," or the network of radicals who dropped out of their regular lives to hide from the police. When the BLA machine-gunned two police on May 19, 1971, on the anniversary of Malcolm X's birthday, her reaction was

> Wow! The tables were turning. As many Black people as the New York Police Department murdered every year, someone was finally paying them back. . . . I felt sorry for [the officers'] families, sorry for their children, but i was relieved to see that somebody else besides Black folks and Puerto Ricans and Chicanos were being shot at. I was sick and tired of us being the only victims, and i didn't care who knew it. As far as i was concerned, the police in the Black communities were nothing but a foreign, occupying army, beating, torturing, and murdering people at whim and without restraint.

"I despise violence," says Assata, but "somebody was doing what the rest of us merely had fantasies about."[40] Did Assata have prior knowledge of the attacks? Her narrative leaves this open to interpretation, although she describes herself as flummoxed at the discovery that the police want to question her in relation to the machine-gunning.[41]

Assata's aunt and lawyer, Evelyn Williams, later asserted that the police repeatedly named Assata as "wanted for questioning" in order to impute guilt and to build public enmity against her.[42] In "Target Blue," Robert Daley described the at-large Assata (Joanne Chesimard) as "a City College girl who was once shot in the stomach during a stick-up and who later said she was glad she had been shot because now she no longer feared police bullets."[43] Whether Assata had ever said such a thing is not clear, and the stickup appears nowhere in her autobiography. According to her aunt, Daley was referring to April 5, 1971, when Assata was indeed "shot in the stomach by a drug dealer she was trying to set up." The shooting led to her arrest and charges of attempted robbery, felonious assault, and possession of a deadly weapon, which may be why Assata preferred to leave the incident out of her book.[44]

Assata's attentiveness to her image, and the vigor with which she appealed to "the people" to distrust state-sponsored allegations of her misconduct, anticipated similar efforts on the part of the SLA. While awaiting trial with Sundiata Acoli for the 1973 Turnpike shootout, Assata recorded a Fourth of July radio broadcast entitled "To My People." After studying the newspaper articles that were being written about her in the wake of her capture, Assata says,

> It was obvious the press was trying to railroad me, to make me seem like a monster. According to them i was a common criminal, just going around shooting down cops for the hell of it. I had to make a statement. I had to talk to my people and let them know what i was about.

Assata directed her radio address to "Black brothers, Black sisters," for whom she declares her love, before adding, "i hope that somewhere in your hearts you have love for me." Recognizing her audience's potential trepidation or anger toward the BLA, Assata strives to humanize and ennoble its members, describing them as "brothers and sisters from all walks of life, who are tired of suffering passively." Assata argues that the BLA has been wrongly vilified:

> I am a Black revolutionary, and by definition, that makes me a part of the Black Liberation Army. The pigs have used their newspapers and TVs to paint the Black Liberation Army as vicious, brutal, mad-dog criminals. They have called us gangsters and gun molls and have compared us to such characters as john dillinger and ma barker. It should be clear, it must be clear to anyone who can think, see, or hear, that we are the victims. The victims and not the criminals.

The conflation of "revolutionary" with "victim" is central to the type of outlawry that Assata would claim for herself for the next thirty-five years. Disavowing any kinship with "gangsters and gun molls" who may have captured the public's imagination, but who broke the law only to enrich themselves, Assata describes herself as wanting nothing more than to subvert the legal and economic structures that many black Americans experience as grindingly unjust. In short, she self-represents as a common person who was compelled, if not coerced, to resist further victimhood, and who did so on behalf of all people of color. Both John Dillinger and Ma Barker were shot dead in FBI ambushes, but that was not the only reason she tried to distance herself from them. Dillinger, at least, may have been a popular criminal-outlaw, but he had no other-directed politics. The Ma comparison was obviously meant to promote Assata as a "mastermind" and dominator of men. Assata disavows connections to either Dillinger or Ma, asserting herself and the BLA as more sincerely popul*ist* revolutionary-outlaws, because they flout the law for the good of a collective.

As she reasoned in her Fourth of July address, the "real criminals" were those exposed as liars by the Watergate trial: "Nixon and his crime partners have murdered hundreds of Third World brothers and sisters in Vietnam, Cambodia, Mozambique, Angola, and South Africa."[45] She argues that the designation of the BLA as comprising murderers, kidnappers, and thieves would better apply to the U.S. government and to all citizens who benefit from racist economic structures. "They [the authorities] call us bandits, yet every time most Black people pick up our paycheck we are being robbed. Every time we pay our rent the landlord sticks a gun into our ribs . . . Black revolutionaries do not drop from the moon. We are created by our conditions. Shaped by our oppression."[46]

In her Fourth of July address, Assata also complained of "being accused of every alleged crime in which a woman was believed to have participated." She offered no further analysis but obviously comprehended the significance of her gender to her outlawry. "The alleged crimes in which only men were supposedly involved, i have been accused of planning," she notes. The statement could be read as an assertion that, as a rare woman member of the BLA, she has been treated more harshly and accorded greater culpability by police. It may also be an oblique criticism of a police effort to emasculate black men by implying they are led by black women. The speech also marked Assata's first official opportunity to declare her African identity, one that she had embraced after her divorce and as part of her revolutionary activity. As she recalled her quest for reinvention:

> My mind, heart, and soul had gone back to Africa, but my name was still stranded in Europe somewhere. . . . At the time, there were little pamphlets being put out listing [African] names and their meanings, but i had a hard time finding one i liked. A lot of the names had to do with flowers or songs or other things like that. Others meant born on a Thursday, faithful, loyal, or even things like tears, or little fool, or one who giggles. The women's names were nothing like the men's names, which meant things like strong, warrior, man of iron, brave, etc.

I wanted a name that had something to do with struggle, something to do with the liberation of our people.[47]

To the listeners of the "To My People" address, she renamed herself "Assata Shakur (slave name Joanne Chesimard)." As she explains in her book, Assata means "she who struggles." The "Shakur," which she adopted in honor of her friend Zayd Shakur (James F. Coston), who died on the Turnpike, means "the thankful." By 1987, she had also added a middle name: Olugbala, which translates as "love for the people."

In the courtroom, of course, Assata Shakur was still identified as Joanne Chesimard. In the press, she was "Mrs. Joanne Chesimard," emphasizing her status as a divorcée; as her trials dragged on through the late 1970s, more newspapers began identifying her as "Miss." Occasionally, a mainstream paper would acknowledge her "Muslim" name, usually to explain the "Free Assata" signs carried outside the courthouse by her supporters. When she finally took the witness stand in 1977 to describe what happened during the Turnpike shootout, Assata was permitted to swear herself in as "Assata Shakur, also known as Joanne Chesimard."[48]

Defendant and Prisoner

Assata was not tried again for her part in the Turnpike incident until the early months of 1977, by which time she was the mother of a toddler (albeit one being raised by Assata's mother) and the subject of 289 articles in the mainstream press.[49] The trial was moved to the state's nearly all-white Morris County but ultimately ended in a mistrial when Assata had to be hospitalized due to pregnancy-related complications. By that time, Sundiata Acoli had already been convicted of the murder of trooper Werner Foerster and was three years into the life sentence that continues to this day.[50]

Assata's reputation grew with each court appearance, trial severance, and mistrial. Some of this was due to her high-profile legal defense team, which included proudly leftist legal stars such as William Kunstler (famous for defending Abbie Hoffman, Bobby Seale, and others during what became the trial of the "Chicago Seven"), Stanley Cohen (who died, midtrial, under suspicious circumstances), and Florynce Kennedy.[51] But Assata's greatest legal asset was her aunt, lawyer Evelyn Williams, who provided the necessary leverage to sustain Assata both in the courtroom and in a difficult prison environment.[52] In her 1993 autobiography, *Inadmissible Evidence: The Story of the African-American Trial Lawyer Who Defended the Black*

Liberation Army, Evelyn Williams describes her concern at the media's portrayal of her niece from 1971 to 1973 and admits to having prepared for her "Joey's" trials years before they happened. "I was suspect of the airtight public indictment against Joey. I screened every newspaper accusation for loopholes, photocopied reports, compared them, and filed them for future reference in the event she was captured alive. I taped radio reports and transcribed them. I evaluated every fragment of information leaked by the police department or the FBI for inconsistencies, unintentionally revealed clues, or suspect sources."[53]

In their respective autobiographies, Assata and Williams both recount a 1975 court appearance in which the judge approved the prosecution's motion that Assata be photographed by FBI agents at the same angle as the woman in the Queens bank robbery wanted posters. Assata and Williams objected, on fears that the FBI would tamper with the photograph by superimposing the wanted poster image on top of it.[54] On the judge's orders, FBI agents on the scene attempted to take the new photo by force. Curiously, Assata and her aunt offered opposing accounts of what happened next. Assata remembered her aunt's composure during the ensuing struggle:

> The FBI, the marshals, and i end up on the kourtroom floor, with me on the bottom. I hear Evelyn in the background. "Let the record reflect that the marshals are twisting my client's arms behind her back." "Let the record reflect that the marshals are choking my client." "Let the record reflect that there are five marshals manhandling my client." Evelyn goes on and on while the marshals twist me, jerk me, strangle me, kick me, and literally try to beat me into submission. The assault goes on and on with Evelyn putting it, blow by blow, into the record.[55]

In Williams's version of the story, recorded in 1993, she recalls herself watching in horror while Assata calmly narrates her own rough treatment for the court record. It is odd that Williams's account does not match Assata's, since she would have had access to Assata's 1987 biography. It may be that one of the women simply misremembered the incident. It is also possible that Assata attributed the calmness to her aunt in tribute to her and/or because her ability to speak during the struggle would make the beating sound too tame.

While Assata's next three trials lurched slowly toward acquittals, she spent most of the next three years either in solitary on Rikers Island or confined, alone, in the basement of a men's prison facility in New Jersey. In the fall of 1977, a judge dismissed what was to have been her final trial (for an alleged robbery and murder) to reflect his disapproval of how she had been "shuffled" from place to place for so long.[56] Assata does not even bother to mention the canceled trial in her book, perhaps because it seemed meaningless—she had, by then, already been given a life sentence in the Turnpike trial—or perhaps because it would have detracted from her story to bring in this anticlimactic moment of clemency. For an outlaw-hero narrative to work, the legal system has to appear uniformly unreasonable.

From the perspective of those in the New Jersey State Police Department, keeping Assata for the Turnpike trial was expensive, stressful, and not producing the hoped-for results of a conviction. Sheriff Joseph DeMarino later expressed bitterness at those years, citing a blown-up police cruiser, bomb threats, and exorbitant amounts spent on security for the jury members and their families.[57] The fear and bitterness were echoed across the river, where the New York Police Department had for years felt under siege by the BLA and the random acts of violence that had by then killed or maimed almost a dozen of their number.[58]

Assata's legal team tried to link police anger to recent COINTELPRO abuses. William Kunstler argued that the New Jersey state troopers had been "psyched up" by FBI propaganda about black militants, and this caused them to react more fearfully to Assata and her traveling companions.[59] In February 1977, Assata's lawyers filed paperwork to have the newly public Church Committee report on COINTELPRO entered into the trial as evidence, requesting that Senator Frank Church (for whom the Church report was named) and FBI Director Clarence Kelley be subpoenaed to testify on Assata's behalf.[60] Her lawyers asked for the court to produce memos, tapes, and other documentation connected to COINTELPRO activities and to require federal and New York law enforcement officials to testify under oath about measures designed to harass and disrupt black activist organizations. The lawyers' motion was denied. As a limited concession to the post-COINTELPRO era, however, the judge forbade the prosecution to cross-examine Assata with documents (a firearm pamphlet, false identification papers, and advice to fugitives from the law) that allegedly connected her to "revolutionary activities." The judge had ruled these documents inadmissible but permitted the prosecution to keep them on hand, in case the defense "opened the door" to presenting them to the jury. The defense did not, and so the documents—along with any discussion of counterintelligence gathering or Assata's BLA activities—remained off the table.[61]

Assata's 1977 trial was held in New Jersey's Middlesex County with another all-white jury of people mostly under age thirty.[62] Sundiata Acoli did not testify at Assata's trial, nor did he submit any pretrial statements about his having already been convicted for shooting trooper Werner Foerster. Trooper James Harper, who earlier testified to having stopped the vehicle carrying Assata, Sundiata, and the late Zayd Shakur for a broken taillight, testified again on behalf of his three investigative reports, which were filed as evidence. According to the reports filed by Harper shortly after the incident, he had ordered Sundiata to the back end of the automobile to show his driver's license to Foerster, who had arrived on the scene after Harper radioed for backup. Harper recorded that he had been studying the car's inside door to check its registration when two simultaneous events occurred: Foerster yelled to him and held up an ammunition clip, and Assata, who was still sitting in the car's front seat, pulled a gun from a red pocketbook and shot Harper in the shoulder. Harper maintained that he fired back at Assata after she emerged from the car and after she began shooting at him from a prostrate position alongside the vehicle.

While under cross-examination at both Sundiata's and Assata's trials, Harper admitted that he had lied in all three of his official reports and in his grand jury testimony. He retracted his statements about Foerster having yelled to him and having shown him the ammunition clip. He also conceded that he had not seen a gun in Assata's hand while she was seated in the car, that she did not shoot him from the car, and that he had not, in fact, seen the red pocketbook. Unresolved in cross-examination (or in the years hence) is why Harper made no mention of Foerster's presence at the scene once he ran back to the New Jersey Turnpike Administration Building to report the incident. According to the handwritten log from the officer on duty that night, Harper reported that he had been wounded in a shootout that began after he stopped a Pontiac containing two black men and a woman, and that the Pontiac was now headed south on the Turnpike. He gave the license plate number, and another set of troopers easily intercepted the car five miles down the road. But it would be over an hour before Foerster's dead body was discovered at the site of the original Turnpike stop.

In her autobiography, Assata offers no details about what might have happened just before Harper retreated or before Sundiata drove the car farther south with a bleeding Assata and a dead or dying Zayd Shakur in the backseat. Stopped by new troopers, Sundiata fled the scene, and this is where Assata opens her narrative. (The very first lines of her book: "There were lights and sirens. Zayd was dead.") She describes herself as limp and lying by the side of the road after being brusquely handled by the troopers, who repeatedly ask, "Is she dead yet?" and who joke about "finishing her off." Trooper Robert Palentchar, who was one of the officers at the blockade, claimed that a bloodied Assata had actually surrendered by stepping out of the car and walking toward him with arms raised.[63]

It should have been difficult or impossible for Assata to raise her arms by the time of the second Turnpike stop. As a result of a bullet that Harper shot under her armpit, Assata's median nerve was severed, paralyzing her right arm. A pathologist testified to the fact of Assata's immediate paralysis at her trial, asserting, "There is no conceivable way that the bullet could have traveled over to hit the clavicle if her arm was down. It was impossible to have that trajectory."[64] The state did not refute this medical testimony, but Harper amended his testimony to suggest that Assata had fired on him while in a crouched position, with her arms resting on the hood of the car. Thus, the prosecution argued, the bullet might indeed have struck her with her arms raised, but they were raised in a posture of aggression. The defense's neurosurgery expert firmly refuted this possibility as "anatomically impossible."[65] Assata's lawyers also pointed to the results of a neutron activation test, which showed that Assata's hands had borne no traces of gunpowder residue.

On the stand, Assata described her injuries in exactly the same manner as she did later, in the pages of her book: "It felt like my entire arm was shot off and was hanging by a piece of flesh." Because her autobiography opens in the immediate aftermath of her capture, it does not repeat her rather unheroic courtroom assertion that she had been so "hysterical" in the wake of the shootout that Sundiata had slapped her.[66] A longtime Middlesex County court reporter described how the nearly inaudible Assata/Joanne resembled "anything but the snarling 'soul' of the revolutionary Black Liberation Army." On the stand, she characterized herself as an innocent bystander to the gunfight. Assata testified that Harper had shot her as she sat in the passenger seat with arms raised, and that he had done so because Zayd Shakur had made a sudden movement from the backseat. Although she did not say so directly, she implied that it was Zayd, and not she, who shot Harper in the arm. She also identified the Llama automatic pistol that injured Foerster as having belonged to Sundiata, contradicting the prosecution's contention that the weapon used to disable the trooper was her own.

While Assata flatly denied having shot Harper or having killed Foerster, she could not explain the three ammunition clips and seventeen loose rounds for the Llama that had been found in her red pocketbook on the night of the killings. She also did not elaborate on why her wallet contained identification cards for "Justine Henderson" (perhaps because that would "open the door" to a discussion of her life in the revolutionary underground) or why her slacks and cuff sleeve were splattered with Foerster's relatively rare type AB blood.[67] None of these elements necessarily proved guilt in connection to the shootings, especially when considered alongside evidence suggesting that she did not have opportunity that night to fire a weapon. But such details do cloud any simple version of the events of May 2, 1973, which is probably why neither she nor her supporters ever mention them. During the trial, her lawyers and supporters repeatedly lauded her as a "warm, sensitive, hopeful young mother, artist, and teacher" who had done nothing wrong.[68] For Assata/Joanne to be a victim of the law required that she also be a woman whose life conformed to prevailing gender norms, norms her defense team hoped would blot out any perception of her as capable of violence. Just as happened at the trial of Patricia Hearst, the two identities—victim and model woman—mutually constituted each other.

On March 25, 1977, the Middlesex jury found Assata guilty on all counts. As the court clerk read the verdicts, Assata addressed the jurors in a low voice: "You're racists—yes, you are. You are unfair. You abuse the law."[69] The comments of her lawyer, William Kunstler, also alluded to a stacked deck: "The reality is, this beautiful young black woman never had a chance. But we, like liberal fools, still had hopes."[70] Kunstler's observation was as self-flattering as it was prescient of what the convicted Assata would become to many of her left-leaning sympathizers: a casualty of a racially and politically biased judicial system whose plight was all the more tragic for the fact of how attractive she is. In a postverdict protest led by activist Silvia Baraldini, demonstrators shouted, "Assata, we're with you. We'll fight until you're free." Baraldini promised the press that "we're going to fight until she's out . . . until every political prisoner is out."[71]

Breakout and Missteps

Almost half of Assata's biography deals with the four years in which she was held in custody during or between trials. Assata records her indignation at the discovery that the Thirteenth Amendment of the U.S. Constitution permits slave labor in prisons and that almost all of her fellow inmates are women of color.[72] For what state and federal police defended as "security reasons," she was for a long time the only female prisoner in the exclusively male Yardville Youth Correction and Reception Center in New Jersey, or

was held, alone, in the basement of the Middlesex County Jail.[73] Assata's unhappy experiences in prison were shaped both by the fact of her sex and by
her notoriety as the "queen" of the BLA. At Rikers, she was kept in solitary
confinement. One of her attorneys, Lennox Hinds, wrote in his foreword
to Assata's biography that she "*understates* the awfulness of the conditions
in which she was incarcerated." As Hinds claimed, "In the history of New
Jersey, no woman pretrial detainee or prisoner has ever been treated as she
was, continuously confined in a men's prison, under 24-hour surveillance
of her most intimate functions, without intellectual sustenance, adequate
medical attention, and exercise, and without the company of other women
for all the years that she was in custody."[74] While Assata's own descriptions
tended to undermine the claim of her never having had the company of
other women, her status as a high-profile prisoner meant that she was frequently in solitary. She describes having forgotten how to speak or to speak
audibly to judges or to her fellow prisoners after long stretches of isolated
confinement.[75]

A chance meeting in prison with a former Black Panther who was soon
to give birth while in prison appears to have formed Assata's feelings about
also becoming a mother while behind bars. Her poem, "Love," suggests
the significance of her own pregnancy to her experience of imprisonment,
as well as to her identity as a revolutionary:

Love is contraband in Hell,
Cause love is an acid that eats away bars.
But you, me, and tomorrow
Hold hands and make vows
That struggle will multiply.
The hacksaw has two blades.
The shotgun has two barrels.
We are pregnant with freedom.
We are a conspiracy.[76]

Assata's daughter was born in the "fortified psychiatric ward" at Elmhurst
General Hospital in Queens, which is where Assata stayed for a few days
before being returned to Rikers. In her book, she describes being beaten by
female guards for refusing a postpartum exam from a prison doctor. Several
of her chapters meditate on the medical treatment available, or not available, to prisoners, particularly in relation to other prisoners' pregnancies
and her own.

Assata's supporters used her pregnancy and her fleeting experience of motherhood—her baby was but a few days old when she and Assata were separated—as a symbol of her innocence and vulnerability. But Assata more often used her maternal identity as one more justification for her hatred and distrust of the U.S. justice system. Because a woman's violence is often countenanced as rational only so long as it happens in defense of her children, Assata reasoned that her obligations to her own child—and to other children like her—required Assata to take drastic action against the law.

In the wake of her 1977 sentencing, Assata was no longer a defendant in government custody but an officially convicted killer.[77] A final appeal failed, and she was sent to West Virginia's Alderson Federal Prison to live in the company of a pair of white supremacists and the "Manson girls" Sandra Good and Lynette "Squeaky" Fromme. (Twenty years earlier, Alderson had also been the longtime home of Kathryn Kelly and her mother, Ora Shannon.) While at Alderson, Assata befriended inmates imprisoned for their radical politics, including antiwar protestor Sister Mary Alice and the Puerto Rican activist Lolita Lebron. In her book, Assata proudly notes her interactions with both activists, who may have been essential to her own self-concept as a people's hero. But Alderson's maximum security division soon closed, and Assata was abruptly transferred back to the Clinton Correctional Facility in New Jersey. Assata attributes a wrenching visit from her young daughter at the Clinton prison as having sealed her resolve to escape.[78]

On November 3, 1979, the headlines blared: "Miss Chesimard Flees Jersey Prison." As the *New York Times* reported, "Joanne Chesimard, a leader of a militant black group who was serving a life term for the 1973 slaying of a state trooper, escaped . . . with the help of three armed men."[79] The FBI immediately offered its assistance in the nationwide hunt for the fugitive Chesimard and helped to distribute the wanted posters that prompted some in New York to respond with signs declaring that "ASSATA IS WELCOME HERE." As a child in Brooklyn, the rapper Mos Def saw the wanted posters and thought they made Joanne Chesimard sound like a "supervillain, like something out of a comic book." He remembers himself as skeptical of the FBI's intentions: "When I looked at those posters and the mug shot of a slight, brown, high-cheek-boned woman with a full afro, I saw someone who looked like she was in my family, an aunt, a mother."[80]

Fury at law enforcement's intrusions into the predominantly black neighborhoods where Assata was presumed to be hiding may have helped protect her from their detection. The FBI likely won Assata more allies during a predawn raid of some Harlem apartments in which they brusquely ordered a woman whom they mistook for their fugitive to hike up her nightgown to reveal an identifying scar. Many of the other tenants in the building were furious at being detained during the hour-long search and complained to New York Representative Charles Rangel, who condemned the FBI's actions as "gestapo-like and disgusting."[81] At least one Brooklyn home in which Assata (then calling herself Cleo) was suspected to be hiding was not invaded for fear of garnering still more bad publicity and negative fallout from the community.

If Assata's prison break hurt the FBI, it also briefly reinvigorated the moribund BLA, which then had working within it white radicals such as Silvia Baraldini, who has since served time for her role in Assata's escape.[82] Years later, former BLA member Safiya Bukhari criticized Assata's supporters for making her a "superstar," arguing that it detracted from efforts to support other people jailed for political activities. As Bukhari told an interviewer in 1995: "[Assata] has survived a lot, she has learned a lot and she has studied and she has developed." But as for her prominence relative to other members: "It was a lot of media hype."[83]

Five years after her escape from prison, Assata again made headlines when she managed to secure political asylum in Cuba. Three years later, she was news again, this time for having published an autobiography. Assata was still living as a "guest" of Cuba when, in a highly publicized media misstep, she agreed to be interviewed by journalist Ralph Penza for an American NBC television profile in 1998.

The televised interview was precipitated by a letter from the New Jersey State Police's Colonel Carl Williams to Pope John Paul II on the eve of the latter's visit to Cuba. Colonel Williams hoped that the pope could somehow persuade Fidel Castro to return the woman he called Joanne Chesimard to prison. (There is no extradition treaty between Cuba and the United States.) Assata responded to media reports about Colonel Williams's correspondence with her own open letter to the pope, in which she referred to her Catholic girlhood and to the high number of people of color in U.S. prisons. Although the pope had no official power to call for extraditions or prison reforms, both Colonel Williams and Assata vied for the attention of his followers and the favor of his influence. The resulting NBC interview was a victory for the New Jersey State Police. It intercut footage of a relaxed-looking Assata strolling along a beach with that of the still-grieving widow of Trooper Foerster.[84] In a second open letter intended for circulation on the Internet, Assata lambasted Penza as having deliberately deceived her and for having edited the interview to revive her reputation as a cop killer. She angrily insisted that she was not a criminal or a fugitive, but a woman hounded by a racist police force: "My name is Assata Shakur, and I am a twentieth-century escaped slave. Because of government persecution, I was left with no other choice than to flee from the political repression, racism and violence that dominate the US government's policy toward people of color. I am an ex–political prisoner."[85]

Assata's open letter could not halt what the NBC interview had already set in motion: New Jersey's governor Christine Todd Whitman announced that she was doubling the reward for the return of Joanne Chesimard to $100,000. By the fall of 1998, Congress had passed a congressional resolution (HR 254) that "call[ed] on the government of Cuba to return to the U.S. convicted felon Joanne Chesimard and all other individuals who have fled the U.S. to avoid persecution or confinement for criminal offenses." Three times on the floor of Congress, the sponsors of HR 254 read an account of Assata's crimes into the *Congressional Record*. Ignoring the findings of Assata's 1977 jury, each account made reference to her having shot and killed a New Jersey state trooper. One account even inaccurately reported that she had been convicted of "first-degree murder . . . for her brutal execution-style murder of Trooper Foerster." No mention was made of her companions on the Turnpike or of the fact that Sundiata Acoli was, in fact, the person convicted for shooting Trooper Foerster. Some of those who voted in favor of the resolution, including California Congresswoman Maxine Waters, later claimed that they had not realized that Joanne Chesimard and Assata Shakur were the same person.[86]

Most of the backers of HR 254 appeared less concerned with what Joanne Chesimard might be calling herself than with her standard of living. The resolution makes repeated references to Assata's "comfortable life." In a press conference, one New Jersey representative imagined Assata/Joanne as having sold her supporters a bill of goods while "sipping piña coladas and walking white beaches, swimming in crystal clear water." As he summarized in the *Congressional Record*, "This escaped murderer now lives a very comfortable life in Cuba and has launched a public relations campaign in which she attempts to portray herself as an innocent victim rather than a cold-blooded murderer."[87]

Eyes of the Rainbow

The version of events laid out by HR 254 and the NBC broadcast stand in stark contrast to *Eyes of the Rainbow* (1997), "a documentary with Assata Shakur" by Cuban director Gloria Rolando. *Eyes of the Rainbow* contains archival footage from the 1970s, including a taped interview with the Afro-wearing prisoner Assata (then Joanne Chesimard) in New Jersey. The rest of the film intercuts on-camera reminiscences of the fifty-year-old Assata with stylistic reenactments of her years with the Black Panthers, her pregnancy, and her experiences as a prisoner.

At the time Rolando began shooting her film, Assata had been living in Cuba for over a decade. *Eyes of the Rainbow* reflects the fondness of both the director and her subject for their shared home. Seated in relaxed posture on the edge of the Havana harbor, Assata laughs at her initial American-bred misconceptions of Cuba as a militarized culture in which "everyone dressed like Castro." After praising the country's climate, schools, and health care, Assata also credits Cuba with deepening her connections to her African roots. "One of the most shocking things to me is how *African* Cuba is." As Gloria Rolando explained to an American journalist in 2000, "In *Eyes of the Rainbow*, I was interested not only in Assata's political history, but in her history as a human being, a human being with roots."[88] Rolando uses Assata's stories to explore the common history of Afro-Cubans and Afro-Americans. She draws repeatedly on Afro-Caribbean Santería imagery, particularly the orisha (goddess) Oya, referred to in the film's press packet as the "goddess of the ancestors, of war, of the cemetery and of the rainbow."[89]

Throughout her career, Gloria Rolando's work has focused on diaspora, Afro-Cuban spirituality, and all that is lost or threatened by emigration. Six years younger than Assata Shakur, and six years old at the time of the 1959 Cuban Revolution, Rolando has few direct memories of the Cuba that predated Fidel Castro and communism. As a young Cuban, she was almost certainly aware of the (qualified) hospitality that her government extended to foreign political exiles, including U.S. Black Panthers such as Eldridge Cleaver.[90] Most of her films offer a hopeful double argument for cultural reclamation and the purposeful redefinition of "mainstream" Cuban culture—two themes that became Rolando's trademark.[91]

The phantasmagoric *Eyes of the Rainbow* was Rolando's third film, and is a bit grainy for having been shot on video. From the outset, the film is intent on elevating Assata's status as a righteous outlaw and near-mythical "woman warrior." When first glimpsed by the audience, Assata walks away from the camera, her face hidden and her back turned. We see only her long braids and the writing on her black T-shirt: "*Killed, Exiled, Framed, Jailed.*" The shirt is a protest against the treatment of American political activists, but those four words also summarize the film's lament for the more general repression of African Americans in the United States. Still with her back to us, Assata walks through a column of light and briefly appears to have dematerialized or become celestial. She will be the film's principal narrator and its hero, as well as an emblem of the group to whom the film is dedicated: "women who are struggling for a better world."

The film loosely matches the chronology of Assata's 1987 autobiography, which Rolando presumes her audience has read; she offers no explication of the events of Assata's life and no reference at all to the 1973 New Jersey Turnpike stop. In a set of extended interviews, Assata narrates several stories almost exactly as she told them in her 1987 memoir. But she is no longer the same woman that she was in that book. Assata wrote her autobiography from the perspective of someone who had just emerged from years of hiding underground. She was then a newly exiled American, working to make sense of her double status as a fugitive and as a black woman who came of age in the United States of the 1950s and 1960s. Although she regarded herself as fighting for collective aims, on the page her story remained one of individual struggle and hardship.[92] By the time Rolando shot *Eyes of the Rainbow* in 1997, Assata had begun articulating herself and her exile in terms of a more global tradition of Afro-women's resistance. In the on-camera explanation of her life, she puts new emphasis on lineage and humility in relation to her elders: "I come from a tradition of women Maroons, *cimarróns*, who didn't just try to escape from oppression but who totally—mind, body, spirit—committed to resisting and committed to winning." Assata hails both Nanny Jamaica and Harriet Tubman as examples of her tradition, and a series of bust portraits depicting both women appear on-screen.[93] Rolando inserts an iconic 1970s image of the jailed Assata at the end of this portrait series, thus anointing Assata as the latest in a noble line of Afro-Diasporic freedom fighters. "I think I come from a very strong tradition," Assata continues. "I simply want to live on this planet and to continue that tradition and to try in my little way to make the ancestors proud."

The film frequently cuts away from Assata's narratives to wordless or near-wordless dance performances meant to represent key moments from her autobiography. The Afro-Cuban and Afro-American music and dance do not so much reenact Assata's experiences as recontextualize them.[94] In her filmmaker's statement, Rolando claimed Assata Shakur as "one of those voices that already forms a part of the history of the African American people." Because Rolando regards both Assata and African Americans as tragically deracinated, her *Eyes of the Rainbow* sought to "create a meeting with

Assata Shakur through the symbols of Afro-Cuban culture, which offer us beautiful songs evoking the ancestors."⁹⁵

Following a sequence in which Assata chops vegetables and then beams from her rocking chair at a circle of singing friends, Assata speaks happily about having become acquainted with the orishas and other African traditions that were better preserved by Afro-Cuban slaves than by slaves in the United States ("I felt like, wow, I was reclaiming just another piece that was stolen from us"). The theme of cultural reclamation is picked up by a musical performance featuring a young male singer wearing a beret and a Malcolm X T-shirt.⁹⁶ Sweat runs down the singer's dark cheeks, which then give way to the image of a bare-chested hunter.⁹⁷ The hunter's body is then superimposed upon the enormous features of a panther cat. (Or, rather, the blown-up features of a soft grey housecat, who, with no hint of intentional irony, stands in for a panther.) The young man and a crowd of other youthful singers sway to the music, swinging their fists into the air in stylized Black Panther salute. As their song concludes, the Panther voices are nearly drowned out by the sounds of sirens and gunshots.

In *Eyes of the Rainbow*, Assata credits J. Edgar Hoover for having "recognized how much the Black Panther Party meant to people." Emphasizing the BPP's broad appeal ("Ordinary street people, working people, mothers, [and] grandmothers, would come to the office and bring clothes, come to the office and make donations"), she explains how it and the BLA "came under the guns of the FBI": "The government just perceived us as a threat because they understood we were serious. They understood we were telling the truth. And they understood also that we were becoming a more sophisticated opposition. We were not just a piece-of-the-pie opposition, but . . . we wanted a real, structural change in the United States." Speaking from the symbolic prison setting in which the film opens, Assata glosses over rankling divisions in the BPP's domestic aims. "It didn't matter what position you took," she claims. "It mattered that people related to those positions, that people understood what you were saying, and that people supported you." She reminds her 1997 audience of the 1970 Panthers' opposition to the war in Vietnam, to apartheid in South Africa, and to "the blockade against Cuba and all of the other U.S. policies that were hostile to the Cuban Revolution."⁹⁸ Alluding to the FBI's counterintelligence program, Assata draws on Hoover's famous language about the Bureau's need to "neutralize" the black liberation movement by sowing paranoia and distrust among its members. She describes the Panther 21 trials and how they diverted most of the time and resources of her BPP unit in New York.

Rolando abruptly shifts to a separate interview, one filmed before a black screen. Assata leans forward and offers this admonishment:

> I think that we cannot look at the Black Panther Party as the past. We cannot look at the Black Liberation Movement as something in the past. African people are still not free. And there are still many, many political prisoners in the United States. It is time for us to demand total and immediate amnesty for all political prisoners and prisoners of war. If we do not take ourselves seriously, if we do not take our movement seriously, then we will have to hang our heads in front of our ancestors.

On her assertion that "African people still are not free," black-and-white portraits of Sundiata Acoli, Mumia Abu-Jamal, and others flash, without identification, on the screen. Assata presumably intends the "we" who must take ourselves seriously and demand total and immediate amnesty for political prisoners to encompass all sympathetic viewers of the film, although she is better able to provide inspiration than specific strategies for that cause. The subject of political prisoners segues into Assata's own experience in U.S. prisons and to a photo of Assata lying on a stretcher with a severely beaten face. This photo was likely snapped shortly after the 1973 Turnpike shootout, although the film does not confirm this. "I was beaten, tortured," says Assata in a voice-over.

> It was a hellish experience. . . . I was in prison altogether for six and a half years in prison. I spent more than two and a half years in solitary confinement. Much of that was in men's prisons. In other words, I was the only woman. Even though they say that there are no political prisoners in the United States, I was kept in solitary confinement, kept in men's prisons, because of my "political beliefs," so you figure that one out.

Assata is again shown walking away, this time in slow motion. She walks through a column of light and billowing smoke and again seems to disappear. The film then cuts to Assata speaking by the harbor, her face streaked with tears.

> What was prison? Prison was hell. It was a new kind of plantation. I feel like a Maroon woman. I feel like an escaped slave. Because what

I saw in the United States in those prisons was slavery. It was black people with chains in cells. It was just poor people . . . just stepped on and smashed. I'll never forget what I saw. I'll never forget what I lived through. I'll never forget what my people have lived through.

Rolando then includes the first overhead shot of Assata, who sits on the cement stairs of the symbolic prison setting, her head slightly turned, as if in private recollection. In the space above Assata's head appears the soft-focus arm of a female dancer, her hand gracefully outstretched. From the other side of the frame, a male dancer reaches toward her and tenderly clasps her fingers. Cut to the image of a traditionally clad woman stirring honey in a bowl, and then back again to the dancers, who enfold each other in a lovers' embrace. In the upper left of the screen, there appears the ghosted image of a laughing, twenty-six-year-old Assata, in her tall Afro. In the lower right sits the Assata of 1997, who softly strokes her own face. The film then cuts back to the interview, which picks up in the middle of an explanation of how Assata happened to become pregnant by Kamau Sadiki (Fred Hilton), with whom she stood trial in 1974. As Assata describes it, "We started to feel tender toward each other. We started to feel an attraction. We started to feel like human beings again."

An extended segment, featuring sensuous close-ups of the dancers' oiled bodies, gives way to a jaunty dance sequence, in which the honey-stirring woman bobs proudly before the camera with a small pumpkin. The roundness of the pumpkin then fades to reveal a pregnant woman's ripe belly, complete with the *linea negra*, indicating an imminent birth. Then both images are replaced on-screen by a quick-fade succession of three portraits in which Assata's daughter is transformed from a bespectacled elementary school student to exultant college graduate. Neither she nor her father is ever mentioned in the film by name, not even in the moment when Assata muses about what it meant to bring a child into a world in which both her parents felt like slaves. "I thought about my mother, my grandmother, my great-great-great grandmothers and what they must have thought about as slaves, bringing life into this world. And, you know, we [Assata and Kamau] just decided that we were gonna live . . . We were gonna struggle. We're not gonna kill our own hopes."

Both Assata and Gloria Rolando repeatedly identify their lives as guided and inspired by matriarchs.[99] *Eyes of the Rainbow* begins and ends with the story of how Assata's 1979 prison break had been foretold by her grandmother. The same story appears at the end of Assata's autobiography: her grandmother had a vivid dream in which she was putting clothes on her granddaughter, and she traveled a long way to visit Assata in prison so she could tell her so. Assata, who was then serving a life sentence, asked her grandmother if her body in the dream had been that of a child or of an adult. As Assata relates the tale for Rolando's camera, "She said, 'you were big.' And I said, oh my god, the only time people dress anybody when they're grown is when they're dead." But Assata's grandmother had a different interpretation: "What this dream means is that you are going to leave this prison!"[100] On the eve of Assata's breakout, she phoned her grandmother, who again exhorted her granddaughter not to become accustomed to life behind bars. "And so when I hung up the phone, it was like a sign. It was . . . It was like my grandmother knew. It was like everything was ready to go. Everything went. And everything went fine."

Assata offers that succinct description of the prison break ("Everything went. And everything went fine.") with a playful smile on her face. To say more might incriminate her accomplices in the escape. Certainly, it would diminish her story's mystique. Rolando recognizes the prison break as having made Assata the political outlaw symbol she became. But Rolando is more interested in how the escape foregrounds Assata's links to her grandmother and her daughter, whom both the film and Assata's book point to as the ultimate catalyst for Assata's breakout.[101] On-screen, the drama of the prison break receives no treatment in dance or song, but only a few seconds of rhythmic harmonica music. The camera swirls over Assata's interview sites, now quite empty. The film jumps back in time, to footage of the 1970s Assata, speaking lightheartedly of revolution. Then it jumps forward again to a wide shot of the fifty-year-old Assata, her long braids and flowing garment silhouetted by the harbor at sunset. The music grows solemn and reflective as the camera skims along the Havana harbor waters, symbol of Assata's freedom, and also of the pain of being separated from her family in the States. Assata appears on-screen one last time. Dressed in black T-shirt and trousers, she confides to the camera that she has just learned that her mother has died. By her account, her mother's passing becomes the reason for having participated in Rolando's film; the death is also an occasion for eulogy, one that justifies Assata's outlawry and exile.

> This [film] was the best homage I could pay to my mother . . . to try
> to carry on her tradition. What she passed down to me, what my
> grandmother passed down to her. And what their foremothers passed
> down to them. I hope I can live up to my mother's example. And I

hope I can live up to my ancestors' expectation of me. Because I really believe that I have a duty to all those who have come before me.[102]

Assata explains that her "duty" commits her to all those of African heritage in the Americas:

To all those who lie at the bottom of the ocean. To all those who lost their lives, whether it's in the cane fields or the cotton fields or hanging off some tree. To continue this struggle. And to continue to love and to continue to believe, and to continue to try to be human, to be giving, to be loving.

While *Eyes of the Rainbow* makes no overt references to the Assata as "outlaw," its recurring themes of the warrior and the political prisoner evoke many traits consistent with a tradition of women's outlawry. Regarded another way, *Eyes of the Rainbow* is an outlaw film keyed to Afro-Diasporic promise. From Assata's decision to become pregnant on the watch of a careless judge to the astonishing ease of her prison break, this film puts forth a story of resistance in the tradition of the persecuted trickster outlaw. It also reinforces the implication that Assata was forced into violence by the state-sponsored aggression against the Black Panthers. But the film makes no allusion to any acts against the state that Assata may have committed, witnessed, or even wished for as a member of the BLA. Indeed, the only brutality depicted on-screen is in the black-and-white archival stills of bloodied and abused Panthers, presumably battered by white police. The only suggestion of an armed Panther retaliation comes in the form of a single still image of former BPP Chairperson Kathleen Cleaver holding a rifle. It is a staged photo and more stylish than threatening. Cleaver smiles behind her dark glasses and tilts the rifle barrel toward the ground. No such photograph of an armed Assata appears anywhere in the film. The BLA and her connections to it are never mentioned.

Eyes of the Rainbow reimagines and rewrites the normal populist appeal associated with male outlaws into something more intimate, more kin oriented. As an American woman of color who took up a gun against her country's law enforcement agencies, Assata is exceptional, but she is also supposed to be typical—another in a line of African American and Afro-Caribbean freedom fighters. In Rolando's vision, Assata's outlawry becomes the expression of love and sacrifice and family ties. Through imagery and music, Rolando presents Assata as having achieved orisha status, meaning that her commitment to ancestor wisdom has reconnected her in a mystical way to the force of nature. *Eyes of the Rainbow* showcases Assata's striking good looks, spotlighting her braids, her cheekbones, and her large brown eyes alongside the opening credits. Assata's features then appear superimposed on clouds and trees, as are the eyes of other dark-skinned women at the beginning and end of the film. A final voice-over makes no direct reference to Assata, beyond an oblique reassertion of her role as a woman warrior.[103] A circle of Afro-Cuban woman and female children performs a traditional dance. As the music accelerates and then is overtaken by the sound of a rushing wind, the camera scans a circle of dancing women before zooming in on the movements of a little girl. The voice-over:

> Women warriors fight when others celebrate. It is only they who see the dreadful colors of suffering. It is only they who can see with the intense splendor of victories to be found. Because women warriors are the eyes of the rainbow.

For a decade, *Eyes of the Rainbow* was banned in the United States. It could not be purchased or exported under the terms of the current U.S.-Cuban embargo, and so screenings in the United States happened only infrequently and under paranoid circumstances. ("We should assume that there are members of the FBI here with us tonight" is how the former Black Panther Rosemari Mealy introduced a hastily organized screening at Amherst College in January 2006.) Seven years after the film's original release, *Eyes of the Rainbow* had its official "premiere" in Havana. Casa de las Américas, the Cuban government's main cultural forum, promoted the event.[104]

In 2000, Assata was featured as a "Cuban Diva" in the PBS-sponsored women's travel series *Adventure Divas*. The nervously edited Cuban episode spent more time on Gloria Rolando than it did on Assata. Show host Holly Morris cautiously summarized Assata as someone who "sees herself as neither sinner nor saint, but as an exile whose notion of revolution is always evolving."[105] Meanwhile, the political culture of the United States was evolving also, and not in Assata's favor. Even before September 11, 2001, there had been rumors that Assata might be exchanged for the six-year-old refugee Elián González, who was one of three survivors of a group of fourteen Cubans who had tried to cross the Florida Straits to seek asylum in the United States.[106] Eighteen months later, the United States was under the leadership of the George W. Bush administration and had entered a very different era. In the wake of September 11, Assata Shakur was briefly displaced from the "Most Wanted" list, where her name had lingered since 1979. Then, along with a number of other 1970s radicals-at-large, her case was reassessed. Assata was moved back onto a new version of the list, this time as one of the FBI's most wanted domestic terrorists.

A victory for the Symbionese Liberation Army. Posters at Berkeley embrace Patty Hearst as "Tania." © Bettman/Corbis.

UNITED STATES DEPARTMENT OF JUSTICE

FEDERAL BUREAU OF INVESTIGATION

WASHINGTON, D.C. 20535

April 19, 1974

RE: DONALD DAVID DE FREEZE   PATRICIA MICHELLE SOLTYSIK   PATRICIA CAMPBELL HEARST
      NANCY LING PERRY   CAMILLA CHRISTINE HALL   MATERIAL WITNESS

TO WHOM IT MAY CONCERN:

     The FBI is conducting an investigation to determine the whereabouts of these individuals whose descriptions and photographs appear below. Federal warrants charging robbery of a San Francisco bank on April 15, 1974, have been issued at San Francisco, California, for Camilla Hall, Donald DeFreeze, Nancy Perry, and Patricia Soltysik. A material witness warrant in this robbery has been issued for Patricia Hearst, who was abducted from her Berkeley, California, residence on February 4, 1974, by a group which has identified itself as the Symbionese Liberation Army (SLA). The participants in the bank robbery also claim to be members of the SLA.

DONALD DAVID DE FREEZE
M/M, DOB 11/16/43, 5'9" to 5'11",
150-160, blk hair, br eyes

PATRICIA MICHELLE SOLTYSIK
W/F, DOB 5/17/50, 5'3" to 5'4",
116, dk br hair, br eyes

PATRICIA CAMPBELL HEARST
W/F, DOB 2/20/54, 5'3", 110,
lt br hair, br eyes

MATERIAL WITNESS

NANCY LING PERRY
W/F, DOB 9/19/47, 5', 95-105, red
br hair, haz eyes

CAMILLA CHRISTINE HALL
W/F, DOB 3/24/45, 5'6", 125,
blonde hair, blue eyes

     If you have any information concerning these individuals, please notify your local FBI office, a telephone listing for which can be found on the first page of your directory. In view of the crimes for which these individuals are being sought, they should be considered armed and extremely dangerous, and no action should be taken which would endanger anyone's safety.

Very truly yours,

C. M. Kelley

Clarence M. Kelley

FBI wanted poster. By October 1974, the FBI had stopped referring to Patty Hearst as only a "material witness" to the SLA's crimes. Courtesy of the Federal Bureau of Investigation.

S.L.A. Memorial poster—"In lonely outrage . . ."

The six SLA members who perished in the May 17, 1974, fire were eulogized as martyr-heroes. Poster image courtesy of J. H. Bryan.

Identification shots of Patty Hearst, San Mateo County Jail, September 18, 1975. Courtesy of the San Mateo County Sheriff's Office.

Political cartoon for the *Duluth News Tribune*, May 11, 2001. The cartoon juxtaposes Sara Jane Olson's crimes with those of Nebraska Senator Bob Kerrey, a decorated Vietnam veteran whose role in the Thanh Phong Massacre had just been revealed. Courtesy of Steve Lindstrom.

The same cartoon, as tweaked by anti-SLA activist Jack Golan. Golan added headstones for SLA victims Marcus Foster and Myrna Opsahl to undermine the assertion that Olson "killed nobody." This unauthorized version of the cartoon appeared on Golan's Lektrik Press web site in 2001. Courtesy of Steve Lindstrom and Jack Golan.

Actress Natasha Richardson poses alongside the real Patricia Hearst in a promotional photo for *Patty Hearst* (1988). Zenith Entertainment/Photofest.

An SLA propaganda photo, as reproduced in the film *Patty Hearst* (1988).
Zenith Entertainment/Photofest.

Melanie Griffith in *Cecil B. DeMented* (2000), John Waters's spoof of the Patty Hearst story and the SLA. Griffith plays a Hollywood diva kidnapped by a band of "cinema guerrillas" who force her to star in their revolution. Courtesy of the Academy of Motion Picture Arts and Sciences.

WANTED
BY THE FBI

ACT OF TERRORISM - DOMESTIC TERRORISM; UNLAWFUL FLIGHT TO AVOID CONFINEMENT - MURDER

JOANNE DEBORAH CHESIMARD

Aliases: Assata Shakur, Joanne Byron, Barbara Odoms, Joanne Chesterman, Joan Davis, Justine Henderson, Mary Davis, Pat Chesimard, Jo-Ann Chesimard, Joanne Debra Chesimard, Joanne D. Byron, Joanne D. Chesimard, Joanne Davis, Chesimard Joanne, Ches Chesimard, Sister-Love Chesimard, Joann Debra Byron Chesimard, Joanne Deborah Byron Chesimard, Joan Chesimard, Josephine Henderson, Carolyn Johnson, Carol Brown, "Ches"

DESCRIPTION

Dates of Birth Used:	July 16, 1947; August 19, 1952	Hair:	Black/Gray
Place of Birth:	New York City, New York	Eyes:	Brown
Height:	5'7"	Sex:	Female
Weight:	135 to 150 pounds	Race:	Black
NCIC:	W220305367	Nationality:	American
Occupation:	Unknown		
Scars and Marks:	Chesimard has scars on her chest, abdomen, left shoulder, and left knee.		
Remarks:	Chesimard may be living in Cuba. She may wear her hair in a variety of styles and dress in African tribal clothing.		

CAUTION

Joanne Chesimard is wanted for escaping from prison in Clinton, New Jersey, while serving a life sentence for murder. On May 2, 1973, Chesimard, who was part of a revolutionary activist organization known as the Black Liberation Army, and two accomplices were stopped for a motor vehicle violation on the New Jersey Turnpike by two troopers with the New Jersey State Police. At the time, Chesimard was wanted for her involvement in several felonies, including bank robbery. Chesimard and her accomplices opened fire on the troopers, seemingly without provocation. One trooper was wounded and the other was shot and killed execution-style at point-blank range. Chesimard fled the scene, but was subsequently apprehended. One of her accomplices was killed in the shoot-out and the other was also apprehended and remains in jail.

In 1977, Chesimard was found guilty of first degree murder, assault and battery of a police officer, assault with a dangerous weapon, assault with intent to kill, illegal possession of a weapon, and armed robbery. She was sentenced to life in prison.

On November 2, 1979, Chesimard escaped from prison and lived underground before being located in Cuba in 1984. She is thought to currently still be living in Cuba.

REWARD

The FBI is offering a reward of up to $1,000,000 for information directly leading to the apprehension of Joanne Chesimard.

ADDITIONAL PHOTOGRAPHS

SHOULD BE CONSIDERED ARMED AND EXTREMELY DANGEROUS

IF YOU HAVE ANY INFORMATION CONCERNING THIS PERSON, PLEASE CONTACT YOUR LOCAL FBI OFFICE OR THE NEAREST AMERICAN EMBASSY OR CONSULATE.

ROBERT S. MUELLER, III
DIRECTOR
FEDERAL BUREAU OF INVESTIGATION
UNITED STATES DEPARTMENT OF JUSTICE
WASHINGTON, D.C. 20535
TELEPHONE: (202) 324-3000

Wanted poster for Joanne Deborah Chesimard, alias Assata Shakur. Courtesy of the Federal Bureau of Investigation.

Assata Shakur in *Eyes of the Rainbow* (1997).

Cover of *Assata: An Autobiography*,
published by Lawrence Hill Books.

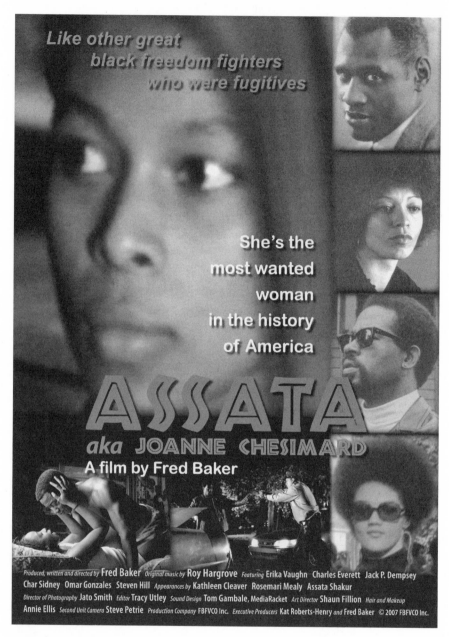

Poster for *Assata aka Joanne Chesimard* (2008). Poster design by Beverly Deutsch. Courtesy of the Fred Baker Film and Video Company.

6

Glorious and Bitter Ends

To drive around St. Paul, Minnesota, at the end of the twentieth century was to witness a silent debate raging on the city streets. Bumper stickers on vehicles around town alternately exhorted the public to "Free Sara" or "Stop Terrorism: Jail Kathleen." Both messages referred to just one woman, who in June 1999 was revealed as the 1970s fugitive and former SLA associate Kathleen Soliah.[1]

By 1999, the SLA had largely faded into history, remembered as the group that had kidnapped Patty Hearst twenty-five years earlier. While Soliah had not really joined the SLA until well after that famous abduction, she and two of her siblings had linked up with the group in time to participate in some of its later activities, including the Sacramento bank robbery in which Myrna Opsahl was murdered.

In the spring of 1974, Soliah had drawn the attention of both the SLA's Emily Harris and the FBI when she spoke at a memorial for the SLA members who had perished in the Los Angeles fire. On camera, Soliah swore her hatred for the "pigs" and urged the rest of the SLA to "keep fighting" before pledging, "I am with you! We are with you!" The FBI immediately visited Soliah to question her. So, too, did Emily Harris, who, along with Bill Harris and Patty Hearst, was desperate for a sympathetic contact to provide food and sanctuary. Soliah, her two younger siblings, and a few other associates helped supply the three fugitives with all they needed to stay underground for another year.

When the FBI captured Patty and the Harrises in San Francisco, Soliah slipped quietly out of her northern Californian life and went underground. In fact, Soliah would spend most of the next quarter century hiding in plain sight. The woman charged with planting pipe bombs under police cars in 1975 was living a comfortable existence in St. Paul's upscale Hyland Park neighborhood—not a place one would expect a member of the rabidly anti-bourgeois SLA to reside. Adopting the plausibly Minnesotan alias "Sara Jane Olson," Soliah married a doctor with whom she eventually had three daughters. Kathleen–turned–Sara Jane had never been officially employed, but had been an active and visible community volunteer for left-leaning causes in the Twin Cities. She had also acted in local theater productions, run marathons, and—to the delight of journalists who broke the story of the fugitive radical—become a certified gourmet cook.

Soliah/Olson thus emerged in the national media as a woman of contradictions, one with a split identity mirrored by the public split over what she deserved. The bumper stickers told part of the story. So, too, did a pair of words that turned up regularly in her pretrial press: "housewife" and "terrorist." Those who regarded Olson as having been the latter urged her immediate incarceration. Those inclined to see her as harmless argued that Olson's criminal actions had been specific to the post-Watergate era and worried that Olson would be made a scapegoat for the perceived transgressions of the 1970s counterculture. Pointing to Olson's decades of good works and middle-class respectability, supporters carefully began referring to Olson as the "church-going mother of three," separated from her family by a vindictive legal system.[2] The most committed of her allies formed "the Sara Olson Defense Committee" and took out second mortgages on their homes to fund her million-dollar bail bond.

If the FBI's capture of Soliah/Olson had disrupted the former fugitive's life, it had also jarred that of Patricia Hearst Shaw, by then a forty-nine-year-old mother of two living in Connecticut. Unlike Olson, Hearst was far too famous ever to elude her SLA past. But Hearst had grown accustomed to her semipublic role of the fetishized housewife-terrorist. Indeed, by 1999, she had occupied that role for most of her life. She had even consented to becoming an object of camp, taking on cameo roles as innocent "squares" in several of director John Waters's satirical films, including *Cry-Baby* (1990) and *Serial Mom* (1994).

As a subpoenaed trial witness against Sara Jane Olson, Patricia Hearst and her rehabilitated image posed the greatest challenge to Olson's defense team. Unlike Olson, Hearst had served some prison time for her affiliation with the SLA and had made clear that she was itching for Olson, whom Hearst had known as "Kathy," to do the same. In the waning months of 2000, each of the two women struggled to publicly discredit the other within the confines of a gag order. Olson's supporters derided Hearst as a "convicted criminal," a charge that lost most of its bite once President Bill Clinton pardoned Hearst on the final evening of his presidency.[3]

Clinton's pardon—which went much farther than President Carter's jail sentence commutation in restoring Hearst's rights of citizenship—reignited interest in Hearst's "outlaw days," her 1982 biography, and the 1988 film *Patty Hearst*.[4] Both of the latter included unflattering portrayals of Soliah/Olson, who was shown either as a breathless hanger-on or as a callous instrument of the SLA's worst impulses. (In *Every Secret Thing*, Kathy Soliah shrugs off the news that a woman was killed during the Crocker Bank robbery. "She was a bourgeois pig, anyway," Kathy says. "Her husband is a doctor.") In *The Ordeal of Patty Hearst*, the Soliah/Olson character nearly out-villains the SLA by becoming a frustrating obstacle to FBI Special Agent Charles Bates. Emphasizing Soliah's credentials as a semiprofessional actress, the 1979 TV movie showed her as a self-serving liar and the main reason that Patty remained with the SLA for another year.

For director John Waters, Soliah/Olson's capture and Hearst's pardon coincided felicitously with the 2000 release of *Cecil B. DeMented*, his gleeful gross-out of a film about "cinema guerrillas" who kidnap a popular Hollywood diva and force her to take a starring role in their "ultimate-reality" movie. Melanie Griffith plays pampered actress Honey Whitlock, who is repulsed by her drug-addled, sex-crazed captors, but who slowly warms to their critique of vapid, big-budget Hollywood movies. The "Sprocket Holes" give Honey a garish makeover and a pair of automatic weapons, which she uses to threaten the makers of *Gump Again* (an imaginary sequel to *Forrest Gump*) and *Patch Adams: The Director's Cut*. Soon, Honey is shouting the Sprockets' revolutionary slogan: "Power to the people who punish bad cinema!"

Film critics joked that the Sprocket Holes' maniacal leader, Cecil (Stephen Dorff), the self-proclaimed "prophet against profit," brought new meaning to the idea of a "cult director." But the *San Francisco Chronicle* called the movie for what it was: a spoof of the Patty Hearst story and of the SLA.[5] After kidnapping the privileged Honey as spokesperson for their cause, the Sprocket Holes trick her into launching a terrorist attack on the Maryland Film Commission. Ever after, the public regards Honey as having allied herself with the Sprocket Holes and their insistence that their anti-Hollywood movie will include "real violence and real terror." Cecil and crew echo the SLA's militant, media-obsessed propaganda when they point their cameras and guns at a panicked Baltimore crowd and declare them expendable extras in a terrorist fantasy. As Cecil declares, "I'm Cecil B. DeMented, and you're in my movie! Do not look into the lens and ruin the shot or you will be shot."

Like the SLA, the Sprocket Holes are obnoxious ideologues, untroubled by the prospect of hurting others for their cause. They are a mixed-race group, with as many women as men, and a completely open attitude toward sex and sexual attraction in all its forms. All have tattooed a favorite niche filmmaker's name to their bodies, and these proudly fringe identities give shape to their lives in the underground. Wielding a megaphone and a horsewhip, Dorff's tyrannical Cecil recalls either a Bill Harris or a Donald DeFreeze (indeed, Cecil's references to guerrilla *cin*ema wickedly recall the sin/cin homophone of Cinque's nickname), and he and the rest of the Sprocket Holes are willing to die for their politics.

Honey's kidnappers are meant to appear ridiculous, but also—in the context of the film's relentless silliness—as vaguely heroic freaks and outcasts. They victimize only the pompous, the powerful, and the insincere. Finding allies at the margins of society (kung-fu fans, shuffling porn show attendees), the SLA-inspired Sprocket Holes struggle against the bourgeois conventions of their upbringing, as in this silly exchange, where the group tries to strengthen the resolve of their youngest member, Fidget:

Fidget: I want to go home! I don't want to be in show business anymore!
Cecil: I knew you were the weak one, Fidget. Just remember, your parents liked *Godzilla*.
Lyle: They wouldn't even let you see R-rated films as a child.
Dinah: They've never even been to a midnight movie.
Chardonnay: They enjoy classic TV sitcoms turned into feature length films.
Cherish: They've never rented a porno movie.
Cecil: And to top it all off, they talk out loud in the theatre once the feature has begun.
Honey: Oh, that really is unforgivable, Fidget.
Fidget: Okay, okay! My parents are the enemies of film!

By 2000, Patricia Hearst had become a regular in John Waters's informal repertory company, along with actress-personalities Mink Stole and Ricki

Lake. In *Cecil B. DeMented*, she plays Fidget's clueless but adoring mother, who at one point goes on television to be interviewed about her child. The scene eerily replicates what Hearst's own parents did during her captivity, and it is not clear whether the performance is meant as condemnation or bizarre homage to the senior Hearsts. At the film's climax, Fidget is shot by the police in both kneecaps and drops from his perch on a drive-in movie marquis to the hood of his parents' car. As Fidget's mom, Hearst reaches lovingly toward her injured son, pressing her fingers against the car's windshield as if it were the glass separating visitors from a hospital's newborn ward.

Patricia Hearst is remarkably unskilled as an actress. (In a 1990s interview, she described Waters as having cast her precisely because she was not a professional and therefore "wouldn't be any trouble.") In all of her Waters film cameos, she plays the sort of wholesome domestic figure that she aspired to as Steven Weed's fiancé and then vehemently rejected in her speeches for the SLA. Often she portrays a mother whose naïveté offends her offspring and pushes them to rebellion. But her characters are never accorded any real blame or forced to undergo any change of heart. With the exception of *Serial Mom*, in which Hearst's sympathetic juror is bludgeoned to death by the woman she has just helped acquit, Hearst's impervious characters typically make it to the end of Waters's films in the same way—cheerful and unscathed.

Because *Cecil B. DeMented* was loosely built around Hearst's real-life experience, her *Cecil* cameo becomes a little more complicated. Hearst plays yet another good-natured naïf, but this time she is parent to a kid who, in some ways, recalls the kidnapped teenager that she was in 1974. There is also the obvious echo of Hearst's story in Honey Whitlock, whom *Rolling Stone* magazine ironically described as "pulling a Patty Hearst" when she renounces her sellout career as a highly paid actress in Hollywood froth.[6] To the delight of crowds at the drive-in movie theater where the Sprocket Holes are shooting their movie's final scene, Honey grants Cecil's appeal that she douse her hair with gasoline and briefly set it afire. As most of the other Sprocket Holes flee or perish around her, the still-defiant Honey is led off to prison—a survivor of the fiery spectacle and, in the context of Waters's narrative, the ultimate good sport.

Christopher Castiglia has observed how Hearst's presence in John Waters's camp projects typically serves as "the unstable threshold between the juridical maintenance of convention and its criminal resistance . . . undermin[ing] naturalized representations of American 'normalcy.'"[7] In the case of *Cecil B. DeMented*, her ambiguous outlaw reputation brings a cheeky doubleness to the script, which Waters wrote as well as directed. On the one hand, Waters defends Hearst as having been the unwitting target of a band of kooky terrorists. On the other hand, he suggests that the terrorists' visions for reforms actually made some sense and that Hearst (like Honey) might have become a better person for having been exposed to them.

Cecil B. DeMented roughly broke even at the box office, rapidly earning back its $10 million budget despite disappointing reviews. Too crude and quirky for the mainstream movie audiences it satirized, the film yet reflected the shifting zeitgeist around the memory of Patty Hearst, who was then unhappily embroiled in a second act with the SLA. By the time Honey Whitlock was terrorizing the multiplex, the former Kathleen Soliah had legally changed her name to Sara Jane Olson. Her legal team touted Olson as the "fifty-three-year-old wife and mother of three from Minnesota" as they battled her murder conspiracy charges for the attempted bombing of two Los Angeles police cars. Before she went underground, Olson had been indicted for having placed the bombs in retaliation for the shootout that had killed five of the original SLA. But Olson steadfastly maintained that she had never worked for the SLA, no matter what Hearst may have written in her memoir.

In the spring of 2000, the Sara Olson Defense Fund Committee began selling copies of *Ungagged*, a video recording of a February forum that had drawn a small number of scholar-activists to Minneapolis to discuss connections between Olson's case and "the use of prosecution and prison to silence dissidents and control minority people." The keynote speaker was Bernadine Dohrn, the former Weather Underground leader who had in 1980 voluntarily emerged from the underground, with fellow Weather leader Bill Ayers and their two children in tow. (The prosecutorial misconduct related to the FBI's illegal surveillance program ensured that neither Dohrn nor Ayers would ever serve time for their Weather Underground activities, although Dohrn did receive probation for various state charges.)[8] By the time she appeared in the Twin Cities on Sara Jane Olson's behalf, Dohrn was a professor at Northwestern School of Law and director of its Children and Family Justice Center. Dismissing the case against Olson as a "witch hunt," Dohrn criticized the United States for going after civil rights leaders and Vietnam War protestors. She argued that women radicals were particularly vulnerable, for they "aroused [in law enforcement] a kind of wrath that other people don't."[9] Tacitly acknowledging the irony of her credentials as a panelist, Dohrn was circumspect: "How did a good girl from Milwaukee . . . end up on the FBI's Ten Most Wanted List? I can't answer that."[10]

With Bernadine Dohrn in her corner, Olson might have hoped to walk the same delicate path toward dropped charges and a secure future. But the icon of the Weather Underground was a strange role model for Olson. Not quite a true "outlaw"—being very much alive and having too emphatic and controversial a set of politics precluded that—Dohrn the middle-aged mother was leading a life that was arguably more consistent with the radical politics of her underground youth. However much certain segments of the public might loathe her, Dohrn also still has a cultural celebrity's cachet. As a relative unknown, Olson relied on her supporters to raise her profile through tongue-in-cheek fund-raising projects like an Olson-inspired cookbook, *Serving Time: America's Most Wanted Recipes.* But the cookbook immediately came under fire for its goofy images of Olson juggling handcuffs alongside spatulas and other cooking equipment. Olson insisted that a photo of herself balancing a stack of baguettes in one hand and a wad of money in the other was just a playful reference to the 1970s slang that referred to money as "bread." Critics read the photo as an inappropriate joke about the SLA's assault on the banks they called "bakeries."

Days after Hearst's January 2000 pardon, Sacramento authorities added to Olson's legal woes by filing first-degree murder charges against her and three other former SLA members for the Crocker bank robbery killing. There were also serious intimations that Olson could, on the basis of the original SLA's "Declaration of War," be charged with conspiracy to overthrow the U.S. government. Olson's "housewife" defense crumbled along with her original defense team, which had repeatedly asked to push back her trial. Finally, it crumbled completely in the wake of the 9/11 terrorist attacks. Despite her lawyers' efforts to convince the public that Olson was a radical poster child on the same order as Leonard Peltier or Mumia Abu-Jamal, the panicked Olson pleaded guilty to the attempted bombing charges on Halloween 2001.

As more revelations surfaced about Olson and the former SLA (Emily Harris worked for Disney! Olson's SLA-era boyfriend, the fugitive James Kilgore, had found work as a university professor in South Africa!), reporters began drawing on Patty Hearst's 1982 accounting of the SLA as an unquestionably reliable source for their reporting. In a reversal of the climate of 1976, when comparisons to the white, middle-class SLA woman cast doubt upon her credibility, by 2001 Hearst's reputation was being redeemed in the press. California's prosecuting attorneys happily fed the media unflattering details about surviving SLA members who apparently had aged into the very sorts of "bourgeois pigs" they had once professed to despise. Worse, they had never expressed regret for their activities as "domestic terrorists," quite a serious charge after September 11. In a CNN interview with Larry King, Hearst did her best to connect the SLA to the United States' worst criminals, comparing the surviving members to Oklahoma City bomber Timothy McVeigh and charging them with orchestrating their "own little jihad" on the United States.[11]

The *Economist* used the SLA story to condemn John Walker, the young "California airhead" discovered in late 2001 as a volunteer for the Taliban forces in Afghanistan. "Why throw the book at him?" the editors huffed. "[Because] Mr. Walker is no Patty Hearst, goaded into his actions."[12] Both Hearst and Walker hailed from the Bay Area in San Francisco—a region widely blamed for Walker's actions—so the comparison may have been inevitable. But it also signaled a sea change in attitude toward Hearst's SLA involvement, even if she might have been "goaded" and not officially "brainwashed" as her defense team insisted in 1976.

The outpouring of scrutiny and scorn heaped on the SLA was accompanied by an outpouring of creativity. Multiple novelists drew inspiration from the Patty Hearst kidnapping and from the dozens of individual stories that radiated from it. Not only did the aims and characters of the SLA make for compelling fiction, they also became a way to probe the 1970s decade, a set of lingering social problems, and even prospects for the twenty-first century, which had opened with another period of war and political upheaval. Susan Choi's *American Woman* (2003) was the first "Patty Hearst" novel to hit the bookstores. But Choi based her protagonist on one of the SLA's more peripheral figures, Wendy Yoshimura, who was best known for having been arrested with Hearst and whose path to radicalism began with her birth in a Japanese internment camp. As happened in real life, Wendy ("Jenny") forms an odd friendship with Patty ("Pauline"), and that friendship ultimately becomes an index of racial and class boundaries. As Choi muses at the novel's close, "Pauline would 'get the book thrown at her' yet somehow be redeemed, or rather be shown to require no redemption, while Jenny would 'get off easy' for somebody like her."[13]

In 2005, Christopher Sorrentino released *Trance*, his phantasmagoric recreation of the SLA and the largely damaged denizens of the middle 1970s. Sorrentino's Patty is Alice Gralton, and his novel's title fits like a blindfold across the eyes of the novel's cover girl, a Hearst look-alike. For five hundred pages, *Trance* eavesdrops on the inner thoughts of everyone from the least SLA associate to Alice's father. Some of the details are fabricated; many are lifted from the HEARNAP case's more obscure texts, including a Los Angeles coroner's report on the charred corpses of five SLA members.

Two years later, Brian Joseph Davis's absurdist *I, Tania* (2007) imagined a Patty Hearst who was the SLA's true ideologue and whose current life is just a brilliant cover for her ongoing guerrilla activities. Davis's intelligent Tania struggles to write a memoir that the public will accept; the result is a wild mash-up of pop references and sly insights, as in the moment that the Los Angeles coroner reports on the events leading up to the deadly fire.

> Tania, on lookout in the waiting van, began shooting into the store from across the street with a submachine gun. Everyone in the store took cover and became confused as they pondered why it was such a distinctly American response to be turned on by the sight of a woman with gun . . . Tania reloaded and emptied the magazine again, only becoming more sexy and more confusing.[14]

Early in the twenty-first century, with the threat of terrorism and two divisive wars dominating headlines, it was perhaps inevitable that both the Weather Underground and the SLA would get their own feature-length documentaries. Bill Ayers's memoir, *Fugitive Days*—which included an account of planting a bomb in the Pentagon—had been reviewed on page 1 of the *New York Times* on September 11, 2001. For the first time, Ayers's reputation began to overshadow that of his wife, Bernadine Dohrn, and both found it wise to keep a low profile for a while before emerging as some of the most fervid voices against the Iraq War. In *The Weather Underground* (2002), filmmakers Sam Green and Bill Siegel do not contextualize the radical group in movement history. Instead, they spotlight individual members and let them reminisce about what they did over Ektachrome footage of their impossibly young selves. The documentary's chief skeptic, Todd Gitlin, dismisses the former Weathermen by comparing them to Bonnie and Clyde. As Gitlin, the onetime SDS president ousted by a Weather takeover, explains, "They were into youth, exuberance, sex, drugs. They wanted action."

In *Neverland: The Rise and Fall of the Symbionese Liberation Army* (2003), director Robert Stone gives the SLA their own chance to explain themselves. Or, more accurately, he lets SLA members Russ Little and Michael Bortin tell their version of the story of Patty Hearst. Little, one of the two SLA members who were jailed for the Marcus Foster murder a month before the Hearst kidnapping, was retried and acquitted of that crime in

1981. In *Neverland,* Little derides himself and the rest of the SLA for taking too seriously the television heroes of their childhood, among them Zorro and Robin Hood and "all these tales of swashbucklers and people who were fighting against the government." Little recalls the original SLA members as having first become acquainted through a political film series that featured titles like *State of Siege* (1972), about a kidnapping and prisoner swap, and *Che!* (1969).

Bortin, who joined the second-team SLA after the 1974 fire, concurs that SLA members' heads were filled with romantic imagery. He also credits the original SLA as having produced some of the best of it. Bortin confesses his astonishment at the black-and-white security camera images in which "Tania" made her debut as a bank robber: "It was Bonnie and Clyde. It was all that kind of thing that's very American at the core . . . These guys [the SLA] are doing it so *artistically.*"

The surreality of movie imagery surfaces repeatedly in the Little and Bortin interviews. Reflecting on what it meant to become a high-stakes prisoner, Little jokes, "We had read about this, watched movies about it. Now we got to be in *Attica,* as revolutionaries, no less." Bortin saw the SLA as representing the best (and most entertaining) hopes for political change. Watching their demands around the People in Need food giveaway "was like watching a movie," says Bortin. "Oh, we were pulling for them so much." Little even theorizes that Patty Hearst's apparent conversion was motivated by the glamour of the celluloid outlaw. He imagines Patty as having jumped at the chance to "join Robin Hood," because "Why shouldn't it be Hollywood for her too?" *Neverland*'s director picks up on the theme, occasionally punctuating the SLA story with clips from the 1939 *Robin Hood,* starring Errol Flynn.

Neverland has an alternative name, *Guerrilla: The Taking of Patty Hearst.* At least one critic raised an eyebrow at the sexual innuendo in that subtitle.[15] It also seemed a misnomer for a movie that, while technically about the Hearst kidnapping, had almost nothing new to say about Hearst herself. *Neverland*'s Patty is more absence than presence, represented primarily by her voice on the SLA audiotapes and a hallucinogenic sequence in which images from her captivity are intercut with a fleeting sequence from a 1930s gangster film. One of the Hearst lawyers reads aloud an affidavit declaring the Patty whom the FBI took into custody as "confused, still unable to discern between actuality and fantasy."

The documentary's coda sums up the fate of the SLA who pled guilty in 2003 for the 1976 murder of Myrna Opsahl. Four SLA members would serve more jail time, it explains, and all thanks to the arrest of Kathy Soliah (Sara Jane Olson), in combination with the post-9/11 crackdown on terrorism. Her formerly red hair now completely white, a sober Olson/Soliah appears in a Los Angeles courtroom with Mike Bortin and the long-divorced Emily and Bill Harris. In their matching orange jumpsuits, the former SLA look haggard and pathetic. Bortin rises to offer an incoherent apology ("The fact that Mrs. Opsahl was murdered unintentionally in the bank is of no consequence"). Opsahl's son grimaces and shakes his head. The *Neverland* title here resonates more clearly in its reference to perpetual youth and an impossible future. The fortunate SLA members—that is, the only ones to retain any dignity—are those who died in the 1974 blaze.

Most fortunate of all is Patricia Hearst, who is almost given the last word in a circa 2000 talk-show clip. Hearst enters atop a TV-set staircase, dazzlingly blonde and wearing a sleek black dress. When the television interviewer opens with a question about growing up in a famous family, Hearst enthuses, "Well, it was great, you know. I think it was really pretty perfect." That is when the film abruptly cuts her off by cutting away to the end credits. *Neverland* halfheartedly celebrates Hearst as a survivor—and one who has made the most of her "Hollywood" opportunity. But it also suggests nobody really wants to hear the truth as Hearst tells it, because that could only spoil the myriad fantasies projected onto Tania.

Hearst's younger self and mysterious alter ego continue to provide the stuff of parodies and fiction. Patty/Tania and the first-team SLA have even become fodder for the Military Channel's *Combat Zone* program, which reviews martial strategies employed in various well-documented battles. In 2007, *Combat Zone*'s producers reenacted the deadly 1974 standoff between a group that included FBI and LAPD members and the SLA's six-person "army." (The dramatization appeared in the same season with episodes entitled "Invasion of Grenada," "Triangle of Death, Iraq," and "Battle of Najaf, Iraq.") Whoever approved the lengthy examination of the SLA shootout must have had a memory of the startlingly combatlike conditions of the four-hour battle. While emphasizing the SLA's remarkable firepower (they modified their M-1 carbines to shoot as rapidly as machine guns), the program is also sprinkled with commentary from former journalists, FBI agents, and law enforcement officials who marvel at the SLA's tenacity in the face of death. Multiple talking heads repeat the tale of how the six SLA cornered in the Los Angeles safe house kept on shooting and would not surrender, not even after the house filled with teargas and then flames.

Rather than using the individual SLA members to explain Tania, *Combat*

Zone uses Tania to explain the SLA. The program frames its story with the question of Patty Hearst's conversion—a question the producers tacitly answer by reenacting the moment when an armed and unattended Patty came to the aid of her captors. As a security guard gets into a scuffle with the program's stand-ins for Bill and Emily Harris, a snarling actress representing Patty/Tania leaps from the SLA van to fire her submachine gun. The program twice repeats this "historical" footage of Patty's swift and strategic response on behalf of the SLA.

Curiously, however, this heavy-handed visual of a savage, turncoat Patty stands mostly at odds with the rest of *Combat Zone*'s narrative. TV journalist Bill Deiz speculates that as soon as the SLA's kidnapping victim had appeared on bank cameras as Tania, the public lost touch with the tragedy of the situation and "immediately fixated on the fact that Patty Hearst was an outlaw." Journalist Bob Navarro seems less convinced that Tania's rebellion was either exaggerated or an expression of the public's desire. He instead attributes any lenience shown to Patty as proof that most of the country has chosen to forget, rather than forgive. This deliberate forgetfulness, Navarro reasons, is analogous to the understanding shown to American troops taken hostage by an enemy. Not long ago, captured soldiers who said or did things against their country would have been scorned. "Now," says Navarro, "they're treated. You understand it. So times change."

Assata aka Joanne Chesimard

For years, a listing for "Assata Shakur" appeared in the Havana telephone book. Then the FBI, in conjunction with the state of New Jersey, declared that they were raising the standing reward for her capture to $1 million. "She's now 120 pounds of money," quipped one New Jersey trooper on the day the new reward was announced in May 2005. An NJLawman.com editorial responded with one word: "FINALLY." It continued, "She will no longer be able to casually saunter down the streets, take in a movie, or do whatever else people living on exotic islands do. In a country where the minimum wage is eight-dollars and forty-cents a month, this excrement will have to look over her shoulder for the rest of her life. Joanne Chesimard, enjoy your new life."[16] Oddly, the 2005 announcement again contradicted the findings of Assata's 1977 jury in pronouncing her, and not Sundiata Acoli, as Trooper Foerster's killer. In a television address that year, Fidel Castro voiced his objections to the $1 million on Assata's head, although he did not call Assata by name: "To make her look like a terrorist is an injustice, a brutality, an infamous lie. This woman was a role model," said Castro. "There are strange things, very strange, mixed up here."[17] Assata's phone number vanished from the public listing.

In the online forum at AssataShakur.org, commenters reacted with anger, some of them pledging to rip down the new wanted posters that the FBI were distributing in English and in Spanish. Galvanized by the $1 million "bounty," members of the Hands Off Assata campaign began distributing low-quality copies of Rolando's previously banned *Eyes of the Rainbow*, via individual DVD sales. The sales began on July 16, 2007, in honor of Assata's sixtieth birthday.

By July 2007, Fred Baker had just wrapped his own film about the contemporary outlaw. *Assata aka Joanne Chesimard* is a film about a young, twenty-first-century man obsessed with Assata Shakur and struggling to complete a documentary about her. The besotted documentarian is clearly a stand-in for *Assata*'s director, who admits to having fallen in love with Assata upon meeting her as a fellow inmate at the Manhattan Correctional Center in the mid-1970s. Baker himself wrote the screenplay, which imagines an impetuous romance between Justin (the filmmaker) and Asha (a graduate student) who come together through their shared admiration for Assata.[18]

Like *Eyes of the Rainbow*, Baker's film enshrines Assata as a freedom fighter dedicated to the rights of black Americans. The narrator explicitly compares her to Harriet Tubman, Ida B. Wells, Paul Robeson, Rosa Parks, Medgar Evers, and Martin Luther King Jr., among others, who "all came to fight." A photographic montage of these luminaries devotes extra time to Malcolm X, who "came to raise his voice and fight for radical change, *by any means necessary.*" Baker's film is bolder than Rolando's in contextualizing Assata's imprisonment in the history of state violence against black men and women. Baker also frames the BPP and its origins as the apotheosis of black struggle in the United States: "The Black Panther Party was born in the 1960s . . . [The BPP's] great freedom fighters were Eldridge and Kathleen Cleaver, Huey Newton, Bobby Seale, Fred Hampton, and many, many others. And yes, many of them lost their lives in the struggle to systematic FBI and police assassination and murder." The montage of heroes is bracketed by images of brutal lynchings and a shockingly long list of Panthers killed by police in the late 1960s and early 1970s. This section, and other of the more didactic sections of *Assata*, are amplified by talking-head interviews with former Panthers Kathleen Cleaver and Rosemari Mealy.[19]

The film offers the first glimpse of its protagonist with a close-up of a woman's bare shoulders and neck. The camera then pans back to reveal a police photo of the twenty-something Assata Shakur, posed to display the dark, round scar from a bullet's exit point. Over the image of the New Jersey State Police web site, on which Assata remains one of "New Jersey's 12 Most Wanted," the narrator introduces Assata this way: "There's one revolutionary still fighting today, despite the many murderous odds brought down against her by her own government. A woman of great beauty and passion. A woman of an undying will, whose voice is still loud and clear in the battle for racial freedom, quality and liberation throughout the world. Her name is Assata Shakur." To make the film's subject, and its politics, absolutely clear, the narrator adds: "Perhaps you know her as Joanne Chesimard. This film is dedicated to her."

In Baker's film, Assata is both an outlaw and a conduit through which the characters Justin and Asha become ersatz outlaws as well. "That girl has revolution in her soul," declares Justin (Charles Everett), who warns Asha (Erika Vaughn) of the hazards of making a movie about their idol: "There's danger in the true telling of this story." Assata's story becomes an emblem of a nest of twenty-first-century concerns, including draconian antiterrorism measures and the Iraq War. ("Don't you realize we're living in a police state?" Justin chides Asha when she suggests that he is paranoid. "They're torturing and killing innocent people today, in our name.") Justin and Asha's first meeting echoes an early scene in *Bonnie and Clyde*, in which Bonnie becomes sexually excited by Clyde's gun. In *Assata*, Justin teaches Asha to use his camera, which becomes the source of innuendo-laced banter and leads to a steamy stairwell tryst. Justin and Asha's mutual regard for Assata (on whom Asha is writing a master's thesis) fuels their attraction and appears to occupy all their conversations, including those that take place while the couple is in bed. At one point, Asha breaks off their lovemaking with a declaration that she must go to Cuba to meet Assata in person, something that Justin has tried to do three times without success. Asha never gets to meet with Assata either—throughout the film, the present-day Assata remains more of a glittering concept than a real woman—and Asha's frustration at Justin's unwillingness to join her in Cuba nearly tears the couple apart.

In 2003, Fred Baker telephoned Assata Shakur in Cuba and asked her to let him meet with her there. She declined but, according to Baker, remembered well their charged encounter at a prison mixer in the Manhattan Correctional Center. In her autobiography, Assata recalls the correctional center this way: "To my absolute surprise i was placed in 'general population,' given a key to my cage, and told that there was no 'lock-in' time. We were supposed to stand by the cell doors at various times of the day to be counted." She relates how male prisoners on the honor floor, which was on the same floor as the female prisoners, could bribe the guards to send out for special foods or even sneak into the women's section for conjugal visits.[20]

As Baker explains, he had been sentenced to serve sixty weekends at the prison for "guerrilla activity." He joked about how incongruous his status was as a part-time prison inmate: "[I was a] Father of three. Filmmaker. Broadway actor. And all of a sudden I'm being set up to be totally busted out for whatever. It was harmless. I had thrown some tear gas back at the soldiers at the Pentagon." While serving his time as prison cook, Baker became known as the "filmmaker who's doing interviews." Assata sent him a note requesting that they meet at the next prison dance. "They had mixers between the female and male prisoners," Baker recalled. "It was like a buffet and some music and you could stand and talk to a woman. Because everything else was pretty segregated."

Baker remembers complimenting Assata: "I said, 'You're a celebrity here.' And she said 'oh, don't be silly'—or I forget. But it was really beautiful, sort of just a nice intimate evening . . . I think she's one of the most absolutely beautiful women I've ever seen in my life." Thirty years later, the memory of "that one night in the joint" prompted Baker to pour $85,000 of his own savings into the making of *Assata*. "Why Assata for the film?" Baker laughed. "I think I'm one of those guys that just loves beautiful women. I found one that I secretly was in love with from that one night in the jail . . . We had great sex in a broom closet. But that's not why you fall in love. I always had a feeling that I'd never forget that night."

According to Baker, Assata could not meet with him because of security concerns but did approve of his film proposal and spoke with him for three hours on the telephone. "She said, 'well, [the film] sounds great,'" reported Baker. "'Ask me anything you want to.'" Baker soon found, however, that there were certain details of her story that Assata refused to revisit. In particular, Assata would not answer questions about the other two guns found at the scene of the incident in which Zayd Shakur and Werner Foerster were killed. When Baker asked for details about the evening of May 2, 1973, "she said, 'that's all gone and forgotten.'" As Baker recalled, "She indicated to me in one of those conversations, 'Look, from what I gather you're talking about making a film about someone who's totally innocent. Are you sure about that?' I said, 'Yes, I am very sure about that. And you don't have to worry about the film. I'll never say anything different.'"

Referring to the trouble that had followed Ralph Penza's 1997 interview with Assata for NBC, Baker noted,

> He [Penza] made a mistake. And I just didn't want to make that mistake. She really, really was fed up with anybody that still had doubts and wanted to ask typical questions about the positioning, blah blah blah. "Where were the guns? Were they in the trunk? Did Sundiata open the trunk and have to pick up a gun cause he would have been caught?" I didn't want to ask any of those questions. By the time that we spoke in 2003, I had envisioned the way I would tell it in the film.

Baker justifies his telling of Assata's story through the dialogue he wrote for Justin and Asha—dialogue in which Justin speaks for Baker and Asha articulates the complaints of an imagined film critic. When Asha mocks Justin for using a "corny" and outmoded swirl of newspaper headlines to sum up Assata's four years of court trials, Justin retorts that he has no choice because he is running out of money. When Asha derides a reenactment of the Turnpike shootout as "theater," Justin indignantly defends his staging of the event as based on police tape transcripts that were playing during Assata's trial and later reproduced in the *New York Times*.[21]

For Baker, as for Justin, the boundaries of reenactment are malleable. After Assata's aunt, Evelyn Williams, tried to discourage Baker from making *Assata*, Baker contrived for Justin to ask Asha to stand in for Williams's part. When the real-life Fred Hampton Jr. demanded a staggering fee to participate in the film's homage to his late father, Baker worked around that as well. ("I said, 'Get me an actor.'") Asha and Justin meet up with a man identified as the junior Hampton who expresses a son's grief upon watching a documentary about the murder of Hampton's father.

From the start of the film, Justin is consumed by the Turnpike reenactment, repeatedly lapsing into reveries in which he imagines how the deadly confrontation played out. Six times in *Assata*, the Turnpike confrontation is replayed, until Patrolman James Harper is revealed to have been responsible for both of the killings that night.[22] Justin portrays Harper as an impulsive man, prone to panic, an interpretation that hinges on Harper's failure to report the shooting of his fellow officer, as well as his later admission of having fabricated portions of the incident report. (As the scene is filmed, it ignores the finding that, after being shot at a short distance by someone on the scene, Trooper Werner Foerster was ultimately executed at point-blank range, by two bullets from his own weapon. It also disregards the fact that a gunshot wound to Harper's shoulder was caused by a gun from the vehicle. In the reenactment, it is Foerster who accidentally shoots Harper when Sundiata Acoli tries to wrest his service revolver from him.) As Baker mused after an early pre-screening, "I looked into the case. I researched it. I read about it. What I show on the screen totally is my opinion. So I'm hoping that I don't get sued for libel by this Captain Patrolman Harper. But probably I will. I'm essentially accusing him of having murdered everybody on the scene. And I truly believe that that's what happened." Baker opens his film with a similar disclaimer, plus a quotation from the writer Janet Malcolm: "The instability of human knowledge is one of our few certainties. Almost everything we know we know incompletely at best. And almost nothing we are told remains the same when retold."[23]

Baker included the disclaimer to acknowledge his own unavoidably incomplete understanding of why Assata was ultimately convicted of first-degree murder and sent to prison. Midway through the film, Justin is shown attempting to access the judicial record of Assata's 1977 trial at the New Jersey State Law Library. Turned away by archivists who declare the record "unavailable," Justin is followed back to his car by two FBI agents who threaten him with bodily harm. ("Listen here, young brother. You're treading on some pretty sensitive ground here, boy.") Baker pointed to this sequence as a more dramatic version of his own failed attempts at gaining access to the court transcript. Like Justin in the film, Baker allegedly was told by library staffers that the documents he sought were unavailable, despite the fact that they are noncirculating material.[24] Later, he and a "lady friend" were visited by FBI agents. By Baker's recollection, "They were very rough. They came and stopped me."

That Justin (and, by extension, Baker) presses on with his film project ascribes to him a heroism that *Assata*'s nearly invisible protagonist would seem to lack. Throughout the film, the character "Assata Shakur" is a fawnlike cipher. Baker attributes this to the actress, Char Sydney, whom he cast for her resemblance to Assata rather than for her acting talent. In her most important moment of the film, Sydney's Assata appears as the terrified, unarmed victim of the irrational Harper, albeit one who stoically bears her injuries by his gun. This portrayal accords with the real-life Assata's own accounting of her behavior on the scene but also undermines her reputation as the "firebrand revolutionary Black Panther" promised in *Assata*'s promotional materials.[25] (Early test audiences criticized Sydney as "too feminine" for the title role.) The film emphasizes Assata's physical vulnerability with images of Sydney's tiny, bandaged form in a hospital bed.[26] Later, she is a stylishly dressed defendant in dark sunglasses, standing mute on the courthouse steps. Only after Sydney's Assata speaks, to limply enunciate the real Assata's furious condemnation of her 1977 court verdict, does the usefulness of her silence become apparent. As long as the character Assata keeps mum, a sympathetic audience may remain in awe of her and project upon her what they will. Baker seems to have understood this when he decided not to include any of Assata Shakur's more recent public statements in his film. For one who is so eloquent on the page, the real-life Assata may be less gifted as an extemporaneous public speaker. While Baker did give the real Assata a fleeting cameo in his film—a Havana marketplace shot lifted from the 1997 NBC interview—he confessed to finding most other footage of her unusable: "There were too many uhs, ums."

The recurring doubleness of Assata finds symbolic expression in the film's full title: *Assata aka Joanne Chesimard.* Baker acknowledged having added the *aka* as a concession to generational, as well as political, divides: "I need both names. Because there's a divergence in the [public] consciousness of who she is." Baker said he knew he would need the second half of the title when his sister, who was an adult in the 1970s, could not identify Assata Shakur. "But," notes Baker, "if I say to my sister 'Joanne,' then she says, 'that girl in Cuba who killed the cop.'" Meanwhile, younger people do not recognize the name Joanne Chesimard. "But you say 'Assata' and they know it. She's like big news." Baker freely admits to wanting to please Assata with his film and to honor her self-constructions: "Assata doesn't like to be referred to as Joanne Chesimard." So by supplanting the *aka Assata Shakur* with *aka Joanne Chesimard,* Baker's film is "saying that [her birth name] is almost discarded."

Assata's courtroom reenactment includes a deliberately anachronistic bit of testimony on Assata's Turnpike injuries—a computer-generated image sequence in which we see two bullets pierce a deliberately light-skinned stand-in for Assata's body. The bullets do their damage; virtual blood splatters on the wall behind the white model's alluringly posed, naked torso. ("I love the idea of mixing the race," said Baker, of the decision to do the graphic on a body with light skin. "What's the difference? It's a body. I thought that was a great political point.") Baker also acknowledged the potency of graphically representing violence done to a female form versus a male form. "To my eyes, the female body is just much more beautiful to look at than the male body and when you injure it or wound it, it's a bit more brutal." Nowhere in *Assata* is there any mention of the pregnancy and motherhood story that was so important to Assata's biography in *Eyes of the Rainbow,* although Justin does make fleeting reference to Assata's granddaughter as one of the reasons she so zealously guards her sanctuary in Cuba.

While *Eyes of the Rainbow* glossed over the details of Assata's prison break, *Assata* dramatizes it as it may have happened. In a placard explaining the breakout, Baker cannot resist the use of the exclamatory: *"After her conviction, Assata was remanded to serve a life sentence . . . Then one day, in 1979, after serving two and a half years, a very remarkable event occurred!"* Although Assata might have wished for more attention to the prison conditions that she decries in her book, she probably would not take issue with Baker's exclamation mark. As Baker reconstructs it, the breakout went off with remarkable—and, for the viewer, almost disappointing—ease. Two male visitors to the prison are not searched. Once inside, one of these visitors holds a gun to a female guard's head until she and another guard are taken as hostages and loaded in a prison van. Over a jumpy, improvisational jazz soundtrack, Assata's liberators find her waiting in a stairwell. Empty-handed, she follows them and their hostages outside; she is never given a weapon. A mysterious, beret-wearing white woman, who earlier brought Assata and her compatriots the automobile for their trip down the Turnpike, now reappears with another car for the getaway.[27]

The metanarrative of *Assata*'s film-within-a-film suggests that Asha helped Justin obtain the money he needed to shoot the prison break scene. From her post in Cuba, Asha requests the funds from "an old lover, who'd do anything for me." The intimation is that Asha, like Assata, permanently enchants those who fall in love with her. This gift for enchantment, and its privileges, will be Asha's contribution to Justin's vicarious outlawry. So it is for Baker's on-screen Assata. She is noble and beautiful and worthy of tribute, but without being particularly daring. While it might be tempting to attribute this objectified Assata to the filmmaker's emotional attachment to her, it would be a mistake to underestimate Fred Baker. After all, the apparent passivity of his heroine makes those who despise her look stupid and oppressive.

As the owner of the Fred Baker Film and Video Company, Baker has long distributed his own films (*Events*, 1970; *Lenny Bruce without Tears*, 1971; *White Trash*, 1992), plus multiple films from the popular Jazz Masters series.[28] "This will be the first film I'm making that is [an] anti-establishment, anti-American, anti-governmental, anti–police state statement," Baker volunteered, before adding that he could not predict how the general public would receive it. "I know that Michael Moore has sold millions and millions and millions of dollars' worth of tickets, but he may be cleverer than I am, I don't know." On a MySpace page set up to promote the film, Baker describes Assata as "a beacon for freedom, and, in her own way, the female Che Guevara."[29] The important phrase there—and Baker knows it—is "in her own way." Because Assata, like all women outlaws, is primarily regarded through the lens of her sex, it may never have been possible for her to occupy the same category as Che, not even if she had been born a member of the United States' racial majority or if she had a more high-profile career as an outlaw. However, like Che, she has become an important figure in Cuba, an icon to whom multiple and conflicted meanings are assigned, and someone whose reputation will likely live on beyond her death. A cynical person might also read her, like Che, as a marketing opportunity. But Baker is earnest in wanting his film to make her a hero for the ages and a window onto an era wracked by racially motivated violence. Of the potential profits to be made from the film, Baker is nonchalant, despite having made the decision to "denude [his] bank account" by making *Assata.*[30]

One early reviewer compared Baker's character, Justin, to the filmmaker Keith Beauchamp, who spent a decade struggling to complete *The Untold Story of Emmett Louis Till* (2005). Beauchamp's documentary ultimately persuaded the Justice Department to reopen Till's murder case. "The martyrs and heroes of the Black Community have a way of inspiring succeeding generations of truth-tellers," wrote Louis Proyect, a self-described "old leftist" who admitted to having previously "assumed the worst" about Assata when she was on trial in the 1970s. He lauded Baker's film for having corrected this impression and for having crafted a story with "more impact than the average Hollywood blockbuster costing 1000 times more."[31] For now, however, *Assata* will have to go a long way before commanding a blockbuster's audience. The film had its official debut in February 2008, at the San Diego Black Film Festival. Baker intends to distribute *Assata* slowly, starting with screenings for left-leaning organizations and for young activists who participate in the Hands Off Assata campaign or other movements like it. He hopes it will resonate with a new generation for whom Assata might become newly iconic and newly relevant, an index of everything from racial profiling to civil liberties abuses under the revised Patriot Act.

In a 2000 interview, Assata said that she now regrets some of her radical political strategies. She was talking not about revolutionary violence but about revolutionary rhetoric. As she quipped, "We do not have the right, in the name of social justice, to bore people to death."[32] Fred Baker surely agrees with her. His "docudrama" is edutainment, a political argument wrapped in romantic confectionary. Kathleen Cleaver may appear on-screen to explain how Homeland Security funds motivated Assata's official categorization as a "domestic terrorist," but it is not long before the film cuts back to Justin and Asha, snuggling together in front of Cleaver's on-screen image. The lovers' bond springs from their shared indignation at the treatment of Assata; their happiness seems predicated on her fate. The film concludes with footage of New York City Councilman Charles Barron speaking at a Hands Off Assata rally. Lamenting the passing of the BPP, Barron summons the power of moviemaking to check police violence against black citizens: "Forget the guns, if we had camcorders, [Amado] Diallo would be alive today. We have to make a way for Assata to come home."[33] With those words, Asha and Justin call a truce to their earlier quarrel and reunite in Central Park. Dressed for the chill of late autumn weather, they walk off arm in arm, girded for more hard times in their campaign for Assata and, by extension, the safety of all people of color.[34]

Baker's film offers another glimpse of the potent fantasies surrounding the outlaw Assata—his own and those of the audience he hopes to reach. In each of his reenactments, Assata is sexually attractive without the complicated overlay of motherhood. She is rebellious without being "castrating." Most important, she is politically committed to the BLA without ever having to fire, or even hold, a gun. This treatment could be seen either as a "typical hetero-male interpretation" or, more fairly, as the prevailing formula for the longevity of an outlaw-hero. Larry Buchanan had his Bonnie Parker, in whom he found a sexy moneymaker, a populist love story, and an opportunity for a political statement. Baker seems to have found something similar in Assata. Like Buchanan, Baker was an actor before he became a director: "As a filmmaker, my strongest feelings are for the remarkable people. For me, as an entertainer, they're the other entertainers." Baker might not go so far as to label Assata a performer. (To do so would come uncomfortably close to an alliance with her angriest critics.) But he obviously recognizes in her a natural star quality that combined felicitously with an exceptional set of circumstances to make her a compelling film subject.

When Kathleen Cleaver saw *Assata aka Joanne Chesimard*, she urged Baker to take it to the college campuses, where audiences would identify with Assata through the characters Justin and Asha, who are both in their late twenties and African American. Apart from being a filmmaker, Baker does not much resemble his on-screen avatar. A self-described red-diaper baby born to Jewish parents who lost family in the Holocaust, Baker is white. *Assata* requires younger characters to sell the glamour of its 1970s icon to a new generation of human rights activists. Jason and Asha might have been any color, so long as they were young and beautiful. But Baker presumes that members of the black community have a more personal investment in a story about racial profiling, police brutality, and a capricious justice system. Baker and Proyect are welcome to support and revere Assata, but she is first and foremost an outlaw symbol for those who have been on the receiving end of white or imperialist oppression (at least by many of Assata's own writings, in which "white" and "imperialist" are nearly synonymous). Hence Baker's need for Justin as his racial "disguise"—which is not intended as a deceit but reflects Baker's pragmatism as well as a heartfelt solidarity. For Baker and for some of his film's audience, it may also be an expression of white liberal fantasy; that is, of disavowing white privilege and joining the ranks of "the people" for whom the noble, aggrieved exile continually professes her love.

As shown in the case of Patricia Hearst, film and other popular entertainments have been integral to the cultural survival of the contemporary woman outlaw. In the case of Assata, popular culture may help ensure her literal survival as well. Long before the announcement of the million-dollar reward for her capture, Assata won the sympathy and support of multiple rap and hip-hop artists.[35] For example, Common's circa 2000 "Song for Assata," on the *Like Water for Chocolate* album, encapsulates the highlights of her autobiography, reiterates her account of having been framed for a murder she did not commit, and marvels at her strength in the face of racist abuse. No troubadour of old could have done better in advertising Assata as an exceptional woman who was forced into outlawry. Declaring Assata free for the fact of her political asylum in Cuba, Common wishes for a chance for the "Beautiful Woman to become soft again." The song's chorus (sung by Cee-Lo) shifts into a direct address intended for Assata: "Your Power and Pride, so Beautiful. May God bless your Soul."[36] Common's song was inspired by Assata's autobiography, but rap and hip-hop communities have also embraced her for having been godmother to the late Tupac Shakur. AllHipHop.com rallied to Assata's aid on May 2, 2005, alerting its readers that Tupac's godmother was being hunted.[37] The announcement of the $1 million reward infuriated Mos Def, who, with the National Conference of Black Lawyers, continues to defend Assata's innocence along with the ongoing Hands Off Assata campaign.

While a student in New York City, Assata attended two different colleges, neither of which has entirely forgotten—or sufficiently remembered—her.

In 1995, the Manhattan Community College was compelled to rename a scholarship that had previously been given in her honor. In 2006, the chancellor of the City University of New York announced that the title of City College's Guillermo Morales/Assata Shakur Community and Student Center was "unauthorized and inappropriate." Guillermo Morales, a Puerto Rican separatist and bomber who pulled off a daring escape from a prison hospital, is another fugitive who lives in Cuba.[38] City College students named the center in his and Assata's honor back in 1989. The decision to remove the names created an uproar among student and alumni groups, as well as an open letter from three city council members, who insisted that "a terrorist is a terrorist . . . period."[39] In both controversies, college officials claimed that they were not aware that Assata Shakur and Joanne Chesimard were the same person.

Talkback in the Afterlife

In his review of another Black Panther's biography, Stanley Crouch observed that "heroes are made by luck, will, circumstance and the kind of exaggerations that always follow exceptional actions of some sort."[40] This formula surely applied in the case of Assata, who may have spent six miserable years in prison, but who had the luck (so to speak) of circumstances that enabled her prison break and made her an international cause célèbre. Certainly, she had the will to point out and resist oppressive structures, but that on its own terms would not make her an outlaw-hero. Nor would that have been enough to make her (to some) a revolutionary, a freedom fighter, a political prisoner, or any of the other identifications that have been read into her particular brand of outlawry. If Assata had not become the exaggerated focus of law enforcement's public relations campaign against the BLA, or if Lawrence Hill had declined to publish her autobiography, or if she had not related her story so compellingly, it is unlikely that anyone outside her own circle would recognize her name today. Likewise, if Assata had not had the benefit of free legal counsel from her Aunt Evelyn, and had her Turnpike trial not coincided with the Church Committee findings that revealed an illegal FBI campaign against black militants, then she might still be in prison today. Finally, if she had not succeeded in eluding the authorities from 1979 to 1984 (when she was finally granted asylum in Cuba), and if she did not have a band of loyal supporters determined to protect her from anyone seeking the $1 million reward, she might today be imprisoned or dead. Certainly, there are many who hope that the official end of Fidel and Raúl Castro's regime will yet invite such an end.[41]

As a woman outlaw of color whose tale began in the late-twentieth-century United States, Assata and her story tapped the Black Panther mystique, racial exoticism, white guilt, and the genuine need for reforms that made the Panthers what they were. (In other words, she had exactly the sort of radical 1970s cachet that the SLA aspired to through their involvement with the prison reform movement and their repeated ham-fisted attempts to win the love of the capital-P People.) Her outlawry was obviously predicated upon and complicated by her status as a black woman. Because Assata is a marginalized representative of an already marginalized group, skin color becomes an implicit bond, a fairly reliable index of how others will receive her. In the opening pages of her book, she describes the surreptitious support she receives from the few African Americans on staff at the hospital where she was taken on the night of her 1973 arrest: a security guard assigned to guard her door covertly flashes her the Black Power sign from his post. A nurse sneaks her novels and poetry to lift her spirits. Assata reports these interactions as evidence of the implicit rationality of her politics and of the affection she inspires in strangers for whom racism has been a personal reality. Of course, skin color can also be a trap, a misleading index of solidarity where there may be none. By Assata's reasoning, this is a tragedy and only happens when people of color mistakenly align themselves with historically white power structures. Thus, even the antagonism that some black nurses or informants show toward Assata becomes, by her telling, further evidence of her righteousness.

Like many of the women outlaws who preceded her, Assata seems to have presented herself as at once larger than she is (in terms of the significance of her actions) and also less than she is (i.e., she may be exceptional but she remains humble in relation to her love for her people). Like Bonnie Parker, Assata wrote poetry, both to make sense of her own experiences and to justify her choices. Had there been only one male companion with Assata on the night of the Turnpike stop, it is possible that she and he would have been dubbed the "black Bonnie and Clyde."[42] Instead, especially once her trial was severed from Sundiata's, she would frequently be misremembered as a woman who acted alone, the BLA's "high priestess," whose passions would be presumed confined to her love of the black liberation movement and her apparent hatred for police.[43]

The language of Assata's story abounds with polarizing dichotomies. The FBI and the state of New Jersey call her Joanne Chesimard because that is the name under which she was convicted as an accomplice to the killing of Werner Foerster. Referring to Assata Shakur exclusively by the birth name she long ago disavowed also implicitly rejects her celebrity and personal reinvention. It may also be intended to dismiss her claims that she was mistreated on the basis of her race. In her book, Assata repeatedly refers to her work in the "struggle" and self-identifies as a revolutionary. In the early 1970s, as today, she was regarded by law enforcement as a terrorist. In 1979, depending on who was telling the story, Assata either escaped prison or was "liberated." In 2005, when the reward for Joanne Chesimard went up to $1 million, Assata's supporters immediately condemned it as a slave catchers' bounty.[44]

The paradox of outlawry, of course, is that such a rancorous split in perception fuels interest in Assata, even as it shores up the determination of her allies. The split also illustrates what the historian Jenny Sharpe called "contending forms of knowledge," or the battles between national and colonial (or racially identified) cultures and between institutional and popular ways of knowing.[45] Assata objects to being called a "criminal," and in the past has described herself as a "maroon" or "twentieth-century escaped slave." The New Jersey State Police refer to her as a "cop-killer" and even, in one of their less official communications, as "excrement."[46] In 2005, New Jersey officials renamed the location of the 1973 Turnpike murder the "Werner Foerster Overpass."[47] A photograph of "Escaped, Convicted Cop-Killer Joanne Chesimard" appears on the New Jersey Police homepage beside a cartoon animation of a blinking red police light.[48] Meanwhile, the Hands Off Assata campaign calls Assata "our mother, sister, comrade, and revolutionary s/hero." On the occasion of her sixtieth birthday in 2007, Assata released to Hands Off Assata a scathing letter in which she condemned the "ruthless, evil, imperialist policies of the U.S. government."[49] Railing against the shoddy treatment of those most affected by Hurricane Katrina and the "unspeakable acts of torture" happening on Cuba's "illegally occupie[d]" Guantánamo Bay, the letter pointedly accuses the United States of using the terrorist label to justify illegal imprisonments.

It is a foreseeable irony that appraising her danger at a million dollars would only enhance Assata's myth. Certainly, the Hands Off Assata supporters who condemn the bounty have also used it to insist on Assata's continued relevance as a symbol of race consciousness and government-sponsored persecution. To her supporters, she is at once an imperiled victim, a political inspiration, and a beautiful, frozen asset. To law enforcement, she is an infuriating scandal, an affront to the law and to the family of

Werner Foerster. To the New Jersey State Police, who have made Assata a focal point of their web site, the fact of her talkback from Cuba is like their site's spinning police light, incessantly throbbing its alarm.

As a generation of 1970s radicals has grown older, they face two predictable risks. They may be accused of being sellouts, traitors to the ideals they once espoused. They may, like Sara Jane Olson, be derided as hypocrites or artifacts, still tied to a dangerous and irrelevant politics. Would the face of Che Guevara be so widely recognized the world over if he had continued to evolve politically or if he had survived to a comfortable old age? To be an outlaw—or to be a truly resonant, enduring brand of outlaw—typically requires youthful male identity and a death trip. Patricia Hearst did not die, but she now occupies a space apart from either "Patty" or "Tania" by virtue of those characters' perpetual ambiguity. At fifty-six, Hearst remains a chameleon and a cipher, which is why her past still lends itself so nicely to fiction and reenactment and why Hearst herself is a perfect instrument of camp.

Assata Shakur also survives, but, through her Cuban exile, she may have achieved "crossover" of a unique sort. She and her supporters have worked to "kill off" Joanne Chesimard, to counteract the efforts of law enforcement to keep Joanne alive. From her once-secure post in Cuba, the fugitive was given the opportunity—as "Assata"—both to be reborn and to manage her own afterlife.

Epilogue

Long before J. Edgar Hoover got into the business of writing about women criminals, dramatic stories of women engaged in illicit and "unfeminine" enterprises had consistently turned a healthy profit. On the U.S. frontier of the late nineteenth century, a few women like Martha Cannery Burke (better known as "Calamity Jane") had gained widespread, if grudging, respect for their prowess with firearms and their insistence on enjoying the same drinking, gambling, and traveling privileges as the almost exclusively male company they kept. The dime-store novels that featured characters modeled on Calamity and women like her coyly tested the limits of a gendered and female identity but ultimately reinforced those limits. Fiction about frontier women with adventuresome lives and no thought of children or family ties typically ensured that their heroines suffered enormously for their independence. Readers could vicariously enjoy their feats of daring while also reassuring themselves of the wisdom of their more ordinary lives.[1]

Still, the popularity of such stories alarmed more than a few critics who worried about how certain female audiences were using the *idea* of the woman outlaw. In 1927, Duncan Aikman set out to redress the romantic folklore that had grown up around women like Calamity Jane, Belle Starr, Lola Montez, and other of what he dubbed the frontier's "lady wildcats."

As Aikman saw it, these undeserving figures had become famous only by a political accident related to the agitation for women's rights. In response to each of Calamity's unladylike transgressions, wrote Aikman, "talented young women in the east and even in England grasped their pens in a tremble of feminist admiration." While such women would never actually choose to live like Calamity, they "wrote of her career, both factitiously and fictitiously, as establishing a new notch in womanly achievement."[2]

Some of the most enthusiastic readers of newspaper stories about women criminals were other women. Or so Maurine Dallas Watkins was able to persuade the editor of the *Chicago Tribune* in early 1924. Watkins was hired at fifty dollars a week, quite a respectable salary in 1924, to write about crime from a "feminine" perspective. She won accolades and front-page billing for her articles on two murderesses, Belva Gaertner and Beulah Annan, whose makeup, apparel, and behavior in court Watkins described in minute detail. Her reporting on Annan, whom Watkins had dubbed "[the woman] whose pursuit of wine, men, and jazz music was interrupted by her glibness with the trigger finger," became the subject of Watkins's stage play *Chicago*. The play became one of the biggest hits of the 1926–1927 Broadway season. Half a century later, it inspired the Broadway musical *Chicago*.

Audiences who enjoyed Watkins's stories or stories like them were drawn to the novelty of a woman acting outside proscribed cultural norms—but, again, not *too* far outside of them. (Of "wine, men, and jazz music," none was quite so transgressive as the jazz, which still held implications of African American culture and, hence, for the white women Watkins covered, scandalous race-mixing.) A woman who killed her children would not likely become the subject of a fashion column or of a musical. But someone like Beulah Annan, who shot her lover and watched him die as she played the foxtrot on her husband's phonograph, was titillating fodder for a writer like Watkins, whose stories ultimately helped make possible Annan's acquittal.[3] Each fanciful reiteration of Annan's deeds downplayed the unpleasant realities of her crime and transformed her into a glamorous caricature of a modern woman run amok. Whether readers identified with her or were shocked by her (or both), they derived vicarious pleasure from the fantasies and social taboos bound up in her case.

Who Wants the "Most Wanted"?

A host of sociologists and folklorists have concluded that a culture's heroes, villains, and fools form what Orrin Klapp dubbed a "social system"—one that delineates that culture's standards by surpassing them, threatening them, and falling short of them, respectively. Meanwhile, plenty of literary and cultural theorists have found different ways to argue how "what is socially peripheral is . . . symbolically central."[4] This book has tried to demonstrate how much less predictable in the "system" are the positions held by a subgroup of socially peripheral women—particularly those of the women outlaws of this study, whose symbolic meaning is repeatedly asserted but also endlessly in doubt.

In the 1970s and 1980s, historians of criminal justice broke new ground by doing what today may seem intuitive—examining crime and criminals in the context of the broader culture that surrounds them. In her study of sixteenth-century French pardon tales designed to request mercy for condemned prisoners, Natalie Zemon Davis described those texts as remarkable not so much for their "made-up" qualities but for what the narration of those qualities happened to reveal. In other words, "the most interesting crimes are those about which the most telling stories were told."[5] Criminology professor Carolyn Strange concurred, defining an interesting crime— and, by extension, an interesting *criminal*—as "a moment when a culture fails in its own terms." In cases of violent murder especially, normally unacknowledged assumptions, such as "feelings about sexuality, ideals of marriage and the family, normative notions of femininity and masculinity are suddenly articulated, even shouted out in dueling narratives."[6]

What is gripping or uncomfortably revealing about any crime depends mightily on its circumstances and the predisposition of the audience that witnessed it. For example, stories of poor people stealing from the prosperous typically evoke strong feelings about class divides and the righteousness (or not) of state power. That is one reason actor Johnny Depp, who played John Dillinger in the 2009 film *Public Enemies*, told the *Los Angeles Times*, "I don't see John Dillinger as an enemy of the public." As Depp said of his film in another interview, "People at certain points just had to take up arms, did they not?"[7]

Depp's comments highlight the necessary contradiction of the criminal whose actions or personal story resonates with different publics, even long after he (or she) is gone: blessed as he was with a bit of cleverness and panache, an entirely self-interested fellow like Dillinger came to stand for an outraged, populist politics to which the outlaw himself would never have subscribed. To those Americans who suffered the worst effects of the Great Depression, Dillinger became a symbolic thumb in the eye of a law that appeared most invested in protecting the privileges of the ruling class.

Ironically, the outlaw also became absolutely necessary to the legitimacy of those who would enforce the law. So it was that outlaw and lawman mutually threatened and created each other.

Writing in 1968, Lew Louderback observed that the 1930s gangsters had left as their monument the G-man, and that they also stood for a natural human response to authority during periods of economic hardship. Louderback argued that the old public enemies had reinforced an esteemed American tradition: "What we see now, under the pearl-gray fedoras and the blue pinstripe suits, are not J. Edgar Hoover's 'craven beasts,' 'public rats,' and 'vermin,' but simply old-style American badmen, sprung from the same soil as Jessie James, the Daltons, and Belle Starr. Theirs were the bucolic virtues, no matter how 'big cityish' they later became. The important things were hardihood, close-knit family ties, fierce independence of outside authority." In providing an entertaining vision of the apparent freedoms of bad behavior, the gangsters were, Louderback argued, "therapeutic" figures who provided relief from the dully moralistic FBI man.[8] Critics from the early 1970s agreed that the G-man had more cultural cachet when portrayed as an avenger than as a straight-arrow guy living under the same constraints as any law-abiding citizen. As Aaron Marc Stein observed in a book about the appeal of the "maverick" lawman who flourishes in times of economic downturn, periods of malaise inevitably produce "a universal itch to take justice into our own hands [and] . . . to let us good guys have a share in the intoxicating joys of sadism." As Stein summarized, "Why should the criminals have all the fun and we, the pure of heart, have none?"[9]

As the number of violent women criminals surged upward in the 1970s, some worried that feminism had given more women a taste for that same brand of fun. In popular entertainments, the purported motivations of women lawbreakers are useful for what they disclose about the preoccupations of a particular age. That is why this book focuses on the fiction and films inspired by notorious women lawbreakers from the 1930s and 1970s, two eras marked by economic woes, a pervasive distrust of government institutions, and plenty of hand-wringing over the apparent decline of women's traditional roles. Gender-defying, gun-toting women became a recurrent obsession for the struggling FBI, the rapidly evolving film industry, and multiple American publics.

Like Dillinger, the subjects of this study fit—or *aspire* to fit, or have been *made* to fit—conventions of an Anglo-Celtic tradition of outlawry, a tradition without much room for the woman outlaw, who is seen primarily through the lens of her sex or race. Each of the chapters has tried to illustrate the rarefied conditions that may make a true outlaw of an otherwise "normal" woman lawbreaker. It is not enough that she rename and reinvent herself, that she profess to break the law in the interest of someone other than herself, or that she attract the attentions of a powerful law enforcement agency. Like Dillinger, it is essential that she be regarded by her supporters as a clever but "regular" woman (which definition is characteristically vague, but which is often enunciated in class terms), and one who was brought down by some sort of trickery on the part of the law.

Historically, the most enduring outlaws have been young, male, and dead. But, as this book argues, the woman outlaw has other means of cultural survival. All of the women in this book sought to create counternarratives to the "official" accounts of themselves by the law. More important, all were sufficiently silenced (through death, imprisonment, or exile) such that fictional and cinematic interpretations of their activities could flourish without interference, maintaining their usefulness to multiple audiences across the years. That is why this book declines to put too much emphasis on the "real" stories and images of any of its subjects, including those who are still alive. What matters are the "Most Wanted" stories and images—which is to say, the invention of the woman outlaw as whatever her various supporters and detractors have needed her to be.

Although the woman outlaw typically originates amid rapidly changing gender roles, none of the subjects of this book have emerged as feminist icons. On the contrary, whatever appealing freedoms were apparent in each woman outlaw's story, popular reenactments of her life typically foreground the compromises (giving up home, marriage, family) that are presented as making her tragically dissatisfied and ultimately *un*free. Quite unlike her male counterparts, the woman lawbreaker has defenders who tend to justify her choices in terms of traditional feminine priorities—boyfriends, husbands, children, and other kin. Both her allies and her attackers highlight her embarrassing lapses as an outlaw, which may include her yearning for motherhood, for luxury goods, or for bourgeois men. Such inconsistencies make for a more interesting story. They may console audiences that the woman outlaw is only playacting. Or they may hint that the capacity to "snap" exists in every woman, no matter how "normal" her aspirations.

Whether she is portrayed as heroic, titillating, deceitful, or dangerous, the woman outlaw sometimes occupies a space less like that of the male folk hero and more akin to that of the witch, upon whom audiences project their "unacknowledged terrifying desires."[10] In short, women's outlawry means—or is most often interpreted to mean—something different than men's, and this has impacted women's relationship to the law. Inevitably, gender influenced how the woman outlaw was prosecuted, either literally (in a barrage of gunfire) or in a court of law. That is why even the sillier re-creations of her story have the capacity to illuminate lingering social prejudices within the legal system.

Women's violence is media-genic, born of the camera's natural affinity for the bizarre, the dramatic, and the emotional payoff of witnessing a justice done. The women of this study work for the screen because they and their crimes represent a pitch-perfect blend of novelty and the familiar. They are novel because they rewrite the traditional female victim as the aggressor. They are familiar because, at least by the filmmakers' telling, the "aggressor" aggresses only in service of a woman's conventional desire or passions. Ironically, all the films come to the same conclusion about their characters, regardless of whether the director intended to impugn or flatter their subjects. By each film's end, the woman outlaw is shown dying, grimly cursing out the feds, or living a ghostly existence in another country. For all the glamour or grit of her earlier appearances, she winds up a figure of pathos and regret, and this actually may be the most important source of her cachet.

For almost a decade, actress Dixie Lee Sedgwick has been channeling Bonnie Parker, first through her one-woman play and more recently through the short film *Bonnie & Clyde—End of the Line*, which she plans to develop into a commercial-length vehicle. The Texas-based Sedgwick describes her first-person account of Bonnie's life as a deliberate refutation of the "sexy, cigar-smoking gun moll." Instead, audiences see Bonnie's transformation "from a bewildered, married, estranged, lonely, giggly, high-strung, articulate teenager, into a hardened, grave, terrified, resolved, addicted cripple. It's not pretty and it's not fun, but it is engaging. People see themselves, their sons, daughters, husbands, wives, friends that have made many of the same choices. . . . This is a cautionary tale."[11]

Like many of her male counterparts, the mythologized woman lawbreaker relies on a potent imagery that becomes synonymous with her image and may even become a shorthand explanation for large cultural and historical shifts. So it was that Hoover's FBI leaned on Hollywood and the new, picture-heavy magazines of the 1930s to advertise the "public enemy." So it is that sequences from old gangster films are spliced without comment into documentaries about the Great Depression, and that a film like *Bonnie and Clyde* becomes a cultural reference point for its era. As American Studies professor Jim Farrell observed, the SLA produced images that "work better for a visual media than would the sorts of social change going on in a [1970s food] co-op." Indeed, but even so, cinematic reenactments of violence risk accusations of poor taste unless they can be shown to have some higher purpose. This is why so many of the films described in these pages have imitated the conventions of documentary. Without the right story lines and photographs, without the right sorts of ambiguity and talkback, each of the women profiled in this book might only have been remembered by her victims. Of course, given her often deliberate self-distortions and those of filmmakers and law enforcement, one might argue that the woman outlaw is, in fact, remembered *only* by her victims, who are most immune to the lore that surrounds her.

Still Inventing the Outlaw

Today, there are as many versions of J. Edgar Hoover as there are of Bonnie Parker, Patty Hearst, or Joanne Chesimard, aka Assata Shakur. Hoover has been celebrated as a national treasure and reviled as its most despicable villain. The morning in 1972 that Hoover was found to have died in his sleep was the day that loyal friends, acting on Hoover's advance directive, destroyed the "official and confidential" records that he had accumulated in his near half century as Bureau director. Speculation abounds as to what these records contained and do much to fuel distaste for the man who for many years was synonymous with modern law enforcement. In 1976, the newly completed J. Edgar Hoover FBI headquarters in Washington, D.C., was named in his honor. Enormously prominent for most of the twentieth century, Hoover was, by the dawn of the twenty-first century, largely erased. In the 2008 *Centennial History* of the FBI, Hoover barely appears by name. He is rebuked twice (Palmer Raids, COINTELPRO), praised once (in a paragraph on his reforms), and tersely acknowledged in the introduction as the Bureau's "long-lasting" director. It is because of Hoover's long-lasting and controversial leadership that FBI directors are today limited to ten-year terms.

In the pages of the *American Magazine*, Kate "Ma" Barker officially began her service as another dissipated female foil to the abstemious G-man. In recent years, however, the FBI has backed away from Hoover's original claims. The *Centennial History* offers no photograph of Ma and no claim about Ma having once been a queen of the underworld. The pithy summary of the Barker-Karpis Gang avoids any clear statement about Ma's guilt or innocence. Only a photograph of the extensive weaponry removed from

Fred and Ma's Florida cottage after the 1936 shootout makes the silent argument that her death, while unwarranted, may have been unavoidable.

Pop artists Beyoncé and Jay-Z borrowed on the *Bonnie and Clyde* glamour and updated it for a new generation with their popular music video *Bonnie and Clyde '03*. Former teen pop star Hilary Duff will play Bonnie Parker in yet another Bonnie-and-Clyde movie due out in 2010. With each new pop-cultural revival of the Bonnie Parker story, the elements of Kathryn Kelly that Hoover inserted in the *Persons in Hiding* script slip further away. Where once Kathryn was the central character, the FBI now omits her entirely from its official history of Machine Gun Kelly.

Assata Shakur remains in hiding in Cuba. The $1 million reward for her capture continues to go unclaimed. Speculation abounds as to what will happen to her case as U.S.-Cuban relations are projected to shift under the administration of President Barack Obama. The New Jersey State Police have vowed to ensure that Joanne Chesimard does not ever again set foot in the United States, unless it is to return to a prison cell. Meanwhile, Assata's supporters continue to tell her story as that of the revolutionary outlaw who has lived the past forty years with a New Jersey trooper's bullet "lodged next to her heart."

By 2009, just six years after their trial for the Crocker bank murder, all the members of the second-team SLA were paroled, even Emily Harris (the original SLA's "Yolanda"), who had been convicted of pulling the trigger.[12] Sara Jane Olson has returned to her home in St. Paul, although the Minnesota governor is supporting efforts by both the Minnesota and California police unions to force Olson to serve the rest of her parole in California. Critics continue to evoke SLA victim Myrna Opsahl as the upstanding wife and mother whose memory Olson desecrates by now having a family of her own. Patricia Hearst, who drove the getaway car, was long ago granted immunity for her role in the bank robbery–homicide in exchange for information on the case. She never did have to testify publicly in any of the twenty-first-century trials of the second-string SLA.

In the wake of September 11, 2001, the central FBI headquarters in Washington, D.C., shuttered its popular FBI tour, citing space constrictions and security concerns. On the occasion of the FBI's centennial in 2008, the Bureau collaborated with D.C.'s popular Newseum to produce a commemorative exhibit on "G-men and Journalists." Focused as it was on cases in which newspapers and TV media played a significant role, the exhibit gave prominent treatment to artifacts from the gangster age and to Patty Hearst's turn with the SLA. None of the Black Panthers were mentioned, save for a small panel of text that acknowledged COINTELPRO abuses and credited them to Hoover. (Another panel on race-based violence in the 1950s and 1960s sought to recuperate the FBI's role as a defender of civil rights.)

The FBI's historian, John Fox, characterized the Newseum exhibit as a chance for the Bureau to show "where we were, where we've come." He explained that the exhibitors' choices were influenced by the visuals in the FBI archives. For example, the gangster age exhibit stood near a glass case overflowing with colorful movie posters, FBI-inspired board games, and other playthings designed for "Junior G-men." As Fox speculated, the SLA bank robbery photos and the carved monkey necklace worn by Patty Hearst were compelling to audiences old enough to remember those artifacts from the 1970s. The HEARNAP case also "came at a time of key change in the way the FBI pursued domestic security investigations." Fox dismissed Bonnie Parker as "but a side note in Bureau history" but acknowledged that his office continues to get regular inquiries about Bonnie and Clyde.[13] Although the FBI has worked to distance itself from the mythmaking of the Hoover era, it knows better than to turn away a surefire promotional tool. On the cover of its *Centennial History*, front and center, is a photo of Bonnie leveling a rifle at Clyde.

NOTES

Introduction: Ten Most Wanted

1. The Federal Bureau of Investigation was founded in 1908 as the Bureau of Investigation. Hoover was appointed its director in 1924. Between 1934 and the fall of 1935, the Bureau briefly became known as the Division of Investigation. After 1935, it became the Federal Bureau of Investigation, and Hoover remained its director until his death in 1972.

2. Claire Bond Potter, *War on Crime: Bandits, G-Men, and the Politics of Mass Culture* (New Brunswick, NJ: Rutgers University Press, 1998), 76.

3. J. Edgar Hoover with Courtney Ryley Cooper, "The *Real* Public Enemy No. 1," *American Magazine* 121 (April 1936): 16–17, 118–123.

4. In the early twentieth century, author Duncan Aikman used this phrase to describe nineteenth-century frontier women who used guns and liquor in "unladylike" fashion and who sought to engage in the same social and business enterprises as male frontier settlers. Duncan Aikman, *Calamity Jane and the Lady Wildcats* (New York: Henry Holt & Co., 1927), 95–96.

5. *News Chief*, "Ma Barker Shootout Re-enacted in Marion County," January 12, 2001, http://www.newschief.com/article/20010112/ARTICLES/301129962?tc=ar.

6. For more on myths "crystallizing" around an individual, see Peter Burke, *Popular Culture in Early Modern Europe* (Brookfield, VT: Scholar Press, 1994), 169.

7. For example, "gender outlaws" may reject the binary categories of maleness and femaleness altogether and be admired or reviled as a result. Paradoxically, however, refusing to comply with the "natural laws" (essential traits and experiences) widely regarded as defining someone as a woman or a man may in some cases further reify traditional sex categories, even as it creates a space from which to discard them. See Kate Borstein, *Gender Outlaw: On Men, Women, and the Rest of Us* (New York: Vintage Books, 1995).

8. Graham Seal, *The Outlaw Legend: A Cultural Tradition in Britain, America, and Australia* (Cambridge: Cambridge University Press, 1996), 2.

9. *U.S. News & World Report*, "Women Catching Up with Men in One More Field: Crime," September 23, 1974, 45–58. For further speculation on the connections between second-wave feminism and women's criminality, see Freda Adler, *Sisters in Crime: The Rise of the New Female Criminal* (New York: McGraw-Hill, 1975); Shana Alexander, *Anyone's Daughter: The Times and Trials of Patty Hearst* (New York: Viking Press, 1979); and Marilyn Baker and Sally Brompton, *Exclusive! The Inside Story of Patricia Hearst and the SLA* (New York: Macmillan, 1974).

10. Emma K. Parker and Nellie B. Cowan, *The True Story of Clyde Barrow and Bonnie Parker: As Told by Bonnie's Mother and Clyde's Sister*, ed. Jan I. Fortune (New York: Signet Books), 1968.

11. Assata Shakur, *Assata: An Autobiography* (Chicago: Lawrence Hill Books, 1984), 40; Evelyn Williams, *Inadmissible Evidence: The Story of the African-American Trial Lawyer Who Defended the Black Liberation Army* (Chicago: Lawrence Hill & Co., 1994).

12. The FBI now keeps multiple "Most Wanted" lists that are divided into subcategories.

Chapter 1. The Girls behind the Man behind the Gun

1. Paul Lomatire, "Cold Beer and Killer Women," *Sydney Morning Herald*, March 6, 2004.

2. For accounts of the ambush, see E. R. Milner, *The Lives and Times of Bonnie and Clyde* (Carbondale: Southern Illinois University Press, 1996), 140–143; John Neal Phillips, *Running with Bonnie and Clyde: The Ten Fast Years of Ralph Fults* (Norman: University of Oklahoma Press, 1996), 196–207; Vicki L. Murphy, "A Louisiana Steel Trap: The Deaths of Clyde Barrow and Bonnie Parker," *Journal of the North Louisiana Historical Association Journal* 24, nos. 2–3 (1993): 51–67. See also multiple articles from the *Dallas Morning News*, May 24, 1934. For accounts that claim Ivan Methvin's involvement in the ambush was not voluntary but coerced, see John Treherne, *The Strange History of Bonnie and Clyde* (London: Jonathan Cape, 1984), 180–191; and Ted Hinton, with Larry Grove, foreword to *Ambush: The Real Story of Bonnie and Clyde* (Austin, TX: Shoal Creek Publishers, 1979).

3. W. D. Jones, "Riding with Bonnie and Clyde," *Playboy*, November 1968, http://www.cinetropic.com/janeloisemorris/commentary/bonn%26clyde/wdjones.html.

4. Hinton, *Ambush*, 190.

5. Alvin Karpis, with Bill Trent, *The Alvin Karpis Story* (New York: Coward, McCann & Geoghegan, 1971).

6. Phillips, *Running*, 132.

7. Jones, "Riding."

8. Censorship summary, *You Only Live Once* file (1937), Academy of Motion Picture Arts and Sciences, Beverly Hills.

9. There have been multiple contradictory accounts of the Kellys' capture. Until recently, the FBI's official version of the Kelly capture maintained that the raiding party consisted of federal agents. In fact, the job was done by local police. The FBI's 2008 *Centennial History* acknowledges the early press reports that Kelly had been hungover and had mumbled, "I was expecting you," to the raiding party. However, "the more colorful version sparked the popular imagination and 'G-Men' became synonymous with the special agents of the FBI." Federal Bureau of Investigation Office of Public Affairs, *The FBI: A Centennial History, 1908–2008* (Washington, DC: U.S. Government Printing Office, 2008), 24.

10. Stanley Hamilton, *Machine Gun Kelly's Last Stand* (Lawrence: University Press of Kansas, 2003), 126.

11. "George 'Machine Gun' Kelly, et al; Kidnapping of Charles F. Urschel," FBI 7-115-714, p. 7, Federal Bureau of Investigation records, Washington, DC.

12. William B. Breuer, *J. Edgar Hoover and His G-Men* (Westport, CT: Praeger, 1995), 106.

13. J. Edgar Hoover, *Persons in Hiding* (Boston: Little, Brown & Co., 1938), 143.

14. Ibid., 159, 162; J. Edgar Hoover, with Courtney Ryley Cooper, "Crime's Leading Lady," *American Magazine* 123 (February 1937): 79. E. E. Kirkpatrick's 1934 history

of the Urschel kidnapping (*Crime's Paradise: The Authentic Inside Story of the Urschel Kidnapping* [San Antonio, TX: Naylor Co., 1934]) appears to have originated the story of Kathryn leaving George in a movie house when he had a case of "the nerves."

15. Hoover, *Persons*, 157.

16. Hamilton, *Machine Gun*, 123.

17. Kirkpatrick, *Crimes' Paradise*, 233–234.

18. Hoover, *Persons*, 160.

19. *New York Times*, November 27, 1935.

20. Hoover, *Persons*, 163 (emphasis added).

21. In its summary of the Palmer Raids, the FBI's own centennial history notes, "The constitutionality of the entire operation was questionable, and [District Attorney A. Mitchell] Palmer and Hoover were roundly criticized for the plan and for their overzealous domestic security efforts." FBI, *The FBI: A Centennial History*, 12. The raids initially received positive publicity, but the tide of public opinion shifted rapidly once more was revealed about the planning and execution of the numerous arrests.

22. Director William Burns was implicated in the Teapot Dome scandal when it was revealed that he had allowed agents to spy on the president's critics.

23. President Herbert Hoover had been reluctant to interfere in local authorities' investigation of the New Jersey kidnapping. However, when the twenty-month-old Charles Lindbergh Jr. was found dead not far from his home, the president asked J. Edgar Hoover (no relation) to coordinate efforts by several federal agencies to catch the killer. (The most important break in the case came not from Hoover's Bureau, but from the U.S. Treasury, which tracked serial numbers on banknotes from the kidnapping ransom.) The Kansas City Massacre began as an attempt by Charles Arthur "Pretty Boy" Floyd, Vernon Miller, and Adam Richetti to use machine guns to free their friend Frank Nash, a federal prisoner. Nash was killed in the July 17 confrontation, which also took the lives of four peace officers. Historians have since argued that the "crime wave" of the 1930s was a fiction, but that highly publicized events such as the massacre made it easy to believe that criminal activity was on the rise.

24. The Urschel kidnapping was the very first kidnapping to apply the Lindbergh Law, which made it a federal crime to transport a kidnapping victim across state lines.

25. The FBI's powers evolved in response to high-profile cases of the early and mid-1930s. Initial congressional resistance to giving agents firearms had melted away after June 17, 1933, the date of the Kansas City Massacre. Athan G. Theoharis, Tony G. Poveda, Susan Rosenfeld, and Richard Gid Powers, eds., *The FBI: A Comprehensive Reference Guide* (New York: Oryx Press, 2000).

26. Allan M. Winkler, *The Politics of Propaganda: The Office of War Information, 1942–1945* (New Haven, CT: Yale University Press, 1978), 21.

27. Kenneth O'Reilly, "A New Deal for the FBI: The Roosevelt Administration, Crime Control, and National Security," *Journal of American History* 69 (December 1982): 638–658. Cummings hired the *Brooklyn Eagle's* Washington correspondent Henry Suydam as a special assistant to the attorney general. From 1933 to 1937, Suydam earned $10,000 a year for his work in embellishing the Bureau's image. In 1934 the entry-level salary for federal agents was $2,900 a year. Once Hoover developed his own press contacts and became a master of public relations in his own right, he may have pressed for Suydam's dismissal.

28. Some have suggested that the "G-man" moniker may actually have been

borrowed from the Irish Republican underground, which referred to undercover and plainclothes detectives of the Dublin constabulary as "G-men." That designation came from the constabulary's departments, which were divided into categories "A" through "F." The "G" was therefore assigned to the force's secret agents. Historian Richard Gid Powers has pointed out that the truth of this explanation is no better documented than the FBI's version. Theoharis et al., *The FBI*, 269.

29. Curt Gentry, *J. Edgar Hoover: The Man and the Secrets* (New York: W. W. Norton & Co., 1991), 174–177.

30. For example, the re-creation of a shootout at the Little Bohemia Lodge in Wisconsin did not end up a fiasco in which the bad guys all escaped and an innocent civilian was killed at the hands of the FBI. Instead, the FBI exterminated most of the gang. In *'G' Men*, the only accidental death is the "good death" of a reformed gangster who needed to pay for past sins. Such changes suited Hollywood's storytelling conventions. They, like the *'G' Men* film itself, also were likely outgrowths of the Motion Pictures Producers and Distributors Association's 1934 decision to begin enforcing the 1930 Production Code.

31. Jonathan Mumby, *Public Enemies, Public Heroes: Screening the Gangster from* Little Caesar *to* Touch of Evil (Chicago: University of Chicago Press, 1999), 33–34; Carlos Clarens, "Hooverville West: The Hollywood G-Man, 1934–1945," *Film Comment*, May–June 1977, 10.

32. After 1933, 11,000 of the United States' 25,000 bans had failed. In that same year, most private citizens' bank savings had become more secure. The passage of the Glass-Steagall Act created the Federal Deposit Insurance Corporation (FDIC) to cover individual accounts. Thus, the mid-1930s bank robber who did not kill anyone could be regarded as committing a "victimless" crime—or even a semipopulist crime, if he made a show of not robbing bank customers and of destroying mortgage foreclosure records.

33. Claire Bond Potter, *War on Crime: Bandits, G-Men, and the Politics of Mass Culture* (New Brunswick, NJ: Rutgers University Press, 1998), 88–89.

34. Lizabeth Cohen, *Making a New Deal: Industrial Workers in Chicago, 1919–1939* (Cambridge: Cambridge University Press, 1990), 101, 157.

35. *New York Times*, "Hoover Asks Press to Help Crime War," April 23, 1937.

36. Quoted in the foreword to Hoover, *Persons in Hiding*, xviii, by Hoover's ghostwriter, Courtney Ryley Cooper. Cooper added that Hoover had concluded his oath with this observation: "If the people don't like it, they can get me fired."

37. Kathleen McLaughlin, "J. E. Hoover Urges Women Aid Work," *New York Times*, May 18, 1938.

38. *Motion Picture Herald*, "Parole Fixer," February 27, 1940, 41.

39. By 1937, the magazine's biggest competitors were *Redbook* and *Cosmopolitan*. Theodore Peterson, *Magazines in the Twentieth Century* (Urbana: University of Illinois Press, 1964), 193–194.

40. J. Edgar Hoover with Courtney Ryley Cooper, "The Boy Who Wanted to Go Fishing," *American Magazine* 122 (November 1936): 54–55, 137–143.

41. President Herbert Hoover expelled thousands of married female government workers in 1932 with his executive order that decreed only one spouse could work for the federal government. In 1930, approximately 29 percent of married women were employed outside the home. By 1940, that figure rose to 35.5 percent. Alice Kessler-Harris, *Women Have Always Worked: A Historical Overview* (Old Westbury, NY: Feminist Press, 1981), 138.

42. Nancy Cott, *The Grounding of Modern Feminism* (New Haven, CT: Yale University Press, 1987), 130–132; Laura Hapke, *Women, Work, and Fiction in the American 1930s* (Athens: University of Georgia Press, 1995), 3–25, 72. As a *New York Times* headline ungraciously phrased it, women had "invaded" nearly all occupations by 1923 (*New York Times*, August 12, 1923).

43. Paula Rabinowitz, *Labor and Desire: Women's Revolutionary Fiction in Depression America* (Chapel Hill: University of North Carolina Press, 1991); Gail Bederman, *Manliness and Civilization: A Cultural History of Gender and Race in the United States, 1880–1917* (Chicago: University of Chicago Press, 1995).

44. Cott, *Grounding*, 132.

45. Bernard A. Drew, ed., *Hard-Boiled Dames: Stories Featuring Women Detectives, Reporters, Adventurers, and Criminals from the Pulp Fiction Magazines of the 1930s* (New York: St. Martin's Press, 1986), xiv–xv.

46. Marge Suskie to Jean Crompton, Pat Cherrington, and Marie Conforti, April 1934, FBI 62-29777-1406, Federal Bureau of Investigation records, Washington, DC. Claire Bond Potter, "'I'll Go the Limit and Then Some': Gun Molls, Desire, and Danger in the 1930s," *Feminist Studies* 21 (Fall 1994): 61.

47. Investigation of Marge Suskie, FBI 62-29777-1406, Federal Bureau of Investigation records; quoted in Potter, "I'll Go the Limit," 42.

48. Walter Noble Burns, *The One-Way Ride: The Red Trail of Chicago Gangland from Prohibition to Lake Jingle* (Garden City, NY: Doubleday, Doran, 1931), 241. Burns's text matched the tenor of a pre-1932 United States, which became far less tolerant of crime and criminals after the 1932 abduction of the Lindbergh baby.

49. Karpis, *Karpis Story*, 209–215; Laura Browder, *Her Best Shot: Women and Guns in America* (Chapel Hill: University of North Carolina Press, 2006), 117.

50. Frederick L. Collins, *The FBI in Peace and War* (New York: G. P. Putnam's Sons, 1943), 21–22.

51. Hoover, *Persons*, 54.

52. Ellen Poulsen, *Don't Call Us Molls: Women of the John Dillinger Gang* (Little Neck, NY: Clinton Cook Publishing, 2002), xv.

53. Hoover, *Persons*, 154.

54. Courtney Ryley Cooper, *Here's to Crime!* (Boston: Little, Brown & Co., 1937), 220.

55. Herbert Corey, *Farewell, Mr. Gangster! America's War on Crime* (New York: D. Appleton-Century Co., 1936), 286–287.

56. David Ruth, *Inventing the Public Enemy: The Gangster in American Culture, 1918–1934* (Chicago: University of Chicago Press, 1996), 90–91.

57. Alan Dundes, a folklorist and expert in the anthropology of humor at Berkeley, called the strategy of attacking the opposition's women "part of the male arsenal of weapons to make your way in the world. . . . Since ancient times, you get at your male opponent by violating his women. If the women's honor is lost, the man's honor is lost. . . . You conquer enemies by feminizing the men and putting down the women" (Maureen Dowd, "Liberties: The Joke's on Him," *New York Times*, June 21, 1998), http://query.nytimes.com/gst/fullpage.html?res=9C00E6DD173CF932A15755C0A96 E958260.

58. Robert Warshow, "Movie Chronicle: The Westerner," in *The Immediate Experience: Movies, Comics, Theatre, and Other Aspects of Popular Culture* (Garden City, NY: Doubleday & Co., 1962), 135.

59. J. Edgar Hoover with Courtney Ryley Cooper, "Crime's Leading Lady," *American Magazine* 123 (February 1939): 54.

60. *Motion Picture Herald*, February 4, 1939, 39–40, 45–46, 51–52; italics in the original.

61. See, for instance, references in film histories, including Carlos Clarens, *Crime Movies: An Illustrated History of the Gangster Genre from D. W. Griffith to Pulp Fiction* (Cambridge, MA: Da Capo Press, 1997), 135–136; and Marilyn Yaquinto, *Pump 'Em Full of Lead: A Look at Gangsters on Film* (New York: Twayne Publishers, 1998), 56. Rare is the author like John Treherne, who notes elements lifted from the Kathryn Kelly and George "Machine-Gun" Kelly story. Treherne, *Strange History*, 227.

62. The Paramount press release sheets made much of this detail. One gushed that "it took a newcomer to the Hollywood crime writing fraternity to bring to the screen the most unusual clue of the year. . . . The name of the fatal scent, 'Tantalizing' was coined by Hoover himself, an inveterate reader of the magazine ads, who thought it typical of the names given perfumes by sponsors" ("Whiff! Perfume Novel Clue in J. Edgar Hoover's New Crime Plot," Paramount Press Sheet File, August 1, 1938–July 31, 1939, Academy of Motion Picture Arts and Sciences, Beverly Hills).

63. As Lucy Fischer wrote of the constraints on women in film, "Female derangement tied to the refusal of motherhood—an 'unnatural' position for women." Fischer, *Cinematernity: Film, Motherhood, Genre* (Princeton, NJ: Princeton University Press, 1996), 20.

64. *Motion Picture Herald*, January 28, 1939, 33.

65. Paramount reportedly paid Hoover $100,000 for the right to turn four of his stories into screenplays. *Persons in Hiding* file, Motion Picture Association of America file, Academy of Motion Picture Arts and Sciences, Beverly Hills. The studio had reason to expect a good return on its investment. The 1938 book had proved so popular that it had to go through several extra press runs in its first year out. The *Persons in Hiding* films also fit neatly with the newly stringent requirements of the Motion Picture Production Code after 1934.

66. According to its leading lady, Patricia Morison, *Persons in Hiding* was also a success in Europe. Patricia Morison, interviewed by Ronald Davis, August 25, 1983, Oral history #289, Ronald L. Davis Oral History Collection, Academy of Motion Picture Arts and Sciences, Beverly Hills.

67. Clarens, "Hooverville West," 14.

68. *New York Times*, "Country's Arrests Are of Women, but Chief Hoover Notes Violence Trend," September 6, 1936.

69. One example is Ethel Rosenberg, whom Hoover had recommended the FBI use as a "lever" to put pressure on her husband, Julius Rosenberg. Hoover did not recommend that Ethel be executed, however, recommending a long jail sentence instead.

70. From that same Hoover interview: "Here is something I will confess. If I ever marry and the girl fails me, ceases to love me, and our marriage is dissolved, it would ruin me. My mental status couldn't take it, and I would not be responsible for my actions." The phrase "mental status" was deleted in reprints of this interview. *New York Times*, November 1939; Anthony Summers, *Official and Confidential: The Secret Life of J. Edgar Hoover* (New York: G. P. Putnam's Sons, 1993), 32. As a high school debater, he had successfully argued for "The Fallacies of Women's Suffrage." Hoover's niece Margaret Fennell remembered Hoover as having little time for women: "I think he regarded

women as a kind of hindrance. You know, they sort of got in your way when you were going places" (Ovid Demaris, *The Director: An Oral Biography of J. Edgar Hoover* [New York: Harper's Magazine Press, 1975], 8). Hoover spent a lifetime believing in a version of "republican motherhood," or the understanding that women citizens' primary political role was to raise virtuous (male) citizens willing to sacrifice individual interests to the common good. This ideology, first popular during the Revolutionary War, imbued motherhood with civic purpose. But it also sentimentalized domestic duties and posited women as private guardians of public morality. Linda Kerber, *Women of the Republic: Intellect and Ideology in Revolutionary America* (Chapel Hill: University of North Carolina Press, 1980); Mary Beth Norton, *Liberty's Daughters: The Revolutionary Experience of American Women, 1750–1800* (Boston: Little, Brown & Co., 1980), 245–250, 298–299; Sara Evans, *Born for Liberty: A History of Women in America* (New York: Free Press, 1989), 246–247.

71. O'Reilly, "A New Deal," 639.

72. Ibid., 645–646.

73. Powers, *G-Men*, 110–111.

74. Hoover, *Persons*, 5.

75. Milner, *Lives and Times*, 149.

76. *Saint Louis Post Dispatch*, "Ex-Ranger 'Hated to Shoot Woman, Especially When Sitting Down' but Had No Choice," May 24, 1934.

77. Hinton, *Ambush*, 173.

78. *New York Times*, "Barrow Is Buried; Thousands View Body," May 26, 1934. Clyde's funeral was a circus, with crowds so eager for a glimpse of the casket lowering that the front-row family members were very nearly pushed into the open grave.

79. Hinton, *Ambush*, 191–192.

80. From the *Dallas Journal*, May 24, 1934, quoted in Murphy, "A Louisiana Steel Trap," 62.

81. *Time*, "Lovers in a Car," June 4, 1934, 16.

82. This and other selections of "The Ballad of Bonnie and Clyde" are taken from Emma K. Parker and Nellie B. Cowan, *The True Story of Clyde Barrow and Bonnie Parker: As Told by Bonnie's Mother and Clyde's Sister*, ed. Jan Fortune (New York: Signet Books, 1968), 167–169.

83. Rosemary Elliot, *Women and Smoking since 1890* (New York: Routledge, 2008).

84. Hinton, *Ambush*, 47.

85. *Dallas Morning News*, "Elusive Dallas Desperados Shot to Death in Louisiana," May 24, 1934; *New York Times*, "Barrow and Woman Are Slain by Police in Louisiana Trap," May 24, 1934.

86. Parker and Cowan, *The True Story*, 171.

87. Breuer, *J. Edgar Hoover*, 59. Breuer does not document the cases he describes, but his acknowledgments section indicates that "most of the research material used in creating this book came from the records of the Federal Bureau of Investigation in the J. Edgar Hoover Building in Washington, D.C." However, in that same section, he also credits contemporary magazines and newspapers for "injecting color, sparkle, and immediacy into [his] narrative." As the original slim FBI file on Bonnie and Clyde makes no mention of the prison break or where Bonnie might have concealed a weapon, we can only conjecture that Breuer took that detail from an archived newspaper clipping.

88. Breuer, *J. Edgar Hoover*, 57–58.

89. Parker and Cowan, *The True Story*, 166.

90. Hinton, *Ambush*, 193; Milner, *Lives and Times*, 160, 168.

91. Parker and Cowan, *The True Story*, 121. See also the story of how the Okabena heist was initially postponed due to excessive ice and snow, in Phillips, *Running*, 67.

92. Jeff Guinn, *Go Down Together: The True, Untold Story of Bonnie and Clyde* (New York: Simon & Schuster, 2009), 285.

93. Hinton, *Ambush*, ix–x.

94. Jacquelyn Dowd Hall, "Disorderly Women: Gender and Labor Militancy in the Appalachian South." *Journal of American History* 73 (September 1986): 355.

95. Parker and Cowan, *True Story*, 99.

96. Hinton, *Ambush*, 194.

97. Poulsen, *Don't Call Us Molls*, 324, 410.

Chapter 2. Mother Barker, Public Enemy No. 1

1. J. Edgar Hoover, with Courtney Ryley Cooper, "The *Real* Public Enemy No. 1," *American Magazine* 121 (April 1936): 16.

2. Ibid., 17.

3. Alvin Karpis, with Bill Trent, *The Alvin Karpis Story* (New York: Coward, McCann & Geoghegan, 1971), 80.

4. Hoover, "*Real* Public Enemy," 17.

5. "The Kidnapping of Edward George Bremer," FBI 7-576-241, Federal Bureau of Investigation records, Washington, DC. In keeping with eugenicist theories that lingered well into the twentieth century, Indian ancestry might account for Ma's apparent lawlessness, an affirmation of the outdated, but still popularly regarded, criminal "type."

6. Hoover, "The *Real* Public Enemy," 17, 118.

7. That Ma believed her son was murdered has been corroborated by numerous other sources, including those based on accounts by George Barker, who still lived with Ma at the time of Herman's death. Upon being told her eldest son's death was a suicide, Ma allegedly screamed, "A Barker don't do things like that!" (Jay Robert Nash, *Bloodletters and Badmen: A Narrative Encyclopedia of Criminals from the Pilgrims to the Present* [New York: M. Evans & Co., 1973], 35).

8. "S.K. McKee," FBI report, June 9, 1936, 198, Hamm Kidnap File 810, sec. 9 (7-77), Federal Bureau of Investigation records, Washington, DC. Karpis, *Karpis Story*, 56, 81.

9. Hoover, "*Real* Public Enemy," 16. The editor's note at the beginning of the article warns, "Don't read it if you're easily shocked." Agent Joseph, critique of the "Mother of Murder" article, January 16, 1936, FBI 62-21526-253; Hoover, reply to Cooper, January 18, 1936, FBI 62-21526-252, Federal Bureau of Investigation records, Washington, DC. The "spawn of hell" comment is reminiscent of a Puritan belief that the female "vessel" was both more susceptible to the devil and capable of passing on its transgressions through fluid transfers. So, for instance, a colicky baby might be suspected of having absorbed through its mother's milk the evil of her sins. The *American Magazine* article frames Ma as having passed on her wickedness to her children, another "crime" that makes her the most culpable of the gang. Franny Nuddelman, "Emblem and Product of Sin: The Poisoned Child in *The Scarlet Letter* and Domestic Advice Literature," *Yale Journal of Criticism* 10 (Spring 1997): 199.

10. Hoover, "*Real* Public Enemy, " 121.

11. "The Kidnapping of Edward George Bremer."

12. Hoover, "The *Real* Public Enemy," 121. In the FBI version of events, George, the "mild, inoffensive, quiet man who seemed somewhat bewildered by his dominating wife," at least gets to be the one who initiates the marital separation.

13. Hoover, "*Real* Public Enemy," 120, 123. In some gangster films from this period, a connection with nature signaled a character's innate goodness or immunity to corruption. In *High Sierra* (1946), Humphrey Bogart's Dillinger-like character happily reminisces about the old fishing hole, a cue to audiences that he is, at heart, a noble guy. In '*G' Men* (1935), Cagney's former gangland boss and mentor dissuades his young charge from the criminal lifestyle and confesses his desire to retire from the gangster racket and buy a cabin in the Wisconsin woods. This, the ultimate sign of reform, makes the gang boss's death a tragedy. Conversely, an ignorance of nature indicated an unredeemable character. In *Show Them No Mercy* (1935), a gangster audiences were supposed to despise appears even more loathsome and ridiculous when he tries to kill a woodpecker he cannot identify. (He calls it a "noisy chicken" and a "seagull.")

14. Cooper mentions his "lecture tour" in a January 20, 1936, letter to Tolson. The letter reveals some competitiveness between Hoover and Cooper, who was soon to lecture in a city that Hoover had just visited. Cooper jokes, "Figure I've got a tough guy to follow in this fellow Hoover. Will have to start getting out injunctions against him if he is going to run much more opposition as a speaking attraction." Cooper to Tolson, January 15, 1936, FBI 62-21526-252, Federal Bureau of Investigation records, Washington, DC.

15. J. Edgar Hoover, *Persons in Hiding* (Boston: Little, Brown & Co., 1938), 22.

16. Hoover, "The *Real* Public Enemy," 121.

17. Richard Hirsch, "Killers Called Him Creepy," *True Detective*, June 1940, 36.

18. Karpis, *Karpis Story*, 91.

19. Ibid., 81–82.

20. Nash, *Bloodletters*, 35.

21. Karpis, *Karpis Story*, 82.

22. Paul Maccabee, *John Dillinger Slept Here: A Crooks' Tour of Crime and Corruption in St. Paul, 1920–1936* (St. Paul: Minnesota Historical Society Press, 1995), 115, 144.

23. Hoover, "*Real* Public Enemy," 121.

24. Ibid., 122.

25. Maccabee, *John Dillinger*, 201–202.

26. Cooper to Tolson, January 15, 1936, FBI 62-21526-252, Federal Bureau of Investigation records, Washington, DC. This letter was reproduced in Cooper's casual memo to Clyde Tolson and stored in FBI files. It is possible that other such letters exist in collections maintained or donated by the Leavenworth Penitentiary, where Lloyd served twenty-five years; the Oklahoma State Penitentiary, where Doc was incarcerated for murder; or the Kansas State Penitentiary, where Freddie served time for burglary.

27. Hoover, "*Real* Public Enemy," 121.

28. Ibid.

29. Cooper to Clyde Tolson, January 15, 1936, FBI 62-21526-252, Federal Bureau of Investigation records, Washington, DC; Hoover, "The *Real* Public Enemy No. 1," 17, 118.

30. Cooper to Clyde Tolson, January 15, 1936. In his communication with Tolson, Hoover's second-in-command, Cooper attributed the quotations he would ultimately

put into Hoover's mouth as having come from an unidentified "reliable source," one who had "got George Barker's trust . . . where it was not possible for another person to get it."

31. Hoover, *"Real* Public Enemy," 118, 121.

32. Herbert Corey, *Farewell, Mr. Gangster! America's War on Crime*, foreword by J. Edgar Hoover (New York: D. Appleton-Century Co., 1936), 66.

33. Hoover, *Persons*, 9; Karpis, *Karpis Story*, 84.

34. Hoover, *"Real* Public Enemy," 122.

35. Hoover, *Persons*, 35.

36. Although interrogators kept Doc handcuffed to a chair for eight days and nights, he would reveal nothing of the whereabouts of other gang members. For his lack of co-operation, he spent the rest of his life at Alcatraz, until he was killed trying to escape in 1939. John Toland, *The Dillinger Days* (New York: Random House, 1963), 338–339.

37. Corey, *Farewell*, 68.

38. Hoover, *"Real* Public Enemy," 122–123.

39. Jim Yandle, "The Bloody End to Ma Barker's Crime Spree," *Orlando Sentinel*, January 19, 1988.

40. "The Kidnapping of Edward George Bremer."

41. *New York Times*, "Barker Gang Man, Woman under Arrest," January 17, 1935.

42. Melvin Purvis, *American Agent* (Garden City, NY: Doubleday, Moran & Co., 1936), 166.

43. Purvis, *American Agent*, 166. Melvin Purvis's *American Agent* and Herbert Corey's *Farewell, Mr. Gangster!* were both published in 1936. It was remarkable that Hoover would write the foreword to the latter work and not the former, authored by one of his most successful and celebrated agents. Athan G. Theoharis and John Stuart Cox speculate that Hoover was jealous of the attention Purvis received during his three years as director of the special agents' office in Chicago. Under Purvis's leadership, the Chicago office brought down Ma, Fred, and Doc Barker, Babyface Nelson, and John Dillinger. According to Theoharis and Cox, Purvis was forced out of the FBI after the Dillinger assassination, "apparently for having the temerity to take credit for the kill." Athan G. Theoharis and John Stuart Cox, *The Boss: J. Edgar Hoover and the Great American Inquisition* (Philadelphia: Temple University Press, 1988), 129.

44. Hoover, *Persons*, 39.

45. Corey, *Farewell*, 69.

46. Hoover, *"Real* Public Enemy," 123; *New York Times*, "Barker Gang Man."

47. *New York Times*, "Barker Gang Man."

48. Harold Martin, embalmer at the Pyles Mortuary, reported that Ma's skin was "just like a piece of leather." It was his job to oil the bodies and periodically remove mold from them, so they could remain on display. Ellen Poulsen, *Don't Call Us Molls: Women of the John Dillinger Gang* (Little Neck, NY: Clinton Cook Publishing, 2002), 378–379.

49. Henry Lee, "The Ten Most Wanted Criminals of the Past 50 Years," *Liberty* (Autumn 1972): 26–40.

50. Italics added; Joseph A. Mulcahy (Justice Dept.) to Joseph Breen, January 16, 1940, and Luigi Luraschi to Joseph Breen, January 22, 1940, *Queen of the Mob* file, Academy of Motion Picture Arts and Sciences, Beverly Hills.

51. *Film Daily, Motion Picture Herald*, and the *New Yorker* reviewed the film favorably upon its release. They also frequently misidentified the story line as strictly based on the facts of the real Ma Barker's life. Only a reporter for *Variety* wondered if the whole

thing were not perhaps "handed a sugary coating in several episodes." *Queen of the Mob* file, Academy of Motion Picture Arts and Sciences, Beverly Hills; *Variety*, "Queen of the Mob," July 3, 1940 (byline: "Wear").

52. Philip Wylie, *Generation of Vipers* (New York: Holt, Rinehart & Winston, 1955), 189.

53. Ibid., 188–189.

54. *Shadow of a Doubt*, directed by Alfred Hitchcock (Universal City, CA: Universal Pictures, 1943).

55. Wylie coined this term for a later edition of the text.

56. Patrick McGilligan, "Introduction: 'Made It Ma! Top of the World,'" in *White Heat*, ed. Patrick McGilligan (Madison: University of Wisconsin Press, 1984), 15.

57. For more on the implied menace of the maternal bond in film, see Michael Rogin, "Kiss Me Deadly: Communism, Motherhood, and Cold War Movies," in *Ronald Reagan: The Movie and Other Episodes in Political Demonology* (Los Angeles: University of California Press, 1987), 243–244.

58. At midcentury, gangster stories had not disappeared entirely from the public radar, as the long-running radio series *Gangbusters* could attest. Phillips H. Lord initiated the series as *G-Men* in 1935, with the cooperation of Hoover and his FBI. Exasperated by the Bureau's insistence that *G-Men* scripts avoid sensational details common to the action-detective genre, Lord terminated the partnership after only thirteen episodes. He then relaunched the series as the unauthorized but far more colorful FBI drama *Gangbusters*, which stayed on the airwaves until 1957. In 1954, it crossed over to television. Richard Gid Powers, *G-Men: Hoover's FBI in American Popular Culture* (Carbondale: Southern Illinois University Press, 1983), 207–216.

59. Karpis, *Karpis Story*, 80–91.

60. Wylie, *Vipers*, 204.

61. Charles Stinson, "Dr. Spock Would Rap Ma Barker's Method," *Los Angeles Times*, February 5, 1960 (A.M. edition).

62. Ibid.

63. *Mirror-News*, "Petty Thievery," February 4, 1960.

64. Sara Evans, *Born for Liberty: A History of Women in America* (New York: Free Press, 1989), 246–247.

65. Charles Champlin, "Crime Saga of Ma Barker," *Los Angeles Times*, 1970.

66. The author specifically cites Hoover's fabricated description of Ma's eyes. Louis Black, "Bloody Mama," *Cinema Texas Program Notes* 19 (October 13, 1980): 86.

67. In a 1969 interview, Samuel Arkoff reflected on the success of American International Pictures since its founding in 1954. "We started looking for our audience by removing the element of authority in our films. We saw the [youth] rebellion coming, but we couldn't predict the extent of it. So we made a rule: no parents, no church or school authorities in our films. If they must appear, then they will be bumbling ineffectual people." Wayne Warger, "Independent Filmmakers Tuned to Youthquake," *Los Angeles Times*, May 5, 1968.

Chapter 3. The Perfectly Ambiguous Bonnie Parker

1. When Alcatraz closed in 1962, Karpis was transferred to the McNeil Island Penitentiary in Washington State. It was there he met Charles Manson, who had not yet become infamous. Alvin Karpis and Robert Livesey, *On the Rock: Twenty-five Years at Alcatraz* (New York: Beaufort Books, 1980).

2. "Fellow travelers" was a term used by Hoover to describe the "five types of sub-versives" he identified in his 1958 book, *Masters of Deceit: The Story of Communism in America and How to Fight It* (New York: Henry Holt & Co., 1958). Tom Wicker, introduction to *Investigating the FBI*, ed. Pat Watters and Stephen Gillers (Garden City, NY: Doubleday & Co., 1973), xv.

3. Robert Sherrill, "The Selling of the FBI," in Watters and Gillers, *Investigating the FBI*, 4.

4. Ibid., 3. This is not to say that the FBI was without critics. Indeed, Max Lowenthal's 1950 book, *The Federal Bureau of Investigation*, argued that the Bureau had become "an American Gestapo" and summarized evidence of civil liberties violations that had already been published in liberal journals such as the *Nation*. Still, a positive image of the FBI prevailed until just before and just after Hoover's death in 1972.

5. Sherrill, "Selling," 12, 15–20.

6. Hoover and his team held complete creative control over the program, dictating its casting, the content of its scripts, and even the sponsorship of the Ford Motor Company. Each episode opened with the FBI seal and concluded with a thank-you to Hoover and his associates for their cooperation. Hoover occasionally appeared during the show's commercial segments, and once a month the show appealed to the public for leads on one of the Bureau's ten most wanted fugitives. Of the bowdlerized story lines, Hoover wrote, "Perhaps we are inclined toward Puritanism in an increasingly permissive world." But such heavy edits were necessary since the program was "telecast into American homes at a 'family hour' on a 'family evening.'" Richard Gid Powers, "The FBI in American Popular Culture," in *The FBI: A Comprehensive Reference Guide*, ed. Athan G. Theoharis, Tony G. Poveda, Susan Rosenfeld, and Richard Gid Powers (New York: Oryx Press, 2000), 287–288.

7. At the time of Hoover's death in 1972, 40 million Americans were tuning in to *The F.B.I.* each week, and it was syndicated in fifty countries. When the show was finally canceled in 1974, it was still in the top ten most-watched programs in the country. In 2009, FBI Director Robert Mueller honored the ninety-one-year-old Zimbalist with an honorary FBI badge for the "friendship and service" he had provided through his involvement with *The F.B.I.* program. "You inspired countless men and women to take up that badge," said Mueller, adding that he himself had been a devoted fan. Sue Doyle, "Actor Who Portrayed Lawman Given Gold Badge for Contributions to Organization," *Los Angeles Daily News*, June 8, 2009, http://www.dailynews.com/news/ci_12549932.

8. Ted Hinton, with Larry Grove, *Ambush: The Real Story of Bonnie and Clyde* (Austin, TX: Shoal Creek Publishers, 1979), 173. The sense of witnessing something momentous or historical may have motivated Hinton to bring a 16mm motion picture camera to the scene of the ambush. Most of the silent footage of Bonnie and Clyde's death car, and the crumpled bodies within, was not to be released to the public until many years later.

9. John Neal Phillips, *Running with Bonnie and Clyde: The Ten Fast Years of Ralph Fults* (Norman: University of Oklahoma Press, 1996), 213; James R. Knight, with Jonathan Davis, *Bonnie and Clyde: A Twenty-first Century Update* (Austin, TX: Eakin Press, 2003), 172.

10. Once the coroner arrived, the streets of Arcadia had to be cleared by highway patrolmen before the wrecker towing the outlaws' car could be driven to Conger's Furniture Store, which also served as the town's funeral parlor. The sheriff ordered the

tow truck to pause in front of the local school in Gibsland. He wanted to show the students what ultimately became of the legendary outlaws with whom many young people seemed fascinated. Rushing from their classrooms, the children screamed and dipped their hands in the blood still trickling from the car. One twelve-year-old girl impulsively leapt onto the car's right-side running board and there came face-to-face with the grossly disfigured Bonnie. The girl fainted, but did not fall, because of the crush of the crowd behind her. For accounts of the crowd's macabre response to the death car and its cargo, see Vicki L. Murphy, "A Louisiana Steel Trap: The Deaths of Clyde Barrow and Bonnie Parker," *Journal of the North Louisiana Historical Association* 24, nos. 2–3 (1993): 61; E. R. Milner, *The Lives and Times of Bonnie and Clyde* (Carbondale: Southern Illinois University Press, 1996), 147–148; Phillips, *Running*, 209–210.

11. Carlos Clarens, *Crime Movies: An Illustrated History of the Gangster Genre from D. W. Griffith to Pulp Fiction* (Cambridge, MA: Da Capo Press, 1997).

12. Thomas M. Pryor, "Hollywood's Oscar Night: Joanne Woodward, Miyoski Umeki 'Star' in Thirteenth Annual Awards Show—Hoover Scores Film Crime," *New York Times*, March 3, 1958; Thomas Doherty, *Teenagers and Teenpics: The Juvenilization of American Movies in the 1950s* (Philadelphia: Temple University Press, 2002), 97.

13. Wayne Warger, "Independent Filmmakers Tuned to Youthquake," *Los Angeles Times*, May 5, 1968.

14. Arthur Lyons, *Death on the Cheap: The Lost B Movies of Film Noir!* (New York: Da Capo Press, 2000), 66–67.

15. As Doherty notes, if the movie itself were not licentious, then the advertising would be. Doherty, *Teenagers and Teenpics*, 9.

16. Robert Pogue Harrison, *The Dominion of the Dead* (Chicago: University of Chicago Press, 2003). Harrison describes funeral rites as separating the corpse from its image. Once Bonnie and Clyde died, their images could more readily accommodate fantasy projections steeped in censure, admiration, or ambivalence.

17. Pauline Kael, "Bonnie and Clyde," *Kiss Kiss Bang Bang* (New York: Little, Brown & Co., 1968), 47–63.

18. At age sixteen, Bonnie Parker married a schoolmate, Roy Thornton. The marriage was short-lived, and Roy Thornton was eventually sent to prison. Bonnie reportedly considered it cold to divorce him while he was in jail and so remained married to him until she died.

19. *Time*'s initial review ("Low-Down Hoedown," August 23, 1967, 13) panned *Bonnie and Clyde* for its "sheer, tasteless aimlessness." Pauline Kael boldly defended the film in the pages of the *New Yorker*. Five months later, *Time* reversed its original evaluation of Penn's movie as part of its December 8, 1967, feature on "The New Cinema: Violence . . . Sex . . . Art." An Andy Warhol–inspired collage of Faye Dunaway and Warren Beatty as *Bonnie and Clyde* appeared on the issue's cover. As the second, laudatory piece explained, "TIME's review made the mistake of comparing the fictional and real Bonnie and Clyde, a totally irrelevant exercise." *Time* further justified the film's unsettling shifts from comedy to violence as making sense to the first-ever TV generation.

20. As Penn reported, "Five Negroes present there [at a 1967 screening] completely identified with Bonnie and Clyde. They were delighted. They said 'This is the way; that's the way to go, baby. Those cats were all right.' They really understood, because in a certain sense, the American Negro has the same kind of attitude of 'I have nothing more to lose" that was true during the Depression for Bonnie and Clyde. It is true

now of the American Negro. He is really at the point of revolution—it's rebellion, not riot." David Newman and Robert Benton, "Lightning in a Bottle," *Bonnie and Clyde: An Original Screenplay* (Burbank, CA: Warner Brothers, 1967), 17.

21. Newman and Benton, "Lightning in a Bottle," 19.

22. Buchanan did contract work for American International Pictures' Sam Arkoff, who hired Buchanan to churn out cheap knockoffs of horror films by AIP's reigning star, Roger Corman. The inexpensive copycat films could then be shown on late-night television or as the lesser half of a cinema double feature.

23. Larry Buchanan, interview with the author, May 26, 2004.

24. Larry Buchanan, *It Came from Hunger! Tales of a Cinema Schlockmeister* (Jefferson, NC: McFarland & Co., 1996), 115.

25. In his 2003 director's commentary, Buchanan twice mentions the saxophone. Buchanan described his Sears Roebuck guitar as having once been his "bread and butter"; the instrument was the ticket to his first-ever film role. It is possible that Buchanan felt a musician's kinship with Clyde Barrow.

26. Marcus Seale signed an acting contract with Twentieth Century Fox, which renamed him Larry Buchanan, the name he would keep for the rest of his life. His wife and children also took the name Buchanan.

27. Buchanan, *It Came from Hunger!* 115. As Larry Buchanan wrote in 2004, "Warren Beatty, at a director's award dinner, complimented my work on B & C. I know he was sincere, because he brought it up and cited chapter and verse. He also confessed to 'lifting' the scene from AIP's 'The Story of Bonnie Parker' [*sic*], wherein the brothers come together and shadowbox; Warren is a great guy. Imagine my surprise when, in front of five hundred members of the [Directors Guild of America], he dropped to his knees in mock prayer asking my forgiveness. When I reminded him that I did not make that picture [*The Bonnie Parker Story*], he spread his hands out from his prayer and shouted, "Jesus, Larry, you spoiled my finish!" Buchanan, correspondence with the author, June 13, 2004.

28. Phillips, *Running*, 133. Other versions of the story report that Buck Barrow handed the couple the five dollars. Milner, *Lives and Times*, 78.

29. Larry Buchanan, "Director's Commentary," *The Other Side of Bonnie and Clyde*, DVD, directed by Larry Buchanan (Dallas, TX: Larry Buchanan Productions, 2003).

30. In *Bonnie and Clyde*, Sophie Stone and Mr. Darby became "Velma Davis" and "Eugene Grizzard," comedic characters played by Evans Evans and Gene Wilder. In 2003, Larry Buchanan misremembered Sophie Stone and Mr. Darby as having been romantically linked, probably because the *Bonnie and Clyde* script had suggested as much.

31. The eyewitness, a local farmer, later claimed that the woman who shot the police officer might have been Billie Parker, Bonnie's sister.

32. The reenactment actually contradicts the account in *I'm Frank Hamer: The Life of a Texas Peace Officer*, which says that it was Clyde who first pulled up a shotgun and killed Constable Cal Campbell. Hamer's biography alleged that Bonnie and another gang member, Henry Methvin, then opened fire on policeman Percy Boyd, who was sitting in the constable's car. (Methvin would later confess to both shootings.) Many histories describe how the trio forced a wounded Boyd to push their car from the mud and took him on a wild, fourteen-hour ride before releasing him with money to get home. Boyd did what Bonnie had asked of him and told reporters that she did not smoke cigars. H. Gordon Frost and John J. Jenkins, *I'm Frank Hamer: The Life of a Texas Peace Officer* (Abilene, TX: State House Press, 1991), 221.

33. Newman and Benton, "Lightning in a Bottle," 19.

34. Buchanan, *It Came from Hunger!* 12, 15.

35. Buchanan, "Director's Commentary."

36. As a very young man, Buchanan became keenly interested in the Nazarene, or historical Jesus. He began filming *The Copper Scroll of Mary Magdalene* in 1972 and tinkered with it on and off for the next thirty-two years. He finally finished the postproduction stages just a few months before his death on December 2, 2004.

37. In our first conversation in May 2004, Larry told me that his father had been *killed* by Bonnie Parker. He may have been teasing, or he may have genuinely convinced himself that this was so. He encouraged me to check the story in his 1996 autobiography, *It Came from Hunger! Tales of a Cinema Schlockmeister,* which reports the shooter as Floyd Hamilton. Hamilton "pumped buckshot into Papa's chest" and from a far enough distance that the injury "was not serious, but it was sobering" (10).

38. Buchanan, correspondence with author, June 13, 2004.

39. Ibid.

40. *New York Times,* "The New Cinema," 73.

41. Newman and Benton, "Lightning in a Bottle," 17, 19. What Newman and Benton saw as an American "underworld" sensibility seems to have had currency in other parts of the world as well. During the events of May 1968, a protestor moved by Penn's movie signed "*Bonnot et Clyde*" beneath a graffiti scrawl on a wall of the Sorbonne: "Yes to organizing! No to party authority!" René Viénet, *Enragés and Situationists in the Occupation Movement* (New York: Autonomedia, 1992).

42. *Economist,* February 7, 1998. This uncredited article was a review of "Police Pictures," a photographic exhibition that opened at the Grey Gallery of New York University in May 1998.

43. *U.S. News & World Report,* "Women Catching Up with Men in One More Field: Crime," September 23, 1974, 45.

44. For example, the investigative journalist Fred J. Cook censured the FBI in the pages of the *Nation* in 1958 and then again in his 1964 book, *The FBI Nobody Knows* (New York: Macmillan Co., 1964).

Chapter 4. Radical Cheerleaders and a Frustrated PTA Type

1. *Network*'s heiress is named "Mary Ann Gifford." Kathy Cronkite, daughter of newsman Walter Cronkite, played the part.

2. Undated "Letter to the People," written by former SLA members, FBI 7-152-464, Federal Bureau of Investigation records, Washington, DC.

3. Michael Stohl, ed., *The Politics of Terrorism* (New York: M. Dekker, 1983), 24.

4. The polarized American electorate was evident in the election results, in which Nixon had taken just 43.4 percent of the vote, compared to Democrat Hubert Humphrey's 42.7 percent and the Independent candidate George Wallace's 13.5 percent.

5. Lucinda Franks, "The Seeds of Terror," *New York Times Magazine,* November 22, 1981. While generally friendly to the Weathermen, Hampton had condemned the Days of Rage, fearing the event would bring a massive police reprisal.

6. *U.S. News & World Report,* "U.S. Unrest, as FBI Chief Sees It," January 12, 1970, 8.

7. John Edgar Hoover, "The SDS and the High Schools: A Study in Student Extremism, Part 1," *PTA Magazine,* January 1970, 2–5. The magazine printed a sampling of the flood of letters they received in response to Hoover's two-part article. Of the fourteen letters printed, four expressed gratitude to Hoover. One approved of his article

but suggested that adults needed to do a better job of addressing the younger genera-tion's complaints. The nine remaining letters conveyed skepticism or derision toward Hoover's arguments about the SDS.

8. Richard Gid Powers, *G-Men: Hoover's FBI in American Popular Culture* (Carbon-dale: Southern Illinois University Press, 1983), 277–278.

9. James T. Patterson, *Grand Expectations: The United States 1945–1974* (New York: Oxford University Press, 1996), 24–25.

10. Jeremy Varon, *Bringing the War Home: The Weather Underground, the Red Army Faction, and Revolutionary Violence in the Sixties and Seventies* (Berkeley: University of California Press, 2004), 293.

11. In March 1971, the Citizens Committee to Investigate the FBI broke into an FBI office in Media, Pennsylvania, stole secret files, and leaked them to the press. In the aftermath, several agents resigned and began talking openly about the Bureau's trans-gressions. The FBI issued a formal apology in 1972. In 1975, Senator Frank Church held congressional hearings that further exposed the abuses of COINTELPRO.

12. Ruth Rosen wrote about the FBI's extensive monitoring of women's groups in the late 1960s and early 1970s and how even the suspicion of having been infiltrated was enough to encourage infighting and a destructive paranoia. Ruth Rosen, "The Poli-tics of Paranoia," in *The World Split Open: How the Modern Women's Movement Changed America* (New York: Viking, 2006), 227–260.

13. The declaration was released on August 21, the second anniversary of the death of George Jackson at San Quentin Prison.

14. As the SLA would write in their declaration, "The name symbionese is taken from the word symbiosis and we define its meaning as a body of dissimilar bodies and organisms living in deep and loving harmony and partnership in the best interest of all within the body."

15. SLA transcript, FBI 7-15200-129, Federal Bureau of Investigation records, Washington, DC.

16. It is possible that the SLA took the name from *The Spook Who Sat by the Door*, a 1959 novel by Sam Greenlee about a black uprising in Chicago. Greenlee foregrounds the concept of "symbiology" in his story of a small commando unit called the cobras. John Pascal and Francine Pascal, *The Strange Case of Patty Hearst* (New York: Signet Books, 1974), 76.

17. Memorandum, "The Symbionese Liberation Army," FBI 7-15200-125, Federal Bureau of Investigation records, Washington, DC.

18. The full quotation: "In the history of terror, in the history of crime, surely no group suffered such excesses of literary manufacture as the Symbionese Liberation Army. Their logorrhea was chronic and possibly fatal. They wrote down *everything*. . . . The members of the SLA were terrorists with the habits of graduate students. They left a paper trail behind them so wide that one might imagine that they were seeking rather desperately to be found out and stopped. The sea of evidence might also be interpreted as a sign of the SLA's overweening contempt for the pigs and for their inability to read or write or to comprehend the paper middens they were wading through." Shana Alex-ander, *Anyone's Daughter: The Times and Trials of Patty Hearst* (New York: Viking Press, 1979), 89–90.

19. The SLA had objected to Superintendent Marcus Foster's support of a plan that would require student ID cards and guards in the public schools, a move they regarded

as "patterned after the fascist Ameriken tactics of genocide . . . in Vietnam, the Philippines, Chile and South Africa" ("Symbionese Liberation Army Western Regional Youth Unit, Communiqué No. 1," FBI 7-15200-26, Federal Bureau of Investigation records, Washington, DC). Other members of the Bay Area community also regarded Foster's proposal unfavorably but were outraged by the assassination of a black leader. The SLA had somehow missed the fact that Foster had publicly withdrawn the ID card plan almost a full month before he was shot.

20. John Bryan, *This Soldier Still at War* (New York: Harcourt Brace Jovanovich, 1975), 238.

21. Sara Davidson, "Notes from the Land of the Cobra," *New York Times Magazine*, June 2, 1974, 39.

22. *Newsweek*, "The Hostage: A Game of Terror," February 25, 1974, 18–19.

23. Patty's impressive weapon was actually a sawed-off shotgun with a black rifle scope taped to its barrel—another detail that underscored the SLA's emphasis on theatrical expressions of violence.

24. Bryan, *This Soldier*, 264.

25. Alexander, *Anyone's Daughter*, 155. Wrote Alexander: "Everybody else in our pop pantheon, from Billy the Kid to Lucky Lindbergh to John Glenn, was a variation on Jack Armstrong, your basic all-American boy. Patty was the first big-time all-American girl, and that, I am certain by now, was part of her original powerful attraction for me."

26. Davidson, "Notes," 36, 40.

27. Several members or former members of Venceremos had been indicted or convicted for participation in the breakout of Ronald Beaty from Chino Prison in 1972. A guard was killed in the ambush-escape. Memorandum, "The Symbionese Liberation Army," FBI 7-15200-125, Federal Bureau of Investigation records, Washington, DC.

28. Accused by more radical groups of "going Establishment," the Black Panthers were moving in the opposite direction of groups like the SLA. As Huey Newton declared in a 1972 interview, "We've rejected the rhetoric of the gun. It got about 40 of us killed and sent hundreds of us to prison. Our goal now is to organize the black communities politically" (Peter N. Carroll, *It Seemed Like Nothing Happened: America in the 1970s* [New Brunswick, NJ: Rutgers University Press, 1990], 54).

29. Davidson, "Notes," 43.

30. Ibid., 40.

31. *Newsweek*, "Patty: Guilty," March 29, 1976, 24.

32. Lacey Fosburgh, "3 Women: Their Paths Leading to Terrorism," *New York Times*, April 23, 1974.

33. Notes from interrogation at Mill Valley, CA, FBI 7-15200, Federal Bureau of Investigation records, Washington, DC. For more on the FBI's surveillance of the women's movement, see Rosen, *The World Split Open*, 227–260.

34. Davidson, "Notes," 40. This is a quotation from Emily Harris's (Yolanda's) letter to her father.

35. Alexander, *Anyone's Daughter*, 142.

36. FBI agents noted how before going to prison, Cinque married a woman with multiple children who were not his own. When Cinque referred to these children as "my babies" in an SLA communiqué, profilers seized on his language as proof that he lacked masculine pride and was indeed the SLA women's puppet.

37. Marilyn Baker and Sally Brompton, *Exclusive! The Inside Story of Patricia Hearst and the SLA* (New York: Macmillan, 1974), 57.

38. Ibid., 81.

39. Ibid., 48, 57. Recalling the makeup discovery, Baker quipped, "Two facts never vary about revolutionaries: They have no sense of humor and the women involved never wear makeup. The second fact is so hard and fast it is almost as if their plainness is a weapon in their war against the pretty and the stylized masses."

40. Les Payne and Tim Findley, with Carolyn Craven, *The Life and Death of the SLA* (New York: Ballantine Books, 1976), 172.

41. The SLA's constitutionally enforced abhorrence for marriage or any other contractual relationship between men and women pleased Joe Remiro (Bo), who declared "guerrilla women—the highest form of woman." He praised their accommodating brand of feminism, because "they took their rights and they left me mine. They didn't bore me with feminist rhetoric." Emily Harris (Yolanda) would later lament that the group's vision of a female guerrilla had been "male-defined." Bryan, *This Soldier,* 177.

42. William Graebner, *Patty's Got a Gun: Patricia Hearst in 1970s America* (Chicago: University of Chicago Press, 2008), 129.

43. Nancy Isenberg, "Not 'Anyone's Daughter': Patty Hearst and the Postmodern Legal Subject," *American Quarterly* 52 (December 2000): 655.

44. *U.S. News & World Report,* "Women Catching Up with Men in One More Field: Crime," September 23, 1974, 45.

45. Alice Kessler-Harris, *Women Have Always Worked: A Historical Overview* (New York: McGraw-Hill, 1981), 144–157; Winifred D. Wandersee, *On the Move: American Women in the 1970s* (Boston: Twayne Publishers, 1988), 127–149; Rosen, *World Split Open,* 63–93.

46. *U.S. News & World Report,* "Women Catching Up," 48.

47. Cinque's name was frequently abbreviated to "Cin," and in the SLA's taped broadcasts it was easily mistaken for "sin." The Cin/sin homophone inevitably supported the image of a demonic possession.

48. Urgent Teletype, San Francisco to Director, April 22, 1974, FBI 7-15200-1468, Federal Bureau of Investigation records, Washington, DC.

49. Powers, *G-Men,* 266–277.

50. Athan G. Theoharis, Tony G. Poveda, Susan Rosenfeld, and Richard Gid Powers, eds., *The FBI: A Comprehensive Reference Guide* (New York: Oryx Press, 2000), 187.

51. Former agent Cril Payne alluded to the Bureau's struggle for reform in his 1979 memoir. "I had served under three Directors since the death of J. Edgar Hoover, and although each tried to institute meaningful reform, the Hoover loyalists at Bureau Headquarters did exactly as they pleased. They seemed to act on the premise that the American people, or for that matter Congress, could not be trusted with the truth, and that they alone knew what was best for the country. Implicit in that notion was the belief that the memory of J. Edgar Hoover should be protected and defended at all costs." Cril Payne, *Deep Cover: An FBI Agent Infiltrates the Radical Underground* (New York: Newsweek Books, 1979), 335.

52. *Newsweek,* "The Saga of Patty Hearst," April 29, 1974, 24.

53. Patricia Campbell Hearst, with Alvin Moscow, *Every Secret Thing* (Garden City, NY: Doubleday & Co., 1982), 83.

54. Howard Kohn and David Weir, "SLA Lost Year, Part Two," *Rolling Stone,* November 20, 1975.

55. Bryan, *This Soldier*, 6.

56. *Neverland: The Rise and Fall of the Symbionese Liberation Army*, directed by Robert Stone (Rhinebeck, NY: Robert Stone Productions, 2004).

57. Hearst, *Every Secret Thing*, 257.

58. Richard Nixon's 1968 presidential campaign had been the first high-tech television campaign in U.S. history and the first to employ "media specialists."

59. *Time*, "The New Cinema" (December 8, 1967): 67.

60. Hearst, *Every Secret Thing*, 151.

61. Jerry Belcher and Don West, *Patty/Tania* (New York: Pyramid Books, 1975), jacket copy.

62. Les Payne and Tim Findley, with Carolyn Craven, *The Life and Death of the SLA* (New York: Ballantine Books, 1976), frontispiece.

63. Janey Jiminez, as told to Ted Berkman, *My Prisoner* (Kansas City, KS: Sheed Andrews & McMeel, 1977), 80.

64. Hearst, *Every Secret Thing*, 361.

65. Jiminez, *My Prisoner*, 104.

66. Hearst, *Every Secret Thing*, 105.

67. Patricia Hearst, interview by Larry King, *Larry King Live*, CNN, January 31, 2001. In her biography, Hearst made no mention of the cropped frames, but she did argue that the SLA members in the bank "could have shot anyone . . . including me" (Hearst, *Every Secret Thing*, 395).

68. Hearst, *Every Secret Thing*, 89–90.

69. Ibid., 206.

70. Judy Stone, "Patty Hearst: The Hearst Family's Cook Provides Still Another View," *Ladies Home Journal*, October 1974, 147.

71. Fred Soltysik, *In Search of a Sister* (New York: Bantam Books, 1976), 233.

72. Ecclesiastes 12:13–14.

73. Vincent Canby. "Schrader's *Patty Hearst*," *New York Times*, September 23, 1988, http://www.nytimes.com/1988/09/23/movies/review-film-schrader-s-patty-hearst.html?scp=1&sq=%22Paul%20Schrader%22%20%22Patty%20Hearst%22&st=cse.

74. Elvis Mitchell, "Patty Hearst: The Movie," *Rolling Stone*, September 8, 1988, 160.

Chapter 5. Panther, Prisoner, Poet, and Prize

1. Assata Shakur, *Assata: An Autobiography* (Chicago: Lawrence Hill Books, 1987), 234.

2. Robert Daley, "Target Blue," *New York*, February 12, 1973, 44.

3. July 4, 1973, radio broadcast, quoted in Shakur, *Assata*, 50.

4. The name "Assata" stands as the badge of her outlawry both to those who love her and to those who despise her. Because she is simply "Assata" in the title of her autobiography and to the Hands Off Assata campaign, this chapter most often refers to her that way. This usage helps avoid confusion with the other Shakurs in the story.

5. On July 10, 1972, New York's *Daily News* ran a full-page reproduction of the wanted poster, which read "Wanted for Bank Robbery, $10,000 Reward." Evelyn Williams, *Inadmissible Evidence: The Story of the African-American Trial Lawyer Who Defended the Black Liberation Army* (Chicago: Lawrence Hill Books, 1993), 4. See also Lennox Hinds's foreword in Shakur, *Assata*, viii.

6. *New York Daily News*, quoted in Williams, *Inadmissible Evidence*, 78–79.

7. Akinyele Omowale Umoja, "Repression Breeds Resistance: The Black Liberation Army and the Radical Legacy of the Black Panther Party," in *Liberation, Imagination, and the Black Panther Party*, ed. Kathleen Cleaver and George N. Katsiaficas (New York: Routledge, 2001), 16.

8. Anannya Bhattercharjee, "Whose Safety? Women of Color and the Violence of Law Enforcement," working paper, American Friends Service Committee, Committee on Women, Population, and the Environment, Philadelphia, 2001.

9. This date happened to be the first anniversary of J. Edgar Hoover's death.

10. Although Joanne Chesimard/Assata Shakur was widely regarded as one of the figures behind the New York City cop killings of the early 1970s, she was never tried in connection to any of those killings. Charges for an attempted murder of policemen on January 23, 1973, were brought against her, but those charges were dismissed.

11. The accomplice ruling was in accordance with New Jersey's felony murder law, which makes anyone present for a homicide a potential accomplice to murder. The twenty-six to thirty-three years in state prison were to be served consecutively with her mandatory life sentence for the murders.

12. Editor Cynthia Sherry described *Assata* as a "popular backlist bestseller" for the Chicago Review Press, which absorbed Lawrence Hill Books in 1973. (Lawrence Hill, who acquired Assata's book, died just two months after it was published.) To circumvent the "Son of Sam" law, which prevents convicts from receiving profits on books or movies detailing their crimes, Lawrence Hill Books first released *Assata* through Zed, a publishing house in England (*Newsday*, "Chesimard Book Out," January 6, 1988, 16). All of the book's royalties go to Zed, who presumably forward them either to Assata or to her representative.

13. Margo V. Perkins, *Autobiography as Activism* (Jackson: University Press of Mississippi, 2000), xii. Assata's former attorney Lennox Hinds lauded her for "writ[ing] about her experiences not as a historical icon seeking to crystallize the 'Official Life' but as one whose experiences searching for change can provide a key to her own life and to all those others, who, as she so vividly puts it, 'have been locked by the lawless. Handcuffed by the haters. Gagged by the greedy'" (Shakur, *Assata*, vi).

14. Her narrator is confident, prone to self-criticism, but ultimately righteous, especially in the moments when she recognizes herself as playing into the hypocritical enforcement of race or class hierarchies. The book is full of stories of pranks, including a significant moment when her mother gains access to a racially segregated zoo by pretending that she and her children only speak Spanish. The lesson: "Anybody, no matter who they were, could come right off the boat and get more rights and respect than amerikan-born Blacks" (Shakur, *Assata*, 28).

15. For more on Shakur's attention to language, and the attention paid by other female authors of political autobiographies, see Perkins's *Autobiography as Activism*.

16. In her book, Assata notes that she contemplated joining in the wake of the Panther 21 trials, in which twenty-one of the most high-profile New York City Panthers had been arrested on conspiracy charges: "I thought about joining the Party right then, but i had some other things i wanted to do and i needed a low profile in order to do them" (Shakur, *Assata*, 204).

17. Shakur, *Assata*, 204.

18. Ibid., 196.

19. Jonathan Jackson attempted the kidnapping with two accomplices on August

7, 1970. He famously shouted, "We are the revolutionaries! Free the Soledad Brothers by 12:30." The "Soledad Brothers" referred to George Jackson and two other San Quentin inmates who had been accused of killing a white prison guard and who were facing the death penalty. On August 21, 1971, three days before he was to go on trial, George Jackson was gunned down in the prison yard during what was officially deemed an escape attempt but which some believe was a setup.

20. Shakur, *Assata*, 206.

21. In her book, Assata describes Davis as "one of the most beautiful women i had ever seen. Not physically, but spiritually. i knew who she was, because I had been keeping clippings of her in my file. She was the sister who got fired from her job teaching at a California college because she told everybody she was a communist and if they didn't like it, they could go to hell" (Shakur, *Assata*, 207). Davis was acquitted of all charges twenty-two months later, on June 4, 1974.

22. Shakur, *Assata*, 207.

23. In the early 1970s, Assata and Zayd Shakur worked to raise the $100,000 cash bail for their future New Jersey Turnpike companion, Sundiata Acoli, a member of the Panther 21 who was then in prison. But the judge for the trial refused to release Sundiata, a fact that Assata includes in her book and has referenced in subsequent interviews over the years. Shakur, *Assata*, 225.

24. Shakur, *Assata*, 224.

25. Stew Albert, "White Radicals, Black Panthers, and a Sense of Fulfillment," in Cleaver and Katsiaficas, *Liberation*, 189.

26. The Panther 21 had written an open letter to the Weather Underground (then the Weathermen) that was somewhat critical of BPP policies. On May 13, 1971, after the longest political trial in New York's history, all twenty-one New York Panthers were acquitted of all charges in just forty-five minutes of jury deliberation. The acquittal of the Panther 21 was a major political setback and embarrassment for the Manhattan district attorney's office and the New York Police intelligence unit known as BOSSI, which had extensively infiltrated and disrupted the BPP's community programs.

27. Assata notes that her telephone kept working long after she had stopped paying for service and offers evidence that her activities were being observed inside and outside her home. Shakur, *Assata*, 226.

28. "Because of police harassment, the Panthers had been ordered not to wear the uniform, except for special occasions" (Shakur, *Assata*, 231).

29. After the assassination of Martin Luther King, the BPP transformed itself from a California-based organization to a national movement. By 1969, which was later recorded as the "Year of the Panther," it had approximately five thousand members in forty chapters, which had sprung up in American cities across the country. One of the most significant of these new chapters was in New York City. Umoja, "Repression," 7.

30. Ruth Reitan, "Cuba, the Black Panther Party, and the U.S. Black Movement in the 1960s," in Cleaver and Katsiaficas, *Liberation*, 169.

31. J. Edgar Hoover quoted in Ward Churchill and Jim Vander Wall, *Agents of Repression: The FBI's Secret Wars against the Black Panther Party and the American Indian Movement* (Boston: South End Press, 1988), 77.

32. Frank Donner, *Protector of Privilege: Red Squads and Police Repression in Urban America* (Berkeley: University of California Press, 1990), 180.

33. Shakur, *Assata*, 228–230.

34. Umoja, "Repression," 10.

35. Shakur, *Assata*, 233.

36. Ibid., 227.

37. Craig Williams, "Reflections of Geronimo: The Essence of a Panther," *Black Panther*, August 29, 1970, 74.

38. Shakur, *Assata*, 222.

39. Ibid., 223.

40. Ibid., 235–236. The shootings happened on Malcolm X's birthday, six days after the Panther 21 were acquitted on charges of conspiracy. A car traveling in the wrong direction on Riverside Drive blasted machine-gun fire into the police car of patrolmen Thomas Curry and Nicholas Binetti. Both men survived but were seriously injured. The attempted murder took place not far from the home of District Attorney Frank Hogan, the prosecutor in the Panther 21 trial.

41. Her comments in response to the police shootings echoed those that appeared in a letter sent to the *New York Times* by the perpetrators: "The armed goons of this racist government will again meet the guns of oppressed Third World People as long as they occupy our community and murder our brothers and sisters in the name of American law and order. The domestic armed forces of racism and oppression will be confronted with the guns of the Black Liberation Army, who will mete out in the tradition of Malcolm and all true revolutionaries, real justice. We are revolutionary justice" (Daley, "Target Blue," 77). In the next chapter of her autobiography, Assata speaks disapprovingly of "do-or-die battle[s] with the power structure in amerika," noting that they are far less important than organizing the underground: "Revolutionary war is a people's war. And no people's war can be won without the support of the masses of people." She concedes, however, that she "didn't feel that armed acts of resistance should be ruled out" (Shakur, *Assata*, 242–243).

42. Williams, *Inadmissible Evidence*, 3–6.

43. Daley, "Target Blue," 44.

44. *New York Times*, "Woman Shot in Struggle with Her Alleged Victim," April 7, 1971. Assata may make an oblique reference to this incident in her description of her adaptation to life in the underground: "I had always been open and trusting and I was finding it really hard to change. It took my almost getting killed for me to develop a more suspicious nature" (Shakur, *Assata*, 235).

45. Shakur, *Assata*, 50.

46. Ibid., 52.

47. Ibid., 185–186.

48. Reginald Kavanaugh, "Chesimard Claims Innocence," *Home News*, East Brunswick, NJ, March 16, 1977; *Home News*, "Slogans Cleaned from Building," March 15, 1977. In April 1977, a reporter covering Assata's postconviction hearing on the constitutionality of her confinement in a men's prison mistakenly referred to her throughout the article as "Schakur," reflecting how infrequently her new name had then appeared in print. Jeff Weatherby, "Chesimard Pleads for Transfer from Yardville Isolation," *Home News*, East Brunswick, NJ, April 1977.

49. Assata was originally to have stood trial with Sundiata Acoli (Clark Squire) in the fall of 1973 on charges of first-degree murder for the killing of Trooper Werner Foerster, second-degree murder for the death of Zayd Shakur, illegal possession of a weapon, armed robbery (of Foerster's revolver), and four assault charges. But Sundiata's

trial had been severed from Assata's on account of her unexpected pregnancy. And then her own trial was postponed for several months after a poll revealed that 83 percent of New Jersey's Middlesex County residents recognized the name Joanne Chesimard and 70 percent thought she was guilty. A judge granted the change of venue from Middlesex to the nearly all-white Morris County, New Jersey, after a candidate in the jury pool revealed that he had been told by the other jurors that "if she's Black, she's guilty." The Morris County trial ended in a mistrial when Assata had to be hospitalized due to pregnancy-related complications. Alix Kirsta, "A Black and White Case," *Times* (London), May 29, 1999.

50. Sundiata Acoli (Clark Squire) received a sentence of life plus twenty-four to thirty years. The New Jersey State Police have sent representatives to each of the parole hearings and have vowed to make sure he is never released.

51. The Chicago Seven trial began as the Chicago Eight. Abbie Hoffman, Jerry Rubin, David Dellinger, Tom Hayden, Rennie Davis, John Froines, Lee Weiner, and Bobby Seale were charged with conspiracy and inciting to riot in relation to the 1968 protests outside the Democratic National Convention in Chicago. Bobby Seale's trial was severed from that of the other defendants after he hurled insults at the judge for denying a postponement of the trial (Seale's lawyer was unavailable) and then for refusing to let him represent himself. The judge ultimately ordered Seale bound and gagged in the courtroom and sentenced him to four years in prison for contempt of court. Seale's refusal to abide by the protocols of the court and his repeated denunciations of the judge as a "fascist dog" and a "racist" may have inspired Assata's own behavior at the first of her trials. Of Stanley Cohen's death in the middle of her 1977 Turnpike trial, Assata writes that Cohen's body had been "found in his home with evidence of trauma" shortly after hinting to Assata that he had a positive new development for her defense. According to Assata, Cohen's widow could not find any of his files for Assata's case until Evelyn Williams found them in the custody of the New York City police.

52. Assata's aunt occasionally joined her niece in a type of juridical outlawry, once being made to serve thirty days for walking out of a courtroom to express her disgust at the judge's actions. In the Bronx bank robbery trial of 1973, Williams and the lawyer of Assata's codefendant deliberately sat mute to protest the short period of time they had been given to prepare the case. After Assata's initial capture, Williams was subject to intrusive strip searches each and every time she visited her niece in her role as counsel. Ultimately, she obtained a court order to stop the humiliating ritual. Kirsta, "Black and White Case," 3.

53. Williams, *Inadmissible Evidence*, 14.

54. In explaining her concern that a FBI photo would be altered, Assata wrote, "If you are unfortunate to have two eyes, a nose, and lips, in more or less the same place, you end up looking like the bank robber, no matter what you really look like" (Shakur, *Assata*, 161).

55. Shakur, *Assata*, 161.

56. In his dismissal, Justice John R. Starkey said, "People have constitutional rights, and you can't shuffle them around" (Max H. Seigel, "Chesimard Murder Case Dropped Because of Delay in Holding Trial," *New York Times*, October 26, 1977).

57. AnneMarie Cooke, "Chesimard Trial Cost $300,000," *Home News*, East Brunswick, NJ, March 28, 1977.

58. New York State Fraternal Order of Police, "New York State Fraternal Order of

Police Criticizes Judge's Decision on the Release of Kathy Boudin," http://www.nysfop .org/Back_Up/events/kathy_boudin.htm.

59. *Home News*, East Brunswick, NJ, "Chesimard Defense Effort to Prove Conspiracy Quashed," March 3, 1977.

60. A few years earlier, William Kunstler had successfully subpoenaed Church and Kelly in the trial of members of the American Indian Movement who had been charged with murdering FBI agents. Joseph F. Sullivan, "Chesimard Attorney Acts to Call Kelley," *New York Times*, Week in Review, February 24, 1977.

61. Kavanaugh, "Chesimard Claims Innocence."

62. Five of the jurors had relatives or close friends who were law enforcement officers.

63. Joseph F. Sullivan, "Panther, Trooper Slain in Shoot-Out," *New York Times*, May 3, 1973.

64. Joseph F. Sullivan, "Doctor Testifies on Bullet Scars in Chesimard Trial," *New York Times*, March 18, 1977.

65. Daniel Hays, "Joanne Shot Me, Trooper Testifies," *Home News*, East Brunswick, NJ, February 22, 1977; Walter H. Waggoner, "Neurosurgeon's Testimony Backs Mrs. Chesimard," *New York Times*, Week in Review, March 17, 1977.

66. Kavanaugh, "Chesimard Claims Innocence." As she told the jury in 1977, "I must have been screaming because Clark Squire (Sundiata) slapped me." In her autobiography, Assata describes herself as having the presence of mind to deliberately misdirect the cops, who demanded to know in which direction Sundiata had run. Shakur, *Assata*, 3.

67. *Home News*, East Brunswick, NJ, "Appleby," March 15, 1977.

68. Lawrence Nagy, "Chesimard Guilty, Gets Life in Prison," *Newark Star-Ledger*, March 26, 1977.

69. Ibid.

70. Walter H. Waggoner, "Joanne Chesimard Convicted in Killing of Jersey Trooper," *New York Times*, March 26, 1977.

71. *Home News*, East Brunswick, NJ, "March," March 27, 1977.

72. Shakur, *Assata*, 64. The Thirteenth Amendment: "Neither slavery nor involuntary servitude, except as a punishment for crime whereof the party shall have been duly convicted, shall exist within the United States, or any place subject to their jurisdiction."

73. Immediately after her Turnpike arrest, Assata was held in the New Jersey State Reception and Correction Center in Yardville, Middlesex County, before being moved to Rikers Island Correctional Institution for Women in New York.

74. Lennox S. Hinds, foreword to Shakur, *Assata*, x.

75. Shakur, *Assata*, 83.

76. Ibid., 130.

77. At sentencing, the judge gave Assata ten to twelve years on four counts of assault, twelve to fifteen for robbery (of the slain officer's service revolver), two to three for armed robbery, plus two to three for aiding and abetting the murder of the officer. The judge dismissed the second-degree murder of Zayd Shakur on the grounds that the New Jersey Supreme Court had recently narrowed the application of the law. For Assata's refusal to rise each time the judge entered the courtroom, he added thirty days in the Middlesex County Workhouse for contempt of court.

78. Shakur, *Assata*, 258.

79. Robert Hanley, "Miss Chesimard Flees Jersey Prison, Helped by 3 Armed 'Visitors,'" *New York Times*, November 3, 1979; Robert Hanley, "F.B.I. to Aid Search for Miss Chesimard," *New York Times*, November 4, 1979.

80. Mos Def, "Assata Shakur: The Government's Terrorist Is Our Community's Heroine," http://www.assatashakur.org/mosdef.htm.

81. *Jet*, "FBI Ransacks N.Y. Apts. in Search for Chesimard: U.S. Probe Ordered," May 8, 1980, 58.

82. Umoja, "Repression," 15. Baraldini, Mutulu Shakur, Sekou Odinga, and Marilyn Buck have all been charged with assisting the breakout. Ronald Boyd Hill was also held on charges of assisting with the escape.

83. *Prison Activist*, "IWD: Interview with Safiya Bukhari-Alston" (New York City, September 27, 1992), http://www.prisonactivist.org/jericho_sfbay/Safiya_Bukhari/Safiya_Bukhari_interview.html. Celebrity outlawry may have boosted the cause of the BLA. It also was at odds with a certain vision of radical political organizing. Bukhari suggested that all the attention paid to Assata was ultimately detrimental to the causes of which she had been a part: "There are a lot of other people out there in exile that no one ever mentions. . . . That is not the way you build movements. If you don't support the people in your movements who made the sacrifices then what incentive is there to anybody else to get involved? I have a real problem with that."

84. Assata Shakur, interview by Ralph Penza, WNBC-TV news, National Broadcasting Co., February 5–6, 1998.

85. Assata Shakur, "Open Letter from Assata Shakur," *Hands off Assata*, http://www.handsoffassata.org/content/assataopenletter-text.htm.

86. In 1998, death row inmate Mumia Abu-Jamal excoriated the Congressional Black Caucus for having recently supported President Bill Clinton during his impeachment trial while not extending the same support to Assata. He also rebuked the CBC for not having read *Assata* or Evelyn Williams's *Inadmissible Evidence*, and condemned HR 254 as a modern-day "fugitive slave law." Mumia Abu-Jamal, "Selling Out Assata," *Assata Shakur*, http://www.assatashakur.org/forum/mumia-abu-jamal/3984-selling-out-assata.html.

87. Committee on International Relations, *Calling for the Extradition of Joanne Chesimard from Cuba*, HR 254, 105th Cong., 2nd sess., *Congressional Record*, May 13, 1998.

88. *Adventure Divas Cuba: Paradox Found*, directed by Holly Morris (Seattle: Adventure Divas, 2000).

89. As part of a once-clandestine religious tradition designed to preserve the traditional beliefs of Nigeria's Yoruba people, Santería spiritual practices were handed down by West Africans enslaved on Caribbean sugar plantations. Given Assata's repeated self-identification as a "twentieth-century escaped slave," and as one who had never really known what it is to be free (a phrase repeated in *Eyes of the Rainbow*), the connection to subversive, culture-preserving Santería goddess tradition makes sense. So, too, do the film's multiple allusions to a female spiritual force (Ìyá Nlá, or "Our Mothers," in the Yoruban tradition), which may bestow upon its believers a renewed connection to their African ancestors. Originally a derogatory term, "Santería" was coined by the Spanish to mock slaves' hyperdevotion to the Christian saints and their apparent neglect of a monotheistic God. In fact, many slaves disguised their orishas as saints in order to preserve their ancestral beliefs and avoid the enforced conversions of the slave masters.

As a reflection of this history, the terms "saint" and "orisha" are sometimes used interchangeably in postrevolutionary Cuba, where until recently both Catholic and Santería rituals were discouraged.

90. "Qualified" because shortly after arriving in 1969 (via hijacked plane), they claimed they were not received "in revolutionary fashion." "Life Worse in Cuba, Unhappy Black Panthers Wail," *Miami Herald*, June 26, 1969, http://www.latinamericanstudies.org/hijackers/raymond-johnson.htm.

91. Rolando's first film, *Oggún: The Eternal Present* (1991), was all about Cuban subcultures seemingly at odds with Cuba's "official" narrative of itself. *Oggún* relates the legend of a Yoruba god as reflected in the spiritual life story of a minor outlaw—Cuba's foremost singer in the Santería ceremonies then discouraged by the Cuban government. In her second film, *My Footsteps in Baragua* (1995), Rolando addresses the ambivalence and nostalgia felt by the descendants of Cubans who migrated from the English-speaking West Indies. *Footsteps* documents the fusion of British and Afro-Caribbean traditions in Cuba's municipality of Baragua (in today's Ciego de Avila).

92. This argument about Assata's individualism is not meant to understate her obvious attention to the collective mistreatment of black people and of prisoners in the United States. But her autobiographical narrative focuses mostly on her individual discovery and coming-of-age.

93. For a useful summary of Nanny Jamaica's reputation as warrior-outlaw, see Kimberly Juanita Brown, "Nanny of the Maroons: History, Memory, and Imagery," Yale University, http://www.yale.edu/glc/nanny.htm.

94. Gloria Rolando's statement for *Eyes of the Rainbow* ended with a comment on its music. "The blues interpreted by Junius Williams and his 'Magic Harp,' the song of Sweet Honey in the Rock, and the Cuban group, 'Vocal Baobab,' give a special stamp to this valiant testimony which defines the spirit of struggle in the African American woman" (AfroCubaWeb, "The Eyes of the Rainbow: Assata Shakur and Oya," http://www.afrocubaweb.com/Rainbow.htm).

95. See ibid.

96. During her visit to Amherst College on January 16, 2006, Rosemari Mealy recollected how Rolando traveled to New York City to fund-raise and shop for costumes for her dancers in the Panther segment.

97. The hunter may represent the Yoruban hunter-god Ochosi, whose stone-cut image also appears fleetingly on-screen.

98. That she does not articulate the Panthers' Black Nationalist platform or their local struggles against racist police practices may be either because these things were not as easily translated in Cuba or because she regarded them as so obvious as to be understood. It is also possible that Assata did mention these things and Rolando chose to leave them out.

99. As Rolando told an interviewer in 2000, "Whenever I have ideas, dreams, difficulties or doubts, I consult with my mother and grandmother. Sometimes people have a dramaturg or a writer to consult, yes? But I consult with them. For me, they are a gift, and dedicating my first film, *Oggún*, to them, was a way to thank them for everything they made possible for me. My grandmother used to clean the floor and I am a filmmaker. How can I not reflect her or her feelings, or her life or her battle?" ("Adventure Divas: Gloria Rolando: Filmmaker," http://www.adventuredivas.com/divas/cuba/gloria-rolando/).

100. In Assata's autobiography, she explains that her grandmother "had been dreaming all of her life, and the dreams have come true." But her grandmother is more of a catalyst than a soothsayer: "My grandmother's dreams have always come when they were needed and have always meant what we needed them to mean. She dreamed my mother would be a schoolteacher, my aunt would go to law school, and, during the hard times, she dreams the good times were coming. . . . She told us what we needed to be told and made us believe it like nobody else could have. She did her part. The rest was up to us" (Shakur, *Assata*, 260–261).

101. In the chapter just before the rumination on her grandmother, Assata writes, "[My daughter] waves good-bye to me, her face clouded and worried, looking like a little adult. I go back to my cage and cry until I vomit. I decide that it's time to leave" (ibid., 258).

102. The fuller quotation: "Separation is a real part of being African in the Americas, being slaves or ex-slaves. In my own case, prison has meant separation. Exile has meant separation. And, well, I'm going to be real right now because I can't be any other way. Today my mother died."

103. In a brief voice-over at the start and the end of the film, the narrator Nehanda Isoke Abiodun (herself a former Panther and fugitive in Cuba) relates a parable, which asks, *"Where are the women warriors?"* The answer: *"They have been scattered. . . . Women warriors are the eyes of the rainbow."*

104. Cancio Isla Wilfredo, "Fugitive a Curiosity in Cuba," *Miami Herald*, December 18, 2007, http://archives.econ.utah.edu/archives/cubanews/2007w51/msg00044.htm.

105. *Adventure Divas Cuba.*

106. Elián's mother perished in the crossing, and Elián swiftly became a symbol of a power struggle between the communist government of Fidel Castro and Miami's Cuban exile community. Attorney General Janet Reno was roundly lambasted for ordering federal agents to take the boy, at gunpoint, from the home of his Miami relatives and to restore him to his father, who resides in Cuba.

Chapter 6. Glorious and Bitter Ends

1. Soliah's capture almost certainly was enabled by a neighbor's tip. On March 3, 1999, and May 15, 1999, she was profiled on the FBI's *America's Most Wanted* television program. Two FBI agents stopped her white minivan a short distance from her home on the morning of June 16, 1999.

2. Sara Olson Defense Committee flyer and cookbook promotion, 2000.

3. Hearst had initially refused to pursue a presidential pardon because of its imputation of guilt. But she ultimately agreed to apply for the pardon at the suggestion of President Ronald Reagan's attorney general Edward Meese. Hearst credits President Jimmy Carter's long-term activism on her behalf for making the pardon finally happen, thirteen years after her initial application. Patricia Hearst, interview by Larry King, *Larry King Live*, CNN, January 31, 2001.

4. On his last day in office, Clinton also pardoned two former Weatherwomen, Linda Evans and Susan Rosenberg. But those pardons did not receive anything like the attention given to Patricia Hearst's.

5. Bob Graham, "Waters' 'DeMented' Offers Giddy Fun," *San Francisco Chronicle*, August 11, 2000, http://www.sfgate.com/cgi-bin/article.cgi?f=/c/a/2000/08/11/DD28654.DTL#ixzz0064IEGQ3.

6. In an angry standoff with members of a family values coalition, Honey quipped, "Family is just a dirty word for censorship!" Peter Travers, "Cecil B. Demented," *Rolling Stone*, December 10, 2000, http://www.rollingstone.com/reviews/movie/5949045/review/5949046/cecil_b_demented.

7. Christopher Castiglia, *Bound and Determined: Captivity, Culture-Crossing, and White Womanhood from Mary Rowlandson to Patty Hearst* (Chicago: University of Chicago Press, 1996), 104.

8. Dohrn eventually served seven months for refusing to testify against another former Weather Underground member for her role in a 1981 armored car robbery.

9. Pat Burson, "100 at Olson Event Talk about Case," *Pioneer Press*, February 13, 2000.

10. Sharon Darby Hendry, *SoLiAh: The Sara Jane Olson Story* (Bloomington, MN: Cable Publishing, 2002), 263.

11. Mark Miller, "From Villain to Victim," *Newsweek*, February 4, 2002, 29.

12. *Economist*, "Treasonous Reflections: Americans—Particularly George Bush—Shouldn't Make Excuses for John Walker," December 15, 2001, 28.

13. Susan Choi, *American Woman* (New York: HarperCollins Publishers, 2003), 355.

14. Brian Joseph Davis, *I, Tania* (Toronto: ECW Press, 2007), 102.

15. Kate Sullivan, "Our Beloved Revolutionary Sweetheart," *City Pages*, February 9, 2005, http://www.citypages.com/2005-02-09/movies/our-beloved-revolutionary-sweetheart/.

16. *NJLawman.com*, "One Million Dollar Reward Issued for Joanne Chesimard," http://www.NJLawman.com/Articles%202/Chesimard-Reward.htm.

17. John Rice, "Castro Defends Fugitive Sought by U.S," *Associated Press*, May 11, 2005.

18. This was Fred Baker's third film about a filmmaker. Baker confirmed that *Assata*'s Jason was based on himself, as were his previous characters: "*Events* (1970) there's a filmmaker, and it's me; *White Trash* (1992) there's a filmmaker living on the streets of California, broke, and can't get it together and trying to get a film off the ground, and it's me" (interview with author, June 15, 2007). In another repetition that may or may not be intentional, both Jason and the character of Assata's lawyer, William Kunstler (played by Fred Baker), use the expression "all over hell and gone."

19. Mealy, who is a friend of Assata Shakur's and was the caretaker for underground screenings of *Eyes of the Rainbow* when it was still banned in the States, later regretted her participation in Baker's film because of Evelyn Williams's opposition to the project. But, according to Baker, both Kathleen Cleaver and Assata Shakur herself still regard *Assata* favorably.

20. Shakur, *Assata*, 209.

21. Jason says he has read the transcripts in the *New York Times*, but the *Times* article he cites only alludes to the recorded conversations; it does not replicate them. Jason says the police-radio tapes prove that the troopers knew who the occupants of the car were before Harper stopped them. In fact, the recorded conversation—about the occupants being black and armed—happened just before the Pontiac was stopped for the second and final time, after an injured Harper had returned to the State Police Headquarters on foot. Walter H. Waggoner, "Jury in Chesimard Murder Trial Listens to State Police Radio Tapes," *New York Times*, Week in Review, February 17, 1977, 83.

22. Like Baker himself, the freelance film critic Louis Proyect compared Baker's treatment of the shootout to the climax of Errol Morris's *The Thin Blue Line* (1988), "in which the police testimony is revealed to be full of holes." As Proyect enthused, "Despite the obvious shoestring budget, the film has more impact than the average Hollywood blockbuster costing 1000 times more . . . If there is anything that can be learned from cases such as Mumia's or Assata Shakur's, it is to take the word of the cops with a wheelbarrow full of salt" (Louis Proyect, "The Unrepentant Marxist," April 10, 2007, "Assata Shakur," http://louisproyect.wordpress.com/2007/04/10/assata-shakur/).

23. The Janet Malcolm quotation was drawn from her 2005 *New Yorker* article on Gertrude Stein. Fred Baker's own disclaimer at the start of his film: "Some of the actual events in my film 'ASSATA a.k.a. Joanne Chesimard' are reenacted strictly from my opinion, based on my research, and how I feel they truly might have happened."

24. As Baker reports, the librarians said, "Well obviously, sir, somebody took them out. We haven't found them yet" (interview with author, June 15, 2007).

25. Of their 2003 phone conversation about the Turnpike incident, Baker reported, "[Assata] said that basically she was cowardly. She was basically out of her mind." The film's plot summary begins, "Assata Shakur, the firebrand revolutionary Black Panther, was falsely convicted and sentenced to life in a widely publicized case involving a 1973 shootout on the NJ Turnpike, which resulted in the deaths of a Panther leader and a NJ State Trooper" (Internet Movie Database, "Plot Summary for *Assata aka Joanne Chesimard* [2008]," http://www.imdb.com/title/tt1186635/plotsummary).

26. Contrary to Assata's biography, in which she describes her right arm as paralyzed by the bullet that damaged a nerve, Sydney's Assata moves both of her arms freely when she hugs Evelyn and turns to display her wounds.

27. Identified only as "White Woman," this character may be a stand-in for Silvia Baraldini, who in 1982 was convicted for driving the getaway car during the prison break. That she wears a beret symbolically connects her to Bonnie Parker, Patty Hearst, Che Guevara, and the Black Panthers.

28. Like Larry Buchanan, director of *The Other Side of Bonnie and Clyde*, Baker is a pragmatic filmmaker, unabashed about using sex to sell movies or about making films about sex. Baker's official debut as a filmmaker, *Events*, is essentially a porn movie about a pair of young men who decide to make a porn movie to raise enough money to make a Lenny Bruce biopic. *Events* came out in 1970. In 1971, Baker and his wife made *Lenny Bruce without Tears*.

29. Fred Baker, *Assata aka Joanne Chesimard*, video at MySpace, http://vids.myspace.com/index.cfm?fuseaction=vids.channel&ChannelID=120183408.

30. Baker says he will give Assata's daughter and granddaughter 15 percent of any profit, "only because I like to share. What the hell do I need it for? I'm not going to hoard whatever comes in on the film. I would like to pay back my kids for seeing me denude my bank account. But the point of the matter is that I did spend *all* my money making a movie" (interview with author, June 15, 2007).

31. See Louis Proyect, "The Unrepentant Marxist," April 10, 2007, "Assata Shakur," http://louisproyect.wordpress.com/2007/04/10/assata-shakur/.

32. *Adventure Divas Cuba: Paradox Found*, directed by Holly Morris (Seattle: Adventure Divas, 2000).

33. West African immigrant Amado Diallo was shot and killed by four officers who thought he was reaching for a weapon when they stopped him outside his house on the

night of February 4, 1999. The officers, who had mistaken Diallo for a criminal they sought, fired on Diallo forty-one times when he reached for the wallet that contained his ID. The four police were ultimately acquitted for their actions.

34. On his MySpace page, Fred calls Assata "a living icon who still, at age 60, represents the struggle against the ugly oppression of racism and injustice to people of color everywhere in the world" (http://vids.myspace.com/index.cfm?fuseaction=vids.channel&ChannelID=120183408).

35. Paris ("Assata's Song"), Digable Planets, Public Enemy, and X-Clan have all recorded tributes to Assata. Charles E. Jones, ed., *The Black Panther Party Reconsidered* (Baltimore: Black Classic Press, 1998), 425.

36. While making his album, Common met with Assata in Havana. His daughter, Omoye Assata Lynn, is named for her.

37. AllHipHop.com bills itself as "The World's Most Dangerous Site"; for example, see "U.S. Government Declares $1 Million Bounty for Assata Shakur, Tupac's Godmother" (http://allhiphop.com/stories/news/archive/2005/05/02/18129965.aspx).

38. Guillermo Morales accidentally blew off all but two of his fingers, prompting his arrest. He later escaped from a prison hospital (where he was set to receive prosthetic hands) by sliding down three stories on a strand of bandages.

39. Karen W. Arenson, "CUNY Chief Orders Names Stripped from Student Center," *New York Times*, December 13, 2006, http://www.nytimes.com/2006/12/13/nyregion/13cuny.html?ex=157680000&en=08a06b950e968815a&ei=5124&partner=permalink&exprod=permalink.

40. Stanley Crouch, "By Any Means Necessary," *New York Times*, September 10, 2006, http://www.nytimes.com/2006/09/10/books/review/crouch.html?ref=books#.

41. Jay Nordinger, "In Castro's Corner: A Story of Black and Red," *National Review*, March 6, 2000, http://article.nationalreview.com/?q=ZTY4oDk4MDRhYzZjODZmMTJhMjVhMTc4ZGJiMWM3YWM=.

42. That she was not presumed romantically connected to either of her companions in the Turnpike stop may have been a function of a predominantly white press for whom her race somehow marked Assata as outside of hetero-romantic norms, or at least outside the immediate identification. Alternatively, the fact that she was traveling with two men potentially tapped racist stereotypes of the hypersexed black woman's body.

43. Frank McKeown, "Squire Guilty of Trooper's Murder," *Daily News*, March 12, 1974.

44. Kathleen Cleaver, "The Fugitive: Why Has the FBI Placed a Million-Dollar Bounty on Assata Shakur?" *Essence*, August 2005. http://www.essence.com/essence/lifestyle/voices/0,16109,1081943,00.html.

45. Jenny Sharpe, *Ghosts of Slavery: A Literary Archeology of Black Women's Lives* (Minneapolis: University of Minnesota Press, 2003), 2.

46. NJLawman.com is maintained by the United Federation of Police Webmasters, which describes the site as "a solely positive place for law enforcement officers to visit." As the site explains, "There will generally be no negative coverage of law enforcement. For that type of reading, please see any of the newspaper websites" (NJLawman.com, "About Us," http://www.njlawman.com/NJLawman%20Important%20Information.htm). See the entry at NJLawman.com for Assata Shakur, "The Story of Joanne Chesimard," editorial from May 2003 (http://njlawman.com/Feature%20Pieces/Joanne%20Chesimard.htm).

47. It was dedicated on Thursday, April 28, 2005, in memory of the thirty-second anniversary of the fatal gunfight.

48. See the State of New Jersey Department of Law and Public Safety, Office of the Attorney General, http://www.njsp.org/.

49. The "Happy Birthday Assata" tour, which HOA organized in honor of Assata's sixty years, featured a traveling birthday card and speeches by Angela Davis, Mos Def, and Sonia Sanchez. It culminated with the public sales of Gloria Rolando's *Eyes of the Rainbow* and a Detroit City Council resolution honoring Assata. Assata's birthday letter appears on the HOA homepage, along with multiple images of Assata, including one circulated by the FBI in the aftermath of her 1979 prison break. See *Hands Off Assata*, http://www.handsoffassata.org/.

Epilogue

1. Henry Nash Smith, *Virgin Land: The American West as Symbol and Myth* (Cambridge, MA: Harvard University Press, 1950), 112–120.

2. Duncan Aikman, *Calamity Jane and the Lady Wildcats* (New York: Henry Holt & Co., 1927), 95–96.

3. After the 1920s stage debut of *Chicago*, Watkins never had another of her plays produced. Over the years, she turned down every request to buy the rights to *Chicago*, out of what some speculated was regret over the role her reporting had played in Gartner's and Annan's acquittals. Watkins died in 1969, a mysterious recluse who never appeared in public without a black veil over her face. Her estate immediately sold the rights of the play to Joel Grey, who turned it into the long-running musical by the same name. Louise Kiernan, "Murder She Wrote," *Chicago Tribune*, July 17, 1997.

4. Orrin Klapp, *Heroes, Villains, and Fools: Reflections of the American Character* (New York: Aegis Publishing Co., 1972), 5; Peter Stallybrass and Allon White, *The Politics and Poetics of Transgression* (Ithaca, NY: Cornell University Press, 1986), 76.

5. Natalie Zemon Davis, *Fiction in the Archives: Pardon Tales and Their Tellers in Sixteenth-Century France* (Stanford, CA: Stanford University Press, 1987), 3.

6. Carolyn Strange, "Murder and Meanings in U.S. Historiography," *Feminist Studies* 25, no. 3 (Fall 1999): 693.

7. Andrew Cline, "Depp out of His Depth," *American Spectator*, July 1, 2009, http://spectator.org/archives/2009/07/01/depp-out-of-his-depth.

8. Lew Louderback, *The Bad Ones: Gangsters of the 1930s and Their Molls* (Greenwich, CT: Fawcett Publications, 1968), 10.

9. Aaron Marc Stein, foreword to *Saint with a Gun: The Unlawful Private Eye*, by William Ruehlmann (New York: New York University Press, 1974), xii.

10. Elizabeth Reis, *Damned Women: Sinners and Witches in Puritan New England* (Ithaca, NY: Cornell University Press, 1997).

11. Dixie Lee Sedgwick, correspondence with author, May 18, 2009.

12. Harris's supporters made the $1 million bail that was supposed to have kept her in prison before her 2003 trial. Gordon Young, "Patty Cakes: Terror, Nostalgia, and the SLA," *Metro*, April 11–17, 2002, http://www.metroactive.com/papers/metro/04.11.02/cover/sla1-0215.html.

13. John Fox, interview with author, June 22, 2009.

BIBLIOGRAPHY

Books and Articles

Abu-Jamal, Mumia. "Selling Out Assata." *Assata Shakur.* http://www.assatashakur.org/forum/mumia-abu-jamal/3984-selling-out-assata.html.

Adler, Freda. *Sisters in Crime: The Rise of the New Female Criminal.* New York: McGraw-Hill, 1975.

Aikman, Duncan. *Calamity Jane and the Lady Wildcats.* New York: Henry Holt & Co., 1927.

Albert, Stew. "White Radicals, Black Panthers, and a Sense of Fulfillment." In *Liberation, Imagination, and the Black Panther Party,* ed. Kathleen Cleaver and George N. Katsiaficas, 188–194. New York: Routledge, 2001.

Alexander, Shana. *Anyone's Daughter: The Times and Trials of Patty Hearst.* New York: Viking Press, 1979.

———. "The Girl in the Box." *Newsweek,* April 29, 1974, 25.

Arenson, Karen W. "CUNY Chief Orders Names Stripped from Student Center." *New York Times,* December 13, 2006.

Ashraf, Rushdy. "Exquisite Corpse." In *The Best American Essays 2001,* ed. Kathleen Norris, 261–269. Robert Atwan, ser. ed. New York: Houghton Mifflin, 2001.

Baker, Marilyn, and Sally Brompton. *Exclusive! The Inside Story of Patricia Hearst and the SLA.* New York: Macmillan, 1974.

Barbato, Joseph. "America Imagines the FBI." *Chronicle of Higher Education,* January 27, 1984.

Barrow, Blanche Caldwell. *My Life with Bonnie and Clyde.* Ed. John Neal Phillips. Norman: University of Oklahoma Press, 2004.

Bederman, Gail. *Manliness and Civilization: A Cultural History of Gender and Race in the United States, 1880–1917.* Chicago: University of Chicago Press, 1995.

Belcher, Jerry, and Don West. *Patty/Tania.* New York: Pyramid Books, 1975.

Bhattercharjee, Anannya. "Whose Safety: Women of Color and the Violence of Law Enforcement." Working paper, American Friends Service Committee, Committee on Women, Population, and the Environment, Philadelphia, 2001.

Blanton, De Anne, and Lauren M. Cook. *They Fought Like Demons: Women Soldiers in the Civil War.* New York: Vintage, 2003.

Borstein, Kate. *Gender Outlaw: On Men, Women, and the Rest of Us.* New York: Vintage Books, 1995.

Breuer, William B. *J. Edgar Hoover and His G-Men.* Westport, CT: Praeger, 1995.

Briggs, Laura. "The Race of Hysteria: 'Overcivilization' and the 'Savage' Woman in Late Nineteenth-Century Obstetrics and Gynecology." *American Quarterly* 52 (June 2000): 246–273.

Browder, Laura. *Her Best Shot: Women and Guns in America.* Chapel Hill: University of North Carolina Press, 2006.

Bryan, John. *This Soldier Still at War.* New York: Harcourt Brace Jovanovich, 1975.

Buchanan, Larry. *It Came from Hunger! Tales of a Cinema Schlockmeister.* Jefferson, NC: McFarland & Co., 1996.

Burke, Peter. *Popular Culture in Early Modern Europe.* Brookfield, VT: Scholar Press, 1994.

Burrough, Bryan. *Public Enemies: America's Greatest Crime Wave and the Birth of the FBI, 1933–1934.* New York: Penguin Books, 2004.

Burson, Pat. "100 at Olson Event Talk about Case." *Pioneer Press*, February 13, 2000.

Canby, Vincent. "Schrader's *Patty Hearst.*" *New York Times*, September 23, 1988. http://www.nytimes.com/1988/09/23/movies/review-film-schrader-s-patty-hearst.html?scp=1&sq=%22Paul%20Schrader%22%20%22Patty%20Hearst%22&st=cse.

Carroll, Peter N. *It Seemed Like Nothing Happened: America in the 1970s.* New Brunswick, NJ: Rutgers University Press, 1990.

Castiglia, Christopher. *Bound and Determined: Captivity, Culture-Crossing, and White Womanhood from Mary Rowlandson to Patty Hearst.* Chicago: University of Chicago, 1996.

Champlin, Charles. "Crime Saga of Ma Barker." *Los Angeles Times*, April 17, 1970, G17.

Choi, Susan. *American Woman.* New York: HarperCollins Publishers, 2003.

Clarens, Carlos. *Crime Movies: An Illustrated History of the Gangster Genre from D. W. Griffith to Pulp Fiction.* Cambridge, MA: Da Capo Press, 1997.

———. "Hooverville West: The Hollywood G-Man, 1934–1945." *Film Comment*, May–June 1977, 10–16.

Cleaver, Kathleen. "The Fugitive: Why Has the FBI Placed a Million-Dollar Bounty on Assata Shakur?" *Essence*, August 2005. http://www.essence.com/essence/lifestyle/voices/0,16109,1081943,00.html.

Cline, Andrew. "Depp out of His Depth." *American Spectator*, July 1, 2009. http://spectator.org/archives/2009/07/01/depp-out-of-his-depth.

Cohan, Steven, and Ina Rae Hark, eds. *The Road Movie Book.* London: Routledge, 1997.

Cohen, Jacob. "The Romance of Revolutionary Violence: The Kathy Power Case." *National Review*, December 13, 1993, 28.

Cohen, Lizabeth. *Making a New Deal: Industrial Workers in Chicago, 1919–1939.* Cambridge: Cambridge University Press, 1990.

Collins, Frederick L. *The FBI in Peace and War.* New York: G. P. Putnam's Sons, 1943.

Commolli, Jean-Louis, and Andrew S. Labarth. "*Bonnie and Clyde:* An Interview with Arthur Penn." In *Focus on Bonnie and Clyde*, ed. John G. Cawelti, 15–19. Englewood Cliffs, NJ: Prentice-Hall, 1973.

Cook, Fred J. *The FBI Nobody Knows.* New York: Macmillan Co., 1964.

Cooke, AnneMarie. "Chesimard Trial Cost $300,000." *Home News* (East Brunswick, NJ), March 28, 1977.

Cooper, Courtney Ryley. *Here's to Crime!* Boston: Little, Brown & Co., 1937.

———. *Ten Thousand Public Enemies.* New York: Blue Ribbon, 1935.

Corey, Herbert. *Farewell, Mr. Gangster! America's War on Crime.* Foreword by J. Edgar Hoover. New York: D. Appleton-Century Co., 1936.

Cott, Nancy. *The Grounding of Modern Feminism.* New Haven, CT: Yale University Press, 1987.

Crouch, Stanley. "By Any Means Necessary." *New York Times*, September 10, 2006. http://www.nytimes.com/2006/09/10/books/review/crouch.html?ref=books#.

Croy, Homer. *Last of the Great Outlaws: The Story of Cole Younger.* New York: Duell, Sloan and Pearce, 1956.

Daley, Robert. "Target Blue." *New York*, February 12, 1973, 44.

Davidson, Sara. "Notes from the Land of the Cobra." *New York Times Magazine*, June 2, 1974, 36–43.

Davis, Brian Joseph. *I, Tania.* Toronto: ECW Press, 2007.

Davis, Natalie Zemon. *Fiction in the Archives: Pardon Tales and Their Tellers in Sixteenth-Century France.* Stanford: Stanford University Press, 1987.

Davison, Bill. "I Wish I Had This Broad's Connections." *TV Guide*, June 8, 1974.

Def, Mos. "Assata Shakur: The Government's Terrorist Is Our Community's Heroine." http://www.assatashakur.org/mosdef.htm.

Demaris, Ovid. *The Director: An Oral Biography of J. Edgar Hoover.* New York: Harper's Magazine Press, 1975.

D'Emilio, John, and Estelle B. Freedman. *Intimate Matters: A History of Sexuality in America.* New York: Harper & Row Publishers, 1988.

Denning, Michael. *The Cultural Front: The Laboring of American Culture in the Twentieth Century.* New York: Verso, 1997.

———. *Mechanic Accents: Dime Novels and Working Class Cultures in America.* New York: Verso, 1998.

Doherty, Thomas. *Cold War, Cool Medium: Television, McCarthyism, and American Culture.* New York: Columbia University Press, 2003.

———. *Teenagers and Teenpics: The Juvenilization of American Movies in the 1950s.* Philadelphia: Temple University Press, 2002.

Donner, Frank. *Protector of Privilege: Red Squads and Police Repression in Urban America.* Berkeley: University of California Press, 1990.

Dowd, Maureen. "Liberties: The Joke's on Him." *New York Times*, June 21, 1998. http://query.nytimes.com/gst/fullpage.html?res=9C00E6DD173CF932A15755C0 A96E958260.

Doyle, Sue. "Actor Who Portrayed Lawman Given Gold Badge for Contributions to Organization." *Los Angeles Daily News*, June 8, 2009. http://www.dailynews.com/news/ci_12549932.

Drew, Bernard A., ed. *Hard-Boiled Dames: Stories Featuring Women Detectives, Reporters, Adventurers, and Criminals from the Pulp Fiction Magazines of the 1930s.* New York: St. Martin's Press, 1986.

Durkeim, Emile. *The Rules of Sociological Method.* Trans. S. A. Solovay and J. H. Mueller. Glencoe, IL: Free Press, 1958.

Economist. "Treasonous Reflections: Americans—Particularly George Bush—Shouldn't Make Excuses for John Walker," December 15, 2001, 28.

Editors of *Look. The Story of the FBI: The Official Picture History of the Federal Bureau of Investigation, with an Introduction by J. Edgar Hoover.* New York: E. P. Dutton & Co., 1954.

Elliot, Rosemary. *Women and Smoking since 1890.* New York: Routledge, 2008.

Enstad, Nan. *Ladies of Labor, Girls of Adventure: Working Women, Popular Culture, and Labor Politics at the Turn of the Twentieth Century.* New York: Columbia University Press, 1999.

Erikson, Kai T. *Wayward Puritans: A Study in the Sociology of Deviance.* New York: John Wiley & Sons, 1966.

Evans, Sara. *Born for Liberty: A History of Women in America.* New York: Free Press, 1989.
———. *Personal Politics: The Roots of Women's Liberation in the Civil Rights Movement and the New Left.* New York: Vintage Books, 1979.

Federal Bureau of Investigation Office of Public Affairs. *The FBI: A Centennial History, 1908–2008.* Washington, DC: U.S. Government Printing Office, 2008.

Fischer, Lucy. *Cinematernity: Film, Motherhood, Genre.* Princeton, NJ: Princeton University Press, 1996.

Fosburgh, Lacey. "3 Women: Their Paths Leading to Terrorism." *New York Times,* April 23, 1974.

Foucault, Michel. *Discipline and Punish: The Birth of the Prison.* New York: Vintage Books, 1979.

Franks, Lucinda. "The Seeds of Terror." *New York Times Magazine,* November 22, 1981, 35.

Frantz, Joe B. "The Frontier Tradition: An Invitation to Violence." In *Violence in America: Historical and Comparative Perspectives; A Report to the National Commissions on the Causes and Prevention of Violence, June 1969,* ed. Hugh Davis Graham and Ted Robert Gurr. New York: New American Library, 1969.

Friedman, Lester D. *Bonnie and Clyde.* London: British Film Institute, 2000.

Frost, H. Gordon, and John H. Jenkins. *I'm Frank Hamer: The Life of a Texas Peace Officer.* Abilene, TX: State House Press, 1991.

Gentry, Curt. *J. Edgar Hoover: The Man and the Secrets.* New York: W. W. Norton & Co., 1991.

Glueck, Sheldon, and Eleanor Glueck. *Five Hundred Delinquent Women.* New York: Alfred A. Knopf, 1934.

Goodman, Ellen. "Mad Mothers and Angry Fathers." *Washington Post,* March 6, 2002.

Graebner, William. *Patty's Got a Gun: Patricia Hearst in 1970s America.* Chicago: University of Chicago Press, 2008.

Graham, Bob. "Waters' 'DeMented' Offers Giddy Fun." *San Francisco Chronicle,* August 11, 2000. http://www.sfgate.com/cgi-bin/article.cgi?f=/c/a/2000/08/11/DD28654. DTL#ixzz0064IEGQ3.

Grieveson, Lee, Esther Sonnet, and Peter Stanfield. *Mob Culture: Hidden Histories of the American Gangster Film.* New Brunswick, NJ: Rutgers University Press, 2005.

Guinn, Jeff. *Go Down Together: The True, Untold Story of Bonnie and Clyde.* New York: Simon & Schuster, 2009.
———. "Notorious." *Smithsonian,* April 2009, 12–14.

Hall, Jacquelyn Dowd. "Disorderly Women: Gender and Labor Militancy in the Appalachian South." *Journal of American History* 73 (September 1986): 354–382.

Hamilton, Stanley. *Machine Gun Kelly's Last Stand.* Lawrence: University Press of Kansas, 2003.

Hanley, Robert. "F.B.I. to Aid Search for Miss Chesimard." *New York Times,* November 4, 1979, 31.
———. "Miss Chesimard Flees Jersey Prison, Helped by 3 Armed 'Visitors.'" *New York Times,* November 3, 1979.

Hapke, Laura. *Women, Work, and Fiction in the American 1930s.* Athens: University of Georgia Press, 1995.

Harrison, Robert Pogue. *The Dominion of the Dead.* Chicago: University of Chicago Press, 2003.

Hays, Daniel. "Joanne Shot Me, Trooper Testifies." *Home News* (East Brunswick, NJ), February 22, 1977.

Hearst, Patricia Campbell, with Alvin Moscow. *Every Secret Thing.* Garden City, NY: Doubleday & Co., 1982.

Hendin, Josephine G. *Heartbreakers: Women and Violence in Contemporary Culture and Literature.* New York: Palgrave Macmillan, 2004.

Hendry, Sharon Darby. *SoLiAh: The Sara Jane Olson Story.* Bloomington, MN: Cable Publishing, 2002.

Hinton, Ted, with Larry Grove. *Ambush: The Real Story of Bonnie and Clyde.* Austin, TX: Shoal Creek Publishers, 1979.

Hirsch, Richard. "Killers Called Him Creepy." *True Detective*, June 1940, 36.

Hobsbawm, E. J. *Bandits.* New York: Pantheon Books, 1981.

———. *Primitive Rebels: Studies in Archaic Forms of Social Movement in the 19th and 20th Centuries.* Manchester: Manchester University Press, 1971.

Hofstadter, Richard. "Reflections on Violence in the United States." In *American Violence: A Documentary History*, ed. Richard Hofstadter and Michael Wallace, 3–43. New York: Alfred A. Knopf, 1971.

Home News (East Brunswick, NJ). "Appleby," March 15, 1977.

———. "Chesimard Defense Effort to Prove Conspiracy Quashed" March 3, 1977.

———. "March" March 27, 1977.

———. "Slogans Cleaned from Building," March 15, 1977.

Hoover, J. Edgar. *Masters of Deceit: The Story of Communism in America and How to Fight It.* New York: Henry Holt & Co., 1958.

———. *Persons in Hiding.* Boston: Little, Brown & Co., 1938.

———. "The SDS and the High Schools: A Study in Student Extremism, Part 1." *PTA Magazine*, January 1970, 2–5.

———. "The SDS and the High Schools: A Study in Student Extremism, Part 2." *PTA Magazine*, February 1970, 8–9.

Hoover, J. Edgar, with Courtney Ryley Cooper. "The Boy Who Wanted to Go Fishing." *American Magazine* 122 (November 1936): 54–55, 137–143.

———. "Crime's Leading Lady." *American Magazine* 123 (February 1939): 54–55, 74–79.

———. "The *Real* Public Enemy No. 1." *American Magazine* 121 (April 1936): 16–17, 118–123.

Inness, Sherrie A. *Tough Girls: Women Warriors and Wonder Women in Popular Culture.* Philadelphia: University of Pennsylvania Press, 1999.

Isenberg, Nancy. "Not 'Anyone's Daughter': Patty Hearst and the Postmodern Legal Subject." *American Quarterly* 52 (December 2000): 639–681.

Jacobs, Lea. *Wages of Sin: Censorship and the Fallen Woman Film, 1928–1942.* Madison: University of Wisconsin Press, 1991.

Jet. "FBI Ransacks N.Y. Apts. in Search for Chesimard: U.S. Probe Ordered," May 8, 1980, 58.

Jiminez, Janey, as told to Ted Berkman. *My Prisoner.* Kansas City, KS: Sheed Andrews & McMeel, 1977.

Jones, Ann. *Women Who Kill.* Boston: Beacon Press, 1996.

Jones, Charles E., ed. *The Black Panther Party Reconsidered.* Baltimore: Black Classic Press, 1998.

Jones, W. D. "Riding with Bonnie and Clyde." *Playboy*, November 1968. http://www
.cinetropic.com/janeloisemorris/commentary/bonn%26clyde/wdjones.html.

Kael, Pauline. "Bonnie and Clyde." In *Kiss Kiss Bang Bang*, 47–63. New York: Little,
Brown & Co., 1968.

Kaplan, E. Ann. *Motherhood and Representation: The Mother in Popular Culture and Melo-
drama*. New York: Routledge, 1992.

Karlsen, Carol. *Devil in the Shape of a Woman: Witchcraft in Colonial New England*. New
York: Vintage Books, 1987.

Karpis, Alvin, with Robert Livesey. *On the Rock: Twenty-five Years at Alcatraz*. New York:
Beaufort Books, 1980.

Karpis, Alvin, with Bill Trent. *The Alvin Karpis Story*. New York: Coward, McCann &
Geoghegan, 1971.

Kavanaugh, Reginald. "Chesimard Claims Innocence." *Home News* (East Brunswick,
NJ), March 16, 1977.

Kerber, Linda. *No Constitutional Right to Be Ladies: Women and the Obligations of Citizenship*. New York: Hill & Wang, 1998.

———. "Separate Spheres, Female Worlds, Woman's Place: The Rhetoric of Women's
History." *Journal of American History* 25 (June 1988): 9–39.

———. *Women of the Republic: Intellect and Ideology in Revolutionary America*. Chapel Hill:
University of North Carolina Press, 1980.

Kessler-Harris, Alice. *In Pursuit of Equity: Women, Men, and the Quest for Economic Citizenship in 20th-Century America*. New York: Oxford University Press, 2001.

———. *Women Have Always Worked: A Historical Overview*. New York: McGraw Hill,
1981.

Kiernan, Louise. "Murder She Wrote." *Chicago Tribune*, July 17, 1997.

Kirkpatrick, E. E. *Crime's Paradise: The Authentic Inside Story of the Urschel Kidnapping*.
San Antonio: Naylor Co., 1934.

Kirsta, Alix. "A Black and White Case." *Times* (London), May 29, 1999.

Kitses, Jim. *Gun Crazy*. London: British Film Institute, 1996.

Klapp, Orrin. *Heroes, Villains, and Fools: Reflections of the American Character*. New York:
Aegis Publishing Co., 1972.

Knight, James. R., with Jonathan Davis. *Bonnie and Clyde: A Twenty-first Century Update*.
Austin, TX: Eakin Press, 2003.

Kohn, Howard, and David Weir. "SLA Lost Year, Part Two." *Rolling Stone*, November
20, 1975.

Kolbert, Elizabeth. "The Prisoner." *New Yorker*, July 16, 2001, 44–58.

Landay, Lori. *Madcaps, Screwballs, and Con Women: The Female Trickster in American Culture*. Philadelphia: University of Pennsylvania Press, 1998.

Lee, Henry. "The Ten Most Wanted Criminals of the Past 50 Years." *Liberty* (Autumn
1972): 26–40.

Lev, Peter. *Transforming the Screen, 1950–1959*. New York: Charles Scribner's Sons,
2003.

Life. "Fugitive in Cuba," December 1987, 9.

Lindahl, Carl, Maida Owens, and C. Renee Harvison, eds. *Swapping Stories: Folktales
from Louisiana*. Jackson: University of Mississippi Press, 1997.

Lomatire, Paul. "Cold Beer and Killer Women." *Sydney Morning Herald*, March 6,
2004.

Louderback, Lew. *The Bad Ones: Gangsters of the 1930s and Their Molls.* Greenwich, CT: Fawcett Publications, 1968.

Lowenthal, Max. *The Federal Bureau of Investigation.* New York: Sloane, 1950.

Lutes, Jean Marie. "Into the Madhouse with Nellie Bly: Girl Stunt Reporting in Late Nineteenth-Century America." *American Quarterly* 54, no. 2 (June 2002): 217–253.

Lyons, Arthur. *Death on the Cheap: The Lost B Movies of Film Noir!* New York: Da Capo Press, 2000.

Maccabee, Paul. *John Dillinger Slept Here: A Crooks' Tour of Crime and Corruption in St. Paul, 1920–1936.* St. Paul: Minnesota Historical Society Press, 1995.

MacDonald, Eileen. *Shoot the Women First.* New York: Random House, 1991.

May, Elaine Tyler. *Homeward Bound: American Families in the Cold War Era.* New York: Basic Books, 1999.

———. "Women in the Wild Blue Yonder." *New York Times,* Op-Ed, August 7, 1991.

May, Lary. *The Big Tomorrow: Hollywood and the Politics of the American Way.* Chicago: University of Chicago Press, 2000.

———. *Screening Out the Past: The Birth of Mass Culture and the Motion Picture Industry.* Chicago: University of Chicago Press, 1980.

McElvaine, Robert S. *The Great Depression: America, 1929–1941.* New York: Times Books, 1961.

McGilligan, Patrick. "Introduction: 'Made It Ma! Top of the World.'" In *White Heat,* ed. Ivan Goff, 9–36. Madison: University of Wisconsin Press, 1984.

McKeown, Frank. "Squire Guilty of Trooper's Murder." *Daily News,* March 12, 1974.

McLaughlin, Kathleen. "J. E. Hoover Urges Women Aid Work." *New York Times,* May 18, 1938.

Melosh, Barbara. *Engendering Culture: Manhood and Womanhood in New Deal Public Art and Theatre.* Washington: Smithsonian Institution Press, 1991.

Miller, John J. "J. Edgar Who? Renaming the FBI Building." *National Review,* September 24, 2002. http://www.nationalreview.com/miller/milller092402.asp.

Miller, Mark. "From Villain to Victim." *Newsweek,* February 4, 2002, 29.

Milner, E. R. *The Lives and Times of Bonnie and Clyde.* Carbondale: Southern Illinois University Press, 1996.

Mitchell, Elvis. "Patty Hearst: The Movie." *Rolling Stone,* September 8, 1988, 31, 160.

Moran, Robin. *The Demon Lover: On the Sexuality of Terrorism.* New York: W. W. Norton & Co., 1989.

Motion Picture Herald. "Parole Fixer," February 27, 1940, 41.

———. "Queen of the Mob," June 22, 1940, 48, 50.

Mulvey, Laura. *Visual and Other Pleasures.* Bloomington: Indiana University Press, 1989.

Mumby, Jonathan. *Public Enemies, Public Heroes: Screening the Gangster from Little Caesar to Touch of Evil.* Chicago: University of Chicago Press, 1999.

Murphy, Vicki L. "A Louisiana Steel Trap: The Deaths of Clyde Barrow and Bonnie Parker." *Journal of the North Louisiana Historical Association* 24, nos. 2–3 (1993): 51–67.

Myers, Alice, and Sarah Wight, eds. *No Angels: Women Who Commit Violence.* San Francisco: Pandora of HarperCollins Publishers, 1996.

Nagy, Lawrence. "Chesimard Guilty, Gets Life in Prison." *Newark Star-Ledger,* March 26, 1977.

Nash, Jay Robert. *Bloodletters and Badmen: A Narrative Encyclopedia of Criminals from the Pilgrims to the Present.* New York: M. Evans & Co., 1973.

Nelson, Jill. "The Soul Survivor: Assata Shakur on the Making of a Radical." *Washington Post*, February 29, 1988.

Neroni, Hilary. "The Men of Columbine: Violence and Masculinity in American Culture and Film." *Journal for the Psychoanalysis of Culture* 5 (2000): 256.

Newman, David, and Robert Benton. "Lightning in a Bottle." *Bonnie and Clyde: An Original Screenplay.* Burbank, CA: Warner Brothers, 1967.

News Chief. "Ma Barker Shootout Re-enacted in Marion County," January 12, 2001. http://www.newschief.com/article/20010112/ARTICLES/406830998.

Newsweek. "The Hostage: A Game of Terror," February 25, 1974, 18–21.

———. "The 'Morality' of Terrorism," February 25, 1974, 21–22.

———. "Patty: Guilty," March 29, 1976, 23–29.

———. "The Saga of Patty Hearst," April 29, 1974, 20–25.

New York State Fraternal Order of Police. "New York State Fraternal Order of Police Criticizes Judge's Decision on the Release of Kathy Boudin." http://www.nysfop.org/Back_Up/events/kathy_boudin.htm.

New York Times. "Barker Gang Man, Woman under Arrest," January 17, 1935.

———. "Country's Arrests Are of Women, but Chief Hoover Notes Violence Trend," September 6, 1936.

———. "Hoover Asks Press to Help Crime War," April 23, 1937.

———. "Woman Shot in Struggle with Her Alleged Victim," April 7, 1971.

NJLawman.com. "One Million Dollar Reward Issued for Joanne Chesimard." http://www.NJLawman.com/Articles%202/Chesimard-Reward.htm.

Nordinger, Jay. "In Castro's Corner: A Story of Black and Red." *National Review*, March 6, 2000.

Norton, Mary Beth. *Liberty's Daughters: The Revolutionary Experience of American Women, 1750–1800.* Boston: Little, Brown & Co., 1980.

Nuddelman, Franny. "Emblem and Product of Sin: The Poisoned Child in *The Scarlet Letter* and Domestic Advice Literature." *Yale Journal of Criticism* 10 (Spring 1997): 193–213.

O'Reilly, Kenneth. "A New Deal for the FBI: The Roosevelt Administration, Crime Control, and National Security." *Journal of American History* 69 (December 1982): 638–658.

Parker, Emma K., and Nellie B. Cowan. *The True Story of Clyde Barrow and Bonnie Parker: As Told by Bonnie's Mother and Clyde's Sister*, ed. Jan Fortune. New York: Signet Books, 1968.

Parrish, Michael E. *Anxious Decades: America in Prosperity and Depression, 1920–1941.* New York: W. W. Norton & Co., 1992.

Pascal, John, and Francine Pascal. *The Strange Case of Patty Hearst.* New York: Signet Books, 1974.

Patterson, James T. *Grand Expectations: The United States 1945–1974.* New York: Oxford University Press, 1996.

Payne, Cril. *Deep Cover: An FBI Agent Infiltrates the Radical Underground.* New York: Newsweek Books, 1979.

Payne, Les, and Tim Findley, with Carolyn Craven. *The Life and Death of the SLA.* New York: Ballantine Books, 1976.

Pearson, Patricia. *When She Was Bad: How and Why Women Get Away with Murder.* New York: Penguin Books, 1998.

People Magazine Weekly. "Once Her Keeper, Now Her Friend, Janey Jiminez Tells of Patty Hearst's Trials," October 3, 1977. http://presslord.com/people100377.htm.

Perkins, Margo V. *Autobiography as Activism.* Jackson: University Press of Mississippi, 2000.

Peterson, Theodore. *Magazines in the Twentieth Century.* Urbana: University of Illinois Press, 1964.

Phillips, John Neal. "Bonnie and Clyde's Revenge on Eastham." *American History,* June 12, 2006. http://www.historynet.com/bonnie-clydes-revenge-on-eastham.htm.

———. *Running with Bonnie and Clyde: The Ten Fast Years of Ralph Fults.* Norman: University of Oklahoma Press, 1996.

Potter, Claire Bond. "'I'll Go the Limit and Then Some': Gun Molls, Desire, and Danger in the 1930s." *Feminist Studies* 21 (Fall 1994): 41–66.

———. *War on Crime: Bandits, G-Men, and the Politics of Mass Culture.* New Brunswick, NJ: Rutgers University Press, 1998.

Poulsen, Ellen. *Don't Call Us Molls: Women of the John Dillinger Gang.* Little Neck, NY: Clinton Cook Publishing, 2002.

Powers, Richard Gid. *G-Men: Hoover's FBI in American Popular Culture.* Carbondale: Southern Illinois University Press, 1983.

———. *Secrecy and Power: The Life of J. Edgar Hoover.* New York: Free Press, 1988.

Prison Activist. "IWD: Interview with Safiya Bukhari-Alston." http://www.prisonactivist .org/jericho_sfbay/Safiya_Bukhari/Safiya_Bukhari_interview.html.

Pryor, Thomas M. "Hollywood's Oscar Night: Joanne Woodward, Miyoski Umeki 'Star' in Thirteenth Annual Awards Show—Hoover Scores Film Crime." *New York Times,* March 3, 1958.

Purvis, Alston, and Alex Tresniowski. *The Vendetta.* New York: PublicAffairs, 2005.

Purvis, Melvin. *American Agent.* Garden City, NY: Doubleday, Moran & Co., 1936.

Quarles, Mike. *Down and Dirty: Hollywood's Exploitation Filmmakers and Their Movies.* Jefferson, NC: McFarland & Co., 1993.

Rabinowitz, Paula. *Labor and Desire: Women's Revolutionary Fiction in Depression America.* Chapel Hill: University of North Carolina Press, 1991.

Rafter, Nicole. *Shots in the Mirror: Crime Films and Society.* New York: Oxford University Press, 2000.

Reis, Elizabeth. *Damned Women: Sinners and Witches in Puritan New England.* Ithaca: Cornell University Press, 1997.

Reitan, Ruth. "Cuba, the Black Panther Party, and the U.S. Black Movement in the 1960s." In *Liberation, Imagination, and the Black Panther Party,* ed. Kathleen Cleaver and George N. Katsiaficas. New York: Routledge, 2001.

Rice, John. "Castro Defends Fugitive Sought by U.S." *Associated Press,* May 11, 2005.

Rich, Carroll Y. "The Day They Shot Bonnie and Clyde." *Hunters and Healers: Folklore Types and Topics,* ed. William M. Hudson, 35–44. Austin, TX: Encino Press, 1970.

Rogin, Michael. *Ronald Reagan: The Movie and Other Episodes in Political Demonology.* Los Angeles: University of California Press, 1987.

Rosen, Ruth. *The World Split Open: How the Modern Women's Movement Changed America.* New York: Viking, 2006.

Rosenfeld, Susan. "Doing Injustice to the FBI: The Negative Myths Perpetuated by Historians." *Chronicle of Higher Education,* October 8, 1999.

Ruehlmann, William. *Saint with a Gun: The Unlawful American Private Eye.* New York: New York University Press, 1974.

Ruth, David. *Inventing the Public Enemy: The Gangster in American Culture, 1918–1934.* Chicago: University of Chicago Press, 1996.

Saint Louis Post Dispatch. "Ex-Ranger 'Hated to Shoot Woman, Especially When Sitting Down' but Had No Choice," May 24, 1934.

Sara Olson Defense Committee flyer and cookbook promotion. 2000. Formerly at http://www.sarajaneolsondefense.org.

Sargent, Lyman Tower. *Extremism in America: A Reader.* New York: New York University Press, 1995.

Schaefer, Eric. *"Bold! Daring! Shocking! True!" A History of Exploitation Films, 1919–1959.* Durham: Duke University Press, 1999.

Schneider, Paul. *Bonnie and Clyde: The Lives behind the Legend.* New York: Henry Holt & Co., 2009.

Schuetz, Janice. *The Logic of Women on Trial: Case Studies of Popular American Trials.* Carbondale: Southern Illinois University Press, 1994.

Schultz, Nancy Lusignan, ed. *Fear Itself: Enemies Real and Imagined in American Culture.* West Lafayette, IN: Purdue University Press, 1999.

Seal, Graham. *The Outlaw Legend: A Cultural Tradition in Britain, America, and Australia.* Cambridge: Cambridge University Press, 1996.

Seigel, Max H. "Chesimard Murder Case Dropped Because of Delay in Holding Trial." *New York Times*, October 26, 1977.

Shadoin, Jack. *Dreams and Dead Ends: The American Gangster Crime Film.* New York: Oxford University Press, 2003.

Shakur, Assata. *Assata Shakur: An Autobiography.* Chicago: Lawrence Hill Books, 1987.

———. "Open Letter from Assata Shakur." *Hands off Assata.* http://www.handsoffassata .org/content/assataopenletter-text.htm.

Sharpe, Jenny. *Ghosts of Slavery: A Literary Archeology of Black Women's Lives.* Minneapolis: University of Minnesota Press, 2003.

Sherrill, Robert. "The Selling of the FBI." In *Investigating the FBI*, ed. Pat Watters and Stephen Gillers, 3–32. Garden City, NY: Doubleday & Co., 1973.

Sklar, Robert. *Movie-Made America: Social History of American Movies.* New York: Random House, 1975.

Slocum, J. David, ed. *Violence and American Cinema.* New York: Routledge, 2001.

Slotkin, Richard. *Gunfighter Nation: The Myth of the Frontier in Twentieth Century America.* New York: Atheneum, 1992.

Smith, Henry Nash. *Virgin Land: The American West as Symbol and Myth.* Cambridge, MA: Harvard University Press, 1950.

Soltysik, Fred. *In Search of a Sister.* New York: Bantam Books, 1976.

Sorrento, Christopher. *Trance.* New York: Farrar, Straus & Giroux, 2005.

Staiger, Janet. *Bad Women: Regulating Sexuality in Early American Cinema.* Minneapolis: University of Minnesota Press, 1995.

Stallybrass, Peter, and Allon White. *The Politics and Poetics of Transgression.* Ithaca, NY: Cornell University Press, 1986.

Steele, Philip W., and Marie Barrow Scoma. *The Family Story of Bonnie and Clyde.* Gretna, LA: Pelican Publishing Co., 2003.

Stinson, Charles. "Dr. Spock Would Rap Ma Barker's Method." *Los Angeles Times*, February 5, 1960 (A.M. edition).

Stock, Catherine McNicol. *Main Street in Crisis: The Great Depression and the Old Middle Class on the Northern Plains.* Chapel Hill: University of North Carolina Press, 1992.

————. *Rural Radicals: Righteous Rage in the American Grain.* Ithaca, NY: Cornell University Press, 1996.

Stohl, Michael, ed. *The Politics of Terrorism.* New York: M. Dekker, 1983.

Stone, Judy. "Patty Hearst: The Hearst Family's Cook Provides Still Another View." *Ladies Home Journal,* October 1974, 147.

Strange, Carolyn. "Murder and Meanings in U.S. Historiography." *Feminist Studies* 25, no. 3 (Fall 1999): 679–697.

Sturken, Marita. *Tangled Memories: The Vietnam War, the AIDS Epidemic, and the Politics of Remembering.* Berkeley: University of California Press, 1997.

Sullivan, Joseph F. "Chesimard Attorney Acts to Call Kelley." *New York Times,* Week in Review, February 24, 1977.

————. "Doctor Testifies on Bullet Scars in Chesimard Trial." *New York Times,* March 18, 1977.

————. "Panther, Trooper Slain in Shoot-Out." *New York Times,* May 3, 1973.

Sullivan, Kate. "Our Beloved Revolutionary Sweetheart." *City Pages,* February 9, 2005. http://www.citypages.com/2005-02-09/movies/our-beloved-revolutionary-sweetheart/.

Summers, Anthony. *Official and Confidential: The Secret Life of J. Edgar Hoover.* New York: G. P. Putnam's Sons, 1993.

Tatum, Stephen. *Inventing Billy the Kid: Visions of the Outlaw in America, 1881–1981.* Albuquerque: University of New Mexico Press, 1982.

Terry, Don. "The Calm after the Storm." *Chicago Tribune Magazine,* September 16, 2001, 11–15.

Theoharis, Athan G. *J. Edgar Hoover, Sex, and Crime: An Historical Antidote.* Chicago: Ivan R. Dee, 1995.

Theoharis, Athan G., and John Stuart Cox. *The Boss: J. Edgar Hoover and the Great American Inquisition.* Philadelphia: Temple University Press, 1988.

Theoharis, Athan G., Tony G. Poveda, Susan Rosenfeld, and Richard Gid Power, eds. *The FBI: A Comprehensive Reference Guide.* New York: Oryx Press, 2000.

Theweleit, Klaus. *Male Fantasies.* Vol. 1, *Women, Floods, Bodies, History.* Minneapolis: University of Minnesota Press, 1987.

Time. "Lovers in a Car," June 4, 1934, 16.

————. "Low-Down Hoedown," August 23, 1967, 13.

————. "The New Cinema: Violence . . . Sex . . . Art," December 8, 1967, 66–76.

Toland, John. *The Dillinger Days.* New York: Random House, 1963.

Tomasulo, Frank P. "Raging Bully: Postmodern Violence and Masculinity in *Raging Bull.*" In *Mythologies of Violence in Postmodern Media,* ed. Christopher Sharrett, 175–179. Detroit: Wayne State University Press, 1999.

Travers, Peter. "Cecil B. Demented." *Rolling Stone,* December 10, 2000. http://www.rollingstone.com/reviews/movie/5949045/review/5949046/cecil_b_demented.

Treherne, John. *The Strange History of Bonnie and Clyde.* London: Jonathan Cape, 1984.

Ulrich, Laurel Thatcher. *Good Wives: Image and Reality in the Lives of Women in Northern New England, 1650–1750.* New York: Alfred A. Knopf, 1982.

Umoja, Akinyele Omowale. "Repression Breeds Resistance: The Black Liberation Army and the Radical Legacy of the Black Panther Party." In *Liberation, Imagination, and the Black Panther Party,* ed. Kathleen Cleaver and George N. Katsiaficas, 3–19. New York: Routledge, 2001.

Unger, Robert. *The Union Station Massacre: The Original Sin of J. Edgar Hoover's FBI.* Kansas City, KS: Andrews McMeel Publishing, 1997.

U.S. News & World Report. "U.S. Unrest, as FBI Chief Sees It," January 12, 1970, 8.

———. "Women Catching Up with Men in One More Field: Crime," September 23, 1974, 45–58.

Varon, Jeremy. *Bringing the War Home: The Weather Underground, the Red Army Faction, and Revolutionary Violence in the Sixties and Seventies.* Berkeley: University of California Press, 2004.

Viénet, René. *Enragés and Situationists in the Occupation Movement.* New York: Autonomedia, 1992.

Vollers, Maryanne. "Was This Soccer Mom a Terrorist?" *New York Times Magazine,* May 20, 2001, 38–43.

Waggoner, Walter H. "Joanne Chesimard Convicted in Killing of Jersey Trooper." *New York Times,* March 26, 1977.

———. "Jury in Chesimard Murder Trial Listens to State Police Radio Tapes." *New York Times,* Week in Review, February 17, 1977, 83.

———. "Neurosurgeon's Testimony Backs Mrs. Chesimard." *New York Times,* Week in Review, March 17, 1977.

Wall Street Journal. "The Gentle G-Man" [Joseph Aloysius Sullivan], August 9, 2002.

Warger, Wayne. "Independent Filmmakers Tuned to Youthquake." *Los Angeles Times,* May 5, 1968.

Warshow, Robert. "Movie Chronicle: The Westerner." In *The Immediate Experience: Movies, Comics, Theatre, and Other Aspects of Popular Culture,* 105–124. Garden City, NY: Doubleday & Co., 1962.

Watters, Pat, and Stephen Gillers, eds. *Investigating the FBI.* Garden City, NY: Doubleday & Co., 1973.

Weatherby, Jeff. "Chesimard Pleads for Transfer from Yardville Isolation." *Home News* (East Brunswick, NJ), April 1977.

Webb, Walter Prescott. *The Texas Rangers: A Century of Frontier Defense.* New York: Houghton Mifflin Co., 1935.

Welsch, Janice R. *Film Archetypes: Sisters, Mistresses, Mothers and Daughters.* New York: Arno Press, 1978.

Welter, Barbara. "The Cult of True Womanhood, 1820–1860." *American Quarterly* 18 (Summer 1966): 151–174.

Wilfredo, Cancio Isla. "Fugitive a Curiosity in Cuba." *Miami Herald,* December 18, 2007. http://archives.econ.utah.edu/archives/cubanews/2007w51/msg00044.htm.

Will, George. "The Waning of 'Terror Chic.'" *Newsweek,* November 12, 2001. http://www.newsweek.com/id/76382/output/print.

Williams, Craig. "Reflections of Geronimo: The Essence of a Panther." *Black Panther,* August 29, 1970.

Williams, Evelyn. *Inadmissible Evidence: The Story of the African-American Trial Lawyer Who Defended the Black Liberation Army.* Chicago: Lawrence Hill & Co., 1993.

Winkler, Allan M. *The Politics of Propaganda: The Office of War Information, 1942–1945.* New Haven, CT: Yale University Press, 1978.

Winkler, Karen J. "J. Edgar Hoover Revisited." *Chronicle of Higher Education,* March 10, 1993.

Wylie, Philip. *Generation of Vipers.* New York: Holt, Rinehart & Winston, 1955.

W.R.W. "J. Edgar Hoover Crimefilm." *Motion Picture Herald,* January 28, 1939, 33.

Yaquinto, Marilyn. *Pump 'Em Full of Lead: A Look at Gangsters on Film.* New York: Twayne Publishers, 1998.

Yardley, Jonathan. "'Generation of Vipers' Loses Its Bite." *Washington Post*, July 30, 2005. http://www.washingtonpost.com/wp-dyn/content/article/2005/07/29/AR200 5072902124.html (accessed June 13, 2009).

Young, Gordon. "Patty Cakes: Terror, Nostalgia, and the SLA." *Metro*, April 11–17, 2002. http://www.metroactive.com/papers/metro/04.11.02/cover/sla1-0215.html.

Zelizer, Barbie. "Reading the Past against the Grain: The Shape of Memory Studies." *Critical Studies in Mass Communication* 12, no. 2 (1995): 214–239.

Film and Television

Adventure Divas Cuba: Paradox Found. Directed by Holly Morris. Seattle: Adventure Divas, 2000.

Assata aka Joanne Chesimard. Directed by Fred Baker. New York: Fred Baker Film and Video Co., 2008.

Bloody Mama. Directed by Roger Corman. Los Angeles: American International Pictures, 1970.

Bonnie and Clyde. Directed by Arthur Penn. Burbank, CA: Warner Brothers, 1967.

The Bonnie Parker Story. Directed by William Witney. Los Angeles: American International Pictures, 1958.

Cecil B. DeMented. Directed by John Waters. Santa Monica, CA: Lionsgate, 2000.

Chicago. Directed by Rob Marshall. Burbank, CA: Miramax Films, 2002.

Citizen Tania. Directed by David Markey and Raymond Pettibone. Los Angeles: Provisional Video, 1989.

Combat Zone. "SLA Gunfight, Los Angeles." Episode 9 (TV). Directed by Andrew Nock and Gerald Massemei. Silver Springs, MD: Discovery Channel International, 2007.

Eyes of the Rainbow. Directed by Gloria Rolando. Havana, Cuba: Imagines del Caribe, 1997.

The FBI Story. Directed by Mervyn LeRoy. Burbank, CA: Warner Brothers, 1959.

'G' Men. Directed by William Keighley. Burbank, CA: Warner Brothers, 1935.

Gun Crazy. Directed by Joseph H. Lewis. Century City, CA: United Artists, 1949.

Guns Don't Argue. Directed by Richard C. Kahn and Bill Karn. N.p., Visual Drama, 1957.

Ma Barker's Killer Brood. Directed by Bill Karn. N.p., Filmservice Distributors, 1960.

Monster. Directed by Patty Jenkins. Los Angeles: Media 8 Entertainment, 2003.

Network. Directed by Sidney Lumet. Los Angeles: Metro-Goldwyn-Mayer, 1976.

Neverland: The Rise and Fall of the Symbionese Liberation Army. (Alternate title: *Guerrilla: The Taking of Patty Hearst.*) Directed by Robert Stone. Rhinebeck, NY: Robert Stone Productions, 2004.

The Ordeal of Patty Hearst. (TV) Directed by Paul Wendkos. New York: American Broadcasting Co., 1979.

The Other Side of Bonnie and Clyde. Directed by Larry Buchanan. Dallas: Larry Buchanan Productions, 1968.

Patty Hearst. Directed by Paul Schrader. Los Angeles: Metro-Goldwyn-Mayer, 1988.

Persons in Hiding. Directed by Louis King. Hollywood: Paramount, 1939.

Queen of the Mob. Directed by James P. Hogan. Hollywood: Paramount, 1940.

Shadow of a Doubt. Directed by Alfred Hitchcock. Universal City, CA: Universal Pictures, 1943.

Show Them No Mercy. Directed by George Marshall. Century City, CA: Twentieth Century Pictures, 1935.

White Heat. Directed by Raoul Walsh. Burbank, CA: Warner Brothers, 1949.
You Can't Get Away with It. Directed by Charles E. Ford. Universal City, CA: Universal
    Pictures, 1936.
You Only Live Once. Directed by Fritz Lang. Century City, CA: United Artists, 1937.

Interviews and Correspondence
Baker, Fred. Interview with author, June 15, 2007.
Buchanan, Larry. Interview with author, May 26, 2004.
————. Correspondence with author, June 13, 2004.
Fox, John. Interview with author, June 22, 2009.
Hearst, Patricia. Interview by Larry King. *Larry King Live*, CNN, January 31, 2001.
Hoffman, Harold. Correspondence with author, June 5, 2004.
Kilianski, Brenda. Interview with author, May 4, 2008.
Sedgwick, Dixie Lee. Correspondence with author, May 18, 2009.

Archival Sources and Collections
Academy of Motion Picture Arts and Sciences, Beverly Hills, CA
    Bonnie and Clyde (1967)
    J. Edgar Hoover
    Paramount promotions
    Persons in Hiding (1939)
    Queen of the Mob (1940)
    Ronald L. Davis Oral History Collection, Oral History #289, Patricia Morison
    You Only Live Once (1937)
Federal Bureau of Investigation, Washington, D.C.
    Barker-Karpis gang
    Bonnie Parker and Clyde Barrow
    Courtney Riley Cooper
    Kidnapping of Charles F. Urschel (George "Machine Gun" Kelly)
    Kidnapping of Patricia Hearst
    Symbionese Liberation Army
United States National Archives and Records Administration, College Park, MD
    Bonnie Parker and Clyde Barrow
    Federal Bureau of Investigation
    J. Edgar Hoover
Library of Congress Motion Picture and Television Reading Room, Washington, D.C.
Minnesota Historical Society, St. Paul
    St. Paul gangster history research collection
National Film Information Service, Beverly Hills, CA
New Jersey State Police Museum and Learning Center, Trenton
    Joanne Chesimard (Assata Shakur)
University of California, Los Angeles, Film and Television Archive, Hollywood

INDEX

Acoli, Sundiata, 150, 152, 154–155, 161, 227n23
Adler, Freda, 123
Adventure Divas, 169
Aikman, Duncan, 197–198
Alexander, Shana, 115, 119
American International Pictures, 80, 81, 90, 217n67
American Magazine
  female readership, 62
  Ma Barker article, 53–55, 56–58, 59–60, 61–63, 64–65, 73
  "Secrets of the G-Men" series, 32–33
American Woman, 178
Annan, Beulah, 198
Anyone's Daughter, 119
Arkoff, Samuel, 90, 217n67
Assata aka Joanne Chesimard, 183–192
Assata: An Autobiography, 143–144
Atwood, Angela (Gelina), 117, 119, 120, 128
Ayers, Bill, 176, 179

Baker, Fred, 183, 184–185, 189–190, 191–192
Baker, Marilyn, 120
Baraldini, Silvia, 157, 160, 235n27
Barash, Olivia, 136
Barker, Arthur. *See* Barker, Doc
Barker, Doc, 55, 60, 64
Barker, Fred, 53–54, 55, 60, 64–67
Barker, George, 55, 56–57, 67
Barker, Herman, 55
Barker, Kate. *See* Barker, Ma
Barker, Lloyd, 55–56
Barker, Ma, 42, 122
  American Magazine article, 53–55, 56–58, 59–60, 61–63, 64–65, 73
  comparison with Assata Shakur, 140–141
  contradicting narratives of, 62–63, 64, 68
  as criminal mastermind, 54, 61, 75, 76, 79
  cultural legacy of, 71, 73
  FBI and, 5–6, 53–54, 64–67, 203–204
  image and counterculture of 1960s, 82, 85–86
  portrayal of in film, 68–71, 73–84
  "real" Ma Barker, 70–71, 77–78
  and sons, 60–61, 63–64
  and Western outlaw, 59
Barker-Karpis Gang, 59–60, 64, 203
Barnes, George Kelly. *See* Kelly, George

Baron, Charles, 191
Barrow, Clyde, 19, 45–46, 88–89, 100–101. *See also* Bonnie and Clyde; Parker, Bonnie
Barrow Gang
  Bonnie and cultural legacy of, 21, 46–48, 101
  crimes of, 3–4, 21, 50, 91, 96–97, 98
  FBI files on, 49
  See also Barrow, Clyde; Bonnie and Clyde; Parker, Bonnie
Bates, Charles, 126
Beatty, Warren, 92, 96
Beauchamp, Keith, 190
Belcher, Jerry, 129
Benton, Robert, 93, 106
Berkman, Alexander, 27
Beyoncé, 204
Black Liberation Army (BLA), 139, 148–149, 150, 151, 154, 160
Black Panther Party (BPP), 143, 144–148, 164–165, 183
Bloody Mama, 80–84, 85–86
Bo. *See* Remiro, Joe
Bonnie and Clyde
  cultural legacy of, 3–4, 21–22, 46–48, 51–52, 86, 91–92, 105, 106, 204
  deaths of, 19, 45–46, 88–89
  early time together, 19–20
  1960s counterculture and, 13, 85–86, 88, 92, 93, 99, 129
  physical size, 21, 45
  portrayal of in film, 88–90, 91–104
  See also Barrow, Clyde; Barrow Gang; Parker, Bonnie
Bonnie and Clyde
  comparison with *The Other Side of Bonnie and Clyde*, 94–95, 96–97, 98, 100, 101, 102–103, 105–106
  comparison with Patty Hearst, 130
  1960s counterculture and, 85–86, 129, 219n20
  portrayal of kidnappings, 97, 98
  portrayal of Frank Hamer, 99
  reaction to, 92–94
Bonnie & Clyde—End of the Line, 202
Bonnie and Clyde '03, 204
The Bonnie Parker Story, 90, 91, 96
Bortin, Michael, 179, 180, 181

Breen, Joseph, 69
Bremer, Edward, 60
Brooks, Cleo Coleman. *See* Kelly, Kathryn
Bryan, John, 127
Buchanan, Larry, 93–94, 96, 102, 104–105, 191
Bulling, Al, 16, 17
Burns, Walter Noble, 35–36
Burns, William, 27

Cagney, James, 30, 73
Canby, Vincent, 137
Carrie, 124
Carter, Jimmy, 134
Castiglia, Christopher, 175
Castro, Fidel, 160, 182–183
Cecil B. DeMented, 173–174
Centennial History, 203–204, 205
Chesimard, Joanne. *See* Shakur, Assata
Chesimard, Louis, 145
Chicago (film), 16–18
Chicago (stage play), 198
Chicago Tribune, 198
Choi, Susan, 178
Church, Frank, 154
Church Committee Investigations, 147, 154
Cinque. *See* DeFreeze, Donald
Clarens, Carlos, 89
Cleaver, Eldridge, 162
Cleaver, Kathleen, 168, 183, 191
Cohen, Lizabeth, 31
Cohen, Stanley, 152
COINTELPRO, 13, 110, 112, 125, 140, 154
Coleman, Kate, 117
Collins, Frederick, 36
Combat Zone, 181–182
Common, 192
Cook, Sophia, 96–98
Cooper, Courtney Ryley, 33, 37, 55–58, 59–60,
    61–62, 64–65
The Copper Scroll of Mary Magdalene, 104
Corey, Herbert, 37–38, 63, 64, 66
Corman, Roger, 80, 90
counterculture in the 1960s and 1970s, 85–86,
    110, 111, 118
Crocker National Bank robbery, 177, 180–181, 204
Crime Does Not Pay, 44
crime fiction, 34–35
Crouch, Stanley, 193
Crybaby, 172
Cujo. *See* Wolfe, Willie
Cummings, Homer, 29

Daley, Robert, 139
Dallas Journal, 46
Dallas Morning News, 49
Dallas Times Herald, 50
Darby, H. D., 97

Davidson, Sara, 116, 118, 120
Davis, Angela, 145
Davis, Brian Joseph, 179
Davis, Natalie Zemon, 199
Def, Mos, 192
DeFreeze, Donald (Cinque), 114, 117, 119–120
Deiz, Bill, 182
Delaney, Dana, 136
Delaney, Dolores, 33, 60
DeMarino, Joseph, 154
Depp, Johnny, 199
Depression, the. *See* Great Depression, the
Dern, Bruce, 82
Dillinger, John, 21, 29, 44, 35, 151, 199–200
De Niro, Robert, 81
Doherty, Thomas, 91
Dohrn, Bernadine, 111, 141, 176–177, 179
Donner, Frank, 147
Dorff, Stephen, 173
drive-in theaters, 91
Duff, Hilary, 204
Dunaway, Faye, 92, 101, 108
Dunlop, Arthur, 59

Economist, 106
Eilbacher, Lisa, 135
"End of the Line (Ballad of Bonnie and Clyde),"
    10, 20, 47–48
Every Secret Thing, 132, 136, 173
Eyes of the Rainbow, 161–169, 183

Fahizah. *See* Perry, Nancy Ling
Farewell, Mr. Gangster!, 63, 64
Farrell, Jim, 203
The F.B.I., 87–88
The FBI Story, 73–74
Federal Bureau of Investigation (FBI)
    and Assata Shakur, 140, 153, 159–160
    backlash against, 106–107
    Barker shootout and, 53–54, 64–67
    and the Black Panther Party, 147–148, 164–165
    and Bonnie and Clyde, 4, 19, 49
    centennial, 203, 204–205
    changing focus during Cold War, 86–87
    counterintelligence programs, 13–14, 110, 112,
        147–148, 154
    cultivation of image, 3, 11, 12, 27–28, 29–30,
        31, 32, 86, 87
    distrust of, 109, 111, 125
    during the Great Depression, 28
    and film industry, 30, 31, 42, 69, 87, 202
    Hearst kidnapping and, 3, 116, 125, 126–127
    after Hoover's death, 125
    portrayal of in film and television, 73–74, 82,
        84, 87–88
    SLA and, 116, 118–119, 125, 126–128
    Uniform Crime Reports, 28

waning status of, 86, 88, 112, 125
  See also G-men; Hoover, J. Edgar
federal crime laws, 28
female outlaw. *See* woman outlaw
film industry in 1950s, 90–91
Findley, Tim, 129
Fisher, Frances, 136
Foerster, Werner, 152, 155
Fonda, Henry, 22
Ford, Gerald, 131
Fosburgh, Lacey, 118
Foster, Marcus, 114, 121, 179
Fox, John, 205
Frechette, Evelyn, 37
Fred Baker Film and Video Company, 189
Fromme, Lynette "Squeaky," 131
Fugate, Caril, 91
Fugitive Days, 179
Fults, Ralph, 21

Gabi. *See* Hall, Camilla
Gaertner, Belva, 198
"Gangbusters," 44
Gelina. *See* Atwood, Angela
gender
  during economic downturn, 34, 54, 122–123
  and the outlaw, 17–18, 39–40, 41–42, 122–123,
    198, 201–202
  role of mother in society, 13, 71–73, 76
  women in the workforce, 33–34, 35, 72, 122–123
Generation of Vipers, 71–73
Gibson, Mel, 104
Gitlin, Todd, 179
G-men, 23, 30, 31, 44, 71, 88. *See also* Federal
  Bureau of Investigation (FBI)
'*G' Men*, 30
Goldman, Emma, 27
Graebner, William, 121
Gray, L. Patrick, 125
Great Depression, the
  anticrime sentiments during, 67
  class and, 34
  female outlaw and, 18
  and increase in crime, 28–29
  shifting gender roles during, 34, 54
  and women in the workforce, 33–34, 35
Green, Sam, 179
Griffith, Melanie, 173
Guerrilla: The Taking of Patty Hearst, 179–181
Guevara, Che, 190, 196
Gun Crazy, 90, 91
Guns Don't Argue, 74–77

Hall, Camilla (Gabi), 117, 124
Hall, F. Paul, 77
Hall, Jacqueline Dowd, 51
Hamer, Frank

Bonnie and Clyde capture, 45, 88
  portrayal of in film, 93, 98–99, 100, 103–104
Hamer, Mrs. Frank, 95
Hamilton, Raymond, 100–101
Hamm, William, 60
Hampton, Fred, 111, 147
Hampton, Fred, Jr., 186
Hands Off Assata, 183, 192, 195
Harper, James, 155, 156
Harris, Bill (Teko), 17, 127, 181
Harris, Emily (Yolanda), 117, 127, 130, 181, 204
Harvey, Jean, 74
Hauptmann, Bruno Richard, 53
HEARNAP, 116, 125, 126
Hearst, Patricia
  as actor in John Waters's films, 172, 174–175
  arrest of, 130–131
  as character in fiction, 178–179
  commutation of sentence, 134
  comparison with Bonnie Parker, 4
  during FBI shootout, 127
  eulogy for fallen SLA members, 127
  and Hibernia Bank robbery, 115, 131
  kidnapping of, 114–115
  and outlaw image, 3, 15, 121–122, 129–130
  pardon by Bill Clinton, 173
  portrayal of in film and television, 134–138,
    173–176, 180, 181–182
  rehabilitation of image, 132–134, 177–178
  relationship with Willie Wolfe, 127, 132
  and Sara Jane Olson, 172–173
  tactic for survival, 14, 138, 196
  transformation into "Tania," 109, 115, 118,
    124, 126, 131
  trial of, 131–132
Hearst, Randolph, 114–115
Hibernia Bank robbery, 115, 120, 131
Hilton, Fred, 166
Hinton, Ted, 51–52, 88
Hirsch, Richard, 58
Hitchcock, Alfred, 72
Hoover, J. Edgar
  capture of Alvin Karpis, 67–68
  cultivation of FBI image, 3, 11, 12, 27–28,
    29–30, 31, 32, 86, 87
  death of, 112
  and dissident groups, 86, 110, 111
  and ideas of women's virtue, 33, 43, 73
  and Kathryn Kelly, 4–5, 24–25
  legacy of, 125, 203
  and Ma Barker, 53, 55–58, 59–60, 61–62, 64–67
  preoccupation with woman criminal, 13, 31–32,
    33, 36–37, 43, 44
  and *Queen of the Mob*, 69, 70
  rise in FBI, 27
  See also Federal Bureau of Investigation (FBI)
Hudson, Rochelle, 67

I'm Frank Hamer, 98
Inadmissible Evidence, 152–153
Independent Publishers Group, 143
I, Tania, 179
It Came from Hunger! Tales of a Cinema Schlockmeister (Buchanan), 102
Ives, Burl, 94, 105

Jackson, George, 145
Jackson, Jonathan, 145
Jenkins, John, 100
Jiminez, Janey, 129–130, 131
John Paul II, Pope, 160
Joint Terrorist Task Force (JTTF), 141

Kansas City Massacre, 28
Karpis, Alvin, 21, 33, 58, 60, 68, 85. *See also* Barker-Karpis Gang
Kelley, Clarence, 154
Kelly, George, 23, 25, 39
Kelly, Kathryn
    acquittal, 90
    arrest, 23
    comparison with Bonnie Parker, 18, 51–52
    creation of "Machine Gun" Kelly, 24
    as criminal mastermind, 24, 25, 26
    FBI and, 25, 29
    and gender roles, 26–27, 38–39
    lack of cultural legacy, 52, 204
    marriages, 23–24
    portrayal of in film, 39–43
Kelly, "Machine Gun." *See* Kelly, George
Kennedy, Florynce, 152
Kent State, 111
King, Larry, 178
King, Martin Luther, 145
King, Stephen, 124
King Brothers, 90
Kirkpatrick, E. E., 26
Klapp, Orrin, 198–199
Kowanko, Pete, 136
Kunstler, William, 152, 154, 157

Ladies Home Journal, 134
Lake, Ricki, 175–176
Lang, Fritz, 22, 89
Lawrence Hill Books, 193
Lee, Henry, 68
Like Water for Chocolate (album), 192. *See also* Common
Lindbergh baby kidnapping, 28, 53
Lipman, William R., 69
Little, Russ (Osceola), 114, 179–180
Look Magazine, 73
Lord, Phillips H., 74
Los Angeles Mirror-News, 77
Los Angeles Times, 77, 199

Louderback, Lew, 200
Lumet, Sidney, 108

Ma Barker's Killer Brood, 77–80
Maccabee, Paul, 60
Machine Gun Kelly, 90
Mailer, Norman, 121
Manson, Charles, 85, 119
Mealy, Rosemari, 169, 183
Methvin, Henry, 19
Methvin, Ivan, 19
McCoy, Horace, 69
Miles, Vera, 73
momism, 71–73, 76
Monster, 16–18
Moore, Sara Jane, 131
Morales, Guillermo, 193
Moran, Joseph P., 60
Morison, Patricia, 39
Morris, Holly, 169
Motion Picture Herald, 39, 42
Motion Picture Production Code, 22

Nash, Jay, 58–59
National Conference of Black Lawyers, 192
National Guard Armory fire, 111–112
National Student Strike Force, 111
Navarro, Bob, 182
Network, 108–109
Neverland: The Rise and Fall of the Symbionese Liberation Army, 179–181
New Jersey Turnpike killing, 141–142, 152, 155–157, 185, 186–187
Newman, David, 93, 106
Newton, Huey, 143, 146
New York News, 58, 140
New York Times, 116, 118, 137, 179
Nichols, Louis B., 29
Nixon, Richard, 110, 111, 112

Olson, Sara Jane
    cultural legacy of, 15, 196, 204
    defense of, 176–177
    as housewife-terrorist, 172
    portrayal of in film, 173
    and role in the SLA, 171–172, 176
    trial of, 181
Opsahl, Myrna, 130, 180–181
The Ordeal of Patty Hearst, 134–135, 173
Osceola. *See* Little, Russ
The Other Side of Bonnie and Clyde, 94–98, 99–101, 102–106
outlaw, 8, 11–12, 30–31, 36, 200. *See also* woman outlaw

Palentchar, Robert, 156
Palmer Raids, 27

Paramount Pictures, 5, 6, 42, 69
Parker, Billie, 50
Parker, Bonnie
 cigar photo, 10, 20, 48
 comparison with Assata Shakur, 140–141
 comparison with Kathryn Kelly, 4–5, 18,
  51–52
 contradicting narratives of, 48–49, 50–51, 101,
  102–103
 cultural legacy of, 3–4, 10, 13, 21–22, 46–48,
  51–52, 86, 91–92, 105, 106, 204
 death of, 19, 45–46, 88–89
 and family, 49–50, 51
 fetishization of, 101–102
 and gender roles, 10, 26–27, 34, 48–49, 89–90
 poetry, 10, 20, 47–48
 portrayal of in film, 88–90, 91–104, 202
 relationship with Clyde, 45, 47–48
 See also Barrow, Clyde; Bonnie and Clyde
Parker, Buster, 19
Parker, Emma, 19, 20
Parole Fixer, 42
The Passion of Christ, 104
Patty Hearst, 136–138, 173
Patty Hearst: Her Own Story. See *Every Secret
 Thing*
Payne, Les, 129
Penn, Arthur, 92, 96, 101
Penza, Ralph, 160
Perry, Nancy Ling (Fahizah), 117, 119, 124
Persons in Hiding (book)
 films adapted from, 42
 G-man in, 44
 Kathryn Kelly in, 24–25, 26, 37, 39
 Ma Barker in, 64, 66
Persons in Hiding (film), 5, 39–43, 89, 204
Potter, Claire Bond, 35
Power, Kathy, 111–112
Powers, Richard Gid, 111
Proyect, Louis, 190
PTA Magazine, 111
Public Enemies, 199
The Public Enemy, 30
Purvis, Melvin, 29, 66
Pyle, Denver, 99

Queen of the Mob, 6, 42, 68–71

"*Real* Public Enemy No. 1," 53–55, 56–58, 59–60,
 61–63, 64–65, 73
Remiro, Joe (Bo), 114, 127
Rhames, Ving, 136
Richardson, Natasha, 136
Rolando, Gloria, 161–162, 169
Rolling Stone, 175
Romero, Cesar, 67
Roosevelt, Franklin Delano, 28–29

Sadiki, Kamau, 166
Sandler, Georgette, 123
San Francisco Chronicle, 127, 129, 173
Santería, 162
Sara Jane Olson Defense Fund Committee, 176
Saxbe, William, 115
Saxe, Susan, 111–112
Schier-Eismann, Ruth, 122
Schrader, Paul, 136
Schroeder, Walter, 112
Sedgwick, Dixie Lee, 202
Serial Mom, 172, 175
Serving Time: America's Most Wanted Recipes, 177
Shadow of a Doubt, 72
Shakur, Assata
 adoption of African name, 151–152
 and Afro-Cuban tradition, 162, 163–164
 and the Black Liberation Army, 140, 148–149,
  150, 151
 and the Black Panther Party, 144–147
 comparison with Bonnie Parker, 140–141
 comparison with Che Guevara, 190
 comparison with John Dillinger, 150–151
 comparison with Ma Barker, 5, 140–141
 cultivation of image, 143–144, 150–151
 exile in Cuba, 160, 196, 204
 and FBI "Most Wanted" list, 14–15, 139, 170
 and gender, 139–141, 157
 incarceration, 157–159, 165–166, 184–185
 and history of Afro-women's resistance, 163
 and motherhood, 158–159, 166
 NBC interview, 160–161, 186
 and New Jersey Turnpike killing, 141–142,
  152, 155–157, 185
 as outlaw of color, 14, 140, 141, 150–151,
  168–169
 as outlaw-hero, 139, 142–143, 191, 193–195
 portrayal of in film, 161–169, 183–192
 prison break, 142, 159–160, 167, 189
 and race, 10, 14, 140–141, 150–151, 163,
  168–169, 194
 removal of name from campus buildings, 192–193
 reward for capture, 182–183, 195
 support from hip-hop artists, 192
 trials, 142, 152–157
Shakur, Tupac, 192
Shakur, Zayd, 152, 156
Sharpe, Jenny, 195
Show Them No Mercy, 67
Siegel, Bill, 179
Sisters in Crime, 123–124
Soliah, Kathleen. *See* Olson, Sara Jane
Soltysik, Fred, 134
Soltysik, Patricia (Zoya), 117, 124
Something Weird Video (SWV), 104
Sorrentino, Christopher, 178
Starkweather, Charlie, 91

Stockholm syndrome, 133
Stole, Mink, 174
Stone, Robert, 179
"The Story of Suicide Sal," 20
Strange, Carolyn, 199
Steinbeck, John, 34
Stewart, Jimmy, 73–74
Students for a Democratic Society (SDS), 110–111
Suskie, Marge, 35, 51
Sydney, Char, 187
Sydney, Sylvia, 22
Symbionese Liberation Army (SLA)
 and class, 11
 Crocker National Bank robbery, 130, 177, 180–181, 204
 cultivation of image, 14, 108, 110, 126
 FBI shootout and, 126, 127–128
 and gender, 116, 121–122, 124–125
 Hearst kidnapping and, 109–110, 114–115
 Hibernia Bank robbery, 115
 media and, 113–114, 129, 177–178
 membership, 117–118
 mission of, 113, 116–117
 People in Need program, 115
 portrayal of in film and television, 14, 134–138, 173–176, 179–181, 181–182
 race and, 102–121
 rise of, 110–111, 113
 second-team, 130
 women in, 118–120, 123–124

Tania. *See* Hearst, Patricia
Teko. *See* Harris, Bill
Theron, Charlize, 16, 17
Time magazine, 46, 129
Tobin, Trish, 131
Trance, 178–179
The Trial of Lee Harvey Oswald, 104
True Detective, 58
Twentieth Century Pictures, 67

Undercover Doctor, 42
Ungagged, 176
Uniform Crime Reports, 28
Universal Pictures, 31
The Untold Story of Emmett Louis Till, 190
Urschel, Charles, 23, 24, 26
U.S. News & World Report, 106, 123

Variety, 91
Vencermos, 116

Vietnam War, 112
Visual Drama Inc., 74

Walker, John, 178
Waters, John, 172, 173, 174–175
Waters, Maxine, 161
Watkins, Maureen Dallas, 198
Weathermen. *See* Weather Underground
Weather Underground, 110–111, 112–113, 176, 179
The Weather Underground (film), 179
Weaver, Dennis, 134
Weed, Steven, 114, 118, 121
West, Don, 129
White Heat, 7, 73
"The White Negro," 121
Whitman, Christine Todd, 161
Williams, Carl, 160
Williams, Evelyn, 149, 152–153, 186
Winters, Shelly, 81, 82
Wolfe, Willie (Cujo), 117, 127, 132
woman outlaw
 within Anglo-Celtic outlawry tradition, 200–201
 appeal of on film, 2–3, 17–18, 44–45, 202, 203
 in cultural context, 199
 cultural legacy of, 6–8, 11–12, 191, 192, 196, 201
 during the Great Depression, 18
 FBI and, 1–2, 27, 31–32, 36–37, 38, 43, 44
 gender roles and, 2–3, 5, 8–10, 17–18, 39–40, 41–42, 122–123, 198, 201–202
 as model of empowerment, 35–36, 51, 197–198
 and race, 5
 and red hair, 26
 rise of in 1960s and 1970s, 106, 122, 200
 and the Western frontier, 197–198
 women's movement and, 123–124
 See also specific women outlaws
women's movement, 123–124
Wournos, Aileen, 16, 17
Wylie, Philip, 71–73

X, Retimah, 115–116

Yolanda. *See* Harris, Emily
Yoshimura, Wendy, 178
You Can't Get Away with It, 31
You Only Live Once, 22, 89
Yurka, Blanche, 69

Zimbalist, Efrem, Jr., 87
Zoya. *See* Soltysik, Patricia